Meet Joe Copper

Meet Joe Copper

Masculinity and Race on Montana's World War II Home Front

MATTHEW L. BASSO

The University of Chicago Press
Chicago and London

Matthew L. Basso is assistant professor of history and gender studies at the University of Utah. He is editor of *Men at Work: Rediscovering Depression-Era Stories from the Federal Writers' Project* and coeditor of *Across the Great Divide: Cultures of Manhood in the American West.*

The University of Chicago Press, Chicago 60637
The University of Chicago Press, Ltd., London
© 2013 by The University of Chicago
All rights reserved. Published 2013.
Printed in the United States of America

22 21 20 19 18 17 16 15 14 13   1 2 3 4 5

ISBN-13: 978-0-226-03886-5 (cloth)
ISBN-13: 978-0-226-04419-4 (paper)
ISBN-13: 978-0-226-04422-4 (e-book)

Library of Congress Cataloging-in-Publication Data

Basso, Matthew L.
    Meet Joe Copper : masculinity and race on Montana's World War II home front / Matthew L. Basso.
        pages.   cm.
    Includes bibliographical references and index.
    ISBN 978-0-226-03886-5 (hardcover : alk. paper) —
    ISBN 978-0-226-04419-4 (pbk. : alk. paper) —
    ISBN 978-0-226-04422-4 (e-book)   1. Copper miners—Montana—Social conditions. 2. Montana—Race relations. 3. World War, 1939–1945.
    I. Title.
    HD8039.M72U62   2013
    331.7'6223430978609044—dc23

                                                                      2012043674

♾ This paper meets the requirements of ANSI/NISO Z39.48-1992 (Permanence of Paper).

For Ang

CONTENTS

ILLUSTRATIONS

ACKNOWLEDGMENTS

This book was more than a few years in the making. One of the consequences is that I have an awful lot of folks to thank for their help and support. I began this project at the University of Montana under David Emmons's guidance. I would like to thank him as well as Dee Garceau and Janet Finn for their advice and friendship. Montana is a state teeming with talented and dedicated public historians, librarians, and archivists. My gratitude to Ellen Crain and Lee Whitney at the Butte-Silver Bow Public Archives in Butte, and Jerry Hansen and the late Robert Vine at the Anaconda-Deer Lodge County Historical Society in Anaconda. Bob Clark, Angela Murray, Jodie Foley, Ellie Arguimbau, Molly Miller, Loreto Pinochet, and especially Brian Shovers at the Montana Historical Society Research Center made my many visits to Helena both intellectually fruitful and delightful, as did Patty Dean, Molly Holz, and Katy Hampton. I would also like to thank staff members at the University of Montana Library in Missoula, the Hearst Library in Anaconda, the Carroll College Library in Helena, the archives of the *Montana Standard* in Butte, the *Great Falls Tribune* archives and the Great Falls Public Library in Great Falls, and especially the Diocese of Helena Archives (where Sister Dolores dug up what became some of the most important documents in this study).

The Program in American Studies at the University of Minnesota proved to be an excellent place to expand this study. I would like to thank the faculty members of the program, who treat graduate students as colleagues and friends instead of minions and nuisances. Special thanks to David Roediger, Elaine Tyler May, Lary May, Jennifer Pierce, and David Noble for being model mentors, and individually, for being model scholars. Likewise, I would like to acknowledge my fellow graduate students in the program for their friendship, kindness, and constructive criticism. They are too many to name, so as a representative gesture I will mention my own cohort: Anne Martínez, Brian Klopotek, Steve Garabedian, Deirdre Murphy, Adam Pagan, Robin Hemenway, and Julie Berg-Raymond. I would also like to acknowledge the fellowship and grant support of the Program in American Studies, the Minnesota Humanities Center, and the Graduate School of the University of Minnesota, the latter of which awarded me a Harold Leonard Film Studies Fellowship, a Leonard Film Studies Grant, and a Doctoral Dissertation Fellowship.

Financial support from the University of Minnesota, the Montana Historical Society, the University of Richmond, and the University of Utah allowed me to spend long periods of time not only in Montana's archives but also at the University of Colorado–Boulder Library Archive, the Library of Congress and the National Archives in Washington, DC, and at the USC Cinema-Television Archives, UCLA Special Collections, and the Academy of Motion Picture Arts and Sciences Special Collections in Los Angeles. I want to thank the staff members at each of these repositories, as well as those at the National Archives, Denver branch. I extend my appreciation also to Geoffrey Swindells at Northwestern University Library for his gracious assistance with illustrations.

I am grateful to my friends at the University of Richmond for making my years at that wonderful institution so enjoyable. I especially appreciate the feedback I received on aspects of the project from my colleagues in the History Department, the English Department, and the American Studies Program. While at Richmond, I spent a fantastic year in New Zealand on a Fulbright fellowship. I became so fascinated by the history of race and gender formation in Aotearoa that instead of finishing this book, I began another monograph on that subject. *Kia ora* to the scholars I met in Wellington, Dunedin, Christchurch, and Auckland for their warmth, hospitality, and feedback, and for offering me a model for how to link community engagement and first-rate scholarship.

The University of Utah has been a wonderful home for my varied research interests, and many of my colleagues here have also given me very valuable input on this project. I give my thanks to them. I particularly want to note my gratitude to Eric Hinderaker and Beth Clement, who I have turned to for their sage counsel on innumerable occasions. Soon after I moved to Utah, I was asked to direct the university's American West Center. Although I knew that accepting this invitation would significantly hamper my progress on the book, I decided that the opportunity the center provided to pursue my passion for community-engaged scholarly projects and training graduate students in public history was too good to turn down. I want to thank my colleagues in gender studies and history for supporting my decision and for encouraging my work at the center. My heartfelt thanks go to Floyd O'Neil and Greg Thompson for their friendship and for teaching me how to be a public historian. Likewise, my appreciation to all the graduate students I have had the good fortune to work with at the center, but especially Annie Hanshew, John Worsencroft, and Vince Fazzi, for reinforcing my sense that in following this somewhat unusual trajectory I made the right decision.

I have had the good fortune to learn about labor history, and the other fields with which my own scholarship intersects, from scholars across the United States. My appreciation goes out to them and to the audience members at conferences, symposia, and lectures that offered helpful insights. For particularly timely advice and help, I want to thank Betsy Jameson, Eileen Boris, Mary Murphy, and Laurie Mercier. (I owe Laurie a second debt for the wonderful oral histories she recorded in Montana's copper communities.) Besides being a remarkable historian, Elaine May has been a remarkable friend and supporter. Thank you, Lany. My appreciation too to Grey Osterud for helping me whip this manuscript into shape and in the process improving it considerably, and to Paul Grindrod for providing similar aid. At the University of Chicago Press, Doug Mitchell has been a steadfast ally—and I mean steadfast. My appreciation goes out to him; the press's anonymous readers, whose ideas have improved this book; Sandra Hazel, whose sharp editing has made it a much better read; and Tim McGovern, Benjamin Balskus, Natalie Smith, Jeff Waxman, and the rest of the staff for seeing it through production.

Finally, I offer my thanks to my family (Bassos and Smiths) and friends— academic and otherwise—for, among many other things, never thinking I was taking too long, or at least never saying so out loud. Jack and Eamon helped convince me that it really was time to finish this book, and Tifani Simmons helped in wrangling them so that I had the time to do it. Nice job, boys, and thanks, Tifani. This book is dedicated to Angela for reading many, many drafts, improving it repeatedly, always believing it would get done, and for everything else: *Arohanui.*

GI Joe and Rosie the Riveter,
Meet Joe Copper!

No book better encapsulates the popular perception of the lives of American men and women during World War II than Tom Brokaw's best-selling *The Greatest Generation.* In it he writes that "the face of war is almost always one of a man," and that World War II was "no different." According to Brokaw, the bombing of Pearl Harbor catalyzed American manhood. Afterward, "Young men were enlisting in the military by the hundreds of thousands. Farm kids from the Great Plains who never expected to see the ocean in their lifetimes signed up for the Navy; brothers followed brothers into the Marines; young daredevils who were fascinated by the new frontiers of flight volunteered for pilot training." The two-thirds of *The Greatest Generation* devoted to telling the story of men during World War II details the military experiences of men like these, leaving little room for doubt that during the war, "the male was in his historic role as warrior."[1]

The other third of the book discusses women's wartime experiences and offers a more varied portrait. Brokaw contends that women's contributions were made in three different spheres: the home front workplace, the military, and the domestic realm. He writes that following Pearl Harbor, "single young women poured into Washington to fill the exploding needs for clerical help as the political capital mobilized for war. Other women, their husbands or boyfriends off to basic training, learned to drive trucks or handle welding torches." *The Greatest Generation* also profiles women who served in the military, and those, like Brokaw's mother, who through their maternal labors kept families together during those challenging years. All these women answered the nation's call to duty and "raised the place of their gender to new heights; they changed forever the perception and the reality of women in all the disciplines of American life."[2]

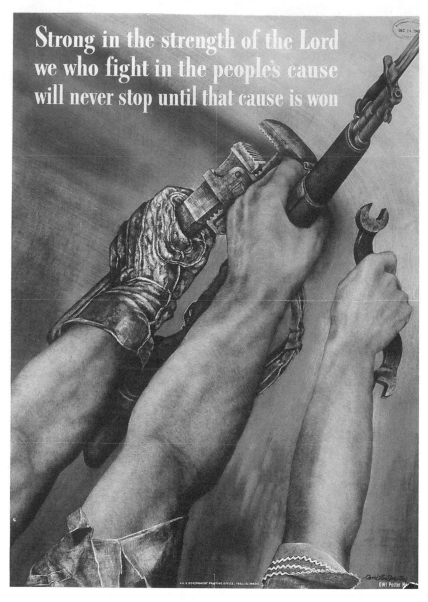

0.1 This 1942 propaganda poster produced by the Office of War Information promoted patriotic resolve and unity among the three major protagonists of America's wartime drama: home front female workers, military men, and home front male workers. "Strong in the Strength of the Lord . . . ," OWI, 1942; courtesy Northwestern University Library.

The Greatest Generation's understanding of what American men and women went through during World War II reflects Hollywood films, national monuments to veterans of that war and to women who worked on the home front, and the vast majority of popular and academic histories. They all emphasize men taking up military masculinity and, by following its dictates, winning the war for the Allies, and women's ability to expand society's perceptions, albeit briefly, of what they could and should be able to do. These stories, especially when they are told with nuance, are rightfully seen as an important part of American history (fig. 0.1). However, this narrative of the war, with its propensity to feature GI Joe and Rosie the Riveter as the sole protagonists of the national wartime drama, has been so compelling that we have missed the story of home front men, a group that was larger than either women who went to work in war industries or men who entered the armed forces.[3]

Tom Brokaw's own father provides a striking example of both the invisibility of these men and their role in the war effort. In his introduction to *The Greatest Generation*, Brokaw describes Anthony "Red" Brokaw as a "Mr. Fix It" who fulfilled the masculine ideal during the Great Depression by working heroically to help his family survive.[4] But the attack on Pearl Harbor did not send him to the enlistment office to join the military and assume "his historic role as warrior." Instead, he pursued one of the new, higher-paying home front jobs created by the war. He and his family moved to an Army Ammunition Depot in South Dakota named Igloo, where he took a position on the maintenance crew that kept the base running. Like all other American men between the ages of eighteen and sixty-five, Red Brokaw had to register with the Selective Service. Twenty-nine years old when the war began, he was in the military's preferred age range and thus susceptible to being called for military duty. But, his son writes, "When he was drafted, the base commander called him back, reasoning he was more valuable in the job he had. When Dad returned home, it was the first time I saw my mother cry. These were powerful images for an impressionable youngster." Nonetheless, because these events do not fit the template of what men did during the war, and because the Brokaw family's experience seems inconsequential compared with that of home front women, this is the last time readers encounter the men like Red Brokaw who spent the duration of the war within the sphere of civilian activity.[5]

Meet Joe Copper seeks to reverse this longtime trend by recovering the history of one group of home front men and analyzing what it tells us about the social politics of the World War II era. It began, however, as a study of Rosie the Riveter. Like many people in the mid-1990s, I was captivated by the fiftieth-anniversary commemorations of World War II. I was especially interested in the depiction of the home front, and after reading the excellent histories of women in that realm I decided that I too wanted to research women's wartime work experiences.[6] I knew that women could find work in an impressive number of fields that before the war had employed only men, and since I was living in Montana at the time, I wondered if they had also been able to enter one of the nation's most challenging and masculine industries: western copper mining and smelting.[7] In searching for the answer, I discovered a set of sources—including remarkable verbatim transcripts of meetings held throughout the war between male workers and managers in Montana's mines and smelters—which confirmed that although women were excluded from the domain of hard-rock mining, they did eventually work in previously male-only occupations at the copper smelter in Anaconda, Montana. One transcript above all, from the spring of 1944, gave me pause. In what was the first significant conversation about employing women at the smelter, the manager told representatives of the plant's unionized white male workers that the government was considering sending either "Mexicans" or "colored fellows from the Islands" to Anaconda to solve the smelter's acute labor shortage. He then added that this could be avoided if they would stop "making a lot of too do [sic]" about employing women at the plant.[8]

I was fascinated by the references in these transcripts to women's taking production jobs at the smelter and to the possibility of introducing black and Mexican men as laborers, but I was struck most profoundly by the words and deeds of Anaconda's home front men.[9] Far from being invisible or inconsequential, they spoke of their anxieties about women and workers of color, and acted to defend what they saw as their own racial and gender prerogatives. Intrigued by the disconnect between what occurred at the Anaconda smelter and the prevailing story of race and gender relations during World War II, I decided to probe the situation in Montana's copper industry in order to discover how beliefs and practices regarding gender and race were contested and defended by white working-class men on the home front.[10]

Joe Copper was the name given by a local magazine to the male wartime copper workers who toiled not just in Anaconda but also in Butte and Black Eagle, the three towns that together formed the Anaconda Copper Mining Company's (ACM's) Montana empire. When the mines were running at full capacity, rich mineral ore, mined deep beneath Butte by between 8,000 and 14,000 men, was delivered by rail to the Anaconda smelter, twenty-five miles to the west of Butte, at a rate of one thousand tons an hour. There, upward of 3,500 men worked to reduce the ore and extract copper and other minerals. Anaconda's smeltermen then sent the processed ore, also by rail, one hundred miles to the north to the Black Eagle plant, typically staffed by 1,400 workers. Smeltermen there used the process of electrolysis to further purify it. The final product, refined copper, zinc, and other metals and minerals, was then distributed to manufacturing plants across the United States, or turned into copper wire and cable by another group of Black Eagle workers at a different part of the facility.[11]

The ACM was already a vast enterprise by the onset of World War II, when demand for copper and other minerals soared due to their use in critical components of airplanes, ships, tanks, bomb sights, ammunition, and an astonishing range of other types of equipment.[12] From the 1880s through the 1940s, this study's broad period of interest, the imperatives of mineral production and the power of the ACM, known locally as simply "the Company," largely defined the lives of the copper men in these three Montana towns and those of their families and neighbors, shaping almost every aspect of their existence, from their work schedules and pay envelopes to their recreational pursuits and politics. During the 1930s and especially World War II, the US government became an equally powerful force in their lives.

Meet Joe Copper provides a different picture of masculinity during the war than that found in the scholarship on the history of American masculinity. These studies ignore home front men, arguing instead that the military masculinity of World War II enabled American men to fulfill society's expectations for masculinity after the Great Depression had eroded their position as breadwinners and, therefore, their manhood. They further suggest that memories of World War II martial valor shored up men's sense of manliness in the postwar era as they experienced the emasculating process of being corporate "organization men."[13]

I argue that Montana's home front copper men viewed the elevation of military masculinity above their own working-class masculinity, which had been bolstered by the labor movement in the 1930s, as a threat to their masculine status and the material conditions of their lives. Prior to Pearl Harbor, mobilization for the war gave Montana's miners and smeltermen steady, full-time employment, enabling them for the first time since the Depression began to consistently fulfill the fundamental requirement for local masculinity by providing for their families. Yet when the United States entered the war, serving the nation in uniform quickly became the predominant expectation for male citizens.[14] Pearl Harbor, then, in contrast to how Tom Brokaw and histories of American masculinity see it, abruptly ended a period of stable masculinity for many working-class men. It definitively changed what constituted ideal masculinity, at least on the national stage, and in so doing ushered in an era defined by a new set of challenges.

Leaders in the government, business, and, to some extent, labor sectors demanded both directly and through popular culture that working-class men modify their behavior to meet the standards of home front masculinity established by those in power. I call this sacrificial masculinity. It required working-class men in the civilian sphere to obediently accept the dictates of the state, renouncing their independent masculine ideology and the related practices they regarded as necessary to protect the power of male workers against the growing power of the state and corporations. The effort by the government and corporations to introduce men of color and women into production jobs once the exclusive purview of white and white ethnic men was a related challenge that held an equal if not greater possibility of disrupting how working-class home front men wanted to see society ordered.

Montana's copper men responded to these threats by following the values embedded in their prewar working-class masculine ideology instead of those of sacrificial masculinity. They claimed that copper work was exceptionally masculine and consequently both unsuitable for women and capable of granting miners and smeltermen elevated masculine status and benefits. And they renounced the interracial ideology for which their own union was among the nation's best-known proponents. They fought a war-long campaign to protect their masculine and white privilege by excluding new workers of color from the mines and smelters and by employing a variety of tactics to contain the effect of women's wartime employment. Though denounced for their actions, miners and smeltermen saw their battle to bolster white working-class male power as a patriotic act that supported their friends, relatives, and other white working men in uniform. The story of Montana's copper men suggests, not only that working-class home front men nationwide played a determinative role in eliminating the revolutionary potential for social change that World War II represented, but also that the working-class masculine ideology of the 1930s profoundly shaped both home front and postwar America.

Meet Joe Copper employs a case-study methodology to add texture to these arguments and to facilitate in-depth analysis, especially concerning the role of place and time in the formation and operation of masculinity.[15] R. W.

Connell's conceptualization of "hegemonic masculinity" has dominated scholarship on masculinity for over a decade. Connell writes, "'Hegemonic masculinity' is not a fixed character type, always and everywhere the same. It is, rather, the masculinity that occupies the hegemonic position in a given pattern of gender relations, a position always contestable." More recently, she has stressed the need for scholars to study the existence of multiple masculinities, the relational character of masculine formation, and the spatial aspects of how that formation operates.[16] In *Meet Joe Copper*, I emphasize the importance of being attuned to context—both time and place—when analyzing the formation and operation of masculinity.[17] I do not dismiss the influence of hegemonic or ideal forms of masculinity, but argue that multiple hegemonic masculinities can and often do exist at a given time. The national masculine ideal, for instance, could be and often was different from a local ideal. I also posit that at the local level, practices shaped ideals as much as or more than ideals shaped practices, and that these practices were often complex and contradictory but nonetheless critical to assessing how various subjects lived and experienced masculine power.[18]

Joe Copper's sense of masculinity had much in common with other American men of the time period, regardless of class or race. For these men, masculinity came with strength, virility, rational intellect, and a perceived superiority to and eminence over women and children. Virtually all miners and smeltermen, and the vast majority of working-class men across the United States, agreed that the ideal of a working-class male breadwinner should be upheld, and differentiated their masculinity from that of middle-class men by emphasizing the physicality of their labor and the fact it *produced* something. With these principles, Montana's copper men created a local working-class masculine ideology that had independence and militance as core values, especially in dealing with the Company. Miners and smeltermen realized that their independence was circumscribed by the industrial capitalist system in which they labored, but they still held strongly to the concept and found multiple ways to exercise it, thereby expressing their working-class masculinity. They did not see it as a contradiction that some of these ways went directly against their producer ethos. Likewise, when they chose to accept the Company's paternalism and form a historic bloc with managers on crucial issues, such as the local gender and racial order, they saw it as a strategy to achieve local working-class male objectives. When copper men asserted their difference from women *and* from men of color, they did so in order to claim the material and psychic dividends that white masculinity conferred, and to uphold their position as workers relative to the undeniable power of the giant corporation that employed them.

For Joe Copper, and for virtually all Americans of this era, masculinity was always intertwined with class and race, but local context determined the specifics of that dynamic.[19] The immigrant identity of Montana's copper workers and copper towns had an outsize role in the formation and operation of whiteness and masculinity, strongly influencing wartime events. From 1880 to 1910, immigrants who had recently arrived from Europe comprised a large percentage of the unionized workforce in the mines and smelters. They and their children continued to dominate working-class culture in Butte, Anaconda, and Black Eagle for the following three decades. Just before World War II, persons of foreign birth or of foreign or mixed parentage still made up just over 45 percent of Montana's entire population. They included Germans, Norwegians, English, Catholics from "the Irish Free State," Swedes, Russians, "Jugoslavs," Scots, Danes, Italians, Finns, Czechs and Slovaks, Protestants from Northern Ireland, and Welsh. First- or second-generation European immigrants comprised an even larger percentage of the population of Butte, Anaconda, and Black Eagle. The most important groups in these three towns were the Irish, English, Welsh, Finns, and Italians, and the Croats, Slovaks, and Serbs who together made up a group called first the "Austrians" and later the "Jugoslavs."[20] These first- and second-generation European immigrants were joined in the copper towns by a number of communities of color, whose influence on local racial formations was far greater than their numbers. Chinese and especially African Americans figured significantly in the local process through which racial-ethnic groups in Butte and Anaconda came to define themselves as white. Mexican Americans too played an intriguing part in Butte's racial politics. Moreover, American Indian communities were visible in and around Butte, Anaconda, and Black Eagle. In Black Eagle in particular, Indians were crucial to the process through which the town's immigrants could assert their whiteness.[21]

Local understandings of race in these towns reflected the nation's pre–World War II conflation of race, ethnicity, and nationality, as well as its racist categorizations. I use the term *racial-ethnic* to reference this conflation. Prominent racial thinkers of the nineteenth and early twentieth centuries used the vernacular of science to rank races based on how supposedly civilized they were, with northern European Anglo-Saxons or "Nordics" inevitably at the top and "Negroids" at the bottom. *Meet Joe Copper* shows that beginning in the 1880s, the national rhetoric of racial ranking—found in pejorative terms like *bohunk*, *dago*, and *wop*, for example—was deployed in Montana's copper communities against and by European "immigrants" as part of a larger effort to create and enforce a highly local hierarchy of races.

The idea of someone being part of a "race," however, also bonded groups of immigrants in Montana's copper towns. Contrary to studies arguing that immigrants in this period felt compelled to assimilate, evidence from Butte, Black Eagle, and Anaconda shows that being Italian or Croatian or Irish remained a central and cherished part of local identity. Equally critically, these groups also fought to gain full access to the benefits of whiteness.[22]

Like a number of recent histories, this book differentiates between "race" and "color" so as to construct a more nuanced portrait of social relations and power. The overarching question in the scholarship on the status of European immigrants in the latter part of the nineteenth and first half of the twentieth centuries is whether those immigrants were considered "non-white," "in-between" white and black, or "white on arrival."[23] In Montana's copper towns, the rhetoric of color was used both against and by immigrants. For instance, immigrants from Serbia, Croatia, and other parts of the Balkans found themselves referred to in Butte as "black men from across the water," and Italians could read in newspapers that they were not "white men." In each town, I argue, comparable discussions demonstrate locally specific differences in the relationships between and among immigrants and so-called native-born whites.

The local racial hierarchy reflected and shaped a local power structure that for decades largely denied southeastern Europeans the best working-class jobs in the mines and smelters. However, even if these immigrants found themselves called "black" or placed outside "whiteness," they were not barred from employment in the mines and smelters or from citizenship, nor were they subject to many of the other forms of racial oppression experienced by the African Americans, Chinese, and Indians who lived in these local communities. *Meet Joe Copper* shows that in Montana's copper communities, the local racial-ethnic power structure that initially worked against southeastern European aspirations began to change significantly in the 1920s, with the result that by the 1930s these groups and other local first- and second-generation European immigrants had formed "pan-ethnic" coalitions. The strength of these coalitions differed in Butte, Black Eagle, and Anaconda, but each helped determine the social politics of the home front and the postwar period in their respective towns. By the end of World War II, the term *white ethnic* had become an accurate description of the location of Butte's, Black Eagle's, and Anaconda's first- and second-generation immigrants in the American racial-ethnic imaginary. But I argue that during the war itself, changes in national norms and the increased power of the government and the ACM meant that those immigrants sometimes doubted their hold on white privilege and, critically, acted on those doubts.[24]

This study, in considering the racial and gender politics of working-class home front men, also enters a scholarly discussion about the characteristics of New Deal liberalism.[25] Montana's miners and smeltermen used their collective strength to assert their power over their workplaces and towns whenever possible. The workers in this industry had a long tradition of union organizing and rank-and-file militancy. Butte's miners and Anaconda's and Black Eagle's smeltermen helped found and also belonged to some of the most radical labor unions in the country, most notably the Western Federation of Miners and its progeny, the International Union of Mine, Mill, and Smelter Workers (Mine Mill), which became a founding member of the Congress of Industrial Organizations (CIO) in the 1930s.

Scholars agree that organized labor was one of the cornerstones of president Franklin Roosevelt's New Deal coalition, but they depict a wide range of union and worker politics. Mine Mill was categorized among the most radical unions in the CIO, especially in regard to racial equality. Its organizing campaigns among black workers in the Southeast and Mexican and Mexican American workers in the Southwest are among the most famous examples of 1930s labor interracialism and the CIO's "culture of unity." The union's ties to the Communist Party USA and the Popular Front, the broad political and cultural alliance of leftist progressives that had significant influence during the Depression, are also a well-known part of its history.[26]

Montana's rank and file seem to exemplify the radical shift on race that took place among some white workers in the 1930s. They were the largest and most powerful bloc within Mine Mill; they helped finance organizing drives to bring workers of color into the union; and they were the former coworkers of the union president who put Mine Mill in the vanguard of labor's progressive racial politics. I argue, however, that Montana's miners and smeltermen supported Mine Mill because of its militant masculine politics and *despite* its racial politics. I also argue that space and place need to be carefully considered when evaluating liberalism. A major reason Montana's copper men did not revolt more forcefully against Mine Mill's leaders was that the union's fight for racial equality occurred a great distance from Montana and did not threaten the copper men's local racial order.

The social changes wrought by World War II are what reveal Montana's rank-and-file copper men's rejection of Mine Mill's progressive politics, as well as Mine Mill's and the CIO's approach to managing labor's relationship with the government. Indeed, home front copper men saw themselves not only as protecting their claims to the "wages of masculinity" and the "wages of whiteness" against corporations, but also as opposed to what they saw as labor leaders' unwillingness to challenge the Roosevelt administration's national home front policies. Among wartime government agencies, the War Department and the Selective Service System, which managed the draft, had the most direct and obvious influence on the lives of working-class home front men.[27] The National War Labor Board, the government entity perhaps most associated with wartime labor issues, did enter the fray in Montana's copper communities, but the War Manpower Commission and the War Production Board, along with its subsidiary, the United States Employment Service, played the largest part in the major events that unfolded in response to the wartime labor shortage in Butte, Black Eagle, and Anaconda. The leaders of the Roosevelt administration drove national policies and are the face of wartime liberalism, but I maintain that regional and local representatives, whose approach to labor problems regularly failed to mirror national policy, were as influential, if not more so, than their bosses. They offer a different view on the New Deal. Montana's copper men found that these officials would often protect the racial and gender privileges of miners and smeltermen, either because they feared a drop in wartime production if they did otherwise, or because they agreed with the stance taken by home front men. The most discerning local and regional officials, and even some officials on the national scene, came to understand that the copper men's wartime politics were deeply rooted in the local racial and gender orders that had developed in the sixty years before the war.

Throughout *Meet Joe Copper*, I use the term *gender order* as shorthand for the social organization of relations among men and women based on expectations of men's and women's behavior. The gender order allocates power and often works through domination and subordination. It governs differential access to resources and institutions and is interpolated through and shaped by race, class, and other aspects of identity. Similarly, by *racial order* I mean the beliefs—and the practices at the personal and institutional levels they underwrote—that provided greater power and access to resources to those who were deemed "white," and hampered or blocked those deemed nonwhite from gaining power or access.

The first section of this book maps the local racial and gender orders, revealing the specific histories and human geographies of Butte, Black Eagle, and Anaconda, respectively, from 1880 to 1940. Each chapter shows how racial-ethnic and gender identities were generated locally through interactions among immigrants and their descendants in the workplace, the union hall, and the community, and between them and working- and middle-class white Americans, including ACM managers. Each chapter, in its own way, asks: How were the forms of white supremacy and privilege that flourished during these years created, propagated, and upheld in such diverse and dynamic places? How did norms, notions, and practices of masculinity mutate when most men were wage laborers rather than independent farmers, artisans, businesspeople, or managers? And how were the dynamics of race and gender linked to each other?

Chapter 1 discusses the masculinity of Butte's hard-rock miners. I argue that while these men, and the city itself, had a reputation for hypermasculinity, the practice of masculinity in the mines reveals a more complex picture, including how intertwined masculinity was with racial-ethnic identity and labor politics. I outline how Irish and Irish Americans dominated Butte and in the process marginalized the city's large southeastern European population, among others, for several decades. The relationship among European immigrants began to improve before World War II, and a shared ethic of an independent working-class masculinity, a deep distrust of the Company, and a desire to claim and protect the privileges of whiteness developed among the majority of Butte's miners during this period. But underneath the surface unity of the 1930s, Butte's miners remained divided among radical and conservative camps. This division, along with related concerns about racial and masculine status, would become dramatically apparent during the war.

In contrast to Butte, Black Eagle was dominated by southeastern Europeans, especially Croats and Italians. Chapter 2 shows how shared neighborhoods, work and social spaces, schools, Catholic faith and values, and marginalization in Great Falls, the larger city just across the Missouri River from Black Eagle, brought these two racial-ethnic communities together earlier and more completely than in Butte or Anaconda. This pan-ethnic sensibility created a level of trust among immigrant men that, along with the especially strong relationship they had with smelter managers, led to the unusual approach—at least in relation to Butte and Anaconda—they took to employment of women at their production facility during the war.

Chapter 3 contends that the relationship among Anaconda's racial-ethnic communities was broadly characterized by an amalgam of trends in the other two towns. Although Anaconda was too small for true racial-ethnic separatism, immigrants initially formed mini-enclaves in the town and at the smelter. By the 1930s, virtually all parts of the plant were ethnically mixed, and smeltermen had developed both cohesiveness around their identity as Anacondans and a masculine ideology that centered the "steady smelterman" and leveraged the union-won seniority system. Racial and masculine practices had an especially local character, revealed by the masculine status tied to specific jobs and the codes surrounding the employment of African American and "mulatto" men at the smelter. The desire by Anaconda's smeltermen to protect this local system emerged even more powerfully during the war.

The second section of *Meet Joe Copper* explores two critical issues that faced home front men in the early war period, and that subsequently framed their entire wartime experience. Chapter 4 illuminates society's new expectations for masculinity articulated in discussions about the military draft, patriotism, and home front versus frontline service from 1940 through 1942. Montana's miners and smeltermen contested the idea that the most masculine and valuable men served in uniform and that they had to jettison their independent working-class masculinity for sacrificial masculinity. At the same time, they strove to protect the masculine reputation of their labor from the threat of men who wanted to use the mines and smelters to hide from military duty, and they dealt with tensions within their ranks over who deserved deferments from the draft and who did not. Throughout, the government's new influence on masculinity framed the wartime landscape for Montana's miners and smeltermen.

The other critical issue these home front copper men faced early in the war further revealed the government's power to impact their masculinity. Chapter 5 discusses the potential workers, including older and disabled men, women, Mexican men, and black and white furloughed male soldiers, all considered by the government and the ACM as possible solutions to the serious labor shortage that almost immediately struck the mines and smelters when the United States entered the war. Each group of potential workers represented a different type of threat to the racial or masculine status of home front men. Copper men responded by drawing on the values at the heart of working-class masculinity. As they did so, they revealed much about the actual practice of masculinity in mines and smelters, and on the home front more generally.

The final section of this book analyzes the three major wartime crises—one in each town—that occurred in Montana's copper communities during the war. Chapter 6 tells the story of the November 1942 wildcat strike launched by Butte miners in response to the government's effort to introduce black soldier-miners underground. The Butte wildcat, in which eight thousand white miners refused to work with black men, reignited earlier ideological splits among miners. Judging from the accounts of a diverse set of local actors, including Hiawatha Brown, the one black man from Butte allowed to work in the mines; Reid Robinson, the remarkable leader of Mine Mill; and Father Michael English, the Roman Catholic priest tasked with solving the impasse, the strike calls into question the reputation of Mine Mill's rank and file as spearheading Popular Front struggles for an interracial working-class movement. Centered on protecting miners' white racial identity and affirming their local masculine values, the events in Butte further revealed the split between federal officials at the national and local levels regarding these issues.

Chapter 7 delves into the dual challenge posed by the presence of soldiers and airmen at Gore Field and the Great Falls Army Air Base near Black Eagle and the hiring of women to perform previously male-only jobs at the town's smelter. By agreeing in the spring of 1943 to the employment of women in production jobs at their plant, Black Eagle's smeltermen showed themselves more willing than Butte or Anaconda copper men to make the sacrifices asked for by the national government, and thus operate more within the parameters of the dominant national home front narrative. A closer look, however, shows that despite this compromise, Black Eagle's smeltermen were able both to avoid the perceived threat posed by the introduction of workers of color and to largely maintain the local immigrant gender order by relying on their close relationship with management, thereby ensuring that only certain types of women were hired. The presence of home front soldiers and airmen near Black Eagle, the only one of the three copper communities that had a military element as part of its local social politics, also played a role in handling the challenge of women in the workplace. Instead of reinforcing the diminished status of home front copper men, comparisons to local men in uniform allowed the smeltermen to assert equivalency to certain facets of military masculinity.

Chapter 8 discusses the last major home front crisis in Montana's copper towns, which occurred in Anaconda in the spring of 1944. There the smeltermen's fight to exclude local women and minority men from their facility brought together aspects of events in Butte in 1942 and in Black Eagle in 1943. It revealed the comparative calculus of both home front male workers and their managers as both parties grappled with the social changes brought by the war. Anaconda's smeltermen relied on the racist worldview they shared with their bosses to exclude men of color from the smelter and the town. They also used this managerial antipathy toward men of color to delay the employment of women in production jobs and to mitigate the disruption of masculine prerogatives at the plant. They justified their actions, which some read as deeply unpatriotic, as serving their fellow workers and relatives in uniform.

The conclusion of *Meet Joe Copper* carries forward the story of home front copper men into the early years of the postwar period. I argue that our current perspective on that time fails to fully account for working-class masculinity, as expressed both by former home front men and by returning veterans. Most veterans from the working class did not follow the path so well defined by studies of postwar masculinity. Rather than going to college, getting a white-collar managerial job, and buying a home and settling down in the suburbs, many of these veterans entered working-class jobs in either the production or the service sector. When they did so, they assimilated back into the militant, independent working-class masculinity that home front men had carried from the Great Depression through the war and into the postwar. Collectively, these men had a powerful influence on the next phase of American race and gender relations.

PART I

Defining Whiteness and Working-Class Masculinity, 1882–1940

ONE

Butte: "Only White Men and Dagoes"

A century ago Butte, Montana, was one of the most remarkable—and remarked on—cities in the nation. The contradictions that defined it meant that disagreements about its character abounded. Mark Twain, who visited the city at the height of its prosperity, thought it surprisingly urbane. Dashiell Hammett, who experienced it during the tumultuous period around World War I, described it as a corrupt, ugly place. To those seeking their fortunes, Butte's astonishing copper deposits made it the "Richest Hill on Earth." To the workers, who organized virtually every sector of the local economy so as to keep some of the vast wealth their labor created, Butte was America's "Gibraltar of Unionism." One of the few assessments that all these parties would have agreed on was that made by Joseph Kinsey Howard, one of Montana's most famous chroniclers, who called Butte "stridently male."[1]

The urbanity that impressed Twain was a result of Butte's having developed much more fully than other western mining towns, the vast majority of which survived for only a few decades. The discovery of gold in the region sparked the initial influx of white men, who in 1864 built the rough camp along the banks of Silver Bow Creek in western Montana that would become Butte. A decade later, the gold that could be found through placer mining was gone, and Butte had almost become a ghost town. In 1875 a silver bonanza reinvigorated the camp, but it was Irish immigrant Marcus Daly's 1882 discovery of a massive quantity of copper that turned Butte into the world's greatest mining city. Copper was the key component in electrical wire; its demand and prices increased dramatically with the country's rapid electrification, making fortunes for the men who owned the mines. Less than ten years after Daly and others began to pour capital into and extract wealth from Butte, it had become an industrial city that had as

1.1 Arthur Rothstein's 1939 photograph, *View from the Center of Town, Butte, Montana*, shows the physical presence of mining in the city. Library of Congress, Prints & Photographs Division, FSA-OWI Collection, LC-USF33-003111-M4 DLC.

much in common with factory centers such as Pittsburgh as with western mining camps such as Virginia City, Leadville, Cripple Creek, Tombstone, and Deadwood. Called by the artist Joseph Pennell "the most pictorial place in America," Butte's appearance reflected both of these tendencies. Office buildings, grand mansions, small houses for miners' families, and saloons were interspersed among the hoist houses, gallus frames, yellow and gray ore dumps, and other surface components of hard-rock mining that Hammett, and many others, found unappealing (fig. 1.1). The most visible aspects of Butte's social world, prostitution, gambling, and liquor, earned it a reputation as a "wide open town." But not only saloons and brothels operated twenty-four hours a day, seven days a week—so did the city's mines. By the beginning of the twentieth century, they accounted for a third of the nation's copper supply.[2]

For miners and its other residents, Butte was a city of neighborhoods with distinct characteristics and specific, though not exclusive, ethnic affiliations. To the north and northeast of downtown, Centerville, Walkerville, and Meaderville developed among the mines and housed most of Butte's miners. Walkerville was known for its sizable Cornish population, and Meaderville, an Italian enclave, for its nightlife. Below downtown, in the valley at the foot of Butte Hill, lay "the Flats," the neighborhood that most of the city's immigrants from the Austro-Hungarian Empire called home. Composed of Croatians, Serbians, Slovakians, Montenegrins, Herzegovinians, and a few other groups from the Balkan region, these immigrants were often called collectively "Austrians" or, more pejoratively, bohunks. Just before America's entry into World War I, when Butte's population peaked due to demand for munitions and other war material that required copper, approximately 85,000 people lived in the city and its surrounding neighborhoods. But 40,000 was a more typical figure in the years between 1900 and 1940, though miners' habitual transience made an accurate count difficult. Like the housing in other mining camps, Butte's residential areas appeared rough. Yet once the sulfurous smoke that blanketed the city cleared after the smelters that produced it were removed, many homes began to sport tidy gardens and feel more permanent. The rate of home ownership by occupants rose throughout the early twentieth century, reaching 75 percent by the late 1930s.[3]

Visitors marveled at the scope of mining operations. All large-scale hard-rock mines required substantial surface infrastructure. However, what could be seen aboveground paled in comparison with that below. Mine shafts provided access to this underground world, taking men and equipment down and material up. Other shafts provided ventilation. The three main shafts at Butte's Leonard Mine were each equipped with an electric hoist able to move twenty-four thousand tons of material a day. Butte's diggings formed a city under the city, as many of the fifteen-plus mines were connected underground. This subterranean world spread both horizontally and vertically at an average rate of 35 miles per year. While 253 miles of streets crisscrossed Butte proper just prior to World War II, over 2,000 miles of mining corridors and tunnels ran under the surface of Butte Hill.[4]

More than any other entity, the Anaconda Company dominated Butte's aboveground and belowground worlds. Daly founded the Company with George Hearst, James Ben Ali Haggin, and Lloyd Tevis, the three San Francisco–based men whose syndicate would eventually own the richest copper, silver, and gold properties in the United States. Able to mobilize almost unlimited capital, Daly spent nearly $15 million in and around Butte over the following several years. Besides purchasing the Anaconda Mine, where at the three-hundred-foot level he had found evidence of Butte's astonishing copper deposits, and the mines adjacent to it, he also built a state-of-the-art refining and smelting plant in nearby Anaconda and secured timber and coalfields around Montana that would be critical to the vast enterprise he and his partners envisioned. During this time, Daly maintained congenial labor relations with his workers. In 1891 he and his partners took the Company public, a decision that would have a profound effect on Montana's three copper towns. Less than five years later, it reorganized again as the Anaconda Copper Mining Company, with James Ben Ali Haggin and Daly, the two remaining original partners, serving as president and superintendent, respectively. (Although this was its official name until 1955, locals continued to refer to it simply as "the Company." I will refer to it as such or by its common abbreviation, ACM.)[5]

In 1899 a number of monopolists, including Henry Rogers and William Rockefeller, who controlled Standard Oil, succeeded in gaining a majority of ACM stock. In a quest to corner copper production as they had oil production, they also acquired two other corporations with significant holdings in Montana's copper industry: the Boston and Montana Company—which ran the smelter in Black Eagle—and the Butte and Boston Company. Rogers and Rockefeller placed all these under a holding company they called the Amalgamated Copper Company. Daly's death in 1900 solidified the sense that the Anaconda Company "was now 'a foreign corporation'" that no longer followed his approach to employee relations. F. A. Heinze, an owner of mines in Butte who fought against Standard Oil's control of Montana, enunciated the perspective of many locals when he said, "These people are my enemies, fierce, bitter, implacable; but they are your enemies, too. If they crush me today, they will crush you to-morrow. They will cut your wages and raise the tariff in the company stores on every bit you eat, and every rag you wear. They will force you to dwell in Standard Oil houses while you live, and they will bury you in Standard Oil coffins when you die." It took Rogers and Rockefeller another half decade, punctuated by myriad legal battles and mine shutdowns and a $12-million payout, to rid themselves of Heinze and fully assert their control over Montana, but they did so. In 1910 Amalgamated reconsolidated its copper holdings under the banner of the Anaconda Copper Mining Company. By 1915 it had severed its ties with Standard Oil and emerged as the most powerful copper corporation in the world, a titan of Wall Street, and an even more formidable foe for Butte's miners, who would battle it with varying degrees of success for decades to come.[6]

In their effort to counter the power of capital, the men who worked underground in Butte organized unions that would become one of the chief components of the city's social, political, and cultural fabric. Hard-rock miners who came to Montana from the Nevada and California diggings formed the first of these organizations, the Butte Workingmen's Union, in

1878. In 1881 it reflagged itself the Miners' Union of Butte City and opened membership to all laborers. When the organization once again reorganized and changed its name to the Butte Miners' Union (BMU) in 1885, it reverted to miners only, but used the strength of its now more than eighteen hundred members to support the formation of unions in other sectors of Butte's economy. Over the next several years, the BMU solidified its reputation as one of the region's most important labor organizations by turning Butte's mines into a closed shop and adding affiliates in other mining communities around Montana. In 1893, with the objective of strengthening organized labor in the mining industry throughout the Mountain West, the BMU took the lead in founding the Western Federation of Miners (WFM), for which it became Local No. 1. The BMU's struggle with Butte's mine owners would not prompt a strike or turn violent for another two decades, but the WFM had to engage in battle well before then. Success in Cripple Creek, Colorado, in 1894 spurred growth, and confrontations in Leadville, Colorado, and Coeur d'Alene, Idaho, gained the union notoriety and its leaders experience. By 1903 the WFM had two hundred locals in thirteen states, but none trumped the BMU in size or influence.[7]

"A Man's Work"

The BMU's rolls were so large because Butte's mines required a huge labor force. On average, ten thousand men worked underground. An extraordinary range of skills was necessary to operate the city's diggings. In nonferrous mining, as in many other industrial workplaces, the labor process was more differentiated than the term *miner* suggests. At the turn of the twentieth century, census takers listed more than twenty distinct underground jobs on their forms. Muckers, nippers, mule skinners, engineers, electricians, and others worked in Butte's mines, but most men employed as miners made holes in rock to access mineral veins. Before the 1930s, miners used dry drills; later they used wet drills. Miners packed the holes they had made with explosives and then blasted. Next they shoveled the ore either into chutes that led to collection points or directly onto ore trains that were hoisted to the surface. Miners put up support timbers as they went and created stopes, or open chambers; these averaged twenty feet in width and had multiple floors approximately ten feet apart that were reached by ladders.[8]

Ronald C. Brown, one of the early historians of hard-rock mining, observed that the first question asked of prospective miners was, "Can you do the work?" The physical demands of mining and the place that physicality had in establishing its manliness were central to this occupational world. Teddy Roosevelt's championing of "the Strenuous Life," which he identified with the West because he feared that office work and the East's genteel Victorian culture were emasculating upper- and middle-class white men, and the rise of bodybuilding and organized team sports illustrate the crucial nature of strong, manly physiques as an aspect of turn-of-the-century American masculinity more generally. Yet, more than most places, Butte's "stridently male" character was rooted in the physicality of miners' work and the culture it engendered.[9]

Along with this physicality, the homosocial nature of mining solidified its reputation as archetypal masculine work. Miners worked in an all-male world, performing and defining their masculinity against one another as well as through the exclusion of women as unsuitable or incapable of handling the difficulties presented by mining. Seen as both physical and mental, these difficulties allowed men to draw firm distinctions between them and women, and to create bonds between each other. In the mines, young men learned what it was to be skilled working-class men, and a large part of that definition centered on working, and at times socializing, in all-male groups. As Mary Murphy notes, boys "learned to work, to fight, to organize, to claim the streets as their own, and to seek the company of other males," the very habits that defined adult masculinity.[10]

Miners' claim to exemplary working-class manhood revolved around a second question, which hinted at masculinity's complex operation by going beyond physicality: "Will you do the work?" (fig. 1.2). Hard-rock mining required a particular kind of courage because of the dangerous conditions that came with the job. Despite the lure of a good paycheck, many men would never consider going underground into a dark, claustrophobic space to toil hour after hour, day after day. The mines were hot, wet, acrid, and highly unsanitary. Water not only seeped organically through tunnel ceilings but was artificially introduced to keep down the dust. At the end of their shift, miners emerged wet, dirty, tired, and relieved to have survived another day. After reaching the surface, they would shower, change, and, as one observer put it, often "appea[r] on the street dressed like the average business man."[11] This sartorial fashion was a way of asserting equality with the city's middle class and reminding other workers of miners' professionalism and status.

Many miners were fatalistic about the risks their jobs entailed. Statistics of deaths and injuries from hard-rock mining were horrific, and Butte's mines were "arguably the most dangerous in the world." Between 1910 and 1913, for example, 162 men employed by the ACM died and 5,233 were injured in Butte's mines. In order to cope with the dangers they faced,

1.2 It took a particular kind of courage to labor at least eight hours a day in difficult and dangerous conditions and hundreds, if not thousands, of feet underground. Photograph by N. A. Forsyth, *Ready to Blast, 1900 Feet under the Butte Post Office*, circa 1905; Montana Historical Society Research Center Photograph Archives, Helena.

miners used gallows humor in referring to the astonishing number of ways they could be injured or killed. For instance, they called a piece of hanging rock that threatened to fall a "Larry Duggan" after the city's best-known undertaker. Yet miners knew that the most common way their work damaged their bodies was less visible: silicosis, better known as miners' consumption, took a devastating toll, as breathing in the rock dust that permeated the tunnels scarred the lungs. A 1916 investigation found that 42 percent of miners examined suffered from this condition and faced an almost inevitable early death. Improved safety measures and the shuttering of mines during the Great Depression led to a decline in the rate of deaths, accidents, and disease, but Butte's mines remained highly dangerous places. Mining endangered workers' families as well. Wives and children suffered when their husbands and fathers were killed or disabled, and diseases that proliferated in the mines, such as typhoid, were contagious on the surface too. At the end of the 1930s, a startling fact about Butte remained true: there were more dead bodies in Butte's cemetery than live ones in the city itself.[12]

Still, men went underground because the benefits seemed to outweigh the costs, especially for immigrants and the native-born sons of unskilled workers. The relatively high wages paid in Butte were their principal motivation. In 1878, following a strike to protest a wage cut for men working in unskilled positions, Butte's first miners' union negotiated a contract that established a base rate of $3.50 a day for all men who went underground. Skilled miners, operating on the contract system, which saw a man's wages increase in relation to the amount of ore he produced, could make considerably more. By way of comparison, between 1890 and 1899 the Bureau of Labor reported the average daily wage (for a ten-hour day) earned by men in various occupations: stone mason, $3.60; plumber, $3.55; hog gutter, $3.15; Linotype operator, $3.00; boot maker, $2.90; boilermaker, $2.60; cigar maker, $2.60; building trades laborer, $1.46; street and sewer contract laborer, $1.46; railroad laborer, $1.14; textile weaver, $1.11; tobacco mixer, $1.11.[13]

Miners' elevated masculine status was based on their having the courage to do work most men refused, as well as the toughness, skill, and mental acuity necessary to survive the mines. So important was the idea of miners' exceptional manliness that it became an essential part of how people thought about the city itself. *Copper Camp*, the popular account of Butte's past published in 1943, described Butte's first miners as "rough, tough, and as hard as the metal they mined, but many of them were the 'salt of the earth.' They worked like slaves, and they played like kings; they asked no quarter, and no quarter did they give; they took their whiskey straight, and they took it often." The poet Berton Braley, who lived in Butte at the beginning of the century, emphasized the miners' masculinity as well as their diverse origins: "It is easy to gird the 'wide open spaces where men are men' but when Ireland, Scotland, Cornwall, Finland, Italy and Serbia, to say nothing of New England, Texas, California, and the Middle West, seemed to have bred their strongest males for the job of mining copper in Butte, the men-ness of men in this rugged town of wide open spaces is just one of the many facts of life that the intelligentsia don't know."[14]

These celebratory accounts provide clues about some of the conflicts inherent in miners' masculinity that could be difficult for those outside the industry to perceive. *Copper Camp* revealed the contradiction between an ethos of hard work and the fact that miners were akin to slaves laboring for a boss, the ACM, that reaped all the rewards. It also implied the strain between

miners' well-known propensity for extravagant leisure and these men's obligations to their families. Braley's commentary more fundamentally questioned whether miners' masculinity was held in high-enough regard by an
"intelligentsia" that he believed had focused on the more romantic masculinity of the cowboy in the West's "wide open spaces." Submerged in his
critique of thirties intellectuals seems to be the idea that too much attention
had been paid to miners' politics. However, Braley's suggestion that he understood the multiethnic and multiregional masculinity of miners is belied
by his celebratory tone, which fails to reflect the host of tensions—including
what sort of actions comprised quintessential miner masculinity, and how
those actions related to ideas about nationality, race, color, and working-
class solidarity—that divided those men.

Most miners sought to minimize the dangers they faced, even if they
did not advertise the fact. They were keenly attuned to safety issues underground. Some attempted to secure the safest and healthiest jobs, usually
by using their personal connections with shift bosses and foremen. BMU
member Joe Shannon, testifying before the Commission on Industrial Relations in 1913, said, "Fine day miners . . . got an easy place in the mine,
where the air is good and they always have a good word for the company
for giving them the job." Shannon expressed some miners' sense that these
men lost masculine credibility not only for hiding from hard, dangerous
work but also for being under the thumb of their employers. Those who
cornered the very safest positions underground found themselves referred
to by an especially emasculating term: *capons*, meaning castrated roosters. At
the same time, Shannon described those miners who refused to seek the safest and healthiest positions as "strong men" who were "weak in the head."
The differing perspectives on craft jobs, which the Irish also had better access to and which were better paying and less physically arduous, reinforced
workers' tendency to create contrasting narratives about the masculinity of
certain occupations. While some contended that the skill involved in being
a craftsman, along with the better pay, provided elevated masculine status,
others argued that these men did not produce anything. One miner opined,
"As long as I was ever underground I never seen a decent shift put out by
a craftsman." He linked craftsmen to office workers and described both as
"deadheading."[15]

The class and racial-ethnic politics embedded in the question of who
worked where in the mines were especially challenging for those outside
the mining community to discern. Such job stratification provides a window into the divisions that structured masculinity within Butte's social and
occupational worlds. The settled men who had chosen to make Butte their

home and raise a family there comprised one side of the divide. For them, a miner's manliness had less to do with his ability to survive the toughest mines and more to do with the related issues of skill level, longevity, and ability to care for his family and support his union, church, fraternal association, and community by drawing a larger paycheck. All these issues were facilitated by tapping into connections that would provide a good place to work in the mines, and all of them spoke to the unique contract system that for decades was detested by more politically progressive labor leaders. Writing in 1939, Howard described the relationship between the contract system and the ideology of Butte's miners.

> Copper miners have always been individualists; as such they have left their stamp upon Butte. They may be—and are—loyal and militant unionists; but they would rather work "on their own" by contracting with the company on a piecework basis than work for the union minimum scale. These men are no slaves of an assembly line: despite the great advance of metal mines technology since the war, their job is still personal and integrated; the contract miner still "breaks" (blasts), shovels the ore into the cars, and timbers the drift—a unified task, complete. His is still a man's work, a man's contest with Nature jealous of her riches, a struggle against dust and heat and fire and gas and death.[16]

Howard's portrait aptly conveys the contradictions that defined settled miners' masculinity and often frustrated the aspirations of less settled miners.

The less settled men were those who moved from camp to camp for economic and ideological reasons, sometimes just because they enjoyed the freedom of not being tied down. This group, which was closely associated with hard-rock mining in the popular imagination, was affiliated politically with the Industrial Workers of the World (IWW, or Wobblies) and its legendary leader, "Big Bill" Haywood. Rather than trying to work within the system by getting a better job, they valued their ability to assert control over their working lives by quitting, going on strike, sabotaging the productive potential of a worksite, or enacting some other form of manly protest. When assessing manliness, like settled men they looked first at a miner's skill, but then they focused on independence from the bosses and political solidarity with the working class, seen especially through the above forms of direct action. Although they did not figure as much in the popular image of miners, the settled men, who were associated with the BMU and its conservative politics, were dominant within the city's working class. Most important, the less-settled men represented a wide variety of racial-ethnic groups, but the settled men were predominantly Irish.[17]

"Mohammed Murphy"

Where a person came from made an enormous difference in Butte, just as it did in the rest of America. Workers originated from as many as fifty different nations and from most parts of the United States. Figures from 1910 show that almost 3,000 "Austrians," mainly Serbians and Croatians, 2,500 Germans, 1,600 Italians, and 1,500 Finns called Butte home. They toiled alongside immigrants from across Europe as well as from Mexico, China, Syria, and Afghanistan. Until the end of the nineteenth century, English immigrants, especially from Cornwall, outnumbered other foreigners; their Protestant faith and Republican Party leanings meant they tended to assimilate easily. But the culture and politics of Butte were dominated by the Irish, stalwarts of the Roman Catholic Church and the Democratic Party. By 1900 the Irish population in metropolitan Butte stood at 12,000, or 26 percent of the total, surpassing all other racial-ethnic groups. It made its power felt in myriad ways, both large and small. The rug merchant Mohammed Akara's decision to change his name to "Mohammed Murphy" for what he called "business reasons" provides an apt illustration. The historian David Emmons's conclusion that Butte "belonged to the Irish in almost the same way Salt Lake City belonged to the Mormons" makes the point succinctly.[18]

The power of the Irish made Butte's racial-ethnic politics distinctive in significant ways. In the United States for much of the nineteenth century, when an individual's "race" was mentioned it often referred to her or his "nationality," not the color of her or his skin. Racial theorists placed each of these nationalities into a hierarchy based on their sense of the merits of particular languages, religions, and national histories. With the increase in Irish immigration to the United States in the aftermath of the potato famine, influential American commentators echoed their counterparts in Britain by deriding the Irish "race" for its Catholicism, its Gaelic language, and its supposedly uncivilized peasant culture. By the latter part of the century, however, Irish immigrants' place on the American racial hierarchy had been elevated based on a number of factors, including their ability to speak English as well as Gaelic and nativists' growing antipathy toward the new immigrants from southern and eastern Europe.[19]

Around this time, the sense of race as nationality and race as color grew entangled. Prominent thinkers placed national races into three categories,

Mongoloid, Negroid, and Caucasoid, with virtually all Europeans located in the last of these. Spurred by their antagonism to immigrants from southern and eastern Europe, some theorists argued that the Caucasoid category did not make important distinctions among the European races. Madison Grant, who saw European immigrants as divided into Nordic, Alpine, and Mediterranean groupings, represented perhaps the most influential early twentieth-century development of this idea of race. Grant produced a complicated taxonomy that used pseudoscientific reasoning to bolster the argument about the superiority of "white" northern and western Europeans. The specificity of these theories did not dampen their racist core and, ultimately, mattered little to a general public—including Butte's Irish—who typically referenced simplified versions as they argued for the inferiority of new immigrants. The overarching precept was that southern and eastern Europeans fell outside the Nordic identity, and, as lower racial-ethnic groups, were on the margins of whiteness and therefore should not have access to the full material and psychological "wages" that it brought.[20]

One of the reasons the Irish were able to secure power in Butte earlier and more fully than in other places was because employers there did not have an anti-Irish bias. Some western mine owners grouped the Irish with immigrants from southern and eastern Europe, whom they considered of lesser intelligence, ability, and worth than "American" men. Others called them "Irish Mexican greasers," rhetorically linking them with another stigmatized group. In both cases, part of the purpose was to promote competition and animosity among workers of different nationalities so as to drive down wages and make union organizing more difficult. But beginning with Marcus Daly, that was not the common practice in Butte. Daly, the most powerful man in the city during its formative period, was himself an Irish immigrant. He sought out Irish workers and helped place a substantial number in positions of authority in both the mines and the town. William Andrews Clark and Fritz Heinze, two of the other Copper Kings, were also favorably disposed toward Butte's English-speaking workers. Even though it arguably went against their economic interests, they publicly declared their opposition to non-English-speaking workers, especially southeastern Europeans.[21]

Butte's Irish also developed a set of local institutions, especially ethnic associations, Catholic parishes, and the BMU, that enabled the enclave to grow and prosper. The BMU was firmly under the control of settled Irish miners and was less responsive to others in the diverse workforce. Still, all Butte's miners enjoyed the benefits of the BMU's major accomplishments: securing a closed shop, winning high wages, and later attaining an eight-hour workday. The union achieved these victories in part by playing members of the city's elite, especially Daly and Clark, off one another. Miners with a more radical working-class perspective, however, called the BMU's Irish leaders "conservative." The charge had validity; it was even asserted, with a complimentary tone, by Butte's businessmen. According to Emmons, Irish union officials "revealed strong craft biases, bought company stock, permitted hiring officers to retain membership, tolerated company stores and subscription 'health plans,' favored corporate consolidation, and declared socialism a 'dead issue.'" The conflict between radical and conservative workers in Butte was, at its roots, about "race" favoritism: radicals contended that conservative Irish labor leaders put their friendship with Irish bosses above their allegiance to the working class. In a period of deep industrial unrest across the United States, especially in the mining communities of the Mountain West, the fact that the BMU avoided going out on strike against the ACM for thirty-six years was Exhibit A in this debate.[22]

Yet factional conflict in Butte should not be allowed to obscure the shared racial politics that sought to shore up the white privilege of native-born and northern European immigrant workers by excluding or marginalizing groups considered nonwhite or of lower racial-ethnic status. Butte's miners, like their peers elsewhere in the region, initially focused not on southeastern Europeans but on Chinese "Mongoloid" workers as the most likely threat to the jobs and reasonable wages they had secured. Chinese who entered mining during the California gold rush, often under the control of a boss, patron, or contractor, found their way to other western mining towns during the late nineteenth century. They faced racist opposition, including violence. In Butte, according to a local newspaper, a "disheartened, yet patriotic" miner lynched "a Chinaman" in 1868. The city's 1882 mayoral race was won by a candidate who championed the ouster of "Cheap Chinese labor," registering the level of ongoing anti-Chinese sentiment and the relationship between racial prejudice and workplace concerns.[23]

Butte's miners succeeded in blocking the Chinese from working in the mines, but most did not want to go as far as some of their peers in other cities who attempted to bar the Chinese entirely. To the consternation of some civic leaders, Butte had a thriving Chinese district from the 1880s through the 1910s where miners could engage in such leisure activities as gambling and commercial sex and find inexpensive services such as laundry. The continued presence of Chinese men in Butte served as one of the foils for miners' racialized masculinity. European men compared themselves with the supposedly effeminate appearance of Chinese men and to their tainted character, represented by the female slavery and opium smoking that were purportedly at the heart of the Chinese masculine ethic. Many non-Chinese men scoffed at the idea that Chinese men were manly enough to do white men's jobs. Still, speeches at a turn-of-the-century Western Federation of Miners' convention show that some continued to fear that mine owners would use Chinese labor to drive down wages or supplant white men altogether.[24]

"The Dark Skinned Invader"

By the 1890s, the Chinese question had been overshadowed by whether southeastern Europeans and African Americans would be allowed to mine in Butte. Small numbers of Italians, Serbians, and Croatians came to the Mountain West to work in the copper industry before 1890. After that their numbers rose rapidly and peaked in the first decade of the twentieth century. In response, northern European and other miners in Butte, as well as their allies, mounted a concerted campaign against the "dago" and the "bohunk." An 1897 editorial in the *Butte Bystander*, the official newspaper of the BMU, argued that southeastern Europeans were "three centuries behind northern Europeans in intelligence," and the prospective miners from that region were "brutish, ignorant men" who willingly accepted wages that no "American could live on." The opposition of English-speaking workers and the organization that represented them to southeastern Europeans was at least as surprising in some regards as the bosses' stance. As an industrial union, the BMU organized and represented *all* underground workers, including a wide variety of immigrants. Thus, the BMU could have been expected to oppose the racial taxonomies that ranked immigrants in relation to a scale that put Anglo-Saxons at the top and sometimes placed the Irish outside "civilization." Yet the union's Irish leaders chose a different approach, implicitly claiming a place among "northern Europeans" and contending that a vast distance separated them from southeastern Europeans.[25] Not only did the BMU want to keep more southeastern Europeans from coming to Butte and entering the mines, but the Irish and other northern European BMU leaders sought to buttress their interconnected claim to racial and masculine superiority over southeastern Europeans. Having others agree with this proposition ensured that the Irish and their allies would continue to receive the best positions in the mines and the highest masculine status in the community.

The battle over the employment of southeastern Europeans in the mines began in earnest in the early twentieth century. As an increasing number of southeastern Europeans arrived in Butte, Irish workers' influence with the Company dissipated following the death of Daly and the emergence of less Irish-friendly management policies as Standard Oil, which at that point owned the ACM, exerted its power over the mines. Around 1910 the Immigration Commission sent to inspect the situation in Butte and other hard-rock mining towns in the Mountain West reported that non-English-speaking immigrants had a reputation for deflating wages, hampering unionization, and hindering efforts to improve the employer-employee relationship. According to the commission, these new immigrants facilitated managers' use of "race competition" to maximize profits. In 1897 Butte had stood outside much of the rest of the industry because bosses protected English-speaking workers from the threat posed by non-English-speaking immigrants. A decade later, though, some managers in the mining city were behaving much more like their peers elsewhere. One North Butte Mining Company official nicely summarized their attitude: "I don't like to see too many of one nationality put together. I would rather keep them mixed. . . . I think you get better results if you don't have all your employees belonging to one clan or nationality." Local labor leaders' contention that Marcus Daly would have barred the new immigrants from the mines drew applause from workers, but only served to highlight the changing ethnoracial politics in the mines.[26]

Further unsettling Butte's social politics, Irish BMU leaders were facing a significant shift within the union's core membership. Many second-generation Irish, following the wishes of their parents, had chosen not to enter the mines, decreasing the enclave's numerical advantage within the union. Those Irish who continued to come to Butte, drawn by its reputation as an Irish-friendly town, could have buttressed older Irish union leaders, but many in this new cohort did not share the earlier generation's perspective on working-class issues or Irish politics. One local Irish leader remarked that Butte had "Home Rulers, Sinn Feiners, physical force fanatics, Ulstermen and Coronians—all pulling in different directions." These conflicts destroyed the unanimity that had been essential to maintaining the enclave's power. As the historian Michael Malone puts it, when "more radically anti-British newcomers joined the earlier arrivals after 1900, the big Irish bloc came to look more like a salad bowl than a melting pot."[27]

Changes within the community and the Company multiplied the challenges to Butte's power structure being posed by new immigrants (fig. 1.3). A long exposé in the July 24, 1910, edition of the *Butte Evening News*, "The Story of the Butte Bo-hunk—The Dark Skinned Invader," articulated this attitude and reflected the increasing conflation of nationality and color in conceptualizations of race. It began: "This story tells of the bohunks, three thousand strong, who are driving the white man slowly but surely out of the

1.3 This cartoon, which ran in the *Butte Evening News* on July 31, 1910, shows the way the language of color informed the racialization of southeastern Europeans in Montana's copper communities. Courtesy of the Butte-Silver Bow Public Archives, Butte.

camp." Pointedly referring to the older immigrant and native-born miners as "white men" or "Americans" rather than specifying their ethnic backgrounds, the article reinforced a sense that they were racially acceptable and well within the national mainstream. It described southeastern Europeans as "some mysterious form of foreigner" and as "low grade" foreigners. The "Bohunk miner" was similar to "a Chinaman." Collectively, these "black men from across the water" threatened the city with "a black peril" akin to the old "yellow peril."[28]

By using these racist terms, the article ascribed a form of enervated masculinity to southeastern Europeans. In contrast—indeed, in opposition—to the masculinity of the upright, family-centered white miners who were Butte's "bread-winner[s]," bohunk men were "ready to slip into every job where a white man is laid off." Even worse in the eyes of Butte's independent-minded miners with their advertised ethic of battling the boss, a bohunk was willing to "buy his job from the foreman and pa[y] him for keeping it." Union men should be especially alarmed, because bohunk men lacked both a sense of workingmen's independence and a sense of class solidarity.[29]

The version of ideal working-class manhood offered by the article was also racialized and aligned with that espoused by settled miners. Beyond the ability to do the work, real men were family-oriented breadwinners. Far from the model established by Butte's settled men, the paper reported, bohunk men crowded together into cabins with "sickening odors . . . [and] unwashed bodies." At night they "curl[ed] themselves up on a dirty blanket on the floor, and [felt] as refreshed when the alarm goes off as if their cot was of feathers." Suggesting the cross-class affinities between settled miner masculinity and local middle-class masculinity, the paper asserted that bohunk men failed to support the community by patronizing local businesses. Instead, they spent their earnings at their own groceries and bakeries, because "the bohunk does not eat white bread." In a city with remarkably diverse culinary habits—Chinese noodle shops and tamales sold by Afghans were widely acknowledged as among Butte's favorite dining options—bohunks were denigrated for eating "dried sausages and dried meats" instead of the fresh meat offered at Butte's older butcher shops. The paper lambasted the bohunk because he "[stole] coal and rustle[d] railroad ties"—another time-honored tradition for many Butte families—rather than providing trade to the city's fuel dealers. The *Evening News* even questioned southeastern Europeans' haberdashery: "the clothier says one suit of clothes lasts a lifetime; the Bohunks are not fancy dressers."[30]

For Butte, the paper asserted, the bohunk invasion would lead to the exodus of white mining families. "Every train that dumps these foreigners off as it pulls in takes just as many old-timers aboard as it pulls out. . . . Up the gulch, 'mother and the kids' watch daily for the postman to see if father has found a place where a white man can live and earn his living. Up the gulch, boys who were born and raised there are kissing their grey-haired mothers good-bye and are leaving for pastures new."[31]

The perspective presented by the *Evening News* was widely shared in Butte. Miners told Industrial Commission investigators that the bohunks were "inefficient," "worthless," "undisciplined," "bullheaded and troublesome," "surly," and "social outcasts." But being thought of as "bullheaded and troublesome" toward employers or docile coworkers was considered a compliment by Butte's radical miners, a faction with which Butte's settled miners associated—to a large extent accurately—these immigrants. Yet that faction could not or would not defend the men targeted by the *Evening News* exposé, which—especially by revealing the "padrone" practices that saw the poorest of these southern European immigrants come to Butte and other western mining districts under contractual control of a labor boss—prompted a brief decrease in the number of bohunks in Butte.[32] However, others, who also faced some resistance to their presence, replaced them shortly afterward. Unlike African Americans, another group of overtly racialized workers, bohunks were nonetheless allowed to labor in Butte's mines, indicating that the language of color, such as "black peril," deployed against these men did not bar them from the most important privilege of whiteness in this local space.

"Just as White a Man as Anybody Would Ever Want"

The experience of African Americans in Butte differs in critical and illuminating ways from that of southeastern Europeans. Like the debate over allowing southeastern Europeans into Butte's mines, the discussion about employing African Americans started in the 1890s. But, unlike its policy toward southeastern Europeans, the ACM categorically barred blacks from its mines. The *Helena Colored Citizen*, one of a number of African American papers in Montana, first publicized the ACM's stance on September 24, 1894. In "The Anaconda Company Employs Only White Men and Dagoes," it bemoaned exclusionary employment policies and the racial order they reflected while also championing the prowess of African American workers. "Montana has just right to feel proud of its . . . colored citizens," wrote the editor, J. P. Ball. "They are the brawn that has unfettered and exposed to the sunshine of our unsurpassed clime the treasured wealth of ages." Most of Butte's male African American residents were employed by the railroads that served the city. Other men worked as waiters, valets, and janitors in places such as the luxurious ACM Club and as butlers in private homes. Black women worked as maids, virtually the only job they could get in the West.[33]

Working-class whites frequently came into conflict with blacks over access to jobs outside mining. In Helena, for example, white and black residents clashed over employment at the poshest private hotels. In Butte, a notable fracas occurred when in July 1911 the mayor appointed Frank Cassell to the city's police force. Cassell, whom the local paper described as resembling Jake Kilrain, a well-known, late nineteenth-century Irish American boxer, became the only African American on the force. Opponents claimed not only that Cassell was the wrong color but also that he was placed ahead of many white men who had put their name on the list of hopefuls. In contrast, the issue of the *Butte Miner* published on Cassell's first day at work described him—especially his body—as equal to the job and to white men who did the same work: "he swung his club with authority," had "the size and build" to "look the part of the regulation copper," and would, according to the mayor, "acquit himself with credit." After being petitioned by prominent African American residents of Butte, including the pastor of one of the city's black Protestant congregations, the mayor decided that this appointment would show "his non-partisan feeling and the absence of any race prejudice."[34] For Butte's African American residents, however, his support of Cassell did not foretell a dramatic change in local race relations.

Black citizens recalled that discrimination was an ever-present part of personal and institutional life. Butte's YMCA, which purportedly cared for the health and education of all Christian youth, was notorious for its segregationist policies. For blacks, the rule in regard to the 'Y' was, according to one resident, "Don't even open the front door." Another added, "Don't even walk on the same side of the street." "It was almost sacrilegious. It was almost the same as if you went out and tried to proposition the Virgin Mary, to ask for a membership at the YMCA," noted a third. Even black professionals such as Dr. Walter Duncan were not allowed to buy a meal at any decent restaurant in town. In an insult that still stung members of the community decades later, African Americans were refused service at one of Butte's Chinese restaurants. One black resident reported that when he traveled he would let out a deep breath as soon as he got on the train, because he knew that when he got hungry he could buy a meal. Another was most frustrated by the segregation she experienced in Butte's movie theaters. A third recalled being told she was not welcome at one of Butte's churches.[35]

In contrast, Butte's schools and neighborhoods provided integrated spaces that fostered interracial interaction and laid the groundwork for an alternative racial politics. Students were not segregated at any grade level; as William Fenter put it, going to class with white children was "no sweat." Residential patterns were even more significant. Butte's Irish, Italians, Finns, and other ethnic groups largely congregated in their own enclaves. But African Americans were not segregated geographically. Class and occupation, rather than race, determined where blacks lived in the city, with lodging cost and proximity to work driving housing choices.[36]

The dynamic created by Butte's racially integrated working-class neighborhoods and schools fostered close associations among a small number of the city's black and white residents. Sometimes, as in the case of Bob

Logan and Hugo Kenck, strong friendships emerged. Logan, a bank janitor, was born into slavery but parlayed his musical ability into a career. Kenck recalled that when Butte's elite found out about Logan's talent, they asked him to sing at an annual board meeting at the Silver Bow Club, the city's most prestigious social organization. Logan agreed and said his wife, who had studied piano at an eastern college, would accompany him. The person who invited him objected: "We couldn't have a nigger woman in the room with us like that," he told Logan. Kenck saw this comment as evidence that Logan and his wife were being judged by their place on the American racial hierarchy rather than their abilities. "They were niggers first and last to many," he concluded. The signifying power of that term reached all the way to the top of Butte's social order. One of the roots of the Daly-Clark feud was Clark's once having called Daly's part-Turkish partner, James Ben Ali Haggin, a "nigger."[37]

Based on their friendships with blacks in the city, Kenck and other liberal whites fought to change Butte's racial regime and, in the process, revealed the challenges to change posed by the racism of others and by their own internalized beliefs. Seeking to refute the negative, race-based assessment of Logan, Kenck described his friend as a well-mannered man who dressed immaculately; "just as white a man as anybody would ever want, maybe whiter than a lot of them. . . . He wasn't really a black nigger—he was more a palmetto." Kenck's comments say much about his own assumptions concerning the relationship between skin color, race, masculinity, and moral conduct, and suggest the powerful set of racial and gender ideas linked to white identity. Immigrants, who sought to distance themselves from any association with blackness, had a more conscious investment in asserting their white identity. Although Kenck's language reified the binary between black and white, his belief in individuals' ability to move between these categories represented a threat to the whiteness of immigrants who did not yet feel secure in their racial identity.[38]

The anger Butte's African American community felt toward the city's segregated institutions was based on a deep understanding of the emotional and material effects of racism. When Kenck tried to take Logan to Gamer's for lunch, they were turned away. Kenck's refusal to enter alone stands as notable protest against segregation. But he vividly remembered the ways other whites enforced the racial status quo in Butte: "You could be called a nigger lover if you had too much to do with the negroes."[39] Native-born whites and northern Europeans did not face a similar charge if they befriended a bohunk or dago, but that did not translate into better relations between workers for quite some time.

The Birth of Bohunkus Day and the Return
of Miners' Union Day

Tensions between new and old immigrants, and the related battle within the BMU and the WFM between radical and conservative workers, increased sharply at the beginning of the twentieth century and came to a spectacular head in 1914, when the Miners Union Hall was dynamited. The BMU imploded alongside it, and the following years saw several workers' organizations, including the IWW, the Metal Mine Workers Union, and the WFM vying to represent the miners. At its 1916 convention in Great Falls, the WFM removed the teeth from its once-radical mission language and changed its name to the International Union of Mine, Mill, and Smelter Workers (Mine Mill). Neither of these two steps, nor others taken by its leaders, were enough to secure the backing of a plurality of Montana's divided copper workers. The murder of IWW organizer Frank Little in 1917 offers a tragic symbol of how caustic local politics had become. Who exactly attacked Little and hung him from a railroad trestle in Butte remains a point of debate to this day, but the leading theories—workers opposed to his radical politics; Pinkerton guards employed by the ACM—speak to the combustible and complex forces roiling Butte at the time. So too does the massive turnout for Little's funeral march through the city by workers of all political orientations.[40]

As they dealt with their own internal problems during this period, organized labor faced off against corporate leaders who were decidedly less influenced by the personal connections between management and labor that had long characterized all three copper towns. Always a one-industry town, Butte had become a company town, and relations between the ACM and its employees grew markedly worse as the Company increasingly brandished its power. In 1912 it fired five hundred miners for their radical beliefs. Two years later, it instituted a "rustling card" system. Management described the cards as permits issued to allow men to look for work. In the view of the working class, the cards were a blacklisting tool and functioned as "a most formidable weapon for intimidation."[41]

The Company's effort to undermine organized labor, coupled with a series of catastrophes, including the death of 165 men at the Speculator Mine in 1917, gave strong support to the notion that the bosses put profits before people. So did the fact that wages for Montana's copper men had fallen from the best in the nation to twentieth, while the notoriously high cost of living in the state's copper communities had not decreased. Following World War I, the ACM instituted more wage cuts, shuttered a number of mines which resulted in job loss, and, along with its allies in local, state, and national government, further cracked down on labor activism. In April 1920, Company guards fired on picketing miners, killing two and wounding fifteen. The ACM managed to blame the IWW for the Anaconda Road Massacre and to convince the federal government to once more declare martial law in Butte. For many workers, it was the Company's undemocratic actions, not the IWW or any other worker organization, that produced the city's labor turmoil. Miners, however, were unable to muster a successful response to Company and government actions, suggesting both the strength of the forces they faced and just how diminished and fragmented worker solidarity had become. In February 1921, the Company shut down all its operations in Montana for nearly a year. The mines and smelters eventually reopened, but the ability of miners and smeltermen to unify and create a strong, independent union was at a nadir.[42]

The 1920s, building on developments during the 1910s that cemented the sense that Butte had entered a new phase of its history, were a dark era for labor in the mining city, just as they were for unions across the country. The ACM, in contrast, continued to be enormously profitable and powerful. Writing in the *American Mercury* in 1925, one longtime Butte observer held that "like the Lord God Almighty in His universe, the Anaconda Copper Mining Company is everywhere. It is all, and in all. Its titular Mercy Seat is on the sixth floor of the Hennessy Building at the intersection of Main and Granite streets, but it is enthroned in the heart, brain and wallet of every man and woman from Nine-Mile to Stringtown, from the Main Range to Whisky Gulch." Attempting to appear more worker friendly and thereby to reduce turnover, the Company instituted a variety of tepid initiatives, especially in the recreational arena, under the rubric of "welfare capitalism." Among them was Miners Field Day, a replacement for Miners' Union Day, the former holiday that for the thirty years before 1914 represented workers' power and solidarity.[43] Miners and their families partook of these new activities, but they did not fundamentally alter the negative view they had of the ACM's hold on their lives.

Yet the decade did see a number of notable social shifts in Butte that would shape the city's social politics for decades to come. The proportion of the city's population under forty-five years of age had declined by 10 percent between 1900 and 1920, but still stood at a striking 78 percent. Although in that latter year there remained almost 120 men for every 100 women in Butte, that was a sizable drop from the almost 150 men for every 100 women in 1900. For the first time, married men outnumbered bachelors. The cohort of settled miners was becoming larger, and simultaneously, in line with national changes, these men were finding their masculinity judged ever more by heteronormative standards for how they performed as fathers and husbands. Still, the homosocial work world of Butte's mines and the homosocial leisure world of its bars and many other entertainment spaces catering to men meant that working-class masculinity there remained outside the American mainstream.[44]

Domestic servant and teacher were still the first and second most common areas of paid female employment, but the 1910s and 1920s witnessed large numbers of Butte women entering clerical positions, a trend that had occurred across much of the rest of the nation earlier in the century. As Murphy cogently notes, "the strictures of domesticity" had been readily apparent for decades in the mining city. But, more recently, Butte's women "also had the example of trailblazing political campaigners" such as Ella Knowles and Jeanette Rankin, and, between the two chronologically, the iconoclastic feminist Mary McLane. In part inspired by these and other local groundbreakers, women sought greater equality. They increasingly took the lead in addressing the social and economic problems plaguing Butte. At the cultural level, through their fashion choices, how and where they chose to socialize, and in numerous other ways, many actively resisted conventional notions regarding appropriate gendered behavior.[45]

During these years, local men put up considerable opposition to what they perceived as women encroaching on the male world. As one Butte man put it, "There's only a few men's towns left. And we aim to stay one." In no area was this more apparent than in the realm of leisure as women began to attend boxing matches, frequent bars, and gamble. One local woman's comment spoke volumes about Butte's gender regime: "It ain't that us women here in Butte are sissies either. It's because they think if they give us anything but a ten-cent keno game there won't be pork chops on the supper table." Butte's men, Murphy concludes, had to "learn to deal differently with women during the 1920s and 1930s, together forging a community more responsive to the needs of both sexes."[46]

If in the leisure realm the 1930s saw a metamorphosis in relations between men and women, in the workplace that was not the case. The fact that working-class masculinity became hegemonic in the United States during the Great Depression should have facilitated the forging of this new gender order. But this shift into a dominant cultural position was fraught more with irony than paradox for working-class men, as the Depression made it difficult for them to remain employed. In 1929 the ACM had faced a labor shortage that drove it to advertise for miners in the East and to pay $6.00 an hour as the base wage for any man who worked underground, but the stock market crash that year and subsequent economic contraction caused 84 percent of men to lose their jobs by 1932. Subsequently, many local women who had been employed found themselves replaced by men. As one local government official noted, "Butte has never been a good town for the employment of women; public and union opinion has forced them out of all jobs that can, by the widest imagination, be called a man's job."[47]

In Butte, as in scores of working-class communities across the country, the government proved to be white men's ally by aiming the vast majority of New Deal programs and key pieces of legislation at shoring up working-class men's status as breadwinners. Butte residents initially resisted going on the direct relief rolls. As one local leader wrote, "To the self-respecting working-man or woman, work is not only desirable but necessary." However, if work was not available, they believed they deserved the government's assistance as much as anyone else. And work was often unavailable. Butte cycled between bad and worse times for the entire decade. The fall of 1937, for instance, found the ACM employing 7,800 men, but after half a year 5,000 of those had been let go. A few months later, only 800 men still worked in the mines. At that point, 6,736 sought jobs with the Works Progress Administration (WPA). The Roosevelt administration came through for Montanans; their state had the second-highest per-capita federal expenditure. And Montanans returned the favor. Although their state had long elected conservatives, between 1934 and 1940 Democrats swept to victory in virtually all electoral contests.[48]

The Roosevelt administration's support of collective bargaining rights for workers, codified in Section 7A of the 1933 National Industrial Recovery Act, was perhaps the New Deal policy that most influenced copper men's ability to remake their world in the 1930s. In the early years of that decade, local labor activists had once again begun to organize an independent union in Butte. They relied on federal support to spur the growth of the movement, but the foundations of their campaign were the new national mood that fostered working-class activism and Butte's own history as a labor town. Predictably, the challenges organizers faced in winning recognition for their new union and making it a powerful force emerged from the same points of tension that had long characterized worker politics in the mining city.

Reid Robinson, who would become president of the BMU and Mine Mill and a vice president of the Congress of Industrial Organizations (CIO) in the thirties, represents the link between Butte's earlier history and the upsurge of worker militancy during the Depression. His experience in that city during the most turbulent era in its history profoundly shaped his approach to labor issues. Because his father, Jim Robinson, was often at the center of these earlier tensions, Reid received a firsthand education on the peculiar politics of Butte's labor movement. Unlike most of the settled northern European immigrant miners whose conservatism had dominated local labor politics into the early twentieth century, Jim Robinson was affiliated with the group of miners loyal to the IWW and the Socialist Party. He saw building coalitions across racial-ethnic and ideological lines as the cornerstone of an effective labor movement. According to his son, he believed that sometimes the ballot failed, and fighting in the streets was the only way for the working class to make progress. Eugene Debs, Emma Goldman, and Elizabeth Gurley Flynn, family friends who were important figures in the American Left, also influenced the younger Robinson. The Robinsons departed Butte during the volatile World War I years and moved to Seattle, where in 1919 they participated in its general strike, an event that Reid remembered as crucial in the development of his perspective on the latent power of workers' collective action and on the difficulties organized labor faced in fashioning long-term solidarity.[49]

The Robinsons returned to Butte in the 1920s, and father and son witnessed the continuing decimation of miners' power during that decade as the ACM promoted inter-ethnic animosity and set up a Company-controlled union. Miners themselves, the Robinsons were among the workers who revived the BMU and Mine Mill in the early 1930s. The ACM opposed this attempt to restore an independent union. According to Reid Robinson, the Company paid agitators to stir up the men and precipitate a strike before the workers were adequately organized. In the end, this ploy served only to reaffirm miners' deep distrust of the ACM. In May 1934, copper men in all three towns successfully struck, reestablishing Mine Mill locals in Butte, Anaconda, and Black Eagle.[50]

Capitalizing on his intelligence, popularity, and family connections, Reid Robinson rose quickly through the BMU ranks, becoming its president in 1936. Less than twelve months later, at the age of twenty-eight, he was elected president of Mine Mill. Robinson's politics were part of the Popular Front—the broad social movement, which had a dynamic cultural presence, that combined radicals and liberals, especially among the working class, into a coalition that became a powerful force within the New Deal. His approach to labor issues attracted wide support among workers who, given the Depression context, were more willing to entertain the possibility of radical social and economic change. Most significantly, Robinson championed the expansion of Mine Mill into new areas, including the Southeast and the Southwest. Successful campaigns in these regions increased the union's membership, especially among black and Latino workers. Robinson strove to bring diversity to the union's leadership and organizing staff, and made the forging of an interracial working-class movement one of his primary objectives. More conservative members labeled him a radical and a Communist, echoing others' assessments of Mine Mill generally and Robinson in particular. Robinson, like many on the American Left during the 1930s, shared the social justice perspective of the Communist Party USA, but he described his own belief system, including his support for equality for workers of color, as "militant democratic unionism" rather than Communism.[51]

The rank-and-file members who unequivocally supported Robinson during the 1930s shared this outlook. Their hope, and that of their Popular Front counterparts across the country, was that they were witnessing the beginning of a labor- and government-led radical refashioning of power relations between employers and employees. This group of Robinson supporters received reinforcement from some of the more conservative workers, who backed Robinson because they saw him as an effective and militant leader. As a whole, Butte's white and white ethnic workers sustained Robinson's efforts to secure good jobs and decent wages for African American and Mexican American workers in the Southeast and Southwest, because they respected the militancy he had shown against the ACM and, more important, because they themselves faced no threat of having to work alongside miners of color.[52]

During that decade, while some men migrated to Butte from other copper camps and nearby states, few came from racial or ethnic backgrounds that differed from those already found in Montana's copper towns. Hence, miners did not feel directly threatened in this area, and evolving attitudes driven by generational change and Popular Front ideals marked the city's racial-ethnic relations at the time. This shift produced the conditions for a developing though fragile pan-ethnic bond that was increasingly advanced by other local changes. The Irish, for instance, while continuing to be the dominant group in Butte during the twenties and thirties, saw their unanimity further ruptured by the Irish Civil War. Once the cornerstone of the city's immigrant separatism, northern, southern, and eastern European ethnic lodges began to use English and to socialize with one another. Southeastern Europeans still sometimes found themselves referred to as "garlic eaters" or in even more derogatory terms, and fights still broke out between them and the Irish. However, as indicated by the growing popularity of Bohunkus Day and its message of poking fun at the bias directed at bohunks, they enjoyed growing acceptance as a core part of Butte society. According to a WPA assessment, by the latter 1930s the Serbians, Croatians, and others known locally as bohunks were seen as "some of the camp's most respected citizenry."[53]

An essential factor in the solidification of southeastern European immigrants' white racial status and in the creation of a pan-ethnic bloc among miners was the continued exclusion in the thirties of African Americans from mining, an aspect of Butte's social politics that long had a profound effect on the city's interdependent racial and gender order. Barring black men from demonstrating their equality with whites by working in the city's best-paying, most masculine working-class job produced a self-perpetuating racist logic which held that black men could not handle hard-rock mining, because none toiled in the mines. Even though continuing animosity partly marked the relationship between it and the miners, the ACM played a determinative role in this logic. By barring African Americans from the mines while it hired southeastern Europeans, in effect it used blackness to whiten suspect immigrants. Although they had grumbled about it, the willingness of English, Cornish, Irish, and other "white" miners to work next to "bohunks" and "dagoes" solidified, if slowly, the bond between white miners of different racial-ethnic backgrounds. Butte's chilly racial climate and economic difficulties drove most of the city's remaining black residents to leave in the late 1920s and early 1930s.[54]

Paradoxically, in the mid-1930s the public ideology regarding African Americans appeared to change in Butte with the revival of the BMU and Mine Mill under Robinson and other progressive leaders. After all, it was Montana's copper men, now even more closely bonded by the reemergence of flourishing local union culture represented by the rebirth of Miners' Union Day, that provided significant funding for the organizing campaigns among African American workers in the Southeast and Mexican and Mexican American workers in the Southwest. These efforts assisted in bringing those workers into the Roosevelt coalition and gave an important adhesive to this somewhat unlikely grouping. On the surface, then, Butte entered the wartime mobilization era as a city with a strong labor movement that was considered increasingly progressive on questions of race and, to a lesser degree, gender. World War II, however, would reveal a different reality. Black Eagle's history of racial-ethnic and gender relations had both similarities to and important differences from those in Butte, but it would no less profoundly shape wartime events.

TWO

Black Eagle: Immigrants' Bond

Black Eagle began as a collection of shanties for housing workers helping to construct the nearby reduction works and smelter built by the Boston and Montana Consolidated Copper and Silver Mining Company, on the northern bank of the Missouri River across from Great Falls (fig. 2.1). Initially inhabited by immigrants from Norway and Sweden but, notably, not Ireland, the town soon attracted large numbers of Croatians and Italians, most from rural areas, who were pushed to leave their homeland by economic and political problems tied to the global industrialization process. For these new immigrants, it was important that the generous wages men could earn at the smelter were complemented by the opportunity to cultivate vegetable gardens and keep chickens, goats, and cows.[1]

Black Eagle was markedly more friendly toward the immigrant groups that in Butte were derided as "bohunks" and "dagoes." Both the Croatians and the Italians came from the northern regions of their countries. That all but two of the twenty-plus members of Black Eagle's famed Croatian Nightingale Band came from Bribir, a town near the northern reaches of the Adriatic "not far from the Italian border," was not an anomaly. Walt Valacich, a local historian, estimated that 75 percent of the original Croatian immigrants came from Bribir. In contrast, Black Eagle's Italian immigrants did not display a chain migration pattern quite as focused on one town, but a substantial number originated from the north-central province of Lucca, particularly the town of Santa Maria Del Guidice. These ties to place played an influential role in Black Eagle. As in Butte with the Irish, Croatians and Italians who had put down roots offered new arrivals from their native country a network with access to housing, work, and a familiar culture. Each wave of immigrants from Bribir and Lucca reminded earlier ones of the shared values of their sending communities, bolstering the immigrant

2.1 The Black Eagle smelter as seen from Great Falls.
Photograph by Robert I. Nesmith, *Plant from across River*, 1942;
Montana Historical Society Research Center Photograph Archives, Helena.

identity of Black Eagle and, through their growing numbers, increasing the power of Italians and Croatians to shape their world.[2]

By the early twentieth century, although a number of other racial-ethnic groups peopled Black Eagle, Croatians and Italians so dominated the town that it was called Little Chi (for Chicago) or Little Milwaukee, after cities known for their large numbers of southeastern Europeans. As it expanded up the northwestern bank of the Missouri River and spread out from its central axis of Smelter Avenue, Black Eagle acquired many of the trappings immigration historians associate with immigrant enclaves in larger cities. Unlike Butte, where Austrians were criticized for patronizing "un-American" markets that offered goods such as dried meats and brown bread, Black Eagle businesses catered to them. Amelia Polich remembered, "The butcher man would go up the street in his wagon. You'd go out and buy your meat, if you wanted to." Some merchants would speak Croatian to her mother, so she did not have to learn to speak English. Black Eagle residents, Italian and Croatian alike, fondly recalled walking down the town's dozen or so streets and hearing Italian operas either being sung by men and women out gardening or emanating from phonographs that seemed to be playing day and night.[3]

These immigrants forged unusually close ties based in part on their experience living as neighbors, in contrast to the spatial dynamics of Butte and other American immigrant cities where racial-ethnic segregation defined many important immigrant neighborhoods. This experience of community united Black Eagle's immigrant groups. Language differences did not pose a significant barrier to forging relationships between first-generation Croatians and Italians. Some knew the others' language because they had lived in the others' country before emigrating—evidence of the often forgotten cosmopolitanism of some immigrants to the United States. Others learned Croatian or Italian so they could communicate with their workmates and neighbors, whether to complain about the climate—as one disgruntled immigrant put it, "When [you] g[o]t up in the morning it was so cold . . . shoes [were] frozen to the floor"—or to gripe about work and the prejudice they faced.[4]

Schooling further reinforced the social bonds among immigrants. Black Eagle residents thought of the Hawthorne School, first called Copper Smelter School, as one of the centers of the community. The connection between the town's two dominant ethnic groups strengthened into a pan-ethnic bond as the second generation learned English at Hawthorne. While kids in Butte reverted to racial-ethnic neighborhood allegiances once they left school, sharing the same classrooms and neighborhoods cemented the solidarity among youth in Black Eagle. Beginning in 1917, when immigrant adults began to attend night classes in "English, civics, and other subjects essential to citizenship," schooling did the same for their parents. Notably, the local public school curriculum did not erase racial-ethnic identity. Claire Del Guerra recalled that Fanny Collins, who taught and then served as principal of Hawthorne, "reinforced more than ever for us the fact that we were fortunate, we were somebody because we had our heritage." Residents considered Collins

a grand lady who gave hundreds of Black Eagle children the fundamental education they need to make the often difficult transition from the sixth grade to junior high school across the river in Great Falls. The transition was difficult, because Black Eagle students were comfortable and secure with the environment Collins School provided. In Black Eagle they shared a common bond as children of first and second-generation immigrants. In Great Falls they were integrated into a school system where there existed prejudice, bias and discrimination by their fellow students and teachers simply because they came from Black Eagle and had ethnic names.

Highlighting the chasm between the two communities during these years, "many Great Falls teachers wondered how she could spend her years of work in such a place as Black Eagle."[5]

While schooling helped weave the town's various nationalities into a pan-ethnic fabric, other aspects of immigrant life in Black Eagle in the first decades of the twentieth century reflected the cultural fissures apparent in Butte and many other American cities. Nationality-based associations strengthened allegiances based on a shared homeland; created a network that in Butte, Black Eagle, and Anaconda kept each community apprised of the racial-ethnic politics in nearby towns; and theoretically stifled inter-immigrant bonding. Like many such associations, Black Eagle's chapter of the Croatian Brotherhood provided life and health insurance, but its best-known activities focused on conviviality. It built a Croatian Hall so the community would have a place to gather, and regularly sponsored festivals and dinners to celebrate "old country" holidays. On Mesopust, marchers would parade through the town with the "Pust," a man made of straw who embodied all the bad events of the previous year, accompanied by revelers and a band playing traditional instruments such as the *supileca* horn and the *mihjer*, which resembled a bagpipe. Black Eagle's version of the holiday also included a dance that could last several days. Like the celebrations in Croatia, Mesopust climaxed with the trial of the effigy "for theft, assault, and other wrongdoings" committed during the year. Even with a respected local woman playing the part of the straw man's mother and defending him from the charges, he was always found guilty and then burned.[6]

Black Eagle's Croatians invited their Italian neighbors and those from other racial-ethnic backgrounds to partake in Mesopust with them. This was only one of many occasions throughout the year when the celebrations of one immigrant group nurtured bonds among them all. In the fall, for instance, the town's Croatian and Italian neighbors gathered for the arrival of between fifteen and twenty railroad cars from California filled with grapes. The men would together sample the sweetness of the grapes and, if satisfied, would purchase the large amount needed for the year's wine supply. Shortly after that, the Cristoforo Colombo Italian Lodge (CCL) hosted a feast and parade for Italian Founder's Day and held a festival on Columbus Day. Between these two periods of intense racial-ethnic celebration fell the Fourth of July, a patriotic occasion shared by all. Ultimately, whereas associations reinforced ties to either Croatian or Italian identity, residents recalled that on countless occasions they broke bread together and with other immigrants, a practice that strengthened the links between all of Black Eagle's immigrants by fostering a mutual admiration of each other's traditions and history.[7]

"The Man Wore the Pants"

Associations, the principal vehicle for promoting pride in immigrants' cultural identity and, in Black Eagle, a shared pan-ethnic sense of self, played a significant part in reinforcing the conservative gender codes that defined this immigrant town even more than they did Butte and Anaconda. Initially, both the Croatian Brotherhood and the CCL barred women members. After women were admitted, both associations maintained separate men's and women's sections, and men and women socialized only in same-sex groups. The bar was an exclusively male space; the Croatian Hall's kitchen was the women's domain except on Mother's Day, when men cooked breakfast for their wives and children.[8]

Although socializing at associations was important in establishing the pan-ethnic sensibility and shared value system that defined Black Eagle, Catholicism served as an even more essential connection between Italians and Croatians. In Butte the Catholic church operated in part as a vehicle for Irish power, and in Anaconda it reflected the city's racial-ethnic and later its class divisions. In Black Eagle the communally written town history underscores the importance of "*common* faith" in linking the "contrasting languages and customs" of immigrant settlers. Before the Blessed Sacrament Catholic Church was built in that town in 1923, Italians and Croatians attended Mass together in local halls and even saloons. On feast days, they crossed the river to St. Ann's in Great Falls. At the height of post–World War I anti-immigrant sentiment, however, they decided to build a church together in their own town, holding dinners and other fund-raisers so that they could build the edifice, buy pews and altar linens, and pay for coal to heat the building during the long winters. Croatian, Italian, and other immigrant tradesmen helped with the construction so as to keep costs down, tying the church even more closely to the town. Indeed, Black Eagle residents remembered that Blessed Sacrament became the center of pan-ethnic community life for both children and adults. The Garrity family, for instance, recalled that when they arrived in Black Eagle in 1929, they "were the only ones at the time of Irish descent and speaking only one language, English." Their Croatian and Italian neighbors welcomed them warmly and invited them to participate in their cultural events, but the strongest bond was the church. Yet although Catholicism trumped racial-ethnic divisions and bound Black Eagle together, church doctrine reinforced gender divisions. Local norms placed women in the home and privileged men as breadwinners and heads of household.[9]

Migration patterns were gendered also. Typically, men migrated from Croatia and Italy to fulfill breadwinner obligations and then either returned home or sent for their families. Theodore Ranieri, like many of the Italian immigrants to Black Eagle, came to the United States, decided he liked it enough to stay, saved money, and then sent for his wife. Their daughter Jennie Ranieri Signori was born in Black Eagle in 1897 and would eventually marry one of the Italian bachelors who lived at her mother's boardinghouse. Inez Rinari, on the other hand, did not come to America until her husband came back and escorted her in the late 1890s.[10]

Jennie Signori recalled that without question, "Italians favor a son more." The "foreigners"—Signori's term for her family and the other immigrants who peopled early Black Eagle—expected hard work from their daughters, and also worried more about their fealty to immigrant values. Most girls were not allowed to stay in school beyond sixth grade, since it would have meant their taking a streetcar to Great Falls. Olanda Vangelisti did not attend first grade until her eleventh year. Her father told her that girls "didn't need that much schooling anyway . . . the boys do, but not the girl." Dances and parties in Great Falls were also out of the question until a girl was older. To an even greater extent than in other immigrant communities, Black Eagle's immigrant parents valued education more for their sons than their daughters, because they hoped it would help these future breadwinners escape the world of poorly paid manual labor and move into either a supervisory role at the plant or, better yet, a white-collar job outside the industry. But even with the favoritism shown male offspring, a smelter-man who began working at the plant in the latter thirties held that he and his friends comprised the first generation of Black Eagle boys to finish high school—a reality that obviously limited employment options for those who came before him.[11]

The world of work in Black Eagle, with its links to gendered ideas about education as well as religious and immigrant ideologies, reinforced the separation between men and women. Women worked hard there, but unlike some other immigrant centers, most did not work for wages. Instead, they performed domestic labor in and around the home, and occasionally held sex-stereotyped jobs such as waitressing. The Palagis had six children and making ends meet proved difficult; but the family matriarch, whom one child described as "the queen of the kitchen," economized, for example by making a dress from the lining of a coat. Other Croatian and Italian women ran boardinghouses—an opportunity that would have been highly circumscribed in Butte, where Irish women monopolized the trade—catering to the large number of single men who came to Black Eagle.[12]

By the end of the 1920s, although Progressivism, women's suffrage, ideas about companionate marriage, and Jazz-Age culture had reshaped male-female relations in the national imagination, Black Eagle's gender order had not changed significantly. Zaira Stefani Lukes was thirteen when she moved to Black Eagle in 1927 from Stockett, another mining and smelting center inhabited by immigrants. She recalled,

> When we first moved to Black Eagle, we hated it! Because when we moved down here the people . . . even the Italian people . . . weren't like the people in Stockett. The people in Stockett were more open-minded. The boys and girls played together and thought nothing of it . . . and our parents didn't think anything of it. . . . But when we came to Black Eagle, oh, we just hated it down here because it was a disgrace for the boys and girls to play together. And if you went for a walk you weren't considered nothing.

She regarded Black Eagle's strict gender codes, rooted in the heritage celebrated by Fanny Collins, as stifling. When first-generation Italian immigrant David Rinari told his daughter that women were "homemakers . . . you're supposed to be home and take care of the house," he summarized the immigrant gender order in Black Eagle.[13]

During these formative decades, immigrant men gained status within the community by being their family's sole breadwinner. However, the evaluation of immigrant working-class masculinity involved much more than a man's ability to form and provide for a family. Religiosity; racial-ethnic identity; sexuality; muscularity and other bodily matters; wealth; education; military, union, and associational experience; and the type of work he did all contributed to the assessment. Neither the evaluation nor the performance of these aspects of immigrant masculinity can be made sense of without carefully considering context. Numerous studies have shown that immigrant working-class men were at various times and in various places seen as meeting, and perhaps even setting, the standard for American manhood. During other times and in other places, they were perceived as lacking the crucial characteristics of manhood, either because of the ways gender was read through their ethno-racial identity and/or because of their subordinate class position.[14] Locally, though, the convergence of the gender order of Black Eagle's immigrants and that of Great Falls in regard to masculine expectations reinforced these men's standing.

Although some men worked in other blue-collar workplaces, few white-collar jobs were available to immigrant men locally. They had two major routes to upward mobility. An immigrant man could choose the path of becoming a foreman at the smelter. Before 1910, however, only a handful of southeastern Europeans had been allowed to occupy those positions. The second route involved owning a small business, such as a restaurant, saloon, or grocery store. In both these occupations, men remained embedded in the working-class community.[15] Employment at the smelter remained central to most local men's claim to breadwinner status. The smelter's refusal to employ women in production jobs enabled Italian and Croatian men to maintain and promote their sex-segregated view of the world. Yet Black Eagle's immigrant men did not control the smelter as they did the rest of the town. There was no guarantee that the pan-ethnic sensibility defining the racial-ethnic order in the community would prevail in the workplace. In Black Eagle, as in Butte, racial-ethnic relations proved critical to how gender worked.

"Hard to Get a White Man to Do It"

The labor process itself shaped identity formation within the smelter. From the early 1890s until 1911, the Black Eagle plant served as both a copper smelter and a copper concentrator. Following its acquisition of that facility and the subsequent realignment of the corporation, the ACM shifted all smelting operations to Anaconda and had the Black Eagle plant specialize in the final stage of the copper and zinc production process. For copper, this meant refining the anodes that arrived as 99.3% pure copper via railroad from the Anaconda smelter and manufacturing copper rods, copper wire, and copper cable. Electrolytic processing of the element involved placing the anodes in chemical tanks where the impurities were separated, next depositing the pure copper on cathode sheets that were then stripped. Black Eagle's electrolytic copper refinery's tank house refined approximately 27 million pounds of copper a month when operating at full capacity. The copper collected off the cathodes was then sent to the furnace refinery, where it was melted and cast into forms easily turned into final products by the plant's rolling, wire, and rod mills. The plant also housed electrolytic zinc and cadmium production areas. The zinc treatment facility included a roasting, leaching, electrolyzing, and casting division and was the largest of its kind in the United States; when going full bore it produced 29 million pounds of zinc a month. The plant also employed myriad other workers in specialized trades, as laboratory samplers, and on the electric tram system.[16]

Racial-ethnic identity framed certain production jobs in Black Eagle, but not others. Charles Micheletti remembered work at the zinc plant as punishing: "Not many smeltermen worked there long." Immigrant men of any nationality could claim significant masculine status by being tough enough to work in a place like the zinc plant. The tank house, on the other hand, was tied to a particular group (fig. 2.2). "The type of work that they had to do" there, commented smelterman Clarence Silloway, who notably was neither Italian nor Croatian, "it was hard to get a white man to do it." But the "husky" Austrians and Croatians were willing. In contrast, Silloway claimed, the Italian men made sure they did "higher-class labor." In so doing, they signified both their whiteness and their masculinity. Racialized masculinity, in this local scenario, echoed what occurred in Butte between the Irish and the southeastern Europeans whom the *Evening News* described as the "black men from across the water." The ideology embedded in Silloway's comment that "it was hard to get a white man to do it" was deeply rooted in a notion of labor that emerged with industrialization and was contrasted to slavery. In American labor discourse, skill, honor, independence, and a stance against degrading tasks defined white man's labor. At Black Eagle and other production sites across the nation, specific tasks or entire categories of labor were interpreted through a racial and gender lens that in Silloway's reading seemed to place Italians inside and Croatians outside white masculinity.[17]

Yet the connections between racial identity, skin color, and job hierarchies were nothing if not complex and mutable. Croatian immigrant William Tonkovich recalled that "being dark complected I'd slip in" to the Italian Lodge's Columbus Day Dance. "They thought I was one of the Italians." A local Italian contended that the northern Italian origins of the town's Italian residents trumped the national conventional wisdom about their racial status. Citing her brother's blond hair and nickname, "Ole the Swede," she argued that "people never thought we were Italians, see, we weren't dark." According to her, Black Eagle's Italians did not suffer from the "bad reputation" Italians had in the United States, because it was applied mostly to Sicilians and Neapolitans, who were "dark" and "a different type." Clearly the relationship between color and race was an issue of some importance to local immigrants, as it was for immigrants across the nation.[18] But in the Anglo-dominated American imagination, shaped more by Anglo-controlled popular culture and intellectual currents than by the maneuvering of individual immigrant groups, Italians and Croatians were by and large equally suspect racially.

2.2 The tank house in Black Eagle's electrolytic copper refinery was one of the places that Italians refused to work. Photograph by Russell Lee, *Great Falls, Montana: Electrolytic Copper Refinery at Anaconda Copper Mining Company; Dipping Copper Cathodes,* 1942; Library of Congress, Prints & Photographs Division, FSA-OWI Collection, LC-USW3-008856-D DLC.

Immigrants' experiences in Black Eagle and Great Falls were quite different from their counterparts in Butte and Anaconda, which were controlled by immigrants and their children. Both Italians and Croatians pointedly recalled being "treated like a minority" on the Great Falls side of the river. Adults and children often heard themselves referred to as "bohunks," "wops," or "dagoes." Great Falls, founded in 1884 by the visionary entrepreneur Paris Gibson as a hydroelectric and commercial center, had become Montana's largest city by the 1950s, and Black Eagle was swallowed up by the burgeoning military and industrial conurbation. But until the end of World War II, Black Eagle's residents saw their small town as a discrete place with a distinct culture, and residents of Great Falls, with the exception of pockets of immigrants around the city, saw themselves as markedly different from the immigrants across the river.[19]

The ACM's employment policies served to counterbalance the effort by some Great Falls residents to define Black Eagle's immigrants as nonwhite. The Company and its predecessors had prompted immigrants to move to Black Eagle, and saw the continued growth of that labor supply as essential to their production plans. Many employers across the United States saw southern and eastern European immigration as a plentiful source of hard workers. Language differences, job competition, and the practice of separating racial-ethnic groups in the workplace made collective action by immigrants difficult to organize, keeping wages low and profits high. At the smelter, however, workers of different racial-ethnic backgrounds were not segregated, nor were native-born and immigrant workers pitted against each other.[20]

Instead, southeastern European immigrants and native-born workers both feared that employers would begin hiring African Americans. Nationwide, immigrants who found themselves placed further down the racial hierarchy had sought to avoid being associated with black workers for fear of the degradation that a nonwhite identity entailed. By the early twentieth century, enough African Americans were in Great Falls for employers to consider hiring them as a way of dividing the working class. But even though the Great Northern Railroad, the other large industrial employer in the area, had done so, and even though the ACM employed black workers at other Company facilities including the Anaconda smelter, the Company had a de facto policy barring the employment of African Americans in Black Eagle, just as they did in Butte. Eugene Cox, personnel manager at the Black Eagle smelter, remembered, "Over here . . . I was just simply told don't hire 'em. And that come from [the head office in] Butte." The ACM's policy of never hiring African Americans at its Black Eagle plant even during periods of labor shortage reinforced the perceived whiteness of the town's immigrants.[21]

"Eliminate the Indians"

The way race worked at the smelter changed around the time of the US entry into World War I, when the ACM hired "a lot of Indians" to replace men who had been drafted. The history of the Indians who began working at the Black Eagle facility influenced racial formation for the town's immigrants. Twelve indigenous nations—including the Crow, Sioux, Blackfeet, Kootenai Salish, Shoshone, Chippewa (also called Ojibwe and Anishinabe), and Cree—had claimed the area that would become Montana. The process of treaty making, treaty breaking, and warfare left the luckiest survivors of these tribes on seven reservations with lands vastly smaller and of an inferior quality than those they had once controlled in the United States and Canada. Great Falls's "Landless Indians," from which most of the smelter's Indian workers came, were not among the lucky. These people had varied tribal affiliations. Some were Métis, of mixed French and indigenous ancestry. Others had ties to the Turtle Mountain Band of the Chippewa, the Little Shell Band of the Chippewa, or, through intermarriage, other tribes and the white community. Regardless of their individual background, each member of the Landless community shared a history of dispossession. As Great Falls grew, the number of Landless Indians residing on its periphery, in areas whites called "moccasin flats," increased. Whites did not welcome this development. First Lieutenant (later, General) John "Black Jack" Pershing's roundup and removal of the community to Canada in 1896 marked only one of the most egregious efforts to expel the Landless Indians from the area. Yet even after they had been placed in chains, jeered by whites, and sent across the border, most of them returned to the makeshift camps on the outskirts of Montana towns. By the twentieth century, these camps had become their permanent home.[22]

In 1916 Great Falls civic leaders, including the artist Charlie Russell, helped establish Rocky Boy's Reservation in north-central Montana in an effort to provide a home for the Landless community. But the new reservation was small and on poor-quality land, so it could not accommodate everyone. A large number of the Indians who could not be resettled at Rocky Boy's returned to Great Falls and took up residence near the town meat plant, where they occasionally found work. Around this time, Indian men found steady employment at the smelter. Why did the ACM bar African Americans, even when many other employers turned to them during World War I, but hire Indians to work at the Black Eagle smelter? Why did the town's immigrants not seek to block the employment of this community of color? In the first instance, Company management shared aspects of the worldview of Russell and other local elites. Russell's paintings portrayed Indians as noble victims of modernity. Most whites in the West still exhibited racial hostility toward Indians, but liberals sought to "help" them.[23] Coupled with the demand for labor at the smelter, this racial ideology motivated ACM managers to offer Landless Indians jobs.

Immigrants' willingness to work alongside Indians possibly stemmed from a number of sources. It could have resulted from still-vibrant working-class radicalism as reflected by the presence of the Industrial Workers of the World (IWW, or Wobblies) in Montana's copper communities during the World War I period. Like the more famous case of Butte workers, some men in Black Eagle responded positively to the IWW's calls for class-based militancy, though it is unclear whether they received the Wobblies' message of interracial cooperation in the same way that some in Butte did. Significantly, however, the mob that lynched IWW organizer Frank Little in Butte in 1917 targeted a mixed-race Indian. But more probably, immigrant men might simply have lacked the power to prevent the employment of Indians at the smelter. During World War I, when immigrants and especially those accused of radicalism came under attack, nonnative workers across the United States lost power in their workplaces. Fractures in Montana's labor movement discussed previously exacerbated this loss of power.[24] In

Black Eagle, these circumstances and the Company's continued antiunion activities sapped immigrant workers' ability to use collective bargaining to either better their lot or fight changes at the smelter they opposed, such as the employment of Indians, for a decade and a half.

During the 1920s the ACM, which had joined employers throughout the nation in utilizing an oppositional management style during the World War I era, shifted toward the "kinder and gentler" but no less coercive style of paternalist labor relations known as welfare capitalism. The elevation of A. E. Wiggin to the head management job at the Black Eagle smelter was central to the return of Daly-style treatment of employees. Besides raising wages, Wiggin established Black Eagle's enormously popular Anaconda Club, with a bar and bowling alley, for employees and their families. He beautified the plant and surrounding grounds and had a golf course built. These benefits, which workers in Black Eagle, like Butte, quickly came to see as less a gift than an entitlement they earned, were in addition to the health care already provided by the Company. By catering to the social needs of his employees, Wiggin provided a classic example of post–World War I paternalistic management techniques that in some places weakened workers' ties to racial-ethnic and class-based associations. In Black Eagle, they may have made it more difficult to resurrect an independent union local, but they did not appear to dilute fealty to such associations, the church, or ethnic identity more generally. The town's immigrant employees perceived Wiggin's changes as evidence that they had returned to favor in the eyes of the Company, and they responded more favorably than did Butte's miners by placing more trust in the smelter's management.[25]

The relationship between Black Eagle's immigrant workers and the plant's managers became more cordial at the same time that a drought struck the northern plains, driving more Indians toward Great Falls. At the onset of the Great Depression, the Landless Indian community occupied shelters in an area just south and less than a mile west of Black Eagle, along the banks of the Missouri River. It was at this camp and at the smelter that the next critical moment in the formation of immigrant racialization occurred. Between 1929, when normal operations at the smelter and wire mill were cut back, and early 1932, when the full effects of the economic disaster were being felt in the copper industry, the smelter's management had cut over 600 men from the payroll. The local press hailed the ACM for keeping 1,100 men employed at its Black Eagle facility: "In sharp contrast to conditions elsewhere, with entire communities blighted by closing of great plants, the local refinery is rotating employment so that work is being provided for practically every man on the payroll." These men shared 703 daily shifts, which meant that each man lucky enough to keep his job worked four instead of six shifts a week. The contract between the union and the Company tied the hourly base wage rate to the price of copper so that when the commodity's price increased, so did wages, and when it dropped, wages did as well. A precipitous decline in copper prices largely continued until 1938, exacerbating workers' hardship by reducing daily pay considerably. Then on May 7, 1932, the ACM instituted what the plant's manager called a "mass shut down." The question became not how many men could share the work, but whether the smelter would employ anyone at all. By the end of the year, operations had once again resumed, but the smelter employed only 684 men, the majority of whom were working even fewer shifts than before.[26]

No matter how much they appreciated Wiggin's corporate welfare initiatives, the shutdown tested the faith of the immigrant smeltermen who remained on the rolls. At this very moment, management helped solidify immigrants' claim to white identity: employees and employer joined to force Indians from the smelter. Nearly simultaneously, whites burned the riverside Landless camps to the ground. We know more about the Indians' exclusion from employment than about the attack on their community, though burning down Chinatowns had been a popular tactic across the West and perhaps served as a template for this assault. One Black Eagle worker's recollections hint at the all-too-familiar mechanism of accusation blended with stereotype used to remove Indian workers from the plant: "The Indians, they stole too many things. In fact they cleaned out one of the welding shops for the Zinc plant. They had all the stuff, but [the Company] found it. Finally we just had to eliminate the Indians, that was all. I'll never forget it." Although competition for work in lean times also caused tensions among Black Eagle's European immigrant groups, Croatian and Italian workers "never forgot" the power they exercised in the ouster of Indian workers. They also used the incident to assert that honesty and hard work, the hallmarks of white masculine labor, were intrinsic to their character.[27] Equally compelling for their claim to whiteness, they displayed their ability to mobilize two the principal tools of white privilege: control over property and access to jobs.

Smelter Hill

Ironically for ACM management, which colluded with workers in the removal of Indians from the smelter and the community, the sense of mutuality that the expulsion reinforced was instrumental in securing an even greater level of worker control over jobs as a result of the plant's first major strike. On June 7, 1934, the 950 daily wage men employed at the smelter banded together in opposition to the ACM-controlled Company union that had been in place for over a decade. Like their fellow copper workers and ACM employees in Butte and Anaconda, and indeed like workers nation-wide, Black Eagle's workers drew inspiration to strike from the National Industrial Recovery Act, which offered federal support for collective bar-gaining. Butte-based activists took the lead in reestablishing the Interna-tional Union of Mine, Mill, and Smelter Workers (Mine Mill) in all three of Montana's major copper production facilities. Mine Mill's renaissance, coupled with the centering of the working class in American culture, served to bring workingmen together across regional and racial-ethnic lines. In Black Eagle, the resurrection of the union along with collective antipathy to American Indian workers appeared to end years of low-level tension and even occasional violence between Black Eagle men and the smelter work-ers of Great Falls.[28] This solidarity bolstered white and white ethnic men's power to control access to scarce jobs. The ability to bring home a decent paycheck during these difficult times, though still sporadic, strengthened both the masculinity and the whiteness of Black Eagle's immigrant men. Ironically, Mine Mill had interracialism as one of its core tenets, yet Black Eagle's strong local helped to secure workers' whiteness. The relationship between immigrant workers and the company they worked for was essential in shaping local racial and gender formation for the next decade.

The continued support of the Black Eagle smelter's paternalistic manage-ment was critical to this linked process of securing masculinity and white-ness during the 1930s. Even after they had lost their struggle to prevent the return of Mine Mill, smelter managers did their best not to allow depressed economic conditions to destroy the nonwage-based benefits of those men they kept in their employ. The Company's favorable relations with its male employees in Black Eagle throughout the paternalistic era began with the wage packet; according to most workers, for the Depression era the ACM paid well. One smelterman hired in the late 1930s, when work was again becoming plentiful, recalled that he made about $4.25 a day, which had "a lot of purchasing power." At the time, a basket full of groceries cost about four dollars, a used car ran less than a month's wages, and gas came cheaply. When this smelterman transferred to the cadmium section of the plant just a few years later, his daily wage rose to $7.20. A fully employed young man, married and even with a few children, earned the "family wage" so critical to masculine and white status in Black Eagle and across the United States. Although the Depression forced the local gender order to flex, in Black Eagle during the 1930s it was still the case that, as one local smelterman's wife put it, "Women stayed home and did their work. Like they say, the man wore the pants." That perspective was reinforced, albeit with a modern spin, in 1933 with the founding of the Black Eagle Home Demonstration Club and the 4-H Club; local women contended that since that time, "most ladies of the Black Eagle community [became] members." In their own history, they explained the common value system they shared by citing the "Creed of the Extension Clubs," which forefronted women's status as "Homemakers."[29]

The Company's role in bolstering "the family" as defined by white masculinity had a multigenerational dimension. Eugene Cox, the smelter's personnel manager, declared, "If there was any [hiring] preference given it would be given to the man whose dad was working there or the other way around." Men such as Lyle Pellett, who moved to the Great Falls area in 1936 in hopes that he might find work at the smelter, lacked the family connections that allowed Black Eagle's young men to obtain smelter jobs relatively quickly even during the Depression. Notably, the Italian and Croatian smeltermen who emphatically told their sons, "Don't come to work [at the] smelter, don't come to work [at the] smelter, go someplace else," did not celebrate this aspect of ACM paternalism.[30]

Smeltermen and their families continued to be well aware of class differences in Black Eagle during the 1930s. Smelter Hill, where managers lived, was graced by thirty-one grand homes, where some local women worked as maids and the smelter's landscape crew delivered fresh-cut flowers daily. A swimming pool and tennis courts were provided by the Company for the exclusive use of management and their families. The superintendent and his wife had at their disposal a chauffeured car, driven by a smelterman assigned to the smelter garage. Black Eagle's working-class residents would not have been surprised to hear one plant manager's wife remark, "Living on the Hill was like living in fairyland. It was beautiful and everything was done for us."[31]

Nonetheless, the personal relationship between immigrant workers and their bosses grew even closer during the 1930s. Managers and their families lived in Black Eagle and not Great Falls, so the two classes had always been near each other, but residents recalled that during the Depression the bosses began to treat some laborers and their families as near equals—a previously unheard-of dynamic. A smelterman's wife said appreciatively, "The people of Smelter Hill were very sociable for being people that were office—bosses and all that, you know. They didn't ignore you. . . . They were just like you were. That's what made Black Eagle so nice. You know, when you go someplace, well, somebody's a little higher than you, they think they're better than you are. The people of Smelter Hill didn't feel that way. . . . No, they didn't think we were just little peons because we lived in Black Eagle. We were just like one whole community." The mutuality between workers and bosses in the 1930s extended to leisure activities: managers and workers both played golf at the course the Company had built in Black Eagle. They also played cards and bowled together, often in the employees' club the Company had built.[32]

The respect that had come to define the relationship between Black Eagle's employers and employees was evident to all by 1937, when Landless Indians, the group that posed the greatest challenge to immigrants' efforts to secure whiteness, reappear in the historical record. After the 1932 conflagration, the Landless camp was moved to a hill owned by an Indian woman a mile to the west of its former site, an area called "Hill 57" for the large Heinz 57 advertisement painted on its side by a pickle salesman. The community does not appear to have been directly targeted by whites or white ethnics, perhaps because job competition had ended with the plant's exclusion of Indian men.[33] Yet the continued presence of the Landless Indians around Black Eagle provided a visual reminder of the difference between the material world of Black Eagle's immigrants and that of the area's largest community of color.

Immigrants' ability to maintain employment at the smelter, gains in union power, and the new emphasis on national citizenship placed them more clearly within the parameters of whiteness. But the Popular Front sought the elimination of prejudice and discrimination against African American, Latino, Asian American, and American Indian workers in the name of class-wide solidarity. The Black Eagle smeltermen's own union, Mine Mill, had become a standard-bearer for the national movement against workplace racism, making the continued exclusion of Indian workers from the smelter an uncomfortable contradiction of the union's platform. Employment was reviving by 1937: monthly employment figures from that March showed 1,282 men paid by the day, a major increase from the 1932 figure. On average, they earned $5.67 a day for a six-day workweek. Just under half the workforce had been employed at the plant for more than ten years, with a sizable number having at least twice that much experience. The others had worked for fewer than four years. Notably, the Company had hired at least 437 men since the beginning of 1937.[34] With the resumption of hiring, the revitalized Mine Mill union might well have seen this moment as an opportunity to contend that Landless Indians deserved access to smelter jobs.

"Peasants," "Loyal Aliens," White Ethnics

However, before World War II Mine Mill's Popular Front–inspired campaigns against racism in the workplace never directly affected Butte, Anaconda, or Black Eagle. Immigrant copper workers from these towns did support national campaigns against inequality, including Mine Mill's quest to organize workers of color in the Southwest and Southeast. But Montana's copper workers gave no indication that they wanted to see similar activity in their own area. Mine Mill's inaction against discrimination in Black Eagle attests to the limits of the Popular Front in the Mountain West—at least as far as union activity was concerned. Instead, the movement made itself felt through the Federal Arts and Writers' Projects and the work of progressive intellectuals such as D'Arcy McNickle.

In early 1937, McNickle, the great Indian scholar and one of the most important Popular Front figures addressing Indian issues, visited Hill 57 as an administrator in the federal Office of Indian Affairs. In an article published in the *Great Falls Tribune*, he pointed to the disjunction between the interracial ethics of the Popular Front and the local value system. Hill 57 was "as barren as a rock," "windy, always windy, and treeless and grassless," with "flapping tents and patchwork shacks." Its physical marginality reinforced the social ramifications of the Indians' outsider position. A number of Landless families had moved closer to Black Eagle, taking up residence on "Mount Royal" along Wiremill Road, which ran next to the smelter's main production area. In this new location, they became even more visible to smelter workers and to anyone in the area interested in comparing Indians and immigrants. "Such derelicts do not make good company for respectable towns," McNickle suggested. "Their living nags on consciences. Their rags are an offense. No doubt they depreciate real estate values. No doubt that many a community has secretly wished that the whole lot of them could be quietly lethalized in some humane way."[35]

McNickle compared the situation facing Indians to a group Black Eagle's immigrant workers knew intimately: peasants from European countries who had themselves been dispossessed. In so doing, he set up an ideal platform from which to argue for the reemployment of Landless Indians at the area's largest employer, the smelter. But McNickle did not push for the integration of Indian workers into industrial employment; instead, he urged locals to "give Indians land, not land to sell, but land to use."[36] He realized that allowing Landless Indians to reoccupy their traditional lands also contested local power arrangements, as the burning of the river camp showed.

But he appeared to recognize that petitioning for industrial jobs had less of a chance for success.

Even in 1937, at the height of the Popular Front and a time when the plant was hiring, the drive to continue exclusionary policies so as to serve white and white ethnic men was too powerful to overcome. Unemployed smeltermen with between five and ten years' service, local boys who grew up thinking they would have a secure job at the smelter, and white and white ethnic men who came in from out of town all enjoyed access to jobs at the plant, while Landless Indians did not. The fluctuating economic circumstances in the last years of the Depression added to this situation. March proved to be the high point of employment for 1937; that fall, over seven hundred men were laid off. Local white and white ethnic men lucky enough to find jobs in the nonferrous industry still could not count on a consistent paycheck. Conditions improved in 1938, with an increase in copper demand and in the price of copper. But employment rates did not elevate dramatically until the national policy of producing munitions for the Allied armies fighting in Europe stimulated copper production in 1941.[37] Until that time, Black Eagle's immigrant smeltermen relied both on their own community bonds and on their sense that they and their town were favored by the Company. Their sensibility differed significantly from that of their counterparts in Butte, where a more antagonistic relationship between employees and the Company prevailed. It also contrasted with the prevailing view in Anaconda, where that city's smeltermen saw themselves as living under the coercive power of the ACM.

THREE

Anaconda: "Husky Smeltermen" and "Company Boys"

Anaconda, Montana, was from its inception a "company town." This status set it apart from Butte and Black Eagle and played a determinative role in the development of its social politics. The town was conceived by ACM founder Marcus Daly, who decided that he could increase profits by locally smelting the ore coming out of Butte. To build his smelter town, Daly bought thousands of acres twenty-five miles from Butte in a valley that had ample water resources.[1]

Officially incorporated in 1883, Anaconda grew rapidly, thanks to the army of skilled craftsmen and laborers Daly recruited to build the smelter. By 1885, only a few months after those workers completed its construction, the plant employed fifteen hundred men. The centrality of the smelter to these men, their families, and rest of the town was vividly reinforced each day by the presence of the massive plant in their midst. According to one smelterman, Anaconda residents "do not look at the morning sky to see how the weather is"; their "first glance is at the Big Stack" to see "how the smoke's coming out." The smelter itself was intricate, interconnected, and overwhelming in scale. As one worker put it,

> It's hard for anyone to comprehend the hugeness of the Anaconda Reduction Works. It's hard for anyone who has spent a lifetime working in only one or two of its many departments. It's almost impossible for one who has never seen it. You can tell people it's the largest non-ferrous smelter in the world. You can tell people that all the ore from the Butte mines—the richest hill on earth—passes through it. But it doesn't mean anything. It's too big.[2]

In planning the town that would surround his massive smelter, Daly envisioned a place that would be different from Butte. Instead of homes

3.1 The town of Anaconda in 1887, with the original smelter in the background. Photograph by Hazeltine, *Anaconda, Montana, 1887*; Montana Historical Society Research Center Photograph Archives, Helena.

haphazardly interspersed with industrial infrastructure, he placed residential areas at some distance from the plant, yet close enough so that laborers could walk to work (fig. 3.1). The 1885 town directory proclaimed that Anaconda was already on its way to fulfilling his vision: "From end to end Anaconda wears a tidy air. Its streets are clean, its homes are cozy, and its dooryards are well kept." Daly's syndicate catalyzed the town's growth by investing over $1 million a year in Anaconda. By 1890 its population had reached 6,000. Thirteen tailors, fifteen doctors, twenty attorneys, and fifty-eight saloon keepers had hung out their shingles by 1896. In 1900 the population stood at 12,000, the town sported forty brick buildings, and most residences had electricity and indoor plumbing.[3]

Even as it expanded at a dramatic pace, Anaconda remained "Marcus Daly's town, owned and controlled by him and those around him." By the late 1890s, his company "owned and operated the smelter, the railroad, the bank, the newspaper, the main hotel, the race track, the street car line, the power company, the foundry company, the firebrick company and a number of coal and timber companies providing wood and coal to both Anaconda and Butte." Personal considerations and business interests motivated Daly's local investments. According to the corporate history of the ACM, "Anaconda lay deep in Daly's affection. Except for his family, his ranch and his race horses, it was his pride and joy." Daly built a grand home for his family in town and brought many of his relatives to live and work there.[4]

Most of Anaconda's workers valued the benefits that came with Daly's devotion. They also respected his rise from a "mucker" in the West's early underground mines and appreciated his working-class sensibility, including his occasional habit of sharing a drink or a chew of tobacco with his employees. However, in Anaconda, as in Butte, Daly was the boss. While some may have regarded his stated support for labor unions and his practice of paying reasonable wages as proof that he put workers before profits, others saw plenty of contradictions. Not until 1906, six years after his death, did Anaconda's smeltermen succeed in reducing a regular day's work from twelve to eight hours.[5]

Indeed, most workers knew that residing in the town had significant drawbacks. One of the major reasons that Anaconda's smeltermen lagged behind their brothers in Butte in achieving workplace victories was the constraints that came with living in a company town. Unlike the situation in Butte until the early twentieth century, Anaconda's workers could not play one company off another or turn to a different employer if they lost their job. These factors, coupled with resistance from smelter management, stymied smeltermen's unionization drives in the 1890s. The ACM's control of Anaconda manifested in so many ways and places that residents came to call the town the "City of Whispers" because of their fear of openly voicing their discontent. The company store the ACM established in 1892 showed one aspect of that dynamic. Matt Kelly, one of the town's early residents, recalled that after the Company opened Copper City Commercial, an ACM official toured the smelter every day and asked "[each] new man how he liked his job. . . . If they did, and wanted to hold it, he suggested they had better trade at the Copper City, and he would give them a charge book." Mirroring the practice in other company towns, the ACM also had the payroll sent to the store, which subtracted the amount owed and paid the balance to the employee.[6]

Still, the workers who comprised the vast majority of Anaconda's residents found ways of asserting their collective power. Echoing their counterparts in Butte, their principal way of doing this was through workers' organizations. With twenty-seven labor unions large enough to have offices there, Anaconda was clearly a union town. The unions' central place in the town's culture bolstered workers' claims. In contrast to many larger cities, which did not celebrate their working-class identity before the 1930s, Anaconda did so from its inception. One of the best expressions of this came from the pen of Charles Eggleston, assistant editor of the *Anaconda Standard*. In the early 1890s, when Anaconda was competing with Helena to become the Montana state capital, Eggleston wrote a satirical tract that he attributed to Helena boosters. Supposedly meant to condemn the smelter city, Eggleston's pamphlet heaped scorn on Helena's elitism and offered Montana's working-class voters a complimentary portrait of Anaconda.

> A town nine-tenths of whose population toil the year round on manual labor; big, strong, coarse working men who could not tell a German from a wheelbarrow; that so far from exhibiting a sense of mortification and chagrin, they seem to take a sort of unconscious pride in going to and from their work in soiled overalls and with huge dinner buckets; laborers, mechanics, artisans, bricklayers, copper-dippers, whose average wage reach only $105 a month. . . . Spending their time cultivating their little sawed-off gardens, going to low picnics and organizing and perfecting labor unions, which, Helena is informed and believes, are the greatest curse of the modern world. The whistles that blow every morning at seven o'clock, so soon after society people have retired, are an intolerable nuisance. It is impossible to walk the streets of Anaconda without seeing working men and their wives and children, and when the streets are crowded one cannot escape brushing up against them.

While statistics about the sizable number of single men in Anaconda suggest that this image of the town as defined by a family-centered working-class masculinity was a bit simplistic, it was oft repeated.[7]

Anaconda, in fact, was both a worker's town and a company town, and the friction between labor and management shaped life there, including its electoral politics. Most workers and bosses in Butte, Black Eagle, and Anaconda identified as Democrats. Anaconda's Daly-owned *Standard* openly "declares itself a Democrat," adding that "a very large majority of the men who built [Montana] are Democrats." There were, however, exceptions. For instance the Cornish, who were among the first to labor in Butte's mines and made up a considerable portion of the workforce at both smelters, voted Republican. Of even greater consequence, the number of workers aligned with the Socialist Party increased as dissatisfaction with the status quo deepened at the end of the nineteenth century. In Anaconda that dissatisfaction was evident in the standing-room-only turnout to hear Eugene Debs, one of the nation's leading labor and Socialist figures, in 1897. It crystallized dramatically in 1901 with the formation of the Western Federation of Miners

(WFM)-affiliated Anaconda Mill and Smeltermen's Union Local 117, and in 1902 with the decision by the town's Central Labor Council to create the Deer Lodge County Labor Party, an organization whose links to the Socialist cause were well known. Only a few months later, the potential power of this political alignment became evident when Labor Party candidates defeated Democrats to win four of the major county offices and five of the six local seats in the state legislature.[8]

By 1903 the Laborites had affiliated with the Socialist Party of Montana, and solidified its challenge to the ACM-backed Democrats by nominating a slate of candidates for Anaconda town elections. The Socialists put forward a platform centered on improving city services and better serving the working class by more fairly taxing local businesses, especially the Company. Ninety-two percent of eligible voters turned out for the spring election, making it a virtual referendum on the possibility of ending Company domination. While even among workers there was a significant split over whether to support the Socialists, a majority of those casting votes responded enthusiastically to the idea, handing Socialists victories in the races for mayor, city treasurer, police magistrate, and four city council positions.[9]

Anaconda became the first municipality west of the Mississippi to see the Socialist Party achieve a victory of such proportions, a development that apparently surprised the ACM. Drawing on the power afforded to it by operating in a company town, smelter management moved quickly to quell what it saw as an uprising against its interests. Only six weeks after the election, the smeltermen's union reported that 150 of its members had been summarily fired for purportedly either having ties to the Socialist Party or shopping in a Socialist store; local craft unions reported a similar trend. When approached with allegations that they had dismissed workers based solely on their politics, Company officials did not deny the charge. Instead, they offered a veiled warning to others who might be considering shifting their allegiance. Not willing to give up but facing a battle with the ACM that it knew it could not win alone, the smeltermen's union asked the two most powerful labor groups in the industry, the WFM and the Butte Miners' Union (BMU), to come to its defense. The WFM, which had been founded in Butte in 1893, complained to the ACM but then told Local 117 that it could do little else, since it was in the midst of fighting employers at Cripple Creek and elsewhere, and its resources were already overstretched. The BMU's conservative leadership told the smeltermen that it did not support their radical politics.[10]

The experiences of the Socialists who had won local offices confirmed that dramatic change in Anaconda would not occur through electoral politics alone. Their efforts to curb the ACM's power in town were quickly thwarted. They were defeated in the next election, as many of their former supporters among the smeltermen had abandoned the cause. Following these defeats, the *Standard* opined that "in all likelihood nothing more will ever be heard of the Socialist party in Anaconda"—a prediction that was strictly correct but failed to acknowledge the continued prevalence of radical political ideas among Anaconda's workers.[11]

East Side—West Side

As in Butte, racial-ethnic identity overlaid the ideological battles that occurred in Anaconda, but typically at a lesser intensity and with salient differences. Perhaps most important, the question of whether a man was transient or stable had less purchase in Anaconda, because it was from the beginning a town that attracted family-centered workers. Yet socioeconomic standing, which was closely tied to when a person arrived in town and to his or her racial-ethnic identity, played a central role in stratifying Anaconda. Indeed, that the electoral base for Anaconda's Socialist candidates had come from the *poorer* immigrants who populated Anaconda's East Side, not the better-off immigrants and their children on the West Side, was telling.[12]

Like Butte and Black Eagle, Anaconda was home to an astonishing range of nationalities. US Immigration Commission investigators who visited the town in 1909 reported that among "the races" found at its smelter were the "Danish, Dutch, English, Finnish, Flemish, French, German, Irish, Norwegian, Scotch, Swedish, [and] Welsh," all of whom the commission defined as northern European. The smelter was also home to "Southern Europeans," including Greeks, northern Italians, and southern Italians. "Bohemian and Moravian, Bosnian, Croatian, Dalmatian, Herzegovinian, Lithuanian, Magyar, Montenegrin, Polish, Russian, Servian [Serbian], Slovak, and Slovenian" workers represented the "Eastern Europeans." Unlike those in Butte, Anaconda's ethnic communities did not form small, geographically distinct enclaves. However, its Italians, French Canadians, and a few other groups did tend to live in particular areas, or even on particular streets, further distinguishing Anaconda from Black Eagle.[13]

Southern and eastern European immigrants had not been among the American-born workers and the émigrés from northern Europe and Canada comprising the very first arrivals at the smelter town, but they were not far behind, making Anaconda more like Black Eagle than Butte in this regard. Sam Premenko, a Serbian who had sold groceries and operated a saloon in Nevada's mining district, opened a similar establishment in Anaconda the year it was founded. George Barich, a Croatian with similar business interests, did the same a few years later, but added a boardinghouse to his enterprise. Both men paved the way for the large number of "Austrians," especially from Croatia and Slovenia, who came to work at the Anaconda smelter over the next decade. Demographic data show that 35 percent of the Croatians working at both smelters had arrived in the United States before 1899, and more than half of those had come before 1894. The first decade of the twentieth century saw a steady stream of recent Croatian immigrants continuing to find work and settle in Anaconda: 183 Croatian men reported arriving in the United States between 1900 and 1904, and another 164 between 1905 and 1909.[14]

In a pattern similar to that among Croatians and Italians in Black Eagle, Croatians and Slovenians in Anaconda, originally from adjacent countries in Europe, bonded and created an impressive power bloc. They formed the town's second mutual aid immigrant organization, the Saint Peter and Paul Fraternal Aid Society, which built its own hall; affiliated with other "Austrian" societies, including the one in Black Eagle; and established a busy social schedule that reinforced racial-ethnic identity. In the mid-1890s, this group sunk even deeper roots in Anaconda and displayed its growing power by successfully petitioning the Roman Catholic Church to establish a religious sanctuary for them on the town's East Side—called Goosetown by many locals—where most had by then congregated. Following a donation of land from Marcus Daly, Saint Peter's Austrian Roman Catholic Church was dedicated in 1898. Initially, it offered Mass only in Croatian or Slovenian. Even though the Austrian community demanded exclusive purview over Saint Peter's, the large numbers of Catholics from other nations, particularly Ireland, moving into this decidedly working-class immigrant part of town at the beginning of the twentieth century prompted the bishop to expand services to all who lived in the area.[15]

The need to serve newly arriving Irish immigrants at Anaconda's East Side Catholic church reflected two opposing forces in the town's social politics. Catholicism, reinforced by many of Anaconda's working-class and middle-class Catholics sending their children to parochial schools, linked a large number of the town's immigrants. But the way parishes were split there also hinted at the ways economic status could trump racial-ethnic group ties in Anaconda's social landscape. Goosetown, the most working-class part of town, had a diverse immigrant character. Residents remembered the sounds of many languages being spoken and sung; the pungent smells of immigrants' cooking and sulfur from the smelter; the sight of teeming family homes on busy streets; and a wide variety of nationalities socializing together.[16]

Evidence from the Immigration Commission bolstered this perception of how class worked in Anaconda. Investigators, fascinated by the differences between Montana's smelters and those in other parts of the West, concentrated on the large number of northern European immigrants working at the Anaconda smelter who had been in the United States for more than two decades. The Irish led the way in this category, but while 37 percent of the foreign-born Irish had been in the United States for more than twenty years and 26 percent for between ten and nineteen years, 37 percent had arrived in the previous ten years, with the preponderance of those emigrating in the previous five years. In 1909 there were, in fact, equally large numbers of new Irish immigrants working at the smelter and living on the East Side among southeastern European immigrants as there were longtime Irish at the plant. Locals spoke about a family's belonging to one class or the other by describing them as "one bathroom" or "two bathroom" Irish.[17] As in Butte, these new Irish immigrants did not necessarily toe the party line established by their earlier arriving "two bathroom" counterparts.

Nonetheless, the early arriving Irish controlled the town. Daly's favoritism toward his fellow countrymen and the strongly Irish character of the ACM provided the bedrock for the establishment of Irish power in Anaconda; the latter had the same effect in Butte. While the Irish comprised approximately 25 percent of the smelter workforce in 1900, they were found in even larger numbers in the foreman, craft, and management ranks. In 1885 Butte's Irish leaders helped found the Anaconda chapter of the Ancient Order of Hibernians (AOH), the first racial-ethnic association in the smelter town. With the help of their brothers from Butte, the Anaconda Hibernians and other Irish organizations quickly and publicly staked out a leadership role in the town's social, business, and civic affairs. At the 1889 United Irish Societies picnic in Anaconda, for instance, Butte's Irish arrived in fourteen train coaches. They chose to stop on the East Side of Anaconda so they could parade through town in what might easily be read as a show of power on their way to the West Side picnic grounds. Once there, combined with their Anaconda countrymen, they formed a contingent of approximately four thousand that celebrated their heritage while also displaying their preeminence in the two copper towns.[18]

The exercise of power by the early arriving Irish was sometimes met with consternation by Anaconda's non-Irish, particularly when it involved economic matters. Commenting on both the Irish place in Anaconda's business world and the link to the ACM, a non-Irish grocery clerk complained in 1892 about the founding of the Copper City Commercial store: "The promoters are all Irish Catholic and will control the trade of their own breed, besides making it hot for any white man holding a position with the Company that does not patronize them. I am sorry to say that the town is getting to be thoroughly 'Mick.'" A few months later, the writer confirmed that all the town's Irish residents had shifted their purchases to Copper City. For him, the way the store had gone about gaining its trade showed that the Irish, like the Company, excelled at mobilizing coercive force. Using another derogatory term for the Irish, he contended, "The average flannel mouth loves to talk about freedom, but when the opportunity arrives that enables him to put on the thumb screws he does not hesitate a moment but goes to work forgetting his previous protestations." Whether Anaconda's Irish used similar methods to gain local political office may have been a matter of individual interpretation; but any question as to the dominant place of the old Irish in its civic sphere at the end of the nineteenth century was put to rest in 1899, when a new AOH building went up across the street from Anaconda City Hall. Funded in large part by D. J. Hennessy, one of Butte's wealthiest and most influential Irish leaders, the AOH Hall, according to one account, "rivaled [the latter building] in grace," providing an apt symbol through its location and grandeur of Irish power in the smelter town. That the exercise of that power would also come through the Anaconda Mill and Smeltermen's Union was suggested by the fact that the five hundred workers who gathered in 1901 to found it met in AOH Hall.[19]

Southeastern Europeans and others who felt disempowered by the town's Irish and other northern Europeans did more than just grouse. Matt Kelly's remark that "smeltermen enjoyed fighting amongst themselves nearly as much as fighting with outsiders" affirms the importance of fisticuffs as a way to assert masculine status among Anaconda's workers. In this they were not alone; both organized and unorganized forms of pugilism were enormously popular among Montana's copper men. The six thousand residents who came to see a fight in Butte on Labor Day 1904 represented a large but not extraordinary crowd. Several copper men had distinguished careers as fighters. By "describing himself as a 'lifelong hard laborer,'" boxer Dixie Lahood, who came from one of Butte's Lebanese families, spoke to the link between the two masculine arenas.[20]

Fights between smeltermen were such a regular event that workers built a boxing ring in a field only a short distance from the reduction works. Some would-be combatants were not willing to wait until after their shift. Kelly recalled the "terrific battle" between "Red Walsh and Yonko, two wonderful specimens of their respective nationalities," outside the converter building near where paint was stored. It took the intercession of "the Big Boss" to stop the men. When he asked why the two were fighting, "Red replied that he was going to put Yonko in the whitewash and make a white man out of him, even if it killed him."[21] The "Austrian" Yonko's response was not recorded, but presumably one of his goals was to demonstrate the equality if not the superiority of his masculinity, and therefore of his race, to the Irishman's.

For southeastern European smeltermen, being perceived as equal to northern European and native-born workers was important not just to the psychological underpinnings of their masculinity but also to the material ones. At the smelter, typical daily pay for a common laborer had increased from approximately $2.25 in 1888 to $3.00 in 1910. More technical jobs, such as crane operators, skimmers, feeders, dippers, and furnace men, earned workers $4.00 per day in 1910. Foremen usually earned significantly more, and engineers and upper-level supervisors had pay rates well above the foremen. Just as in Butte, native-born and northern European immigrants filled the majority of these higher paying labor positions at the Anaconda plant and dominated the even more lucrative foreman, mechanic, engineer, and supervisor positions as well as the craft jobs. Just under 20 percent of native-born whites and just over 20 percent of the first-generation immigrants from northern and western Europe and Canada at the smelter worked as engineers, mechanics, or foremen. Only 1.6 percent of first-generation Croatians, 1.5 percent of Slovenians, and zero percent of Dalmatians, Herzegovinians, or Montenegrins held similar positions.[22]

The Immigration Commission pondered what these numbers said about developing racial-ethnic relations in Anaconda. Investigators, tracking what they called "Race Changes," a term they used for an evolution in the racial-ethnic composition of a workforce, reported that in comparison with other western copper towns, far fewer native-born and northern European workers had left the Montana smelting industry in search of "more pleasant or more remunerative employment elsewhere." What vacancies did occur in the higher-paying jobs this group tended to occupy, southern and eastern European immigrants were increasingly filling, but not in numbers seen at other smelters in the West. Commission investigators argued that the reasonable wages and hours at Anaconda explained why native-born and northern European workers were still represented in large numbers, and thereby provided the chief reason why more "race changes" had not taken place by 1909. Yet several other factors clearly played a role. These families also had sunk deep roots in Anaconda, and there were not many other op-

portunities in town. Prejudice within the smelter and on the part of the
ACM contributed to this racial-ethnic hierarchy. Croatian American smelterman Joseph Bolkovatz recalled that he was unable to secure a job in one
part of the plant because it was controlled by the Irish—another crucial
reason why more "race changes" did not occur.[23]

The ethno-racial tensions that existed among Anaconda's European immigrant and native-born residents were in place from the beginning, but so
were some of the processes that would eventually create a pan-ethnic white
Anaconda. The founding of the town had coincided with one of the most
virulently anti-Chinese moments in US history. Casual, often unreported
violence, as well as more organized assaults against Chinese, were commonplace in Anaconda and the rest of the West over the next two decades.
The peak occurred in the early 1890s, in conjunction with the debate over
whether the Chinese Exclusion Act should be extended. Among Montana's
copper towns, Butte saw the most horrific expression of this impulse with
the murder of three Chinese by a large gang in 1891. While it did not have
as high-profile a case, anti-Chinese agitation in Anaconda matched that in
Butte. The dynamiting of a Chinese washhouse in 1890 and the brutal beating of two Chinese by a local "thug" in 1892 were part of a concerted effort
to drive out the Chinese from the smelter town.[24]

As in many other parts of the West, organized labor took the lead in
this anti-Chinese campaign. Workers in Butte and Anaconda affiliated with
the Knights of Labor formed committees that argued for a boycott of all
Chinese businesses in both cities. The local Knights chapter ran a notice
in the *Anaconda Standard*, announcing, "Any member found patronizing
hotels, restaurants, boarding houses or laundries that employ Chinese will
be fined five dollars." Suggesting broad support beyond the working class,
the *Standard* carried favorable coverage of the boycott. Nearly a decade earlier, Butte's miners and Anaconda's smeltermen had both secured a pledge
from management that it would not hire Chinese. Hence, the smeltermen's
opposition to the Chinese had more to do with defining Anaconda and the
workers who called it home as white than with fears of job competition. A
local businessman's decision to name his restaurant "White Labor" with
the thought that it would attract a large clientele speaks volumes about the
racial dynamic in Anaconda at the time. As in Butte, anti-Chinese sentiment
continued into the twentieth century there.[25] But unlike Butte, it was not
overtaken by the anti-bohunk movement, reinforcing the different status of
Austrian immigrants in the two cities.

Along with Butte and Great Falls, Anaconda had a Landless Indian population on its outskirts that played a part in its developing racial-ethnic

order. The Nez Perce, Salish, Kootenai, Pen d'Oreilles, Blackfeet, Crow, Pawnee, Bannock, and Shoshone nations all considered the Deer Lodge Valley an important hunting ground and campsite. For some years even after the US government forced them onto reservations, these tribes continued to come to the valley. By then the landless Chippewa under the leadership of Rocky Boy had the most consistent presence around Anaconda. That situation ended with the formation of Rocky Boy's Reservation in 1916. Indian men may have worked at the Anaconda smelter in very small numbers, but local histories mention only their being paid to participate as stereotypical "warriors" in Fourth of July and Labor Day parades.[26] Their being used in this way in these ceremonies allowed Anaconda's immigrants to partake in a ritual of American citizenship that turned on the presence and dismissal of Indians.

"Anaconda's Own Steady Smeltermen"

In the first two decades of the twentieth century, then, Anaconda's Croatians and Slovenians continued to solidify their standing in the town. Likewise, the early arriving Irish continued to assert their preeminence, while newly arriving Irish both reinforced the overall Irish character of Anaconda and represented a growing diversity of Irish perspectives on class politics and Irish nationalism. Other residents, especially the northern Europeans and native-born whites, also continued to exercise significant economic and political power.[27] During this period, Anaconda's European immigrant world was neither as fractured as Butte's nor as unified as Black Eagle's.

Although racial-ethnic identity remained important to Anaconda's social politics, a group of male workers who had worked together for a significant time; who had roots in all parts of Europe; whose families, especially the younger generation, socialized together; and who tended to align based on socioeconomic status as much as on national identity when contentious issues arose began to exert a growing influence. Matt Kelly aptly called this core group, along with the cohort among the new generation of smeltermen who would labor at the plant for decades, "Anaconda's own steady smeltermen." They would prove to be pivotal to the evolution of ethno-racial politics at the smelter, but during the 1910s they, along with other men who would work at the plant only for a short while, experienced the same sort of unrest as did their peers in Butte. A small number were instrumental in the ultimately unsuccessful effort to shore up the position of organized labor in Montana's copper industry.[28] During this period, it is telling that while tensions among Anaconda's immigrant groups did not evaporate, ideological and tactical divides were paramount.

A major demographic transition under way in the town itself played a decisive role in creating inter-ethnic fellowship. The census indicates that the number of residents who were native born with foreign parents increased from 3,488 to 5,021 between 1890 and 1920. Among smeltermen, the 1909 figures show that approximately 70 percent were native born; those with "foreign fathers" outnumbered those with "native white fathers" only slightly.[29] Over time this nativity shift, along with changes in local, regional, and national culture, resulted in immigrants and especially their children considering themselves as "American" and, equally important, "Anacondan" as much as from a particular immigrant group.

Nowhere was this transition more apparent—and nowhere was the intersection with manhood clearer—than in the realm of sports, particularly competitions with Butte. Initially, some of the city-versus-city contests reinforced mono- instead of pan-ethnic identity. Anaconda's and Butte's Irish each fielded Gaelic football teams that for decades saw "natives of the 'Old Sod'" lock horns. One account of the 1911 game in which Butte's Wolftones defeated Anaconda's Emeralds contended, "The Emeralds took consolation in the majority of victories achieved by their backers in the fist fights that took place among the spectators." These fights, described as "a fine old Irish time," and the physicality of the game reinforced the idea that Irishmen showed particular "aggressiveness" and, in the calculus that dominated Anaconda and Butte, were especially masculine compared with men of other racial-ethnic backgrounds.[30]

Significantly, by World War I the annual match was no longer played because of a lack of interest among the younger generation in both cities. This turn away from immigrant-identified sports was spawned in part by the growing popularity of American sports such as baseball, bowling, and football. Anaconda teams in the latter were multiethnic. Equally telling, when the Gaelic football matches were revived by the next generation of Irish Americans, they invited their "Croatian, Italian, English, Scottish, and Lithuanian friends to join them. The original Irish players rated the game that ensued as "sissy goin' ons," offering both a racial-ethnic and a gender critique of Anaconda's shift toward a pan-ethnic sensibility.[31]

The process of creating a pan-ethnic identity in the town through sports also involved the workplace. Anaconda and Butte union locals were closely connected and often celebrated Labor Day together. But they also competed against each other. Anaconda's smeltermen sent teams to vie in events held on Miners' Union Day, and Butte's miners sent their representatives to the annual Smeltermen's Picnic. This rivalry provided another avenue for other allegiances to be formed alongside racial-ethnic identity, with both groups interpreting the contest between their various representatives as a way to assess and assert the relative manhood of the two occupations. Among the most popular team challenges was the tug-of-war, which was taken seriously enough for the local press to cover each team's training sessions. Whereas the final word theoretically went to the victor, smeltermen and miners were known to engage in a verbal to-and-fro before the match. When asked by a reporter about his bragging that his team needed no practice to defeat the smeltermen's squad, Butte miner Jim O'Brien, speaking "in a heavy Irish brogue," replied, "Ah, ya got us wrong, lad. Sure we're gonna practice. It's just that it's so expensive." Befuddled, the newspaperman asked O'Brien why practicing tug-of-war required such expenditures. "'The ropes ya' know. They cost a lot of money and me lads keep breakin' 'em.' After a long pause to let his full meaning sink in, he continued, 'But we're gettin' a steel cable that we're gonna cover with rope. As soon as that's ready, we'll start practicin.'"[32]

The posturing that accompanied the contests between smeltermen and miners could escalate beyond banter. In 1912 the Butte Miners' Union and the Anaconda Mill and Smeltermen's Union held their annual picnic on the same day at the same location. As was the custom, many attended the event with their families. Organizers billed the tug-of-war as "the sporting highlight of the joint affair." According to *Copper Camp*, after a testy battle Anaconda's "husky smeltermen" were declared the victors, at which point, "with the courage inspired by some several thousand quarts of beer," the two sides heatedly argued about the result. "Somebody swung a fist. Someone else threw a bottle," and the melee was on. A reporter covering the event wrote that so many miners and smeltermen engaged the enemy with the weapon that was closest at hand that "the afternoon sun was hidden from sight by the clouds of flying bottles." *Copper Camp* recapped what happened next: "The smeltermen, outnumbered, but fighting valiantly as ever did their Croatian, Austrian and Polish ancestors, were finally forced by sheer numerical superiority to retreat in defeat to the sheltering glades of the nearby hills." Although this account painted a racial-ethnic portrait of the smeltermen as exclusively southern and eastern European—a detail that reminds us of Butte's strongly Irish sense of itself—Irish smeltermen fought next to their Anaconda compatriots. Anacondans, if they *did* admit defeat in the fight as *Copper Camp* proposed, would have no doubt loudly proclaimed their victory in the tug-of-war. Nonetheless, Anacondans certainly lost more competitions against Butte than they won. Their town's identity in relation to Butte had more to do with how their teams carried themselves. Patrick Morris, who grew up in Anaconda, summarized this sensibility: "Undaunted Anaconda . . . never asked for quarter."[33]

Attitudes about the place of racial-ethnic identity in the social ordering of Anaconda shifted further during the 1920s. This development is evident in the remarkable Butte-Anaconda creation known as Bohunkus Day. Originated by youth in both towns, Bohunkus Day, which quickly became widely popular, was a carnivalesque occasion that made fun of the racist stereotypes that earlier generations once aimed at immigrants from the Austro-Hungarian Empire (pejoratively called bohunks). The changes in attitude the event represented were also reflected especially strongly at the smelter in the early 1930s. As they struggled together to establish a strong, community-centered union movement, second-generation ethnic workers made sure that older divisions did not undercut their unity. Their decision to demand a seniority system that would eliminate racial-ethnic and other hiring biases best represents this commitment.[34]

Yet Anaconda's "steady smeltermen" did not help change the gender order in their town in the first decades of the twentieth century as they had the racial-ethnic order. Like Black Eagle and Butte, Anaconda's firmly established male culture had a profound effect on the lives that immigrant women led. The smelter's practice of employing only men in production jobs reinforced the dominant male breadwinner ideology that had women, from morning to night, performing the unpaid domestic labor that kept their families afloat. Those who did venture into the world of paid work found the same limited opportunities within the service economy as did women in Butte, but perhaps the prospects were slightly better than in Black Eagle. Once a woman married, even these options more or less evaporated. In addition to all their other domestic duties, married women were expected to take boarders. In Anaconda the perception was "if you didn't have boarders then there was something the matter with you," contended longtime resident Annie Novis Miles. Perpetuating the local gender order, expectations like these were passed on to boys and girls by both immigrant men and women.[35]

The historian Laurie Mercier has persuasively argued that into the 1920s, "segregated work and community life" still defined Anaconda's gender order. According to one resident, "Men and women socialized with friends of the same gender." Although the town had a more pronounced family sensibility than Butte's, its leisure activities, like Butte's, were organized with men in mind and included many establishments that for decades reinforced homosociality by refusing female patrons. Within this framework, immigrant women used ethnic associations, churches, and neighborly proximity to create a network that influenced Anaconda's day-to-day politics. Eventually, social and work opportunities did expand for the next generation of Anaconda's female citizens. As Mercier notes, by 1930 "in the clerical, service, professional, and retail trade categories, Anaconda women were found in greater numbers than their . . . counterparts" in Montana as a whole. However, the shared gender politics of three of the town's most powerful institutions—the smeltermen's union, the Catholic Church, and the ACM—served to circumscribe more dramatic change. For instance, the Company maintained an exclusively male clerical workforce, except for the "few girls" lucky enough to land jobs at the bottom of the pay scale, even though companies nationwide were hiring women in large numbers for these positions.[36]

During the 1920s, the ACM employed the same paternalistic welfare capitalist strategy in Anaconda that it did in Black Eagle. Simultaneously, the Company, which had played a decisive role in the destruction of legitimate unionism at the smelter, sought to block any effort to reinstate the union, including using men whom other workers considered "company stooges" to spy on its meetings. Managers continued the practice of sporadically laying off employees, causing workers to worry about being labeled a troublemaker and getting fired as a result, and ensuring that the Company could turn a larger profit. Although smeltermen appreciated some of the benefits that came with the paternalistic system and respected *some* of the managers who oversaw it, Anaconda's "steady smeltermen," of both the older generation and the newer, were ready to take on their employer and revitalize independent unionism when the opportunity arrived in the following decade.[37]

"Company Boys"

The Great Depression and the New Deal, which restructured the lives of all Anacondans, strengthened working-class male identity in ways that would have a major impact on the local social politics of the World War II home front. As Mercier concludes, the "Depression brought prolonged unemployment, and the community altered its pace to confront the crisis. But survival was made possible, many believed, only because the federal government provided emergency relief and work programs." Anaconda's history of suffering, survival, and eventual renewal found a parallel in the story of its local house of labor. Most workingpeople did not initially see unionism as a viable mechanism for handling the woes of the Depression. Then the June 1933 passage of the National Industrial Recovery Act, whose Section 7(a) bolstered collective bargaining rights, changed their minds. Local organizers resurrected Local 117 of the International Union of Mine, Mill, and Smelter Workers (Mine Mill) and joined their fellow activist copper workers in Butte and Black Eagle in reenergizing it. Following Mine Mill's 1934 strike, in which workers won the right to a closed shop, the end of the sliding wage scale, and a formal grievance system, Anaconda smeltermen returned to being staunch union advocates. They also increased their support of President Roosevelt, the Democratic Party, and the Popular Front.[38]

Anaconda's shift toward a more openly progressive politics in the 1930s, occurring as local women were becoming a greater presence in the paid workforce, did not mean a significant change to those jobs to which women could aspire. As Mercier notes, "The community's debates and decisions about relief reveal gendered assumptions about poverty and a commitment to dedicate scarce resources to male breadwinners rather than women." Scholars have found the same situation in other union towns. Although women made some inroads through their own activism, neither they, the government, nor the difficulties men faced in fulfilling the breadwinner role changed the fact that the local culture of Butte, Black Eagle, and Anaconda—like the national culture of thirties more generally—centered on bolstering the status of workingmen.[39]

Beginning in the midthirties, their membership in a reinvigorated union and the support they received from local and national culture allowed Anaconda's smeltermen to more aggressively confront their bosses. In so doing they asserted their sense of themselves as "independent" laborers whose manhood was superior to their bosses' and who were willing to fight for their due. In places across the United States, this effort could occasionally include fights and other forms of physical violence. The same was true in Butte and Black Eagle, but contests with specific foremen and other managers also led to other equally telling reactions. In Montana's copper facilities, foremen, clerks, and other lower-level managers consistently heard workers refer to them not as "company men" but as "company boys." Sometimes workers used this term jokingly to kid men who had left labor's ranks, but at other times it became a way to emasculate clerks and managers, particularly those who seemed either overly beholden to the Company's upper echelon or unwilling to deal with workers fairly. A similar trace of derision accompanied other examples of local vernacular for white-collar workers, including "Book miners" or "Fifth floor guys"—mining technicians who worked on the fifth floor of the ACM headquarters in Butte—and "Pencil pushers" or "Ink slingers"—timekeepers who kept track of the workers' hours. On the other hand, local terms like "Brains" for a smelter's assaying and chemical department, or "Big Boss" for the smelter superintendent, seemed laudatory. "Big Boy," another name for the superintendent, was more ambiguous.[40] The term could have been seen either as akin to "Big Boss" or as a way of suggesting the superintendent was the most distant of the "company boys" from smeltermen's true manhood. As a whole, these more subtle forms of assertion saw workers championing their "productive" masculinity with its physicality over the intellectual labor and uncertain productivity of their bosses.

In this same period, workers who regarded productive labor as a foundation for their manhood were able to step up a longtime campaign to assert their masculinity, but in a contradictory way: by being less productive. Men who knew they would spend a lifetime in the confines of a plant doing typically hot, dirty, noisy, tedious, and sometimes dangerous work often felt exploited by the ACM. Smeltermen's desire to feel some sense of control over their lives, to make their working day as easy as possible, and, echoing an aspect of the radical manhood associated with the Industrial Workers of the World, to strike back against their employer, prompted many to avoid work whenever possible. Similarly, an ethos of "if the company has it, why buy it" flourished in the thirties. Men who rejected this approach or who consistently worked too hard were scorned.[41]

Also increasing in the thirties were arguments over who controlled the space in which workers and bosses most often interacted, an old area of contention between both parties that spoke particularly strongly to the practice of working-class masculinity. Labor historians use a geographic metaphor in describing these arguments as fights over control of the shop floor. In a plant the size of the Anaconda Reduction Works, there were numerous areas where employee and employer met besides the places where production occurred (fig. 3.2). The first interaction took place at the company's downtown employment office. The white-collar labor represented by its staff challenged blue-collar male employees as they sought to claim the financial and psychological wages that combined to help form their masculine status.[42]

In the ethnographer and former smelterman Edward Reynolds's story about working at the plant in the latter part of the Great Depression, the protagonist's anger over the work assignment he received from the employment office aptly conveys this point. He had been "grumbling ever since the clerk in the employment office downtown had given him a work card for the Stack. The Stack! Rappin' treaters or dumping flue dust. That was a job for sodbusters and greenhorns. Not for a guy that had been born and raised right here on the ground, here in Anaconda."[43] Besides highlighting the divide between blue- and white-collar men, Reynolds's characterization

3.2 Within the plant, the first place to be contested by employee and employer was the area between the entrance gate and the timekeeper's window, where workers encountered a management representative: the guard. The guard was also the last person associated with the ACM whom workers encountered on their way out of the Anaconda Reduction Works after their shift. The practice of employing guards to scrutinize workers as they entered and exited the plant marked this particular space as one that the Company owned and controlled, while also, like the gate itself, serving as a reminder that the entire facility was owned by the ACM. However, as this photograph shows, workers often responded to this projection of power by studiously ignoring the watchman and, arguably, the ACM's claim of control. Photograph by Russell Lee, *Anaconda Smelter, Montana: Anaconda Copper Mining Company; Men on the Day Shift Leave at End of Work*, 1942. Library of Congress, Prints & Photographs Division, FSA-OWI Collection, LC-USW3-008528-D DLC.

of whom management should assign to the plant's worst jobs confirms that whether a man was from Anaconda and had experience as a smelter-man or whether he was an outsider—a migrant from anywhere outside the copper communities—had become a measure of difference that eclipsed racial-ethnic identity, at least for Anaconda's European immigrants and their descendants.

Reynolds's comments about "the Stack" indicate that the construction of masculine status also occurred through workers' perceptions of jobs associated with certain machinery or areas of the plant. Contemporary commentators, including the workers themselves, frequently argued that the machine dehumanized the entire workplace. In the mid- to late nineteenth century, the rhetoric typically referred to the death of the artisan and the birth of the factory worker. By the time of the Depression, the factory worker had become the quintessential figure whose toil defined what it meant to labor. The revival of the labor movement and the intervention of federal policy makers saw both an elevation of working-class culture nationally and a renewal of concern about the deleterious effects of the machine age. At a number of points, Reynolds's account echoes these others by suggesting that machines dominate men. But unlike *Modern Times* and a plethora of other texts from the era that treated all machines as similar, he depicted the varying emotional responses elicited by specific machinery at the plant.[44]

When Reynolds's smelterman gazes upon the hot-metal section, readers glimpse one of these intense responses.

> His eyes dwelt on the smelters with a mixture of respect and hatred. The blackened buildings with their giant stacks looked like the charred remains of a forest fire. Down there was the hot metal; with its menace that fascinated him. He could see the calcine being dumped into the reverberatory furnaces along with charges of dust and unroasted concentrates. He could hear the roar of the gas used for fuel. From the door of each furnace came a wild red glow like the blood-shot eye of a Cyclops.

For the former smelterman, the "mixture of respect and hatred" brought on by the hot metal's "menace" imbued the place with the ability to confer a status that was seemingly not shared by any other location within the plant.[45]

The two jobs, either of which Reynolds's protagonist expected to be assigned upon reaching the Stack, rapping treaters and dumping flue dust, reinforce the site-specific response of workers and the variety of jobs that smeltermen considered deserving of particular masculine status (fig. 3.3). Both jobs certainly shared the traits of danger and dirt with working the hot metal, but they were not evaluated equally. The treaters recalled "stories of the smell of burning flesh, of the blue hole where the juice had passed through a man's feet on out of his body, of rigid forms toppling from the cat walk." As the narrator notes, "Somehow, death by electrocution seemed tawdry after the violent, threatening spectacle of the hot metal." If the treaters come up wanting in comparison with the hot metal, the danger inherent in dumping flue dust was seemingly even less worthy of masculine status. Although "there was always the chance of getting burned," dumping dust "didn't bring violent death." Apparently worse than burns, however, were the "nasty sores" that men who worked the flue dust could develop. Using language that clearly ties masculine status to the particulars of this job, Reynolds wrote: "There is something unpleasant and humiliating about these sores—under the arms, between the legs, around the waist. You look at them and treat them in the privacy of your room. You're ashamed of them." Returning to his touchstone for manly labor, he explicitly compared these

3.3 A smelterman assigned to work at the stack, wearing the necessary protective equipment. Although working in this part of the plant paid premium wages, the position was among the lowest in status. This was one of the places where black men could work. Photograph by Robert I. Nesmith, *Stack Worker and Stack*, Anaconda, Montana, 1942; Montana Historical Society Research Center Photograph Archives, Helena.

wounds to "the hot metal, where the leaping, roaring flames and the fiery glow of molten metal places danger on a high level." Even after the protagonist goes through the process of dumping flue dust and feels the panic associated with the possibility that "the side of his face" would look like it "was eaten off by cancer," the risks of the job have not elevated it in his estimation.[46]

Reynolds's decision not to mention how race intersected with the status of treater and flue dust jobs is especially intriguing given that the Anaconda smelter was the only Montana copper facility that employed African American men at this point, and Mine Mill's campaign against racial prejudice in the workplace was in high gear. While the "tawdry" danger associated with the treaters and the "humiliating" sores and potential facial disfigurement associated with the flue dust contributed to making working at the Stack "a job for sodbusters and greenhorns," the fact that the Stack was one of only a few places African Americans were allowed to work at the smelter played an equal role in its being perceived by smeltermen as low status. The way that white and white ethnic men in Anaconda racialized arsenic work emerges from the comments of an ACM personnel manager and a smelterman who both claimed that exclusively African American men worked in the arsenic and were allowed to do so only because "their black skin, it didn't hurt them like it did a white person."[47] Such fallacies about the differences between black and white bodies suggest that antiblack racism was a part of the racial landscape at the smelter, but the place of black workers in the dynamics of race and masculinity there was far more complex.

African American men had first come to Anaconda in 1889 to work as porters and waiters in Marcus Daly's lavish Montana Hotel. Their occupying these positions was not unusual in Montana, as plentiful evidence from Helena, Butte, and other cities shows. The historical record is silent, however, regarding the critical question of exactly when and how black men succeeded in gaining and keeping employment at the Anaconda smelter when they were barred from copper work in Butte and Black Eagle. By the early twentieth century, the ACM had hired eighteen as common laborers in a number of places within the plant, including the acid section and the tram railway or air line. In both areas, as in the arsenic section, black men worked next to white men. Some smeltermen described the acid section as the worst place to work at the plant because of the intense heat, cramped space, dirt, and exposure to powerful chemicals. Consequently, black men's work in this job could be explained along the same lines as their labor in the arsenic section. But that opinion of the acid section was not universally shared. Manning the crushers, ovens, and furnaces also had backers among the smeltermen for the least desirable jobs to be assigned at the plant. Black men did not work in these places, but they did labor on the tram railway, making sure that the superheated calcine made its way from the roaster to the reverberatory furnace. Workers tended to describe the tram railway as among the "most dangerous places on the smelter," but as Reynolds noted, other parts of the smelter were considered equally dangerous, and that danger offered masculine status.[48]

Illogic, contradiction, and inconsistency suffused the calculus used to determine the masculine status of each job at the Anaconda smelter, but smeltermen knew that calculus, and race played a part in it. If a white or white ethnic smelterman held a lower-status job, he and his fellow workers may have argued against these perceptions in order to gain more respect for themselves. Given the racial ideology of the day, that argument was much less convincing if the man worked at a job that Anaconda's few African American workers also held. But it was not impossible to make, because black workers were required to work on segregated crews under white supervisors, to negate any sense of white-black equality within the smelter. Most important, white and white ethnic men could use their seniority to move to different positions within the smelter, but black men could not. Notably, the progressive interracialism of Mine Mill during the 1930s did not prompt white and white ethnic smeltermen to include their black cohorts in the seniority rule negotiated with the ACM during this period. The long-used local approach to managing racialized masculinity and affirming white manhood at the smelter remained in place.[49]

The racial heritage of Edward Reynolds gives even more powerful evidence of the often capricious, highly local, and interwoven operation of race and gender in Montana's copper communities on the cusp of World War II. Both of Reynolds's parents held prominent places in Anaconda in the 1910s and 1920s. Born in Kentucky, his father, Claude, lived in the smelter town for thirty years and served for a period as president of its smeltermen's union. According to the *Anaconda Standard*, Reynolds's mother, Marie, was born in New Orleans and "came to Anaconda as a young woman and during her 24 years' residence here gained by her noble character and charming personality the friendship of all with whom she came in contact." Upon her untimely death, she was mourned throughout the city and in Butte. Marie Reynolds's maiden name was Roxborough, and although her Montana Certificate of Death lists her as "White," her family appears in the Ohio and Louisiana census as black. Her sister Cornelia was a prominent member of the "Sisters of the Mysterious Ten . . . A Negro Order" based in Kentucky. Under the "one drop rule" that became codified into law in numerous states nationwide during the first decades of the twentieth century, these circumstances made Edward and his siblings either black or "mulatto."[50]

In fact, the 1910 Montana census lists not only both Marie and Cornelia but also all the Reynolds children and Claude himself as "mulatto"; a former Anaconda resident confirmed that locals knew about the family's racial background. Such a classification typically would have barred them from the privileges that came with whiteness, such as better working conditions and higher pay, and the masculine status that came with such positions. But that is not what happened with the Reynoldses. The family saw themselves shifted to the White category in the 1920 census. Locally, they had been effectively treated as white for over a decade before that. And the Reynoldses were not alone. A careful examination of census records indicates that a remarkable number of men who worked at the smelter had been once classified as "mulatto." And just as they did with the Reynoldses, the locals treated these men as white, and the census eventually reclassified them as such. Also like the Reynoldses, but unlike locals classified and treated as "negroes," Anaconda's "mulatto" smeltermen were allowed to work in some of the best jobs at the plant.[51] The difference between them and the black smeltermen, who were spatially marginalized in the community, had no mobility, could work only in low-status positions, were often the first fired, and were not allowed to accrue seniority, appears to be only how networked each was with those in town who decided who was to be considered a racial insider and who was not.

Local Racialized Masculinity and the Coming War in Butte, Black Eagle, and Anaconda

Reynolds's account of working at the smelter—through either commission or omission—highlighted key aspects of historically rooted social politics in Montana's copper towns that would have a profound impact on how local men approached the challenges of the World War II home front. The importance of being attuned to the locally specific operation of masculinity was the first of these. Butte's miners more than Black Eagle's and Anaconda's smeltermen saw asserting their independence as a crucial part of their masculinity, but all three groups of workers valued this aspect of working-class masculinity. Montana copper men also fought to assert some control over their workplace, and saw the ability to do so as an equally if not more important aspect of establishing masculine status. Each of these three groups gave varying levels of credence to the social and cultural changes in the United States that provided some women with greater access to a variety of jobs in the decades before the war. Local women in Anaconda and Butte found a small number of jobs available to them in the smelter and mine offices, but that was not the case for Black Eagle women. Women in all three towns continued to find the higher-paying, higher-status production jobs at the smelters and mines closed to them. As a whole, the working-class immigrant gender order that revolved around buttressing the male breadwinner and that had long dominated all three towns remained intact heading into World War II.[52]

The ongoing eclipse of racial-ethnic divisions—but not race—among the native-born white and first- and second-generation European immigrant working class, seen in a contextualized reading of Reynolds's story, also characterized all three towns on the cusp of the war. The thirties saw the emergence, albeit at different levels of development, of a pan-ethnic white identity among immigrants from southern, eastern, northern, and western Europe and their descendants in Butte, Black Eagle, and Anaconda. This bond was strongest in Black Eagle and was built on a long history of fellowship, communication, the shared experience of marginalization in Great Falls, and a shared religion and church home. In Butte, the city where the links among immigrants were the weakest, the continuation of racial-ethnic hierarchies, especially in the workplace, was most apparent. Though fractured, the Irish there continued to exercise their ability to secure the best spots in the mines and the trades for themselves and their kin. The language of color, however, was no longer being used against southeastern Europeans. Likewise, the rebirth of the BMU and Mine Mill and the presence of the Congress of Industrial Organizations' culture of unity made working-class identity a strong adhesive among Butte's white multiethnic miners. Butte's miners called on that solidarity as well as their continued belief in "independence" as they increased their militance against the ACM. Those dynamics were also at play in Black Eagle and especially in Anaconda, where class bonds had long served as a vital connection among smeltermen of different nationalities. But Mine Mill's interracial politics also challenged copper men in all three towns. It remained to be seen what would happen if all Montana's copper men were asked to put into practice the philosophy that had become the hallmark of their parent union.

Edward Reynolds's employment history offers yet one more vantage point from which to view the changing socioeconomic climate facing Montana copper men in the two decades before World War II. Thanks to the dominance of local codes over national ones, Reynolds was treated as a well-connected white local when it came to securing a position at the smelter. Instead of seeing the smelter as the limit of his work opportunities, he took the locally atypical step of pursuing a university degree, then securing a job as a writer for the *Montana Standard*. Yet this white-collar position did not protect Reynolds from the Great Depression. After being dismissed by his employer, like many men in the copper towns he sought government relief work. However, instead of doing manual labor for the Works Progress Administration, he gained a position with the Federal Writers' Project. As the Depression came to an end, Reynolds faced the same choice as many American men. Wartime mobilization expanded employment opportunities dramatically, but the United States' almost certain entry into World War II shifted masculine expectations, forcing men to decide whether they should enlist in the armed forces or seek stable, secure employment. The decisions they made on this issue, as well as the other choices made by men working in Montana's copper communities during the war, were deeply influenced by what had occurred in Butte, Black Eagle, and Anaconda over the previous sixty years. Thirty-four-year-old Edward Reynolds took the option that most copper men did not—he entered military service. It is to that story that we now turn.

PART II

Copper Men and the Challenges of the Early War Home Front

FOUR

Redrafting Masculinity: Breadwinners, Shirkers, or "Soldiers of Production"

On a single remarkable but now largely forgotten day in October 1940, approximately 16 million American men between twenty-one and thirty-six years of age registered with the US Selective Service System, the government agency responsible for conscripting male citizens into the nation's armed forces. That act marked a new relationship between American men and their government, as the state came to serve as the final arbiter of whether a man was doing his masculine duty. President Franklin D. Roosevelt, along with secretary of war Henry Stimson, initiated the lottery that established the order in which the Selective Service called men for the United States' first "peacetime draft." The six-thousand-plus local draft boards quickly evaluated men with lower draft numbers for their physical, mental, and moral fitness to serve and recorded relevant personal and occupational details, especially their marital status and current employment. Based on the combination of these factors, men who appeared before their local board received a classification that identified their availability for induction into the military. At the end of October 1940, newspapers across the country published lists of the eligible men in their area in the order that the Selective Service would draft them.[1]

The *Great Falls Tribune*'s section on the peacetime draft list noted that the two local draft boards processing men from Black Eagle, Great Falls, and the surrounding area had ranked 5,107 potential draftees. The paper featured stories about the first man called by each board. For Board No. 1, that honor belonged to Joseph H. Sanders, a college-educated twenty-five-year-old. Board No. 2's first inductee was Samuel M. Cislo, a twenty-two-year-old Polish American railroad worker who had not attended high school. The *Tribune* asserted these unmarried men's willingness "to serve their country anytime the nation sees fit." Sanders, the paper emphasized, had already applied for flight training when he learned he would be among the first two local men called. Cislo, in contrast, was "hesitantly noncommittal" about his new status. He "nervously laughed" as his workmates told him, "So long, Sammy" and "Don't forget to write." Cislo's physique impressed the reporter, who pronounced him "a strapping big fellow." After explaining that he lived with and helped to support his mother, the article concluded by reinforcing the idea that, as "a good American," Cislo's responsibility now was to serve the nation in uniform rather than his mother at home.[2]

The *Tribune*'s insistence that military duty came before other masculine imperatives signaled several significant shifts in the American gender order—social expectations about men's and women's behavior—that are the subject of this chapter. A careful examination of the two years between October 1940 and October 1942, the final year of the United States' mobilization and the first year of its entry in the war, uncovers the complex world of masculinity experienced by the copper men of Montana and other working-class American men during this pivotal period.

Contemporary Americans' impressions of the draft typically reflect the controversies that marked the Vietnam War, when the system was so widely regarded as unjust that the US government felt compelled to shift to an all-volunteer army in 1973. During World War II, perceptions of conscription were very different. The draft drew men from all segments of society into the military, creating a sense of shared sacrifice. The fairness of the draft and, just as important, men's willingness to become "citizen soldiers" are among the main reasons Americans continue to think of World War II as the "good war." Historians of masculinity have argued that World War II, unlike the war in Vietnam, provided a brief period in which men knew and could meet national masculine expectations.[3] What occurred in Montana's copper communities, however, suggests that issues of masculinity, the draft, and military service during World War II were far more fraught with ambivalence than scholars have assumed.

Beginning with the initiation of the peacetime draft, men felt mounting pressure from popular expectations that they belonged in the armed forces. Because public opinion still opposed entering the war, the Roosevelt administration limited the number of men drafted to nine hundred thousand and their active duty service commitment to one year. A Gallup poll taken in the fall of 1940, however, found 62 percent of Montanans in favor of conscription. This view of masculine duty found reinforcement from an especially compelling place in early 1941, when some local copper men decided to leave their workplace and volunteer for the armed forces.[4]

Instead of acceding to this pressure, many Montana copper men, bolstered by local culture, responded by defending their roles as essential workers and family providers. The Japanese bombing of Pearl Harbor dramatically raised expectations that men would place serving the country ahead of breadwinning. Yet, as a close look at Selective Service policies and responses to those policies indicates, Americans were still negotiating the relative importance of competing masculine duties even after the war began. Federal government propaganda inculcated the idea that the most important men were those in uniform. But local propaganda produced in or for Montana's copper communities did not always mimic this message; it regularly offered a noticeably different perspective. The debate over draft deferments for Montana's copper workers articulated these sometimes complementary and sometimes contradictory strains in wartime propaganda. It illuminates many of the ways that Montana's white and white ethnic "soldiers of production" negotiated the new, wartime meanings of masculinity.[5]

By the fall of 1942, Montana's copper workers, especially Butte's miners, had settled on a strategy built around the notion that they were exceptional home front men and deserved special benefits and praise for their wartime duty. But, as in the case with the draft, and foreshadowing a pitched battle over who would be allowed to work in Montana's copper facilities, miners and smeltermen found that the federal government played an increasingly powerful role in their lives and in judgments about their masculinity.

White Ethnic and Working-Class Masculinity, from Mobilization to Pearl Harbor

The peacetime draft did not initially remove the perception that some men from immigrant communities held less of an allegiance to the United States. After all, the eastern European–descended Cislo, not the Anglo Sanders, felt the need to declare himself "a good American." Cislo's statement hints at the undercurrent of racial-ethnic difference framing individual men's relationship with the state, recognizing that some might question his patriotism and even his fitness for duty. Yet while men of color, particularly African Americans, found themselves rejected by prejudiced wartime draft boards, men from southern and eastern European immigrant communities did not face a similar bias. The two decades that had passed since World War I had changed their status dramatically. On the cusp of World War II, they were still thought of as "ethnic," but they were also typically considered "white." Alongside other contemporaneous initiatives such as the "Americans All, Immigrants All" campaign that promoted the idea of an inclusive America, draft boards reinforced this whitening process by assessing ethnic men on the same terms as Anglo men. Although it was not entirely clear at the time, this shift demonstrates that eugenic ideas that had deemed white ethnic masculinity inferior to Anglo-Saxon masculinity had largely been sidelined. The draft created an important opportunity for communities outside the national mainstream a generation before to assert their equality and implicitly claim whiteness.[6]

The peacetime draft had more problematic effects on working-class masculinity. Conscription had long been condemned by labor activists, who saw it as a device for corporate leaders to compel working-class men to fight wars that would make employers vast fortunes while costing workers their lives. Some men in Montana's copper communities shared this view as they considered how to respond to the draft, and there is no question that beginning with the peacetime draft the Selective Service System gave bosses the ability to influence whether the government conscripted a man or not. But the majority of men had more pragmatic, though related, concerns. Wartime mobilization had returned virtually all white ethnic working-class men to full-time work. For the first time since the onset of the Great Depression, workingmen were consistently earning enough money to see themselves as adequate breadwinners—an essential criterion of manhood at the time.[7]

The peacetime draft meant the government was telling men to prepare for military service that, in addition to its other drawbacks, paid significantly lower wages than many industrial jobs. Cislo's ambivalence about the draft reflects this reality. On the one hand, his concern about providing for his mother echoed the worries of many draft-eligible, working-class men about who would care for their dependents. On the other hand, Cislo and many other men from immigrant communities wanted to be seen as manly Americans. As one second-generation Italian American from Black Eagle remarked, "You can't imagine how privileged . . . and patriotic it would be to be in the service. It was our responsibility, our commitment as a result of our parents being immigrants to defend our country." Such after-the-fact reflections align well with the popular understanding of men's responses to the war, but they veil the complicated relationship many working-class men had with the draft and military service.[8]

Indeed, as momentum gathered behind a shift in national attitudes, the hesitancy men felt toward the draft was fed by the sense that their duty during peacetime remained unclear. Working-class men derived masculine status both from the physicality and productiveness of their work and from their ability to be the main provider for their families. "Hot Metal," an essay submitted in late spring 1941 by Edward Reynolds, a former Anaconda smelterman, for *Men at Work*, an anthology compiled by the Federal Writers' Project, echoed this idea of working-class masculinity while responding to the conceptualization of manly duty as intrinsically linked to military service.[9] "Hot Metal" defended smeltermen against the charge of being cowards because they were at the plant instead of inside a tank, battleship, or plane.

> Certainly, I'm registered for the draft. What do you think? Anytime Uncle Sam needs me he knows where I am. But I've got a hunch he's going to need me a lot more right where I'm at. . . . Why, I'm working in the hot metal at the Anaconda Reduction Works. That's where they smelt the copper out of the ore from the Butte mines. . . . No, I'm not afraid people will think I'm yellow. I told you I work in the hot metal, didn't I? People that are yellow just don't work there.[10]

Masculine status, however, did not accrue solely through performing physically difficult or dangerous work.

The narrator's invocation of his father's career in the Anaconda smelter moves from facing danger to returning to breadwinning after an injury. "One of the earliest things I can remember as a kid was when they brought my old man home from the hospital. . . . He worked in the hot metal, too. . . . They told me he was wearing gauntlet gloves and some hot calcine spilled in. That's why you don't see me wearing gauntlets now. I got a good memory. Anyway, when the old man came back his hand was shriveled like an overdone pork roast. It was almost a year before he could use it again." The hard-won lesson is not to avoid the dangers of the hot-metal section (fig. 4.1), but rather to be smart about how you work. Continuing his father's story, the narrator informs the reader that his father "probably never would have been able to use it again because he thought it was paralyzed. But my mother knocked it up in the air to show him it wasn't. The old man almost fainted, but he got the idea."[11] In other words, doing dangerous work meant little if a man could not provide for his family, which is exactly what he was expected to do.

Entering the military would make being the family breadwinner more challenging, but instead of focusing on this masculine standard, "Hot Metal" attacked the more fundamental perception that military service was more dangerous or important than work in the copper industry. While military service in peacetime entailed some danger, many miners risked their lives every time they went underground. Hard-rock mining was among the most dangerous work in the country. Fatality statistics for Butte were staggering:

4.1 Office of War Information photographer Russell Lee's September 1942 photograph of the hot-metal section of the Anaconda smelter captures the danger associated with this part of the plant. Photograph by Russell Lee, *Anaconda Smelter, Montana: Anaconda Copper Mining Company; Sometimes the Molten Copper When Poured . . . Splashes Violently*, 1942; Library of Congress, Prints & Photographs Division, FSA-OWI Collection, LC-USW3-008895-E DLC.

one man a day died of tuberculosis, called miners' consumption; one man a week died in an accident. The numbers of injuries and deaths at the smelter and refining plant were also substantial. The men were well aware of these somber facts. Moreover, it seemed likely that, as in World War I, most Americans in the military would never see combat.[12] The odds of coming home from military service seemed pretty good, begging the question of which was manlier, copper work or soldiering?

Although men working in the Montana copper industry as a whole claimed an equivalency with peacetime soldiering, they regarded some jobs in their field as manlier than others. In fact, an elaborate hierarchy of masculinity had long operated within the smelter, just as it had at the Black Eagle refining plant and the Butte mines. Smeltermen, miners, and community members had discussed among themselves the relative manliness of particular jobs before the wartime emergency. Some of their conclusions became a permanent part of copper culture, such as the widespread practice of calling men who worked aboveground "softies." Reynolds's narrator's declaration that "people that are yellow just don't work" in the smelter's hot-metal section suggests that the shifting expectations of 1941 prompted some men to assert more publicly that their jobs made them manlier than other workers.[13] What was at stake in these discussions about relative worth changed when the United States entered the war.

While more permanently altering how men negotiated their masculine status, the run-up to the war and particularly its onset also briefly challenged the standing of some European immigrant communities. Wartime mobilization made immigrants a target for a section of the population that questioned their patriotism and, more nebulously, even their fitness to be Americans. Echoing aspects of this, on June 29, 1940, President Roosevelt had signed into law a measure requiring the registration and fingerprinting of all resident "aliens." Though he contended it would provide for the "mutual protection of this country and loyal aliens who are its guests," the chief proponents of the bill advertised it as a way of protecting the United States from immigrants' "'fifth column' activities." Instead of the 3.6 million immigrant aliens authorities expected to register nationwide, 5 million submitted the requisite paperwork.[14]

Some depictions of immigrants in Montana during this period echoed the derogatory late nineteenth- and early twentieth-century stereotypes of Italians and other southeastern European immigrants that suffused American national culture and also appeared prominently in local popular culture, such as the Butte Evening News's bohunk exposé. Earlier in the century, these stereotypes had been mobilized by white Americans—and by other immigrants from Europe struggling to secure their own place in the US racial hierarchy—to exclude southeastern European immigrants from the full psychological and material privileges that being considered "white" brought in the United States. Indivisible from this racial project was a gender project that simultaneously placed some immigrants outside masculine and feminine norms. Unlike that era, the early 1940s saw southeastern European immigrants successfully fight this campaign without having to forsake their ethnic ties. Although the agency of these communities themselves had the most to do with this, organizations such as the American Institute of Fraternal Citizenship, which supported immigrant claims to American identity at the national level, played a part as well. Locally, following the paternalistic management practices by then long in place, ACM managers had also quickly and repeatedly come to the defense of their immigrant employees.[15]

Pearl Harbor hindered efforts to have immigrants and their descendants seen as mainstream white Americans. On December 19, 1941, General John DeWitt reported in a confidential letter to Montana governor Sam Ford that the government thought the state's 4,401 German-born, 2,265 Italian-born, 227 Japanese-born, and 281 Japanese American residents were the most likely to mount "fifth column activity and sabotage." He urged Ford to "bring to bear every possible means for combating this insidious danger," particularly at a time when citizens might be distracted by "fairs, fiestas and public gatherings." On December 23, 1941, DeWitt instituted a curfew from 8:00 p.m. to 6:00 a.m. for all enemy aliens and Japanese Americans in "critical military zones"—including copper production sites in Butte, Anaconda, and Black Eagle—and urged citizens in all affected areas to report violations. Ford followed this by requesting the assistance of federal troops in this effort.[16] The concern about European immigrants and their descendants being "enemy aliens" shook the communities in question. But it quickly dissipated, thanks mainly to the continuing support of the immigrants by the ACM, national organizations, and the vast majority of locals, and the entry of a large number of white ethnic men into the military after Pearl Harbor, partly because they wanted to prove that they and their families were "good Americans."

News reports from Pearl Harbor and the Philippines, where the Japanese first attacked US bases on December 7 and 8, 1941, brought about what would be the more powerful effect of the beginning of active hostilities on local communities: in popular discourse, military masculinity instantly trumped any form of civilian masculinity. At least seven Montana men died and numerous others were taken prisoner in the first days of the war. Butte, the hometown of three of the dead, exemplifies how the state's copper communities responded. News about these men circulated by word of mouth and in the media, continually emphasizing the costs of military service. Every local newspaper article referred to the men as heroes.[17]

The story of Private First Class LeRoy Carpenter and the recollections his relatives later shared about him provide greater detail about how the initial war reports were interpreted in Montana's copper communities. When his family learned that the United States Army Air Corps had sent Carpenter to the Philippines, they were relieved. The Pacific Islands seemed like a backwater, the sort of place where war would come late, if at all. Moreover, in August 1940 Carpenter had enlisted in the Air Corps as a mechanic, thereby joining the large majority of men in uniform who supported the actual fighters. When he arrived in the Philippines, his assignment removed him even farther from frontline duty: he served as chauffeur for his commanding officer, ferrying him around base, taking him to meetings, the briefing room, and onto the flight line so that the commander could talk to the men who soon would fly into harm's way. On December 8, 1941, the day after Pearl Harbor and two months into his tour in the Philippines, a bomb fragment from a Japanese air strike against Clark Air Force Base killed Carpenter. The twenty-three-year-old was well liked in Butte. His cousin described him as "a mild-mannered man . . . full of fun," but "tough as nails, too." Smiling, she remembered that he was "pretty popular with the girls." Carpenter was also a talented boxer who had won several amateur bouts. Except for the fact that he had not yet worked in the mines, he was the classic Butte boy.[18]

In the first six months of the war, Butte, Anaconda, and Black Eagle, like communities across the country, lost many LeRoy Carpenters. In World War I, airpower, which wreaked havoc on troops and civilians far in the rear, had been a novelty. But in World War II, hostilities expanded even further beyond combat troops. A significant number of those who died in the war served in combat theaters rather than on the front lines. Hence, the argument that only a small proportion of those in uniform were in danger was no longer convincing; even hypermasculine jobs like those in the copper industry paled in comparison with military service.[19] This new reality, with its implications for families of servicemen and for the manhood of copper workers, settled in on Butte, Black Eagle, and Anaconda just when the government was ramping up the wartime draft.

Classifying Men under the Wartime Draft

While the draft touched residents of every region in the country, it was particularly fitting that Lewis Hershey was traveling through the Mountain West at the moment when the United States entered the war. From 1940 to 1945, in his role as director of the Selective Service System, Hershey oversaw the induction of over 10 million men into the army and navy and the classification and deferment of another 10 million. The draft occupied a prominent place in discussions about citizenship, service, and masculine duty. People in the West, which had a history of contradictory responses to wartime military service, were particularly concerned about this nexus. Based on concerns rooted in the previous world war, western congressional representatives led by Montana's Burton Wheeler had strongly opposed both the draft and US involvement in World War II before the bombing of Pearl Harbor. Yet as one Great Falls newspaper had proudly reminded the state's citizens, in proportion to its population, Montana contributed more men to the armed services during World War I than any other state.

After the country's official entry into World War II, western states, including Montana, Idaho, and Utah, had the highest per-capita voluntary enlistment rates.[20]

Despite westerners' pride in these patriotic enlistees, most men *did not* rush out and enlist on the day after the Pearl Harbor bombing. The story of a Butte miner's son, William T. Paull, illustrates the sudden, dramatic change in home front attitudes toward soldiering, the draft, and manhood. Paull, like many young men, had been fascinated by the version of military service presented in Hollywood's romantic and patriotic fare. He remembered being bewitched by the 1935 movie *Shipmates Forever*, starring Dick Powell as a suave Annapolis midshipman who courts the "sweet young ingénue," Ruby Keeler. Years later he recalled Powell crooning, "Shipmates stand together, / tho it's a long, long trip; / Fair or stormy weather, / we won't give up, / we won't give up the ship." Seeing *Shipmates Forever* prompted Paull to apply for an appointment to Annapolis, which he received in 1936 from Democratic senator James Murray. But Paull failed to pass the Naval Academy physical because of hypertension. Dejected, he enrolled in the School of Mines in Butte; but when the Fuller Paint Company offered him a full-time job earning $75 a month, he bought a hot little Chevy coupe with a rumble seat and started work.[21]

Five years later, when Paull found himself subject to military conscription, his gung-ho attitude evaporated. "When the draft came along, I felt smug. I knew I had high blood pressure and wouldn't pass the physical." But his notoriously fickle blood pressure was just fine the day of his physical, so he was classified 1-A. On December 8, 1941, knowing he would be called soon and not wanting the army to "get him," Paull and a friend enlisted in the marines. If it had been immediately clear that mining would be considered so critical to the national defense that it conferred a deferment, and that being a "soldier of production" would be valued as highly as being a soldier on the front lines, Paull might have gone to work as a miner. His description of his family and friends "huddled" around him on the train platform, with others "surrounding their departing heroes" as "clouds of hissing steam from the locomotive, and an over-all . . . sense of doom" pervaded Butte's Union Pacific Depot, aptly conveys the "somber" national mood and the elevated status enjoyed by military men in early 1942. To the townspeople on that platform, it did not matter that Paull and many other men were unenthusiastic enlistees; once in uniform, they were all heroes doing a man's duty.[22]

For American males, going through the Selective Service process was an obligation. By the end of the first year of the war, 43 million men had registered. In Montana, a vigilant community made sure that young men did not evade the draft. Two months into the war, a posse "wounded and captured" Walter M. Franklin, who was "charged with failing to register under the selective service act." The Associated Press photograph of the bruised and cut captive published in regional newspapers served as a vivid visual reminder of what was at stake. Franklin was part of a large cohort of nonregistrants whom the government pursued as soon as war was declared. Some had been required to go through the Selective Service System before the war but failed to do so. Others found themselves eligible for the first time when the Selective Service extended the system to all men under the age of sixty-five.[23]

Draft Classifications[24]

1-A: Registrants available for general military service.

1-A-O: Registrants who are conscientious objectors available for noncombatant military service when found acceptable to the land or naval forces.

1-C: Registrants who have been inducted into, enlisted in, or appointed to the armed forces.

2-A: Registrants who are necessary or essential in their civilian activity.

2-B: Registrants who are necessary or essential to the war production program, excluding agriculture.

2-C: Necessary or essential men in agriculture.

3-A: Registrants with dependents, engaged in less essential industry or less essential agriculture.

3-B: Registrants with dependents, engaged in an activity essential to the war production program.

3-C: Registrants with dependents, engaged in essential agriculture.

4-A: Registrants who before induction have become forty-five years of age since they registered.

4-B: Registrants who are aliens not acceptable in the armed forces or who have waived their rights to become citizens to avoid military service.

4-D: Registrants who are ministers of religion or divinity students.

4-E: Registrants who are conscientious objectors available only for service in civilian work of national importance.

4-F: Registrants who are mentally, morally, or physically unacceptable to the armed forces.

4-H: Registrants who are thirty-eight to forty-five years of age.

As the number of men eligible for the draft increased, so did the complexity of the draft classification system (see above), and it did so in a manner indicating the hierarchies of masculinity wrought by the war. At opposite ends of the Selective Service spectrum were classifications 1-A and 4-F. At least on paper, 1-A men were paragons of masculinity, physically and mentally fit to wear a uniform. The lyrics for "He's 1-A in the Army and He's A-1 in My Heart," a popular song recorded just prior to the beginning of the war, trumpeted the 1-A man's bravery and patriotism and noted his favor with women. Similarly, the song "4-F Charlie," released the same year and especially popular among men in uniform, derided those receiving this classification as lacking courage and being a "complete physical wreck," and even called a 4-F's procreative abilities into question: "his blood is as thin as water, / He can never be a father." 4-F, which labeled a man as "mentally, morally, or physically unacceptable to the armed forces," was given to an astonishingly high proportion of draftees. In their first twelve months of operation, draft boards across the nation rejected fully half the men who appeared before them. In April 1942 Montana's governor, Sam Ford, wrote to Secretary of War Stimson, complaining about the number of men who had been rejected. Ford, like many others, questioned the government's evaluation system more than the quality of American manhood. Boards responded to official and public criticism by lowering their standards. Nonetheless, by 1945 over 5 million of the 18 million men examined had been classified 4-F.[25]

Whereas 1-A and 4-F were the most obvious indicators of masculine status, other categories reveal the thorny relationship between the draft and manhood. Most Americans saw conscientious objectors (COs), classifications 4-E and 1-A-O, as cowards, because they would not fight for their country. A poll taken in January 1940, when many citizens still preferred staying out of World War II, found that more than 85 percent of respondents favored COs being forced to serve in the military; 9 percent wanted them either "shot or put in jail." Only a small minority believed that COs showed remarkable bravery for standing up for their convictions in the face of public condemnation. The Selective Service differentiated between men categorized as 4-E, who refused to enter the armed forces, and those who merited 1-A-O, who had declared their willingness to serve in uniform and even put themselves in harm's way, often as medics, without carrying a weapon. Sergeant Alvin York, the World War I hero whose story was retold in the highly popular, eponymously titled film of 1941 starring Gary Cooper, helped to valorize the draftees who were classified 1-A-O.[26]

Classification 4-B, given to "registrants who are aliens not acceptable in the armed forces or who have waived their rights to become citizens to avoid military service," seemed the most likely to affect Montana's immigrant copper workers. By making all aliens who had filed initial applications for permanent residency subject to the draft, the 1940 Selective Service Act effectively placed virtually every copper worker in the conscription pool. Category 4-B was created in response to protests from neutral countries regarding this policy. In 1941 Congress amended the act, but also made any alien's petition to be placed in 4-B grounds for "permanent debarment from United States citizenship."[27] In effect, though not in intent, the category offered white immigrants an opportunity to emphasize their equality, patriotism, and aspirations for citizenship.

Although COs and aliens represented the extremes, deferment from induction because of marriage and fatherhood, represented by the 3-series classifications, and/or because of employment in an essential industry, the 2-series classifications, affected far more draft-eligible men. These categories proved contentious in governmental and public deliberations about men's obligations in wartime. Subject to the peacetime draft and anticipating hostilities, many young men and women correctly surmised that married men would be protected from induction. Combined with the Depression-era trend for young adults to delay marriage until they were financially stable, the introduction of peacetime draft legislation in May 1940 sent couples to the nearest altar or justice of the peace in unprecedented numbers. The marriage rate—the proportion of unmarried females over fourteen years of age who married in a given year—rose meteorically from a low of 56.0 in 1932 to 73.0 in 1939 and 82.8 in 1940. Anecdotal evidence reinforced the point. In August 1940, just a month before Roosevelt signed the Selective Service Act, civil authorities in Brooklyn and Staten Island reported people queuing up for marriage licenses at 6:30 in the morning.[28]

Getting married to avoid the draft continued unabated well into the war. A contemporary estimate that 40 percent of the twenty-one-year-olds drafted at the end of 1940 married within six weeks was only mildly, rather than wildly, exaggerated. The marriage rate rose to 88.5 in 1941 as the United States prepared for war; in the year after Pearl Harbor, when marriage still conferred an exemption, it hit a wartime high of 93.0. Taken together, these statistics confirm Lewis Hershey's blunt assessment that American men were using marriage as a way to escape induction.[29]

The draft and deferment process profoundly shaped ideas about sexuality and its link to masculinity. Induction served as a powerful catalyst for the growth of homosexual identity by prompting gays and lesbians to leave their small towns and find communities in the armed forces. For gay men, stereotyped as effeminate by the dominant heterosexual culture, the irony was manifest. But many, like their straight counterparts, had no interest in serving in the military. Their search for wartime jobs that would provide them with deferments led them to larger cities, spaces that also facilitated the creation of gay communities. For heterosexuals, propaganda depicted entering the military as a way to defend the other two cogs of the heterosexual family, women and children.[30] But in practice, it was the effort to stay out of the military by gaining a deferment that strongly promoted heterosexual marriage and procreation in the early war period.

In the fall of 1942, as the need for even more men in uniform became apparent, the issue of whether age or marital status should provide the most protection from the draft came to the fore. The question of how old was too old for military service provoked little public controversy, though it would trouble many home front men for duration of the war. First those over the age of 45 and then those over 38 were classified as 4-A. Military leaders agreed that men older than 28 were less capable of frontline duty, but could still serve effectively in other capacities. Nonetheless, a substantial number of men older than that age enlisted or were drafted. In contrast, the Selective Service's proposal to conscript 18- and 19-year-olds before married men, made in the fall of 1942, prompted a heated national debate. Previously, men under 20 were supposed to wait before donning the uniform, although considerable numbers of younger men lied about their age in order to enlist. But the military's manpower demands meant that leaders had to choose between protecting young men from the horrors of war or honoring married men's obligation to provide for their wives and children. Congress instituted the teenage draft, signaling its belief that protecting the male-breadwinner family model was more important than treating older youths as immature.[31]

Next, military leaders sought to convince the government that deferring married men who had no dependent children had catastrophic effects on the manpower supply. Of the 16.1 million men who had been classified by October 1941, 10,102,000 had fallen in category 3-A, men with dependents, which conflated marriage and fatherhood. In early 1942, Hershey had begun to question the principle that marriage necessitated deferment, while holding firmly to the idea that it was "in the interest of the government to maintain, if possible, the family as a basic social unit." Poll data indicated that Americans believed men with dependents should be shielded from the draft, but enough voices were raised in opposition that married home front men were forced to wonder how others perceived their masculinity. Hershey warned, "Public opinion is going to demand that married men do not hide behind wives and children." A number of wives even publicly urged draft boards to induct their husbands, reinforcing the idea that all men were obligated to serve their country in wartime.[32] Ultimately, the decision to draft married men who had no children went some way toward reinforcing the primacy of military service in the hierarchy of masculine duty, but also underscored the priority placed on shielding men with dependent children from the hazards of combat.

Congress's continued insistence on the protection of fathers meant that having children became the surest protection against conscription for men of draft age. Hence, rapidly rising birthrates during the early 1940s indicate motives more compelling than the new financial wherewithal, or the passions many commentators argued were brought on by the war. Suggesting the continuing power of fatherhood as a definition of masculinity and, once again, the role of the state in forging that definition, most members of Congress did not back the "work or fight" directive from US War Manpower Commission head Paul McNutt, which would have ended blanket deferments for fathers and allowed only deferments based on critical skills. During the final two years of the war, however, exigency meant that draft deferments for fathers ceased, and nearly a million of them entered the armed forces.[33] The government's decision to require fathers to meet their military obligation placed men who stayed on the home front under even greater scrutiny.

A third category of deferments, those for essential home front work, dominated draft debates among Montana's copper men and many other workers across the nation. Controversy swirled primarily around three classes of workers: government, agricultural, and industrial. In October 1942, when Representative Dewey J. Short (R-Missouri) sarcastically complained that "thousands of young government officials are crowding thirsty congressmen out of Washington cocktail lounges," fully 5.5 million men held government jobs. Deferments for federal employees raised such a furor in the hustings and on Capitol Hill that in November 1942, a Senate committee urged the government to fire one-third of nonmilitary employees in Washington, DC, and to revoke deferments for federal workers. Some of those workers agreed with the committee's recommendations. One bureaucrat "characterized his supervisors as draft-dodgers who appeared 'to do nothing but harass and needle'" those employed in war production.[34]

Agricultural deferments caused equal consternation. The high wages paid by war plants induced a mass exodus from the nation's farms. Six months before Pearl Harbor, the secretary of agriculture was already warning about a shortage of farmworkers. In Congress, the powerful farm bloc petitioned the administration to exempt farmers and farmworkers from the draft. Hershey feared the effect of such an exemption on both military manpower and the reputation of the farm men. He argued that a blanket deferment would attach "a stigma to the farming industry which they could not easily eliminate." Despite Hershey's opposition, in November 1942 Congress passed legislation effectively keeping a disproportionate number of male agricultural workers out of uniform for the duration.[35]

Industrial deferments affected Montana's copper workers most directly. By early 1942, six hundred thousand men across the United States had received such deferments. One year later, that figure stood at 1 million, a relatively modest increase that signaled resistance to increasing industrial deferments and skepticism about the argument that men could serve the nation as well on the production lines as on the front lines. Nonetheless, an enormous number of home front men wanted deferments, and throughout 1942 many industries and their workers lobbied to have the government list an occupation as essential. By the beginning of 1944, 3,204,000 men had been categorized as holding essential jobs; another 1,052,455 joined them by the end of that year.[36] In Montana's copper towns, the debate over these deferments occurred in the context of rapidly evolving ideas about masculinity that were disseminated nationally through government propaganda but had distinctive regional and local cultural manifestations. Analyzing this war of words provides critical context for assessing how Montanans viewed industrial deferments and wartime manhood.

Ambivalent Analogies between Soldiers and Industrial Workers

Wartime propaganda comparing soldiers to industrial workers permeated home front culture. The federal Office of War Information deployed sophisticated advertising techniques to inculcate messages ranging from such practical matters as the importance of women's work in war plants to xenophobic notions of the inscrutable evil of the Japanese.[37] Butte, Anaconda, and Black Eagle had their own powerful propaganda apparatus aimed at copper workers. The main cog in this local machine was the ACM Victory Labor-Management Committee and its award-winning twice-monthly newspaper, the *Copper Commando*, distributed to current employees and sent to former employees in the armed forces and their families. Like similar committees across the country, the ACM committee emerged primarily from a government initiative early in the war to curb labor unrest by having employees and employers meet regularly. The committee not only provided a vehicle for management and labor to resolve problems without interrupting production but also served as a conduit of public opinion to government decision makers regarding issues such as the draft. Subcommittees comprising managers and workers from each section of the three production committees met every two weeks.[38] The *Copper Commando* and transcripts of these meetings provide an unparalleled window into the concerns and beliefs of local men.

Documents from the initial meetings show that the federal government intended to use the committees to persuade workers to accept controversial policies, especially organized labor's no-strike pledge. Officials worried that workers would see these committees as mouthpieces for corporate leaders hoping to maximize profits at workers' expense, or for antilabor positions championed by those who saw any wartime labor activism as seditious. Workers had good reasons for their suspicions. The government and the ACM worked together to an unprecedented degree during World War II. The ACM's profits were tied to various government policies, but especially the "premium price policy" which was set in January 1942, and later changed to make it even more advantageous for the Company. A War Production Board statement quoted by smelter manager W. E. Mitchell at the first Victory Committee meeting sought to counter those concerns.

This drive is designed to increase the production of weapons now and not further the special interests of any group. It is not a plan to promote company unions. It is not a device to add to or tear down the power or position of any union. It does not interfere with bargaining machinery where it exists. . . . It is not a management plan, a labor plan, or any other plan. It is the War Production Drive plan. It is a perfectly simple, straightforward effort to increase production.[39]

The same effort to increase production and shape opinions on the home front permeated the *Copper Commando*.

In almost every issue, the *Copper Commando* featured messages from the nation's civil and military leaders to Montana's copper workers, demanding increased production and promoting a version of home front masculinity that valued obedience and sacrifice and was championed by the government and corporations. The message from Lieutenant General Brehon Somervell, commander of the War Department's Services of Supply, is representative. He called on the mine, mill, and smelter workers of Butte, Anaconda, and Black Eagle to see the nation through the emergency.

Our soldiers, fighting for our right to live as free men, depend . . . on every last one of you men of Montana no matter what your job . . . to get out the copper they must have. I know you will not fail them. They are your men. Around the world Montana boys face the most cruel and ruthless armies of all time. They cry for copper . . . more and more copper. No matter how much you produce, it cannot be too much.[40]

Somervell played on notions of fraternal citizenship and on the guilt he thought copper men must feel for not risking their lives in defense of their country. His request served the needs of both the nation and the Anaconda Copper Mining Company. It did nothing to reinforce the self-worth of the worker, making it difficult for a man on the home front to feel he had fulfilled his manly duty.

Comparing the life and, implicitly, the masculinity of soldiers with those of home front workers was a propaganda staple that sought to direct men toward particular ideas of wartime duty. Flanked by two large photos of men cleaning weapons, writing letters, eating, and performing domestic chores in tents, "Boys away from Home," an article in the September 5, 1942, issue of the *Commando*, declared that "life isn't very sweet for men in the fighting forces." The text suggested that copper workers too often took soldiers for granted and failed to realize that absenteeism and low production "handicaps" the troops. "[A] soldier cannot lie down on his job. No matter how poor his tools may be, he must still stay at work." While home front men have the privilege of seeing their families and resting when their shift ends, men on the front lines "work twenty-four hours a day at their jobs."[41]

The *Commando* also propagated racist stereotypes to define home front masculinity in terms of war production, the protection of family from sexual and other threats, and its relation to military masculinity. The *Commando* editors illustrated an October 7, 1942, story, "A Dying Jap Speaks . . . ," with a large photo of a Japanese soldier and smaller ones of the destruction of American property in the Pacific theater of operations. The caption says that the article contains the words of a "Jap soldier gasp[ing] out his scorn for our country and our people . . . for the Japs consider us soft and weak and easy to conquer." The editors implored local copper men to take the threat of a Japanese victory seriously and to "get fighting mad" before the Japanese "tear down the Stars and Stripes." The monologue the paper ascribed to this Japanese soldier is a classic piece of anti-Japanese propaganda meant to shame home front men into following the dictates of the government's version of home front masculinity.

I assaulted captive women, dozens of them, and if I'd lived to get to your country I would have invaded YOUR home and done the same thing. I almost did get there. My people believe we'll STILL get there. Because you Americans don't realize we Japs have been planning this war for years. Even today we work at war twenty-four hours a day. You people still play, still laugh, still think lightning can't strike you.

After using the supposed sexual threat the Japanese posed against local women—a threat the article suggests copper men, with their enervated masculinity, would not have been able to stop—to further impugn the manhood of home front men, the article lambasted copper men for ignoring the needs of the real men who heeded the call to arms: "You send your soldiers into battle with scant equipment, and we shoot them down like dogs. . . . You are willing not only to let your soldiers and sailors fight for you; you waste time in giving them the things they need to fight WITH. How many Americans have already died with the thought that their country let them down!"[42]

In August 1942, the *Commando* reported on another mode of propaganda seeking to reshape home front masculinity: a soldier's in-person plea to copper men. Lieutenant Marion Beatty was one of the men in uniform the Office of War Information and the War Department employed to travel to work sites, exhorting men to avoid absenteeism and act honorably toward those standing in harm's way on their and their families' behalf. In Butte, Beatty stood on a platform with a large sign just over his left shoulder noting that "112 employees were absent from war production yesterday!" and asking, "Were you?" Miners listened respectfully to Beatty's talk at the collar of a mine shaft. He told them: "A few thousand extra tons of copper in 1942 and 1943 can possibly end this war a few months sooner and save a million American lives. One miner staying away from his job one day means 5,000 fewer cartridges for some American soldiers somewhere on the firing line." Beatty appealed to the guilt these men were supposed to feel: "You must not send these men against the enemy in a hopeless or helpless condition. When the enemy attacks and pours out tons of burning hell from planes and tanks and guns they must have the means with which to defend, resist and counter-attack. . . . We cannot fail them." This plea, and the others that spoke to the experience of military men, referenced the homosocial bond between men on the home front and those on the front lines. Homosocial bonds had long been a common feature of masculine practice in Butte, Anaconda, and Black Eagle that served to reinforce a working-class masculine value system among copper men.[43] But now the homosocial bond being referenced was between workers and military men, and the goal was to convert workers fully to the government's home front masculine ideal.

Some copper men echoed Lieutenant Beatty's sentiments. Men like "Tubie" Johnson, a Butte native who began working for the Company in 1927 and whose writings and cartoons were published in the *Copper Commando*, emphasized the superior sacrifices being made by soldiers and demanded the same discipline of his fellow workers that corporations and the government championed (fig. 4.2). In "Remember Our Boys," Johnson reminds his coworkers that men from Montana's copper communities who joined the military had "pledged their lives to defend us / And we workers cannot let them down— / In our unity, might and strength lies, / In those efforts, true security found." Johnson also deployed the "soldier of production" metaphor that was commonly used on the home front.

> To battle stations, prepare[,] workers,
> You, in factories, mines or mills,
> Keep that war production rolling
> All wartime orders must be filled.
> Those boys of ours, our very own,
> Need planes, arms, mechanical mounts.
> Work hard the day and have no delay,
> Remember every precious second counts.
> So unite and pledge to do your job
> Because the sacrifice made is small
> Compared to our boys way over there
> Who are fighting and giving their all.[44]

Johnson acknowledged that for workingmen, what the nation was asking was a sacrifice of principles, but in his mind it was a sacrifice that they must make to support "those boys of ours, our very own."

A related staple of propaganda aimed at home front men was the patriotic performance of their coworkers. As Beatty was touring Montana's copper production centers, the *Commando* attacked absenteeism, among the most highly charged home front issues and one also referenced by Johnson, by reporting that three men at the St. Lawrence Mine had struck "good blows" against the Axis powers by not missing a single shift during July's five-week contract period. Ernest Tambling, born in Cornwall, England, in 1878, had come to Butte in 1920 and had worked in the mines continuously ever since. Thomas Perez, a native of Spain, came to the United States in 1919 and to Butte in 1936. William Koniw, who emigrated from Austria in 1913, entered the mines in 1922. These three men, who each received a $25 war bond, attest to the continuing strong immigrant presence in Butte and the other copper towns. The article reinforced the "Americans All" theme that pervaded wartime ideology. An illustration showed Tambling, Perez, and

4.2 Cartoons drawn by Butte miner John Powers, which were given to miners on every payday during the war, provide another example of local propaganda. Most of the more than 150 war-era cartoons Powers created engaged home front masculinity. These examples are from 1942. Drawings by John Powers, Montana Historical Society Research Center, Helena.

Koniw holding a giant "Buy a Share in America" war poster. The *Commando* expressed its desire "to be able to congratulate many more in the future who are helping to win the war," and by drawing attention to the men's elevated ages implicitly questioned the masculinity of younger men who claimed the difficulty of copper work caused them to miss shifts.[45]

Miners and smeltermen also faced pressure from other community members with considerable social capital. A letter from Bishop Gilmore of Helena, which he intended clergy to read from the pulpit, declared that copper workers "should serve as earnestly and as honorably [as the troops] by reporting faithfully for work." As Gilmore acerbically put it, "Absentee-ism is, to say the least, a mild form of sabotage." He added that absentee-ism posed a major risk to the male-headed Catholic family ideal, because it placed industrial deferments in jeopardy. His linkage of the preserva-tion of "the normal life of the home" to war production provided further ammunition for men who wanted to stay out of uniform, but required these men to renounce one of the cornerstones of local labor masculinity: independence.[46]

In seeking to refute such claims about their performance at work and their manhood, and in an effort to promote their own masculine ideals, copper men turned the master's own tools in their favor by repeating the common theme that war workers were performing a critical duty, perhaps even equivalent to that of soldiers. A "Defense Bulletin Board" radio segment featuring Donald Nelson, chairman of the War Production Board, which appeared in early 1942 on KGIR in Butte and KFBB in Great Falls, provides a classic example of government propaganda referencing this trope. Nelson discussed the importance of creating "two Armies by '43. . . . we'll have a fighting army of 4,000,000 men, and we'll have a working army of some 15,000,000 men and women engaged solely in production for war." By publicly endorsing and distributing a pledge that was originally written and sent to President Roosevelt by 613 workers at the National Transit Pump and Machine works in Oil City, Pennsylvania, the Victory Committee used similar rhetoric to exalt workers' contribution to the war effort.

> I realize that I am a soldier of production, whose duties are as important in this war as those of the man behind the gun.
> I will do my work well and efficiently and will stay on my job, producing to the best of my ability, until my shift ends.
> I will carry out my duties in accordance with instructions.
> I will think before I act.
> I will endeavor to save material by avoiding mistakes and spoilage.
> I will be careful of my health and prevent accidents, to avoid loss of time.
> I will keep my working place tidy and in order.
> All to the end that we may succeed in our efforts to increase production and attain the goal set as necessary to carry us to the final decisive victory over our treacherous enemies who now are threatening the homes of our children and the liberty of our nation.[47]

Likewise, when the president of the ACM rebuked the miners and smeltermen for their demands during the fall 1942 contract negotiations by saying "tell it to the Marines," the labor negotiators made clear their tie to military manhood and the support of military men for copper men's continued championing of working-class masculine ideals. They did so by using one of the government's methods: they had a soldier deliver the message. A former Butte miner who was on furlough came with his home front mates to the next day's labor-management negotiating session so he could "personally" report the Company's claim that miners were not doing their part "to the rest of the Marines."[48]

In resisting the implication that unless they marched in lockstep with the committee's, government's, Company's, and clergy's wishes, they were traitors, copper men demonstrated their commitment to local prewar masculine codes. They had fought for decades to gain a modicum of control over their work. Some workers saw the accelerated pace of wartime production as dangerous. Others felt they had the prerogative to skip a shift, and did so as an exercise of worker autonomy that would help maintain equality with management despite the no-strike pledge. Still others felt that the Company and its managers, as well as government officials, had failed to make an equal sacrifice to that demanded of workers.[49] For these men, showing their autonomy in the face of Company and government power, much as they had done during the 1930s, reinforced both their sense of manhood and a work culture that empowered workingmen and their unions, providing stability for workers' families and an appropriate reward for men in uniform returning to the workplace after the war.

Still, government propaganda had powerful effects on the home front. Men who did not join the armed forces were harangued to acknowledge their subordinate masculinity and comply with the dictates of the state and its business partners. Coupled with the no-strike pledge and wage freezes, this propaganda suggested that corporations were once again gaining ascendancy in Washington.[50] Nonetheless, male home front workers did not give up the fight. For the last eighteen months of peacetime mobilization and the first year of the war, draft deferments for industrial workers became one of the most contentious sites for negotiating between the prewar standards of manhood evoked by "Hot Metal" and the new standards of manhood inculcated by propaganda.

Industrial Deferments and Home Front Masculinity

Even as the state demanded sacrifices from them, many copper men sought to dictate the terms of their wartime service by gaining industrial deferments. They turned to the Victory Labor-Management Committee, the same group that the government wanted to use to control workers, as their primary conduit for putting forward their position on the draft. Fundamentally, miners and smeltermen argued that considering the difficulty, danger, and skill associated with their work, they embodied exceptional manhood. While contending that they could do more for the war effort on the home front, Montana's copper men began to increasingly acknowledge that combat soldiers were at the top of the masculine hierarchy. These industrial workers, however, wanted the government and their fellow citizens to treat them as the pinnacle of home front manliness and provide them with benefits associated with that position.

In August 1942, Joe Marcille and Fred Grey, two longtime copper workers who came to represent men seeking protection from the draft, were the first to ask why workers in ACM's employ were not being deferred by the Selective Service System, while men from other parts of the country were getting deferments and then coming to Black Eagle, Anaconda, and Butte to work. Marcille argued that skilled copper workers were worth more in the workplace than they would be in the armed forces, so the Victory Committee should work on getting deferments for them.[51] In addition to reflecting their obvious anxiety about industrial workers' masculine status, Marcille and Grey's comments evoked the major themes typifying copper men's interaction with the Selective Service and the administration: uncertainty about the draft apparatus; concern over other men "beating the system"; the special worth of men who worked in the copper industry; and fear about postwar economic and social security.

Two months passed before the union-management committee officially addressed Marcille and Grey's concerns about the draft. Much research and discussion among the copper men had occurred in those sixty days. A Butte Miners' Union representative reported that the head of the deferment board in Helena had agreed that miners, smeltermen, and other essential workers deserved deferments if they continued to labor in the copper industry. His remarks cheered the Victory Committee. But the union leader also revealed what would become one of the most difficult issues for miners, smeltermen, and other essential workers, and for the committee's effort to negotiate the draft deferment process for copper men: some deferred men would prefer to serve in the military, and others would fight to be deferred even though their work was not considered essential by the government. He asked, "What about oilers and other men like them: Are they going to take them? They might have to take the place of an engineer should he die." Although they did less technical work, oilers were often cross-trained to take the engineer's place if necessary. His emphasis on the danger of copper work echoed Edward Reynolds's narrator in "Hot Metal." But eighteen months after Reynolds had written convincingly about smeltermen's attitude toward the draft, the fear of looking "yellow" had been trumped by a desire to stay on the home front rather than serving wherever Uncle Sam wanted.[52]

Victory Committee members concluded that the number-one priority should be ensuring "that everyone is given the privilege of going into the Army or working in the mines as he wishes." This rhetorical maneuver placed mining and military service on equal footing as the two forms of wartime labor that would guarantee masculine status. But both union and management were more concerned about the reputation of copper men who wanted to stay on the home front than about the possibility that men would get trapped in deferred jobs. Society, of course, might see men in either group as akin to Walter M. Franklin, the Butte man who was hunted and beaten for allegedly dodging the draft.[53]

The movement of men from other parts of the region and the country to positions in Montana's copper production facilities that allowed them to avoid induction complicated the mine, mill, and smelter workers' ability to navigate community values regarding wartime service and masculinity. Producing copper had long been considered the epitome of men's work, and copper men reveled in the psychological wage that status provided. The war had already seen soldiers like William Paull, who had previously worked for a local paint company, supplant copper men. Now other men were coming to the mines and smelters in order to dodge the draft. Long-time copper workers, already bombarded with propaganda that questioned whether they were doing their utmost, felt that their own manhood was being besmirched.

Two workers raised the issue of men using the mines as a refuge during an early meeting of the Victory Committee. The first commented that within the community, "there has been a lot of doubt as to the attitude of men who have transferred from other industries into our industry. I have heard rumors criticizing a man who never worked for the Company, who was working up town and went to work in the mines." The second worker elaborated, "I have heard of two, the Harkins kid and Chappelle. The two of them worked a few days in the mines and both quit already. One of them is now working in the iron works as a welder and Harkins is back on the old man's truck." Because the War Manpower Commission directed local men to seek work in the copper industry, men who had mined before the war had little power to stop others from seeking a deferment by entering the mines. To show their disgust at Harkins, who had got a job in the mines to gain a deferment and then quit, miners agreed they would not accept any deliveries from him. Mines manager E. S. McGlone responded to the situation by saying that the Company would make every effort to keep employees in the mines, and would not be satisfied with replacements from out of state or local men trying to beat the system. McGlone's indication of cross-class agreement on this issue did not jibe with the ACM's actual need to recruit more workers so as to meet obligations to the government and increase profits. But it did assuage his workers.[54]

Paradoxically, in a bid to elevate themselves above all other local men, miners criticized both other home front men who entered the mines to avoid the draft and those who did not. Bert Riley, a union representative, told the Victory Committee that he thought service workers in town should have to sign the same pledge cards that miners had signed acknowledging their responsibility to the war effort. Riley wanted the cards given to dealers at gambling halls, presumably to emphasize that the dealers were not fulfilling their masculine obligations. A Company representative replied that "some of [the dealers] have taken the position that if they applied for a job [in the copper industry] they would be considered as draft dodgers." There was truth to this assertion. One deferred Butte man recalled that locals "resented [deferees] hanging around and getting out [their] skis in the wintertime when everyone else was off fighting in the war." Copper men were seeing a primary fear realized: many locals regarded industrial deferments as a way for men to avoid the military. For those on the home front who held this view, men who remained in nonessential positions and waited for the Selective Service to call them were actually being manlier than the men in the mines.[55]

Copper men fought the idea that that they were using their jobs to hide from military service by questioning the manhood of others. Riley demanded to know why the dealers, and by implication other men in nonessential positions, did not enlist in the armed forces. But the choices afforded men during this trying time were not so simple. Few, including many of the most patriotic copper workers, wanted to enlist. As a longtime miner and an older man, Riley did not face the same predicament as other men. Because of his age and because he already occupied an essential job, it was unlikely he would be labeled a draft dodger. Yet Riley's continued criticism of the dealers indicated his refusal to accept the complex choices many men had to make and to recognize that some men believed mining during the war was suspect.[56]

The notion put forward by Riley and other workers—that local men who wanted to do their wartime duty needed to either go into the military or become copper workers—veiled the reality that many working in the copper industry faced a predicament similar to the dealers'. In Anaconda, Black Eagle, and Butte, determining which jobs the government deemed essential, and thereby which workers would be deferred because of the "essential" role they played, quickly became a hot topic. Under Lewis Hershey's signature, the Selective Service issued "Occupational Bulletin No. 12" on July 28, 1942, to clarify the jobs within the mining industry it considered essential to the war effort. The bulletin stipulated that draft boards would be the ultimate judge of whether a job required enough skill and experience that a replacement worker would need six months or more of training. If it did determine this, then the man holding that job should gain a deferment. Because the list did not specify every job classification recommended for deferment, it forced employers and employees "to point out to local draft boards the parallel between the degree of training, qualification or skill required for occupations not specifically listed and some of those included in the critical list." Those arguing for deferments should make sure that draft boards understood that the bulletin was "not a direct order" but merely a guide, and "should not be considered ground for refusing deferment," advised the American Mining Congress, which represented the nation's nonferrous mining industry.[57]

"Occupational Bulletin No. 12," and documents like it, showed how deeply the federal government had inserted itself into debates about the comparative worth of men on the home front, but such documents also reinforced the importance of *local* perspectives on the actual practices of the wartime New Deal state. Hershey designed the Selective Service System to promote local control. His biographer writes that Hershey felt "the key to America's republicanism was decentralized government. In the local community people learned and practiced the virtues of cooperation and assumed the responsibility of citizenship." Notably, by late 1942 several other branches of the government were following the Selective Service lead and moving to a decentralized management model that put increasing power in the hands of regional and local officials. This shift would have a profound effect on how Montana's copper men faced the challenges of the home front later in the war.[58]

The arguments among local draft boards, managers, and workers about which men deserved deferments also served to make more public some discussions that previous had been less so. When asked about surface jobs, for instance, the Butte manager, E. S. McGlone, indicated that many of the men working on the copper tanks, a position that typically required less skill and drew less pay, would not be protected, because these men could be replaced relatively easily. A union representative disagreed: "The day we were over in Helena we were told you can get deferments for men on the Copper Tanks."

McGlone, underscoring his middle-class sensibility, responded that these men were easy to replace, and their experience on the tanks or their employment history with the ACM made no difference. He summarized the supposed ACM view on this wartime change by noting, "A man is a man with us now." The copper men, who had staked so much of their self-worth and claim to masculinity on their experience and expertise and the respect of fellow workers and managers, fought back against this notion by arguing that each man had a special set of skills. But McGlone said the government did not see it that way. "If you were working as a surface laborer and Harry here was a handicapped man and could do your work, and we could not sign an affidavit that you could not be replaced when he was available, you would be out of luck." One of Riley's coworkers countered that the surface workers "are very dissatisfied on the proposition." Nonetheless, the ACM pushed forward with its effort to have surface men move to jobs underground that would guarantee them deferments. Some government officials, on the other hand, privately vacillated on their position because of their concern about mineral production. At points these officials went so far as to coach ACM managers on how to request deferments and appeal negative decisions.[59]

The perspective of the surface men, gleaned from suggestions sent to the Victory Committee, more fully reveals the central place of class and its entanglement with age and masculinity in the politics of deferment (fig. 4.3). James L. Barnicoat, John Lasky, William Rozenski, Martin Kovacich, and Pete McDonald wrote,

> In regard to having all young top men go underground to work and replacing them with older men on top, we (the top men) are willing to accept such changes in order to aid in production for the war effort, but on certain conditions. We want only old Butte miners to replace us in our present jobs, and we want all "special watchmen," who are as physically fit as we, to give their jobs to old Butte miners also, and accept underground work. If these men who are composed of salesmen, etc., and who, for the most part, never worked in a mine and many not even at a mine before, are willing to accept such terms, we will go underground gladly but otherwise we will protest.[60]

The five men made it clear that working underground was the most prestigious and dangerous position in Montana's copper communities. They believed in the code of manhood, but they also knew that being considered at the top of the masculine hierarchy meant nothing if a man was not around to support his family. Going into the mines was risky and, in their eyes, a sac-

4.3 Surface workers, such as these laboring at Butte's Leonard Mine in the fall of 1942, illuminate the complexities of home front masculinity especially well. Their jobs were safer than those performed underground, but they carried less masculine status. Surface workers did not receive industrial deferments, so the ACM and the federal government urged them to shift to underground mining jobs. But many of these men resisted. Mobilizing an "equality of sacrifice" argument, they said they would go underground if men in white-collar positions around the mines did so as well, and if older Butte miners who had been released by the ACM were given their surface positions. Notably, women worked in surface mining jobs in other places around the West during World War II. Photograph by Robert I. Nesmith, *Scene at Base of Leonard Frame Safety Sign*, 1942; Montana Historical Society Research Center Photograph Archives, Helena.

rifice, one they believed that fairness dictated white-collar men should also have to make. They also wanted to make sure that only men who had earned their status and proved their manhood—old Butte miners—replaced them on the surface. At the core of this demand was a claim for their own masculine and class worth. They were telling the Company and the community that white-collar workers were not good enough to replace surface men.

Even if a man transferred underground, there was no guarantee that he could stop worrying about community perceptions of his manhood. After the release of "Occupational Bulletin No. 12," another worker on the Victory Committee remarked that "the laborers of the copper tanks think if they transfer underground or anything else, they would be considered draft

dodgers" even though the head of the local deferment board issued a statement declaring that men who transferred to war production jobs from those
in nonessential fields were not neglecting their duty.[61]

Draft and deferment debates in Montana's copper communities uncover
the importance of local ideas and standards in negotiating wartime masculinity. In light of the history of these towns, that is not surprising. But
historians have also not been wrong to note that World War II was a key
moment in the process of local norms being eclipsed by national norms,
which were broadcast effectively by popular culture and propaganda. The
friction produced by this transition was keenly felt by home front men. It
often left them unsure of where to turn, how to act, and whether they could
influence how others saw them.

Exceptional Masculinity and the Wartime State

The war clearly brought about a substantial shift in the state's role in adjudi-
cating masculinity, as the draft and deferment process dramatically showed.
In fact, the acceptance of the Selective Service System and the government's
power to direct men into industry or uniform not only signified this shift
but also arguably initiated it. As the government's role in everyday life increased, particularly during the first year of the war, the copper men's desire
for state support also grew, especially regarding what they viewed as their
exceptional home front masculinity. The miners' and smeltermen's primary
defense against being grouped with draft dodgers and other slackers was to
promote the old idea that copper work was much more difficult than other
occupations, so copper men deserved special advantages and recognition
from the government.

Most evocative of this effort was the Meat for Copper Production drive,
one of the Victory Committee's most labor-intensive and well-received activities. The campaign sought to get a larger weekly meat allowance from
the government for the hardworking men of the copper communities. Dennis McMahon, a Butte Miners' Union man and member of the Rationing
Sub-Committee responsible for procuring more meat for the workingmen,
reported to the Victory board that the subcommittee had gained substantial
media coverage, including a radio piece, on the topic. It also organized a
mass rally at Butte's Fox Theater, attended by an estimated one thousand
people and dignitaries including Montana's governor, in support of the
Meat for Copper Production drive. According to McMahon, "Residents of
the community were asked to send cards to Washington representatives,
pointing to the need for more meat for copper workers." He added that

"upwards of five thousand cards have already been sent to Washington, and it is our hope that we may reach the figure of twenty-five thousand within the next week." The drive suggested that the community, at least subconsciously, knew that the men who remained behind as soldiers of production needed to be reassured of their own worth. The philosophy behind the drive—men need meat; the more manly the work, the more meat; the more meat allotted, the worthier the man—in manifesting the larger strategy copper workers employed to reassure themselves of their exceptional home front masculinity, says even more.[62]

The Victory Committee also pushed for special certificates of recognition from the government for the men of the mining industry, an initiative whose purpose paralleled that of the meat drive. These certificates would record each six-month period of faithful home front industrial duty, and were meant to provide not just reassurance but physical proof that deferred men were considered equal—in both future worth and current manhood—to their comrades serving in the armed forces. The committee's effort in this regard ably represented the paradoxes in the relationship between western industrial manhood and the state during World War II.[63]

Government officials acknowledged home front men's concern that soldiers would have government-sponsored preferences in hiring and in other areas available to them after the war that home front workers would not. Major Walter Mendelsohn of the Manpower Division in Washington, DC, wrote in response to one of the Victory Committee's letters on this matter: "Since the discontinuance of voluntary enlistment, however, the fact that a man is not in uniform should be no reflection on his patriotism." The workingmen forcibly deferred by the government agreed fully with this sentiment, but their experience indicated that others on the home front did not. It is unlikely, however, that miners and smeltermen concurred with another of Mendelsohn's points: "If he is in business clothes or in overalls, it is probably because the Government wants him that way. The entire effort is now to get the right worker into the right war job, and that war job may be either in uniform or civilian clothes."[64] Perhaps such a formulation, which equated men in "business clothes" with men in "overalls," made sense in the East, but as evidenced by the earlier acerbic observation by surface workers regarding "salesmen," it did not carry any weight in the industrial West. Tellingly, the very government civilians who supposedly saw all men within the war manpower system as equivalent revealed in their internal exchanges the depth of the symbolic masculine hierarchy that infused the nation after Pearl Harbor. To cite only one example, a War Production Board leader told members of his Pacific Northwest staff that they should aspire to create among themselves "a real civilian Marine Corps made up of tough leathernecks."[65]

The bureaucrats in the nation's capital ultimately pointed to the draft in explaining why they did not see the need for the certificates of recognition requested by the Victory Committee. As Major Mendelsohn wrote, "Every man now registered has a registration card as evidence that he has presented himself for service, whether he was accepted, rejected, or deferred." "Selective Service," he continued, "has been described as an act of volunteering en masse, and as people come to comprehend the basic good sense and philosophy of this statement, the situation which promotes the desire for insignia should cease." The men of management and labor quickly agreed that the men in Washington were far removed from the reality of being a worker and a man in the West (fig. 4.4). As one Victory Committee member put it, "Young fellows . . . working in the mines . . . were deferred and for that reason they couldn't join the armed forces if they wanted to. These young fellows were called slackers at different times." Another member of the committee responded that "all the people are not as well informed about these things as selective service is. The fact . . . that [these men have been deferred] is not so well known here."[66]

Just how deeply the home front men's concerns about the draft and deferment ran and just how much they needed the government's support emerged as Victory Committee discussions turned to planning for the postwar period. The committee worried that in the postwar scramble for jobs likely made worse by a depression, soldiers of production, deferred for legitimate reasons or not, would be considered second-class citizens in comparison with those soldiers who actually fought. Miner Bert Riley noted, "We have seen the time when, if you didn't have a certificate of discharge from the last war, you were just out of luck." Perhaps in an effort to strengthen the masculine bond between working-class and middle-class home front men, ACM managers said they were willing to give copper men certificates. But, they acknowledged, a certificate "will not suffice to get a job if [a worker] applies at Hoover Dam, for instance"; only federal recognition could achieve that. Yet even as workingmen recognized and sought federal authority, doubts emerged over whether they should still consider the Roosevelt administration a benefactor. Many on the Victory Committee felt that the government itself was "the worst offender" when it came to acknowledging the work of men on the home front. As another worker noted, the government said that "ex-service men shall be preferred" over home front men tied to the production line.[67] Everyone knew that Lewis Hershey was

4.4 Young male copper workers, even though they received deferments based on the essential jobs they performed, found their manhood consistently questioned because they were not in the military. Robert Nesmith, the talented newspaperman hired to run the *Copper Commando*, took this and many of the other photographs featured in *Meet Joe Copper*. Photograph by Robert I. Nesmith, *Fred Schmooke and Phil Larson Setting Up*, 1942; Montana Historical Society Research Center Photograph Archives, Helena.

among those stating their belief that returning soldiers deserved preference for jobs over home front men.

Thus, only a year into the war, home front copper men already found themselves relying increasingly on a government more interested in assuring benefits to men who had served in uniform than protecting the "soldiers of production" who had been the cornerstone of Roosevelt's New Deal coalition. Before December 8, 1941—the point of formal US entry into World War II and hence the start of a new gender regime that placed soldiers at the pinnacle of manhood—masculine duty, it could still be argued, lay with home front production. Men's principal obligation during this "Arsenal of Democracy" phase was to provide for their families after years of hardship caused by the Great Depression. Yet the anxiety surrounding the draft and the ambiguous role of state power in assuaging that anxiety indicated the dramatic changes wrought almost immediately by the war. In some cases, Montana's copper men disagreed among themselves regarding the degree to which they should accept new national norms of masculinity that called on home front men to sacrifice their ideal of independent working-class masculinity and accept their subservience to government mandates. But virtually all copper men felt it was crucial to assert their masculine ideals to some extent, especially as they saw corporations continue to gain power and build an alliance with the government. Draft and deferment problems were the first flashpoint for this fight, but they proved to be only the beginning of the challenges for working-class men in Montana's copper towns. While concerns about masculinity continued to revolve around the draft, deferment, and the employment of men in the copper industry who appeared to be shirking their wartime masculine responsibilities, another issue—the possibility that men of color or women would be used to address the worsening labor shortage—began to take center stage in the summer of 1942.

FIVE

The Emerging Labor Shortage: Independent Masculinity, Patriotic Demands, and the Threat of New Workers

In March of 1941, Lewis Remark, a twenty-one-year-old miner whose family had deep roots in Butte, left the mines and voluntarily enlisted in the military. One year later, his family heard that he had been taken captive in the Philippines, site of some of the most intense combat faced by US forces early in the war. Determined to find work that would contribute directly to the war effort, Remark's mother quickly discovered that the copper industry did not employ women, despite the growing labor shortage in the mines. So she, followed by her daughter, left for Tacoma, Washington, where they joined the tens of thousands of women who went to work in West Coast shipyards and participated in one of the great industrial efforts in US history. (This remarkable endeavor was symbolized, in part, by the production of the ten-thousand-ton Liberty ship SS *Robert E. Peary* in one week, a record that still stands.) On February 24, 1945, the *Montana Standard* reported that after almost three years in a POW camp, Lewis Remark had been freed. His father, who had remained in Butte and had worried about his son ever since Pearl Harbor, died a week before his son's release. Remark's mother and sister heard the news in Tacoma, where they continued to labor in wartime production jobs.[1]

Women like Remark's mother and sister, who have been celebrated for doing their part for the war effort by working in formerly all-male industries, taking the places of men who had gone into the armed forces, and swelling the labor force to increase production, posed a challenge to home front men. They were, however, only one of the groups of potential war industry workers that threatened, through their possible entry into these bastions of masculinity, the white and white ethnic men who had long dominated the industrial workforce in the United States. This chapter recovers the forgotten links between the battle over who would fill critical labor shortages in the West's copper towns and masculine identity formation on the home front early in the war.

Montana's copper facilities were critical to the war effort—only the Manhattan Project had a higher urgency rating. In 1942 they produced over 250 million pounds of copper, 144 million pounds of manganese, 47 million pounds of zinc, almost 6 million ounces of silver, and 10 thousand ounces of gold. Consequently, labor shortages in the three copper towns—Butte, Anaconda, and Black Eagle—were an issue of national importance. In Butte, the focus of this chapter because its mines had to deal with these labor shortages first and most intensely, the ACM employed 9,250 workers and ran fifteen interconnected mines two months after the war began. The Company, driven by rapidly increasing demand and by prodding from Washington, planned to open two more mines as soon as possible, and estimated the need to hire at least 415 more miners over the next year. Employment rose to 9,482 by the spring of 1942. But by August, as men left for the armed forces, agricultural work, construction jobs, including on the Great Falls Air Base outside Black Eagle, and higher-paying war production jobs on the West Coast, only 8,293 men remained on the payroll. ACM managers shuttered one mine instead of opening two more. Several members of Roosevelt's cabinet were so concerned about declining production, which managers ascribed to labor shortages, that they became directly involved in Butte's labor situation.[2]

Company managers and federal officials pursued various solutions in their attempt to address the labor shortage. They sought to improve the discipline and productivity of Butte's miners, particularly in relation to vacations and absenteeism. They considered introducing new workers into the mines from a variety of local and regional labor pools: older and disabled former miners; blue- and white-collar men not employed in an essential wartime industry; local women; Mexican braceros; and, eventually, African Americans. And they had two other groups available to possibly draw from: Japanese American internees and American Indians.

The controversy that erupted over filling these labor shortages does not conform to the popular narrative of the West that features aircraft factories and shipyards staffed in part by women who resembled "Rosie the Riveter" and by African Americans who had previously been excluded from heavy industry. In their demographic profiles and their racial, gender, and labor politics, West Coast cities housing these production facilities differed significantly from Butte, Anaconda, and Black Eagle. The predominance of a single industry, company, and union in the copper towns, and the strong presence and long history of Irish Americans and southeastern Europeans there, altered the negotiations over the composition of the wartime work-force, with proposals to introduce women and African American men into the workplace precipitating especially intense debate. How copper men responded to these proposed incursions, and how seriously the government and Company actually considered each of these groups for employment in Montana's copper industry, reveals the sometimes complementary and sometimes competing notions of who should and could work in the industry. As they sought to shape how the labor shortage would be addressed, Butte miners showed some flexibility in allowing the introduction of new groups of workers that they viewed as posing little threat to the independent working-class masculinity copper men continued to champion. However, they opposed initiatives that would threaten either that value system or the mine's white and male status. Intriguingly, local government and Company officials also chose to defend the last of these.

Disciplined Miners

Before they attempted to introduce new wartime workers into the mines, the government and the Company sought to increase production by disciplining miners' independent ways. The respect demanded by and often accorded to Butte's miners during the first sixty years of industrial mining fostered a distinctive local culture that deeply influenced the reaction of these white and white ethnic men to this effort and to other home front labor issues. In their interactions in both the workplace and the community, these miners projected an especially strong sense of themselves as a collective of skilled, manly workers who proudly claimed a measure of independence from the bosses (fig. 5.1). Along with their ability to quit one mine and go work at another, the Butte mines contract system, which paid contract miners a base hourly wage and a premium for bringing in ore above a certain weight threshold, was the cornerstone of the miners' sense of themselves as independent. In 1942 approximately 80 percent of miners worked on contract, but all men who worked underground—whether as muckers, nippers, electricians, or the numerous other occupations that supported the removal of ore—earned a psychological wage in the form of masculine respect because of the danger they faced in the mines.[3]

Profoundly influencing the wartime actions of Montana's copper men were the labor struggles of the 1930s. After nearly twenty years of Company-controlled locals, the Butte Miners' Union (BMU) was reborn as part of the International Union of Mine, Mill, and Smelter Workers (Mine Mill). Mine Mill leaders, like some other labor leaders of Butte's past, saw the contract

**FREE LABOR
WILL WIN**

5.1 This 1942 poster, featuring a male worker with a muscular body and serious, competent countenance, captures how home front men wanted to be seen. It circulated nationally, suggesting that an ideology of independence was critical to home front working-class masculinity not just in Montana but across the nation. "Free Labor Will Win," War Production Board; courtesy Northwestern University Library.

system as a hindrance to the creation of true working-class solidarity among the copper men. But even in the midst of the Popular Front's collectivist culture, most miners refused to turn against the contract system. They believed that a strong union culture and the independence that they saw as part of the contract system were not contradictory but rather part of the historic identity of Butte miners. These miners did, in fact, band together and form a strong local during the 1930s, but the structural conditions of the Great Depression nonetheless sharply curtailed the autonomy and financial rewards tied to the contract system. Like virtually every other group of laborers, Butte miners' work hours were cut substantially, and men gladly took shifts whenever the Company offered them. Only wartime mobilization brought steady, full-time work back to the Hill. The mines had employed 5,579 men in October 1939, but by the time war began that number topped 9,000. Miners saw full employment as key to their ability to reassert their status as a collective of independent workers who, because of the difficulty and importance of their labor, deserved to be well compensated and well regarded.[4]

Even as the war provided the structural conditions that enabled Butte's miners to bargain more effectively with the Company, it also created a situation in which any demand by copper men or other home front workers could be considered selfish, unmanly, and unpatriotic. The Roosevelt administration, which during the Depression had been workers' most critical ally, came to be viewed more ambiguously. In the case of Butte's hard-rock miners, the War Manpower Commission (WMC) and the Selective Service System acknowledged the unique nature of their work by classifying all underground workers as skilled and deferring them from the draft because of the essential part they were already playing in the war effort. At the same time, the government criticized the commitment of home front men, including miners and smeltermen, to the war effort. Partly to counter the idea that male workers were unpatriotic, the Congress of Industrial Organizations and the American Federation of Labor both agreed to a no-strike pledge. Despite that pledge, work stoppages across the country continued, and their numbers even rose. Workers who engaged in wartime wildcat strikes did not think of their actions as counter to national ideals but rather as a form of "working-class Americanism," to borrow the historian Gary Gerstle's phrase.[5] Tensions over wages, benefits, and working conditions that did not lead to strikes illuminate the even more subtle negotiations—in terms of not just labor but also masculinity—that characterized assertions of working-class Americanism on the home front.

In Butte the right to take paid vacations, one of the most important gains won by Mine Mill just before the war, became a particular point of contention between workers and corporate and government leaders, who believed the war effort required sacrifices of home front working-class men. When the ACM had finally acquiesced to the union's demand, managers reasoned that this new benefit would "provide an incentive for steady employment." Yet with the onset of war, the Company chastised workers who wanted to take vacations. Union leaders, with the support of the rank and file, contended that vacations were a necessity for hard-working miners, that time off would increase the men's productivity, and that neither the government nor the Company was asking managers to make similar sacrifices. The BMU's effort to uphold worker prerogatives and protect benefits troubled ACM and government officials. An April 1942 report by the United States Employment Service (USES)—the federal agency whose nationwide network of offices served the WMC during World War II—argued that the contract system was part of this pattern. It reinforced the individualistic tendencies of miners, making them unwilling to work with new men, thereby creating an obstacle to one of the solutions to the labor shortage: the introduction of untrained workers. Miners countered that new men, who they called "greenhorns," not only were dangerous but also slowed down experienced workers, hampering their productivity and costing them money.[6]

The debate over Butte miners' high rates of absenteeism further elucidates the philosophical and political divide between and among workers, Company officials, and government officials. Many factors contributed to absenteeism, including the sheer difficulty of the work, the decision of many of the most physically able miners to enter the armed forces, and the loss of others to war work on the West Coast or to seasonal agricultural labor. New men, who were attracted to the mines to obtain draft deferments but were unprepared for the grueling conditions underground, were among the most frequent absentees. Still, even men with a long history in the mines had high rates of absenteeism, suggesting that some might have skipped shifts in order to assert their autonomy and to set an example of independent worker masculinity for other men in the mines (fig. 5.2). Secretary of war Robert Patterson saw another aspect of the homosocial world of copper men at work in absenteeism. He believed that the miners' penchant for heavy drinking was a significant cause of missed work days, and requested that Montana's Republican governor, Sam Ford, close Butte's bars on Sunday nights. Ford, who shared Patterson's distaste for miners' expression of independent manhood during the war, knew that taking such a step would anger not only the miners—perhaps even to the point of a revolt—but also

5.2 Like several of the other illustrations in this book, this photograph taken at one of the Butte mines shows the ubiquitous presence of propaganda—note not just the large sign but the posters on the bulletin board—that compared the sacrifices asked of home front men to those asked of soldiers. Propaganda like this questioned the masculinity of home front men and relied on masculine guilt for its effect. The large sign reads: "73 Employees Were Absent from War Production Yesterday! Were You One of Them?" Photograph by Robert I. Nesmith, *Sign 73 EMPLOYEES ABSENT*, 1942; Montana Historical Society Research Center Photograph Archives, Helena.

potentially the ACM leadership, some of whom saw Butte's homosocial drinking culture as a safety valve that reduced miner militance. Ford did not include that information in his response to Patterson. Instead, he said that he did not have the power to close Butte's bars, and that the United States Army should do so if it wished.[7]

The government did not close Butte's bars, instead intensifying its on-going propaganda campaign against absenteeism. In a radio address only three months after Pearl Harbor, War Production Board chairman Donald Nelson had warned workers that they would incur "public wrath" if absenteeism did not decrease. The WMC told absentee copper workers, "You . . . must hold yourself to the same standards that a soldier has. He wouldn't take time off from a 'shift' without reason. If he did, he would know that he was playing fast and loose with the lives of his comrades . . . and his family and neighbors at home. He would take dangerous chances in this war for freedom; he would be risking his right to hold up his head as a free man. The same goes for you." Copper men heard similar sentiments throughout 1942 and beyond. ACM officials reinforced this message, and also sought to put local public pressure on miners, by declaring, for example, that every shift a worker missed reduced the national supply of copper by nearly one hundred pounds.[8]

The ACM Victory Labor-Management Committee, comprising representatives from labor and management who supported the government's wartime production program, also relied heavily on propaganda in its summer and fall 1942 local campaign against absenteeism. At an October 15, 1942, meeting, some committee members proposed asking the men to sign a pledge, "To the Armed Forces of the United States." The pledge was read aloud by E. S. McGlone, one of the ACM managers on the committee: "I pledge myself wholeheartedly to every phase of our Industrial War Production Program. I will work to my full ability to meet every demand of our country's war effort; and so far as it is humanly possible, I will work every available shift to meet those demands." McGlone noted that a copy of the pledge would be given to each worker, and that it would be posted on bulletin boards throughout the workplace. He did not explain that the plan involved using surveillance to compel appropriate behavior: a subcommittee would be responsible for ascertaining why anyone who had signed the pledge did not give his maximum effort. In keeping with this approach, a number of Victory Committee members from management suggested issuing buttons to men who signed the pledge, thereby advertising their allegiance to the government's agenda and their opposition to absenteeism.[9]

BMU representatives on the Victory Committee questioned whether the pledge was designed to address the root causes of absenteeism or to once again pressure copper men to tow the government and Company line. Charles McCarthy declared, "We will take it up with our union members," but "right now they want the $2.00 or $1.25 increase in pay or whatever it will be. They are not in very good humor until that issue is decided." One worker put it succinctly: "Pay some wages and get your miners." Another argued that the men were angry that a new contract had not been signed, and "feel they are working for less wages than any other place." McCarthy summed up the problem as he saw it: "A lot of them think they are getting the 'run around'. . . . They think their patriotism is being imposed upon at the present time."[10] Miners supported the war and saw themselves as patriotic Americans, but a substantial number thought the best way to assert patriotic working-class masculinity was to respond to an injustice, such as the deflated wages they were earning on the home front, by demanding change using one of the few methods—withholding labor—at their disposal.

Despite their frustration that the pledge cards did not address what they believed to be the causes of absenteeism, the majority of the miners finally accepted the pledge-card plan. In fact the labor members of the Victory Committee soon realized that similar cards might provide a solution to another problem that was of deep concern to the rank and file. The committee created a new set of cards, issued by the Copper Division of the WMC, signifying that a worker had served as an essential wartime laborer and worked consistently for a six-month period. Stars would be added to the card for every six-month period for which they maintained the standards of production stipulated by the Victory Committee and the Copper Division. Workers hoped that this official acknowledgment of their service would help them compete against veterans in the expected scramble for jobs after the war.[11]

As their refusal to discard previously won gains and their effort to use patriotic devices for their own purposes indicates, copper workers did not passively accept the government's new role in their lives. Indeed, as often as not they countered government criticisms that blamed miners and smeltermen for lagging production by complaining that the government had not provided copper men with the necessary equipment. The workers attributed some absenteeism to shortages of government-controlled resources such as rubber boots, watches, and meat. The tightly fitting, seventeen-inch boots that bureaucrats substituted for the steel-toed, Terra Haute boot worn by copper men injured miners. The failure to get miners watches to coordinate blasting was a life-threatening problem. And the inability to supply copper men an appropriate amount of meat meant they did not have the energy to do their required work. It was, therefore, middle-class federal officials who failed to do their jobs and should be censured, not working-class miners and smeltermen.[12] Copper workers' pleas for resources were not, however, only about material provisions or critiquing government men; they carried with them copper men's desire for respect and recognition, and their fear that these incidents signaled a larger loss of power akin to their diminishing ability to influence shop floor issues, including the composition of the labor force.

The government's power to define wartime masculinity was palpable in its ubiquitous propaganda depicting men who stayed home as shirkers, cowards, or traitors. The pledges and buttons concealed similar messages under a more positive tone. Despite the miners' determination to maintain their independence, to wrest higher wages from the Company, and to persuade the government materially to acknowledge their preeminence, the men were conscious that the war had significantly altered local and national notions of masculinity in ways that were beyond their control. They knew that when they were taken to task for their absenteeism and apparent lack of patriotism, their manhood was being questioned. In the face of this, it took considerable resolve for them to continue to follow the dictates of working-class Americanism and of their own definition of wartime patriotism, rather than one that they believed favored corporations.

Neither the government's efforts at persuasion and coercion nor the men's campaigns for better wages and working conditions succeeded in remedying the labor shortage. While miners were generally resistant to any change in the type of workers employed, they accepted white and white ethnic men from other mining districts around the United States with only a few grumbles, but their numbers were not large enough to solve the shortage. In the summer of 1942, the government began to suggest that the mines hire workers from outside the pool of white and white ethnic men who had customarily had a monopoly on employment. Butte men quickly sought to preempt this effort by favoring two local groups: former Butte miners, whom they called "old timers," and disabled men who had been injured in the mines. Miners knew that many of these men struggled to live on their often meager pension and Social Security stipends, and believed their employment would be least disruptive to local men's control in the workplace.[13] Negotiations over the reemployment of these groups of men highlight the salience of the body to working-class masculinity on the home front. Notably, some miners saw even this approach as a component of the state's effort to shape new social and labor norms, as an infringement on local notions of masculine independence, and as a reinforcement of their employer's power.

Older and Disabled Miners

The Selective Service System and the WMC made the relationship among men's age, physical capacity, and citizenship obligations into a matter of public policy. In February 1942, the government created a roll of 38- to 45-year-old men, and in April it formally announced that men between the ages of 45 and 65 must register with local draft boards. Men over 38 from Montana's copper communities both volunteered for the military and were drafted over the following year. Locally and across the United States, however, most older men believed that they could be more useful in industry than in uniform. As a sixty-five-year-old wrote to his congressman, "There is a class of high grade citizens in this country, called OLD PEOPLE, folks who are 60 years of age and more, that in this 'all out' war program, occupy a 'no man's land,' so far as real accomplishments are concerned. By that I mean men who are too old for combatant service and yet with plenty of strength, ability and endurance for suitable jobs in defense production, either manual labor or office positions." WMC head Paul McNutt and other officials urged older men to register with the USES. When the Selective Service decided to defer all men over the age of thirty-eight, it spurred the incorporation of older men into the industrial workforce. USES offices in the West were among the first to place older men in critical jobs, including in copper work.[14]

In mid-1942, state and national employment service offices also began to promote the hiring of "physically handicapped" workers. McNutt stated that disabled men and women who were "once barred from many industries because of unnecessarily strict hiring practices . . . are doing an important job today." Statistics provided "conclusive proof, if proof is still needed, that a man is not necessarily through as a productive citizen because he happens to have lost a leg or because he once was afflicted with infantile paralysis." Citing the performance records of disabled workers, McNutt concluded that they were as efficient as "the physically normal worker." Propaganda promoting the employment of disabled men and women often put the relationship between "able" and "disabled" bodies more colloquially. A commentator on a summer 1942 radio segment reminded the audience that "few of us are Tarzans or Supermen. Nearly every one of us has some sort of physical imperfection." These pitches initiated a sporadic, often localized, and occasionally problematic effort to promote the hiring of disabled workers in the first year of the war. Despite some increases, the total remained about 1 percent of USES placements nationally. *Manpower Review* concluded, "Most employers, even during this war emergency, have refused to hire physically handicapped workers," citing their perceived inefficiency, higher absenteeism, and rates of sickness, injury, and turnover.[15]

Before the war, the ACM had a well-earned reputation for engaging in age discrimination and favoring the fully able bodied. As in other industries, some older men had been forced out of mining and smelting during the Depression, particularly when unions were nonexistent or weak. The war changed this situation dramatically.[16] Despite Butte's reputation as a place where young workers were preferred and physical capacity was central to men's standing, the Company welcomed older and disabled workers to fill the labor shortage.

In Butte the disabled and older men under consideration were former miners with recognized experience and skill. Former miners who returned to the shafts did so partly for patriotic reasons, but most also needed the paycheck. As the *Miner's Voice*, the BMU's newspaper, put it, these men wanted to "be useful to our country, and incidentally be able to eat regular." Many wartime miners believed that these men had earned the right to work through their long years of dedication and the risks to which they had exposed themselves. Others knew miners who had successfully returned to work after disabling injuries. Indeed, two of Butte's most famous miners had been blinded in an underground explosion and subsequently toured the country putting on hard-rock drilling exhibitions, demonstrating their perfect timing and technique.[17] Because of the respect afforded them, the hiring of older and disabled local men was also the least threatening of the proposed solutions to the labor shortage.

Employing older and disabled men, however, did potentially harm the reputation for physicality associated with copper work. The wartime iconography of hard-rock copper mining, like the iconography of male workers more generally, featured both the heroic, idealized, muscular masculine body that had dominated the 1930s and the less muscular, often older, "normal" body that increasingly represented home front men (fig. 5.3). Certain features of local worker culture in Butte, such as the drilling and mucking competitions held on Miners' Union Day each year, promoted the link between muscularity and mining. But to locals, these competitions highlighted skill and experience as much as brute strength. Tellingly, men over the age of fifty predominated among the winners of mucking competitions. Published photographs of exemplary miners did not clarify what constituted an ideal miner body, but instead showed a variety of body types, uniform only in their whiteness and short hair. "Greenhorn Miner," written for the Federal Writers' Project, offered a "little, weazened fellow . . . [who] looked like he might be about sixty years old" as an exemplar of productive masculinity.

5.3 One of the many older men who worked at the Anaconda smelter during World War II. Photograph by Robert I. Nesmith, *Pouring Metal at Foundry* (August Vidro), 1942; Montana Historical Society Research Center Photograph Archives, Helena.

Indeed, the younger, physically fit new hires often struggled to match the output of smaller, more experienced men. World War II–era miners derided the abilities of "greenhorns," no matter how closely their bodies fit the national masculine ideal. At the same time, ACM personnel records show that the work managers asked of these older and disabled men was often beyond their physical capacities. Notably, older smeltermen appeared to be more successful than older miners at staying on the job.[18]

The question of what kinds of work older and disabled men should perform generated tense discussions, because it directly related to the value and masculine status of specific jobs within the mines and threatened the ability of some copper men to control where they worked. The BMU found itself in a difficult position by supporting the return of these men to the mines. On the one hand, labor leaders saw this policy shift as justified by a potent combination of patriotism and financial need. On the other, it soon became apparent that the kinds of jobs for which the older and disabled men were most suited, including surface work and repairing equipment and track underground, were already filled by younger and more able-bodied workers who did not wish to vacate their positions. The union had long upheld the right of men with seniority to choose their jobs and even accepted the practice of "deadheading," whereby men elected to stay on at a relatively easy job rather than accept promotion. Although most copper men agreed on which jobs demanded the most skill, and many asserted their masculinity through performing these demanding tasks, some accepted a bit of ribbing as a trade-off for their ability to deadhead. After all, deadheading gave them a better chance to draw a paycheck for longer, and they could argue that they were displaying true working-class masculinity by controlling the system instead of letting it control them. These men consequently resisted having their jobs labeled as suitable for elderly or disabled men, because it would force them to move to more difficult jobs or risk losing their deferment.[19]

The Company responded to workers' efforts to defend seniority and exercise autonomy by once again invoking the ideal of sacrifice. Its Operations Department declared, "During this present emergency it is the patriotic duty of every able-bodied employee on a job [in] which he could be replaced by an oldtimer or a man incapacitated for other reasons to transfer to a mining job. This proper distribution of manpower would not only increase the employment of oldtimers but it would place more men on production and increase the output of vitally needed copper." Working-class men who held comparatively easy jobs on the surface responded by demanding that the Company also force workers in jobs located between labor and management, such as watchmen and timekeepers, to take production jobs.[20]

Thus, while some workers regarded surrendering comparatively easy jobs for more strenuous labor as an abdication of their hard-earned privileges, others took exception to men occupying such positions who were fit enough to fill other jobs. Copper workers resisted officials' assumption that all jobs in the industry were equal, and opposed their efforts to continue to alter prevailing notions of masculinity. The workers' distrust of the Company's and the government's decisions about who should work in which jobs reveals a class-based concern that white-collar workers, including middle-class managers and salesmen, were being unfairly favored. Miners felt that the government exercised more control over their lives than over those men in the management class. One miner's comment about the ever-increasing number of bosses during the war suggests that the topic was aired in the shafts and saloons. When white-collar men were not directed to work underground or undertake other forms of more arduous labor, the men in the mines keenly felt that "equality of sacrifice" was an illusion, and that the greatest sacrifices demanded on the home front were falling to working-class men—even as their claims to masculine autonomy were being eroded.[21]

Butte miners' resistance to the efforts of the government and the Company to replace them with older or disabled miners reveals multiple areas of friction and points toward the competition for masculine status among Montana's copper men. The proposal to employ women in and around the mines offered an even greater challenge, because it threatened both a radical disruption of local gender norms and the increasing incursion of government into the workplace.

Women Miners

The national trend toward the employment of women in war industries aroused an intense controversy that reached a decisive stage by the late summer of 1942. During the wartime mobilization period, despite employers' awareness that they would likely soon need a multitude of new workers to replace men who were going off to war, companies had hesitated to hire women. Publicly, employers said they worried about the high cost of building restrooms, locker rooms, and lunchrooms for females. Many contended that they would need to change production methods in order to accommodate women, who supposedly lacked men's physical strength and skills. Indeed, employers declared that very few industrial jobs—29 percent, to be exact—were suitable for women. Initially sympathetic to employers' concerns, the Roosevelt administration included just 595 women among the first 300,000 workers in the government's Training Program for Defense Industry Laborers. But the bombing of Pearl Harbor and the subsequent loss of men to the military changed the situation dramatically. Industries found themselves suddenly needing laborers. Although significant resistance continued to be a hallmark, within seven months employers decided that women were fit for 55 percent of defense industry jobs.[22]

On September 10, 1942, labor secretary Frances Perkins held a press conference to publicize the successful entry of women into defense industries. She predicted that in just a year, the number of women employed in the aircraft industry would rise from 2,000 to 250,000. Drawing her data from a nationwide survey conducted by the Women's Bureau, she highlighted the wage equivalency between men and women. The *Wall Street Journal* responded to Perkins's claims by referring to female industrial workers as "petticoat soldiers" and objecting to the report's "faint but nevertheless noticeable tone that women are better workers than men."[23]

The leadership and the rank and file of Mine Mill were well aware of the growing use of women in previously all-male workplaces, including the copper mines and smelters of the Southwest. In the two days after Perkins's press conference, newspapers across the country reported that mine bosses were working with the USES to hire 150 women to work as copper miners in Globe, Arizona, and *Business Week* publicized the employment of women in a Colorado metal mine. Moreover, the USES and other government agencies knew that Montana's copper communities had a sizable surplus of female labor. Although members of the Roosevelt administration held widely divergent perspectives on "the woman question," at the national level the agencies responsible for labor mobilization consistently presented women as a solution to the labor shortage. For instance, the WMC chastised a San Francisco American Federation of Labor (AFL) local for refusing membership to women welders and ordered that the women be put to work immediately. Two weeks before Perkins's press conference, the War Labor Board (WLB), in a decision it acknowledged had national implications, mandated equal pay between men and women for equal work at the Brown and Sharpe Manufacturing Company in Providence, Rhode Island. The WLB ridiculed Brown and Sharpe's contention that women should be paid less because of their physical inferiority, remarking, "If this panel may have a small part in demolishing the fictions and the fallacies which have arisen from certain facts of female physiology, it will have served a worthy purpose."[24]

The employment of women could have been an ideal solution to the "manpower" problem for the government and the Company. According to the Federal Security Agency, at least thirty-six hundred women in the Butte area were immediately available for work. For the ACM, women could well have constituted a stable pool of laborers who would have increased its production and profits at a time when, at least in the government's eyes, production overrode the considerations of male workers and their unions. The Company might even have thought that it could continue employing women after the war, allowing it to move toward a double wage-earner system: employing women and men in mining and paying both less rather than the higher single wage-earner "family" wage that male workers had fought for. An article in the *People's Voice*, a Montana-based farm-labor weekly, warned workers that corporate leaders were already thinking about such issues as they planned for the postwar period.[25]

In fact, allowing women to work in and around the mines would have also benefited, at least in the short term, some groups of male workers. Of those currently working at the mines, married men had potentially the most to gain from this arrangement. In September 1942, the USES cited Selective Service System director Lewis Hershey's testimony that "married women who replace single men in war industries prolong the draft deferment of married men generally 'by exactly the number they release for military service.'"[26] In other words, if a married woman replaced a single man in a critical position, his induction into the armed forces would mean that a married man would not have to be drafted. Single men who were willing to move from surface to underground work could benefit financially as well. Above all, opening relatively well-paid jobs to women would have been a positive development for women themselves, who were otherwise confined to low-paid, insecure jobs in the service sector. Even surface workers earned much higher wages than the vast majority of women could earn elsewhere in Butte.

Yet the Butte USES office never proposed the employment of women as a practical solution to the city's labor shortage. Local USES reports repeatedly held that "the physical strength required and the hazardous nature of mine work prevents the utilization of women to alleviate the labor demand." In a subsection entitled "Employment of Women," USES representatives mirrored the perspective of most miners; they rated women as less capable than disabled and older workers who were already being recruited to do surface work. In contrast, even though Colorado's female miners did "hard, dirty work" on the surface, the mine's general superintendent found them "adaptable and dexterous," according to *Business Week*. At the same time, USES officials were encouraging the ACM to employ women at its neighboring Anaconda Smelter in jobs similar to those on a mine's surface.[27]

Butte's mine bosses were unanimous in their objections to female employment. Some argued that employing women was prohibitively expensive because of the cost of training new workers and building new facilities, such as washrooms. These objections were usually overcome, because the government absorbed these costs. The ACM began to hire women at its Black Eagle smelter in early 1943 and at its Anaconda smelter in 1944, indicating that expense was not the real problem locally. Employers' belief in women's innate unsuitability for certain kinds of labor is a more compelling reason for USES officials' reluctance to promote the employment of women around the mines. Companies that balked at hiring women were often headed by men who thought that women could not perform the required tasks. The ACM asserted that women had never, and could not ever, work around the mines, and the local USES representative supported the claim.[28]

Government and Company men shared copper workers' view that hardrock mining was an extreme form of labor that ranked high in the hierarchy of masculinity. Just as copper work trumped other forms of wartime labor, so mining trumped other occupations in the copper industry. Although women were accepted into smelters across the United States during the war, the hiring of women at hard-rock mines, as occurred in Arizona and Colorado, though high profile, was much rarer. In Butte, opposition to women's employment helped maintain the sense of mining as the epitome of masculine labor. USES authorities appeared to share this gendered view of mining. And if they did not, they seemed to suspect that advancing the cause of women in the mines might generate such opposition among the workingmen that the disruption would outweigh potential production gains.[29]

Bosses and workingmen in Butte shared not only the conviction that mining was essentially masculine work but also a gendered view of social relations more broadly that contributed to the unlikelihood of female employment in and around the mines. Their normative outlook on gender permeated the *Copper Commando*, the wartime publication that the Victory Committee distributed to all copper men, whether in the mines or away in the military, and their families. In August 1942, for example, the *Commando* reported that the Women's Auxiliary of the BMU had agreed to find six hundred women to work alongside men as daytime wardens. The paper reassured readers that while each female warden would be trained in general first aid, handling victims of a gas attack, and fighting incendiary bombs, "the work is not as strenuous for women as for men wardens." The editors acknowledged women's desire to contribute to the war effort, but argued that "not all of us can do active work in defense." Seeking to eliminate any ambiguity, they chose a parable to illustrate their point: "There was a woman in a small town in England who wanted to do something for the cause. She was told to keep a kettle of water boiling on her stove at all times. She did—and when the village was attacked, her kettle was the only source of sterile water in the town! The women of Butte can keep their kettle boiling by being wardens." The local Catholic press echoed this gendered worldview, and the Women's Auxiliary also promoted other "campaigns to protect and advance the interests of our families," particularly in the area of patriotic working-class consumption of goods.[30]

Nonlocal federal officials, in contrast, increasingly advertised women's ability to do work formerly considered exclusively male and contended that the hiring of women was a national necessity. In November 1942, President Roosevelt's suggestion of a national campaign to register women for employment in the wartime workforce captured public attention. Vice president Henry Wallace's support of "democracy between the sexes," based in part on the example of Russian women's contributions as industrial workers, suggested to the syndicated columnist Westbrook Pegler that the administration advocated fundamental changes in national gender norms. Paradoxically, although union members detested the conservative, antilabor Pegler, many Butte men found themselves agreeing with his declaration: "Assuming that men and women are equal in numbers and equally employed, there would be no American home."[31]

Men's fears regarding changes in gender relations were encapsulated in a revealing editorial in the Butte-based *Montana Standard* that appeared two and a half weeks before Pegler's column. Under the alarming headline "The Amazons among Our Women," the editors began by noting, "It is a long, long time ago when we used to think, with an air of fancied superiority, that woman's place was in the home, while the man was the self-reliant and sturdy breadwinner for the family." Woman had "for a long time now . . . claim[ed] her place of equality in the world of business and industry." Now women were "taking a prominent place in the industry of war," which the editors saw as "a strange development." Yet, they added, "not even there have women stopped. Now there are women in the Army and women in the Navy . . . leaving only one field open for the men—the fighting fronts." Concerned about the masculinity of male civilians and men in uniform who were not on the front lines, the editors expressed their greatest fears for what these changes might mean for life after the war.

> Our women, under such training and service may become Amazons and the men may gradually become the weaker sex—but we hope not. If the present trends keep up, men some day may be the nursemaids, tending the babies while the women run the world. Such may be the fate which man's failures will bring upon him. May it all be merely a fanciful and fearful dream.[32]

Miners and their white-collar allies in Butte intended to do whatever they could to make sure that this nightmare of gender inversion did not become a reality.

The ACM-owned *Montana Standard*, which ran the "Amazons" editorial, provided a template for appropriate femininity only four days later. In a full-page, lavishly illustrated piece entitled "Don't Try to Be 'The Perfect Wife,'" it presented eight rules for women to follow in order to please their men. The author—who announced his credentials by noting, "For more than two decades, I've had a lot to do with women!"—exclaimed that "the happiest homes are those where the man of the house is head of the household! Or thinks he is! One senses something wrong when a wife wears the pants!"[33]

For many men in the city, Butte's nationally renowned American Women's Voluntary Service (AWVS) represented the ideal of wartime womanhood. Annually, approximately half a million service men and women who were in transit to their military assignments or heading home on leave accepted hospitality from the AWVS. Four hundred local women participated in the organization's Train Service, which became a model for similar undertakings across the nation. Indicating the cross-class agreement on gender norms that often characterized Butte's white- and blue-collar residents, the AWVS Train Service emerged after Mrs. C. F. Kelley, wife of the ACM's chairman, recommended the program (fig. 5.4). However, by celebrating men in uniform and by enlisting local women to serve them, it also reinforced the dominance of military masculinity over civilian masculinity.[34]

The few instances in which women discursively or actually entered into the masculine space of the Butte mines were easily recontained upon later telling. The masculinity of the mine workforce extended to its offices, where men typically performed even low-level clerical jobs. During the war, however, the Company hired women for certain office jobs. One miner laughingly remembered that a few of these women used to talk like the copper men, using colloquialisms such as "It's deep enough" to signify the completion of a job and then suggesting that it was time to head to a bar for a drink. In finding women's adoption of masculine language and ritual incongruous, perhaps even troubling, the miner suggested the strength of male language and male spaces in creating a homosocial bond among copper men. The use of such language and the invasion of such spaces by women added to the diminishment of a masculine culture that so many miners cherished. And yet, by also recalling that the incident was humorous, the miner reaffirmed the difference between men's and women's work and worlds in Montana's copper communities, as well as the tactics men used to reinscribe those differences. Similarly, local lore had it that women had physically entered the mines on one or two occasions: allegedly, a few women had dressed as men and worked with their husbands in Butte's Stewart Mine, and some girlfriends of motormen had supposedly come down into the mines to bring their men a case of beer. Both stories narrate women's incursion into the mines as transgressive acts that reaffirm the masculinity of that space.[35]

The prevailing gender norms in Butte and the assumption that mining was inherently masculine labor were so entrenched that government officials and the Company made only minimal efforts to employ women in and around the mines, despite the plan's apparent advantages and its adoption by neighboring smelters and at least two other western mines. Miners' privileges and status were premised on the exclusion of women from their working environment, grounded in an inherent belief that women were physically incapable of performing mining labor and that it would contravene their "natural" place as wives, mothers, and girlfriends.

5.4 Among the acceptable wartime duties for women in Montana's copper communities was entertaining soldiers. However, this too challenged copper men, as it suggested that servicemen ranked above home front men in the national masculine hierarchy. Photograph by Robert I. Nesmith, *Soldier and Girl*, 1942; Montana Historical Society Research Center Photograph Archives, Helena.

Surprisingly, the International Union of Mine, Mill, and Smelter Workers, the parent organization of the BMU, made one of the more compelling arguments in support of women's employment. In April 1942, Mine Mill's official newspaper, the *Union*, featured a photograph of the women of the Scovill Brass Workers Local 569. In July it beat Vice President Wallace to the punch by printing a column entitled "Soviet Women and the War." In mid-October, the paper announced that "women must be freed for industry," and elaborated on that sentiment in a long story. On November 9, 1942, underneath an illustration of a female Mine Mill member reading the *Union*, union president Reid Robinson, a vice president of the Congress of Industrial Organizations (CIO) and a Butte man, called on male workers to win equal wages and benefits as well as child care and protective legislation for "thousands of women coming into our industry."[36] Rather than suggesting a shift in local ideology, Robinson's statements and the paper's articles indicate a growing split between Mine Mill's leadership and Montana's miners and smeltermen.

In late 1942, the CIO leadership echoed Robinson in pressing the government to provide child care to facilitate women's entry into the workforce. Historians have highlighted the importance of this initiative, focusing especially on the Lanham Act, which subsidized day-care programs. Butte was one of the many communities that applied for Lanham funds, but its rationale made no mention of employing women in the mines or any other industry. Instead, Butte officials referred to the need for more women in offices and the "over crowded conditions in homes, where fathers cannot have proper rest, thereby causing poor health conditions, unnecessary mine accidents, causing a slowing down of the production of essential war materials."[37]

Miners' determination to block women from the mines succeeded, but the intertwining ideologies of gender and race meant that men's efforts to shore up their standing on the home front also depended on the maintenance of white privilege. With the labor shortage unresolved, Butte's men still had to deal with the possibility that men of color might be brought to work alongside them. Here Reid Robinson's and Mine Mill's social progressivism had the most dramatic consequences.

Mexican Braceros, Japanese Internees, and American Indian Workers

Early in the war, the WMC began investigating the possibility of creating formal mechanisms for the "importation" of Mexican citizens to work in understaffed industries, including copper mining and smelting. These laborers, who would come to be known as braceros, are often associated with the history of agriculture in the West. Yet of the approximately 167,000 braceros who worked in the United States over the duration of the war, at least 67,000 were engaged in industrial work.[38]

Shortly after Reid Robinson heard that the government was considering using Mexican nationals in the copper industry, he wrote to Secretary of Labor Perkins, voicing the union's concerns. Mine Mill, Robinson said, was uniquely positioned to comment on potential problems because of the union's strong record in the Southwest of organizing Mexican and Anglo workers into integrated locals. The union held that the importation of Mexican workers could "aggravate the widespread discrimination against Mexican workers that already exists" in the United States and possibly "create a new army of underpaid underprivileged workers." Robinson stipulated that only an agreement that had the full support of the Mexican government and Mexican and American trade unions and that guaranteed minimum wages, maximum hours, and decent accommodations and labor practices would ensure that "Mexicans brought into this country [would] not be used as peon slave workers."[39]

By the late 1930s, Mine Mill had established itself in the vanguard of CIO unions in the fight against workplace discrimination. In organizing African American workers in Alabama's steel and iron industry, Mine Mill had demonstrated its commitment to fighting discrimination and forming an interracial union. It counted more African Americans among its elected leadership than any other CIO union. And in its work among Mexicans and Mexican Americans in the mines, smelters, and mills across the Southwest, it had broken down the racial barriers that continued to plague other unions.[40]

But the respect the union enjoyed among workers of color and its national reputation as a leader in the fight against racism hid serious internal tensions. Reid Robinson, perhaps better than any other American union leader, knew that interracial organizing often entailed a protracted struggle that divided union locals. In Alabama, reactionary white workers fought side by side with antiunion employers to defeat Mine Mill's interracial platform. In the Southwest, as Carey McWilliams later reported, the continuing problem of race-based wage differentials rested as much with Mine Mill's white workers, who wanted to continue benefiting from the higher material and psychological wages the two-tier system brought them, as with employers. After a long struggle, Mine Mill had made inroads against workplace racism, persuading some white workers to join in fighting for improved wages for their Mexican and Mexican American colleagues. But Robinson knew that the introduction of a large reserve army of Mexican labor into the region could destabilize this precarious solidarity and provoke hostility among white workers. He concluded his letter to Perkins by noting that it was still unclear whether a labor shortage even existed in the Southwest, since that view was based exclusively on corporate claims; he suggested that companies had the most to gain by bringing in large numbers of workers to whom they could pay lower wages. He urged the government to make a complete survey of available labor in the area before moving any further with its industrial bracero plan.[41]

The prompt reply by D. W. Tracy, Perkins's assistant labor secretary, to Robinson's letter stated broad agreement with the approach suggested by Mine Mill. Tracy wrote that Mexican nationals would initially be used primarily in agriculture. But his letter mentioned that the department was considering the use of Mexican nationals in the Midwest and Northwest.[42] Robinson, who was born and raised in Butte, knew that his town was home to the first, largest, and strongest local in the International, but it was dominated by a white ethnic workforce that had long been resistant to workers of color.

Butte, like other copper camps in the Mountain West, had occasionally seen migrant Mexican and Mexican American workers arrive in town. World War I brought an increase in their presence, as well as that of another group of miners of color: Filipinos. One history of the town reports that during this period, "several hundred Mexicans and Filipinos" lived in Butte's "Cabbage Patch" neighborhood, where supposedly "McNamara, an old country Irishman . . . with an iron hand ruled" over them. Reports of violence against Filipinos in the mines suggest why they did not stay long in Butte, but a small number of Mexican workers settled their families there and worked, largely together, in the Leonard Mine. Miner William Bartholomew remembered that a diverse ethnic mix continued to prevail at the Leonard into World War II. Though Serbian and Croatian "bohunks" dominated this part of the diggings, the proximity of the Leonard to Meaderville, a neighborhood controlled by Italians and with a significant Slav presence, attracted other immigrants. Perhaps its ethnic diversity explains why the Leonard also hired the majority of Butte's Mexican miners. One hint at the basis for cross-ethnic alliances at the Leonard comes from a collection of mining jargon: in Butte, "bohunks" were defined as "Miners of Latin race." Bartholomew had glowing memories of all these men. The "bohunks" incorporated Bartholomew into their social circle, inviting him over to their hangout, the Queen Club. Vic Martinez, nicknamed "King of the Mexicans," made sure the other Mexicans spoke English around Bartholomew when they were working at the Leonard together, a practice that the white miner acknowledged pleased him.[43]

The ACM did not hide the fact that Mexican men mined, and the city generally regarded them as just another immigrant group. Indeed, the Leonard was Butte's "dude mine" because it had a stope, or mining wall, that ACM officials used for showing visitors a working mine and miners. When Ronald Navarro, a sergeant in the United States Army Air Corps, returned to Butte for a brief visit with his family at the beginning of November 1942, the *Montana Standard* publicized his return just as it did for many other soldiers. His ethnicity made no difference in how the paper reported on his visit. The *Standard* did not note that Navarro was a member of one of Butte's older Mexican American families. This fact stands out in particular, because the city was at the moment being criticized for racism in opposing black soldiers working as miners. The Navarro family lived on the East Side of town, as did quite a few other Mexican American families, though as one Navarro boy put it, "they didn't all just live next door to each other." The neighborhood also housed Finns, Serbians, Austrians, Italians, and "just about everything else." Ethnic kids in Butte fought each other only because "there wasn't anything else to do," recalled miner Joe Navarro, Ronald's brother. He reported that when they were in school they coexisted peacefully, just as they appeared to do in the mines. But whether Butte's white ethnic miners would perceive Mexican workers "imported" by the WMC as similar to the Mexican American miners who had long called Butte home worried those who were familiar with the city's history of racism. Federal officials seemed to think that the incorporation of Mexican braceros into Butte's mines would cause little local consternation. In April 1942, the USES reported that while Butte mines did not employ black workers, "Spanish-American will be employed if available."[44]

As it turned out, the complexity of the binational negotiations and resistance to the initiative within both the United States and Mexico stalled the importation of Mexican laborers. Approximately four thousand braceros entered the United States in 1942, but they worked in agriculture rather than industry. In December of that year, Brigadier General Frank McSherry, director of operations for the WMC and the highest-ranking government official to visit Butte during the labor crisis, informed copper executives that the WMC was in the process of arranging with the Mexican government to employ Mexican miners. McSherry stressed that "the program for the utilization of Mexican workers is highly confidential," and that any publicity would be dangerous.[45] Finally, on April 23, 1943, the United States and Mexico signed an agreement regarding the employment of braceros in nonagricultural work. By July 1, fifteen thousand Mexican workers were slated to take industrial jobs in the West. But instead of being used to alleviate shortages in the region's nonferrous mines, the braceros were all contracted for railroad work. A supplementary agreement in the summer of 1943 allowed for the employment of 2,051 braceros in the copper industry. The use of this pool of laborers would not be proposed in Montana's copper towns again until the spring of 1944, when the ACM's threat to employ them at the Anaconda Smelter prompted a strong reaction from white workingmen.[46]

American Indian workers should have been seen as another possibility, particularly considering their significant numbers in Montana and their history at the Black Eagle smelter. Indian workers were certainly willing to fill the labor shortage. The Blackfoot Nation, one of the closest tribal communities to Black Eagle, went so far as to volunteer all available tribal members for defense work. The Crow Nation, located in southeastern Montana, offered the Roosevelt administration all "tribal resources . . . to use as [the president] sees fit in the prosecution of the war." Moreover, American Indians from reservation communities across the United States moved to war production centers, especially in the West, and both men and women found industrial jobs open to them in those places. There is, however, no evidence that Indians were being considered as a possible solution to the labor shortage in the copper industry.[47]

Japanese American internees were used elsewhere in the Mountain West to alleviate labor shortages and represented another possible resource for addressing this problem in the copper industry. After President Roosevelt had signed Executive Order 9066 in February 1942 ordering the forced removal of Japanese Americans on the West Coast, western farmers and growers had turned for assistance to the War Relocation Authority (WRA), the government agency in charge of internees and internment camps. Employers, as a Washington State farmer put it, believed that "it takes three white men to do the work of one Jap." Many agricultural employers requested interned Japanese Americans to perform farm labor. By October 1942, the WRA had given "seasonal leave" to ten thousand internees who agreed to fill the positions, and one of every twelve internees had volunteered to help save the West's crops.[48]

Not everyone embraced the opportunity to employ the internees. Many farmers were unwilling to think of Japanese Americans as anything but the enemy. Industrial employers apparently shared this sentiment, for there is no record of internees being sought to alleviate labor shortages in western industry, including in mines or smelters, even though Japanese had proved to be adept smelter workers earlier in the century. Likewise, the War Department decided not to employ persons of Japanese ancestry, arguing that Executive Order 8972, which allowed the military to protect domestic national defense facilities, trumped Executive Order 8802, which prohibited racial discrimination in the defense industry. For western copper workers, Japanese Americans represented racial foils against whom whiteness and Americanness could be confirmed, and patriotism and rights of citizenship asserted. In the same month that ten thousand internees toiled in the region's fields and orchards, a member of Butte Miners' Union No. 1 became incensed at reports that the government was shooting surplus elk in Yellowstone National Park to feed the internees. He put forward a motion that the BMU send a flurry of postcards to Washington to protest this action, noting that the meat could be better used to feed copper workers. The motion was passed unanimously. Black Eagle workers reacted similarly.[49] Butte miners would have staunchly opposed any effort to employ Japanese American internees.

Conclusion

When the copper industry was desperately short of labor, the fact that many of the possible solutions considered locally and adopted elsewhere were not even attempted in Butte testifies to the miners' power to maintain the white and masculine character of their workplace, and to the staying power of locally dominant ideologies of race and gender. Ironically, the war itself, even as it prompted calls for a more disciplined workforce, created conditions that allowed workingmen to assert their autonomy and reestablish their manhood in working-class terms. During the Great Depression, miners often had to limit their resistance to objectionable employer practices to simply grousing after work or breaking or "borrowing" Company property. But the wartime labor shortage meant that if a foreman or some other boss said or did something irritating, an independently minded miner could drop tools and walk off the job. In Butte's massive complex of copper works, a white man could easily rustle up another job at a different mine the next day. Even the reemployment of former miners who were aged or disabled generated some discontent on the part of younger and more able men, who strove to hold on to their privileges. The reluctance of some miners to embrace the employment of former miners served as a clear warning that more radical developments, including the introduction of women, Mexican, American Indian, or Japanese American workers would meet even greater resistance.

It was not just the will of rank-and-file workers that blocked the introduction of new groups of laborers in Butte, but also the actions and inactions of federal, Company, and union leaders. USES officials, the ACM, and the Mine Mill union might have pushed for the employment of any of these other groups for their own reasons. Yet despite the fact that local USES officials supported the introduction of women to the area's smelters and to Arizona mines; despite the fact that the ACM owned copper facilities where Mexicans and Mexican Americans constituted a large part of the labor force; and despite the fact that Mine Mill had fought fiercely to protect the rights and improve the working conditions of Mexican and Mexican American workers in the Southwest, none of these groups strongly advocated any of these solutions in Butte. USES officials had received local information that warned against trying to bring about the kinds of changes in the Butte workforces that it was introducing in other places. The Company chose not to follow the examples of other major mining operations such as Phelps Dodge, which had hired over one hundred women and African Americans for its El Paso smelter, even though copper camp managers broadly believed that the hiring of these groups would split the workforce, increase management power, and possibly lead to the defeat of unions, as one Mine Mill organizer recalled.[50] ACM's decision not to bring in women and Mexican workers to Butte indicates that a degree of solidarity characterized the relationship between management and workers. This relationship was predicated on the protection of whiteness and masculinity. In the union, even an avowed integrationist like Reid Robinson knew the strength of local whites' racial prejudices and the danger of pushing for racial equality. For all these reasons, federal, Company, and union representatives supported the town's racial and gender status quo during the first nine months of the war.

But with absenteeism still rampant, women ignored, Mexicans unavailable, and Japanese Americans and American Indians unwelcome, the government's search for other solutions to the labor shortages in the copper industry grew ever more earnest. On the national scene, unlike in Butte, racial and gender norms were rapidly changing in response to the wartime demand for labor. The highest-profile racial shift occurring throughout the United States concerned African Americans. Their history of racial oppression was being more broadly discussed than ever before, and it was becoming apparent that racism was preventing their full contribution to the US war effort. This transformation in the social politics of race contributed to another proposed solution to Butte's labor shortage that would dramatically affect the miners of Butte and their bulwark against the incursions of men of color into their workplace.

PART III

Making the Home Front Social Order

Butte, 1942: White Men, Black Soldier-Miners, and the Limits of Popular Front Interracialism

Hear me, white brothers,
Black brothers, hear me:

I have seen the hand
Holding the blowtorch

To the dark, anguish-twisted body;
I have seen the hand
Giving the high-sign
To fire on the white pickets;
And it was the same hand,
Brothers, listen to me.
It was the same hand.

Hear me, black brothers,
White brothers, hear me:

I have heard the words
They set like barbed-wire fences
To divide you
I have heard the words—
Dirty nigger, poor white trash—
And the same voice spoke them;
Brothers, listen well to me,
The same voice spoke them.

—Robert Hayden, "Speech," 1940

On September 12, 1942, amid the acute manpower shortage in the copper mines of Butte, Montana, Hiawatha (Hi) Brown and Lewis Stewart wrote Paul McNutt, head of the US War Manpower Commission (WMC), to complain that the ACM had barred Brown from working as a miner. Brown, a twenty-seven-year-old father of two and a native of Butte, and Stewart, his pastor, were members of the town's once thriving but now quite small African American community. They contended not only that the Company refused to abide by Executive Order 8802, forbidding racial discrimination on federally contracted work, but also that McNutt's own on-site representatives, including John McCusker, had "confessed" to "a committee representing the colored residents of the city" that they were powerless to rectify the situation. "This information came as a distinct shock." As Brown and Stewart understood it, "Corporations are the creatures of the state," yet they "enjoy the prerogative of absolute refusal of the request of the national government." They asked McNutt,

> Do you believe that the United States Government should exercise absolute authority over the God-given life of our sons but must play the beggar in dealing with creatures of the state? Do you think that one's neighbors should have the power to expose their fellow-citizens to loss of their lives and at the same time be impotent in determining the conduct of the corporate interests in that same community? Do you think that this is "freedom and justice for all"?

Referring to the all-black regiments preparing to head into harm's way, Brown and Stewart told McNutt that the stated position of the WMC representative in Butte would in no way "inspire hope and beget fortitude in the souls of colored men who are asked to give their all" for the nation.[1]

The men urged McNutt to enforce the Roosevelt administration's policies and also to join the Butte Miners' Union (BMU) and the city's and state's religious and labor leaders in supporting Brown's application for employment. Shortly thereafter, the ACM hired Brown, making him the first African American to work in the Butte mines. He and later his brother Bill—who, as Brown and Stewart emphasized in their letter, was one of three Brown brothers then serving in uniform—worked underground for over twenty years.[2]

On November 4, 1942, just two months after Brown was hired, thirty-nine furloughed black soldiers sent to Butte by the War Department and the WMC reported to work at the Tramway Mine. While the ACM accepted the black soldier-miners, the eight-thousand-strong, all-white rank and file of the BMU refused to work with them and walked off the job. For the next month, the Roosevelt administration sent one emissary after another to try to convince the miners to change their mind, but to no avail. Although some of the black troops remained in Butte until March 1943, they never mined the copper there that was so critical to the nation's war effort.[3]

The refusal of Butte's miners to work with black soldier-miners seems surprising. Not only had the BMU endorsed Hi Brown's quest to work underground, but it also had supported the strong stance of its parent union, the International Union of Mine, Mill, and Smelter Workers (Mine Mill), in opposing racial discrimination in the workplace. Moreover, all the black soldiers had mining experience, and some had even been members of Mine Mill before the war. The miners' action is all the more puzzling because it defied Executive Order 8802, which prohibited racial discrimination in industries with federal contracts. Franklin Delano Roosevelt—a president virtually all the miners had strongly supported—had issued the order, and Mine Mill had formally backed it.

The Butte walkout, called a wildcat strike because the miners' union did not endorse it and a hate strike because it was meant to exclude workers based on their race, raises important questions about racial politics at the national and local levels. Did the government foster or fight racial prejudice during World War II? Were corporate bosses the greatest obstacle to racial equality on the home front, or were unionized workers? Was it Brown's community-supported entry into the mines or the community-supported hate strike against the black soldier-miners that was the anomaly? Who was more representative of Butte labor: those who fought against discrimination, or those at the Tramway Mine who refused to work next to the black soldiers?

These pairings are not questions that can be resolved but paradoxes that characterized wartime racial politics in Butte and, perhaps, other places in the Mountain West and the nation more generally. To analyze the way race worked in Butte, this chapter considers the complex web of relationships between the ACM, local African Americans, the BMU's white and white ethnic workers, Mine Mill's national leaders, local religious figures, and government officials at the local, regional, and national levels. Ultimately, instead of fulfilling the poet-essayist Robert Hayden's hope that black and white working-class men would see each other as class "brothers," the war—even as it amplified calls to end racial prejudice—revealed the limited hold the Popular Front's class-based racial progressivism had on Butte's white ethnic men, as well as on their allies among community leaders and officials.[4]

Reid Robinson and the Politics of Interracialism in Butte

On October 19, 1942, the War Department announced that it would release approximately five thousand soldiers who had mining experience from active duty and send them to the nation's highest-priority nonferrous mineral mines. This unprecedented step bolstered miners' claims that their work was at least as important as military service and that they should therefore be honored for doing their masculine duty. "At last the miners have received the recognition they are entitled to," wrote one furloughed soldier. It also proved that the labor shortage was intractable, and underscored the importance of nonferrous minerals to an enormous range of war material. The ACM's Butte mines, whose ore in 1942 alone yielded over 250 million pounds of copper, 144 million pounds of manganese, 47 million pounds of zinc, almost 6 million ounces of silver, and 10,000 ounces of gold for the US war machine, reported needing one thousand miners. They were among the first mines to receive these furloughed soldiers.[5]

The government did not publicize the inclusion of approximately four hundred African Americans among the five thousand soldier-miners. When the ACM heard about the plan in mid-October 1942, its officials, along with those from other western copper companies, told the War Department they opposed the inclusion of black troops. While assuring government officials that they themselves had no objections to employing black men, they explained that the region's copper workers and their unions would oppose it. They added that housing and recreational facilities, which they presumed would be segregated, were inadequate. The War Department dismissed that problem, noting that steps were already being taken to secure temporary housing, and that, unlike the South, "segregation [was] not necessary" in the West. It set aside the more serious concern regarding resistance on the part of labor by arguing that Mine Mill, the dominant union in the industry, had a strong antidiscrimination policy that would win the day—"unless" workers were "provoked."[6]

The government informed Mine Mill president Reid Robinson that "several hundred of the 5,000 [were] Negroes" well after telling ACM executives. Union officials immediately asked why these men would be "living and working in the Rocky Mountain area for the first time in their lives," instead of returning to the mines near their homes in the Southeast. Manpower officials responded that the coal and iron ore that came from southeastern mines were not on the critical minerals list. The union then registered its displeasure that the government had chosen to communicate exclusively with corporate bosses and had not consulted it regarding preemptive solutions to any potential problems with the employment of black men in western mines. However, after being assured by WMC officials that the soldiers would be bound by each bargaining unit's contract and must join the local just like all other workers, Mine Mill leaders said they would "cooperate in any way possible."[7]

The Roosevelt administration based its confidence that Butte's copper men would accept black soldier-miners on its assessment of Mine Mill and Robinson. By World War II, Robinson was not only the former president of the BMU and current president of the international union but also a vice president of the Congress of Industrial Organizations (CIO). Under Robinson in the 1930s, Mine Mill had become a national leader in the fight for equality for workers of color. The union launched major organizing campaigns among black workers in the Southeast and Mexican and Mexican American workers in the Southwest. Its effort to build an interracial working-class movement remained the public face of the union into the war, as a perusal of Mine Mill's newspaper from this period indicates.[8]

The labor shortage created by World War II challenged the racial-ethnic order in Butte, changing the relationship between Robinson and the majority of the city's miners in ways the government appeared not to realize. The soaring demand for workers, combined with the government's prohibition on discrimination, catalyzed large numbers of African Americans to move west to obtain jobs in war plants. The government's decision to bring black soldier-miners to Butte was a deliberate extension of a pattern that was occurring across the nation.[9] But local miners saw the arrival of black workers as a direct challenge to their power and prerogatives. They knew that full employment resulted from the wartime emergency, not any fundamental change in the economic structure, and feared that unemployment would return after the war and that the increasing influence corporations enjoyed would not recede. Butte's white and white ethnic miners sought to position themselves and their brothers-in-arms to hold on to their monopoly on good jobs underground, and were ready to take on the Company, the government, and changing national norms in order to maintain that position.

The government's use of propaganda, especially film, to spread new racial norms for American society reinforced and amplified the direct challenge posed by home front labor and racial policies. The Roosevelt administration's effort to use the motion picture industry to mold public opinion about World War II began as early as 1940. The War Activities Committee of the Motion Picture Industry and the Bureau of Motion Pictures, the chief Hollywood arm of the Office of War Information (OWI), coordinated the government's effort to shape popular cinema, but the informal relationship between liberal government officials and motion picture industry executives played an equally critical role as Hollywood became "the preeminent transmitter of wartime policy."[10]

The best example of Hollywood's projecting a liberal vision of race relations near the time of the Butte walkout crisis is the Warner Brothers drama *In This Our Life*, which played in Montana's copper towns in the summer of 1942. Advertised as a fight for the same man between two Southern sisters—Stanley Timberlake, played by Bette Davis, and Roy Timberlake, played by Olivia de Havilland—the plot included such controversial topics as infidelity, divorce, suicide, and murder.[11] Those who objected to the film focused on its racial politics, however. Mrs. Alonzo Richardson, Atlanta's censor, described the movie as "dynamite" because of scenes between Davis, de Havilland, and the African American actors Hattie McDaniel, playing the sisters' housekeeper, Minerva Clay, and Ernest Anderson, cast as her son, Perry. Stanley frames Perry—a serious and mature young man who aspires to be a lawyer—for a hit-and-run murder she committed (fig. 6.1). Roy, shocked to learn that Perry is in jail, visits Minerva at her small house in the city's African American quarter, where she hears that Stanley is framing Perry because she believes no one will take the word of a young black man over that of a white woman. Roy, convinced that Perry is innocent and her sister is lying, tells the police that Stanley, not Perry, committed the crime. Realizing that her cover is unraveling, Stanley flees the police, only to die in a fiery wreck in the film's final scene.

Richardson told Joseph Breen, head of the Production Code Administration and one of the major figures involved in more closely linking the government and industry, that she had already "learn[ed] that trouble has come from many southern cities" when *In This Our Life* was screened, which "was to be expected" in light of the racial politics of the time. "Everywhere I go," Richardson said, white southerners were blaming Warner Brothers and other Hollywood studios for the rising tensions in interracial relations. Linking the motion picture industry's depiction of African Americans to "the increased impertinence of the negroes, in spite of things done for their own good," Richardson predicted that "race riots . . . will come at any minute under more than slight provocation." In the censor's view, the uncut version of *In This Our Life* was just such a provocation.[12]

African Americans also saw wartime films as an influential part of the campaign to change national racial norms. In contrast to Richardson, they hoped that *In This Our Life* would improve race relations. As W. A. Robinson put it, *In This Our Life* "sounded an entirely new note in motion pictures so

6.1 The contrast between the stereotypical image of black masculinity that appeared in 1930s films, and that which Ernest Anderson depicts in *In This Our Life*, is striking. It makes this 1942 film a benchmark for changing race norms in the United States. *In This Our Life* (dir. John Huston, Warner Bros. Pictures, 1942).

far as the Negro people of America are concerned, and it will undoubtedly do an inestimable service in emotionalizing the position of the American Negro as an oppressed minority." John S. Holley of Washington, DC, wrote Warner Brothers that the example set by *In This Our Life* "[was] worthy of emulation by other major Hollywood companies who, through their portrayals of the Negro and other racial types have long contributed to the misinformation and narrow-mindedness which forms the basis of American race prejudice." Other African Americans echoed Holley's focus on the difference between the black characters in the film and the hideous stereotypes that had pervaded the movies before World War II. Private James E. Samuels, stationed at Fort Bragg, North Carolina, expressed his appreciation that *In This Our Life* depicted "Negroes as flesh and blood human beings, and not as clowns." Edith McDougald of Philadelphia proclaimed the film "outstanding . . . because for the first time in the history of the cinema, a Negro is depicted as a normal, intelligent, clean-living human being. . . . Too long has the movie world shown the Negro as a pitiable burden of society. Thousands of us are working, to the best of our abilities, to build and maintain this American civilization. We only ask an opportunity to learn and to be judged on merit."[13]

In countering racist images of African American men as Sambos, Uncle Toms, Bucks, or Zip Coons and of African American women as Mammies or Jezebels that Hollywood had been so central in creating, and in implicitly laying bare the power of those fictions in bolstering white power, *In This Our Life* signaled a significant, though incomplete, industrywide change in portraying African Americans' place in the polity. *Somewhere I'll Find You*, which played in Butte during the black soldier-miner crisis and starred Clark Gable as an intrepid reporter, underscored that change for Montana's copper men. Striking out against theories of racial difference and specifically the Red Cross's controversial practice of segregating donated blood, Gable cabled back from Bataan "that white men and brown men have fought together" and that "the blood was the same color." Government-produced short films, which became a stock feature of wartime movie programs, provided an even more direct message. *Manpower Missing*, an OWI short documentary released at the same time as *Somewhere I'll Find You*, begins with scenes of massive crowds in cities across the United States spliced into scenes of hundreds and sometimes thousands of workers leaving industrial plants. The narrator intones, "There are one hundred million of us, men and women of fighting age. To fight this war ten million more people must go to work by the end of 1943. . . . For every machinist available, twenty-two are needed. For every riveter, four are needed." *Manpower Missing* lists various factors slowing the influx of workers into wartime production, including the unwillingness to allow certain groups of workers to enter war plants. The film cuts to an image of black men hanging out on a stoop as the narrator remarks, "Unemployed or employed below their best capacity are a million Negroes." Then the film shows a well-dressed black man sweeping a floor and a white man telling a black trainee he's doing "O.K."[14] The government's message was clear: workplace racism was not just irrational—it was unpatriotic and might cost the United States victory.

An inclusionary message also appeared in the newsreels that played alongside *In This Our Life*. Showing a montage of scenes from I Am an American Day celebrations across the country, newsreels purposefully focused on the populace's ethnic and racial diversity. Cameramen captured shots of whites, Chinese, and blacks celebrating together in San Francisco, Chicago, New York, and Boston. As the camera showed a close-up of a person of color, the narrator announced, "These are all Americans, these, and these, and these." Scenes from the celebration were spliced between shots of soldiers, factory workers, a woman holding up a ration book, national monuments including the Statue of Liberty, and a suburban home.[15]

These examples of shorts and newsreels are anomalous; African Americans rarely appeared in them, especially early in the war. As Michael Rogin puts it, they were an "absent presence." *In This Our Life, Somewhere I'll Find You,* and other representatives of the government-backed effort by the motion picture industry to denounce discrimination in American society did not satisfy the NAACP and other racially progressive organizations that had been critical of Hollywood. They deplored the newsreels' practice of ignoring African Americans' contribution to the war effort and also films like *Holiday Inn,* which continued to traffic in minstrel images.[16] From another perspective, however, Hollywood was promoting the dangerous changes in racial norms sponsored by a liberal administration that had forgotten its core constituencies: southern whites and working-class white and white ethnic men.

In this charged context, as the government tried to shift the racial climate and to employ black workers in war production, Mine Mill's interracial platform threatened local men in their own backyard for the first time. The men who had supported Reid Robinson during the 1930s primarily because of his success in building the union responded by joining those miners who were suspicious of his social politics in challenging his leadership. This latter group repeatedly put forward candidates to oppose him in Mine Mill's biannual elections. They had long believed that Robinson put leftist ideological goals ahead of what was best for men in Butte.[17]

While support for interracialism diminished during World War II, the inter-ethnic bonds among Butte workers of European ancestry continued to strengthen—a shift that ultimately aided the campaign against Robinson and influenced the response to home front social change. The ethnic tensions that had long characterized the BMU did not disappear during the 1920s and 1930s. Robinson recalled that some of the Irish workers who dominated mining unions in Montana continued to be unfriendly to Slavs and other southeastern European workers and downright hostile toward blacks. Still, miner Joe Navarro, from one of Butte's few Mexican American families, contended that ethnic conflict among whites ceased to be a dominant force during the Great Depression. The friendships that the American-born children of immigrants developed in Butte's public schools and brought with them to the mines were complemented by the renaissance of the BMU and Mine Mill and the birth of the CIO. In these organizations, cross-ethnic affinities based on shared class concerns generated what the historian Lizabeth Cohen has called a "culture of unity." Butte's white ethnic residents, even those who did not befriend those outside their own ethnic group, learned to live in a productive pan-ethnic harmony.[18] The shift in racial identity from being seen as outside whiteness to being "Caucasian" did not occur simultaneously for the Irish, Slavs, Finns, and Italians, but it provided a critical basis for establishing class unity in the 1930s.

By the time Robinson and Mine Mill began to grapple with the changes wrought by World War II, many Butte miners, including the leaders of the BMU, no longer perceived those from other white ethnic groups as the most serious threat to their position. Instead, along with the power of the ACM and the government, they considered political factions associated with Communism and supportive of interracialism as the most significant danger to the ability of all white ethnic Butte workers to secure long-term racial privilege.

Responses to a flyer for a Win the War May Day Rally in late April 1942 illuminate this evolution. The source of the flyer was unknown, but it was made to look like it came from the BMU. Whether those who produced it were motivated by a leftist agenda or by a desire to make leftists look bad was also unclear, but the BMU responded as if the leftists were behind the flyer. The first paragraph announces a rally to honor union members serving in uniform, particularly "the heroes who have sacrificed their lives." It then lists some of those men: "our force on Bataan, the Philippines; Colin Kelly, the Negro; Doris Miller, of national fame; and our own Norman Featheroff and Lowell Jackson, and others." "Colin Kelly, the Negro" infuriated many union officials and ethnic Irish workers. Kelly was white, an Irish American who had become a hero to many when, three days after Pearl Harbor, legend had it that he ordered his crew to bail out of his stricken bomber and then purportedly flew the damaged plane into a Japanese battleship.[19]

Writing on behalf of the BMU, the union's recording secretary asked the *People's Voice*, Montana's most widely read progressive newspaper, to respond to the claim that Kelly was a "Negro." He told the editor that "this crap" had "caused quite a stir here in Butte." The *Voice* obliged. In a story headlined "Reds Dishonor One of the Greatest of Our Heroes," the editor attacked Butte's "little group of Communists and their fellow travelers" and angrily denounced the "shockingly false statement" against "the great hero, Captain Colin Kelly II." "No greater libel can be committed against any man . . . be he white or black, than to classify him as the member of a race to which he does not belong. In resenting this gross wrong . . . we cast no aspersion or reflection upon members of the Negro race. They are rendering magnificent service to the nation in its hour of peril." Nonetheless, the newspaper was determined to make Kelly's identity absolutely clear: "Of

Irish, Scots, and English descent—but mainly Irish—Colin Purdie Kelly II, the first of our war heroes, was of purest Anglo-Saxon blood." This language reinforced the whiteness of the Irish and reminded white readers of the importance of defending whiteness at a time when racial hierarchies appeared to be eroding.[20]

In castigating Butte leftists for playing fast and loose with racial identity, the *Voice* was implicitly targeting the racial ideology of Reid Robinson, the city's best-known "fellow-traveler." Officially stating its opposition to the racially inclusive stance of a union leader was unwise, especially in light of Executive Order 8802. Instead, union leaders in Montana, along with others in Mine Mill, stepped up their attacks on Robinson for towing the internationalist, un-American Communist Party line, and thus for no longer being an independent militant. As Robin D. G. Kelley has remarked, during this period "charges of communist domination were more than a red herring for union busting. . . . Anti-communism was also a veil for racism."[21]

Well aware of racial attitudes in the city because of his history there, Robinson did not share the government's view that progressive social politics had a strong enough hold on Butte's rank-and-file workers to guarantee the acceptance of the black soldier-miners. He and others repeatedly urged the government to do everything in its power to furlough and return to home former Butte miners in the military. Yet Robinson did not let his qualms stop him from committing himself and Mine Mill's leadership to facilitating the employment of the black men.[22]

Robinson and Mine Mill secretary-treasurer James Leary, another former Butte miner, wrote the BMU on October 27, 1942, to urge the acceptance of black soldier-miners. Providing a classic elaboration of progressive views on race, Robinson and Leary recounted the history of Mine Mill's interracial unionism in the 1930s and early 1940s and the BMU's support of those initiatives. They assured the union that the black soldiers were all experienced iron ore and coal miners from the Southeast, and noted that some were "undoubtedly members of the Mine, Mill and Smelter Workers." These union brothers had "pioneered in unionism and have brought improved conditions to both white and colored alike in the South." Thus, they deserved the respect and support of white miners.[23]

Acknowledging that black men had never before worked in the Butte mines, Robinson and Leary stressed that their "primary interest [was] the winning of the war, making democracy work for all of the people regardless of their race, color or creed." Since its inception, Mine Mill had made opposition to discrimination one of its guiding principles by enshrining it in the union's constitution. The union had affirmed Executive Order 8802 and passed resolutions urging the hiring and promotion of black workers. Moreover, members had instructed the International's executive board "to revoke the charter of any local which practices discrimination against any workers." Butte had long provided leadership on "all progressive matters," and it was now time to put those principles into practice. Robinson and Leary concluded by emphasizing that they were writing as fellow members of the BMU to "express [their] own viewpoints," but they challenged Butte men to "carry on a relentless struggle against any and all manifestations of discrimination against the negro people."[24]

Both managers and miners warmly welcomed the initial group of furloughed soldiers, comprised entirely of white men. When the thirty-nine black soldier-miners arrived for their first shift at the Tramway Mine on November 4, however, the all-white crew walked off the job. Shortly thereafter, the rest of Butte's miners laid down their tools. At a BMU meeting that evening, after hours of heated debate, members passed a motion requesting that the government withdraw the black workers from Butte's mines "in the interest of production" (fig. 6.2). If no black workers were present at the start of the regular day shift on November 6 and if the government and the ACM did not punish the Tramway men who started the wildcat, the Butte men would return to work.[25] Clearly worried about production first and foremost, government and Company officials decided to meet these conditions.

Significantly, neither BMU leaders nor local members had notified Robinson about the November 4 walkout. Mine Mill's president learned about it from undersecretary of war Robert Patterson, who contacted him at the CIO national convention in Boston and told him, "Go out there, Robinson, and get that mine open." When Robinson demurred, Patterson insisted. Leary interjected, "Reid, you can't go to Butte and insist that those Negroes go to work in the mines. You've got an election coming up." Robinson later recalled that Leary's statement "was the clincher that said to me to go to Butte." He told Leary and Patterson, "In times like these it seems to me that there is something more important than my personal welfare."[26]

After flying cross country in an army bomber provided by Patterson, Robinson and Leary spoke to the BMU membership at an "emotionally charged meeting of 1,100" on November 8. The two explained why it was the duty of Mine Mill members to support interracialism, and they introduced a resolution calling on BMU members not to let anyone "stampede [them] into taking any action, such as a refusal to work, that would hamper production so vital in the saving of lives of our own brothers . . . on the fighting fronts." They asked the assembly to welcome the black furloughed

6.2 Office of War Information photographer Russell Lee took
this photograph of a Butte Miners' Union meeting in October
1942, just before the black soldier-miner crisis began. The large
poster above the table onstage is of President Roosevelt.
Russell Lee, *Butte, Montana: Miners' Union Meeting*; Library of
Congress, Prints & Photographs Division, FSA-OWI Collection,
LC-USW3-009619-D DLC.

soldiers "so they can through our friendly and fraternal treatment give their
utmost in this battle for production." Neither these sentiments, nor those
offered by United States Army officials also in attendance, impressed Butte's
rank-and-file workers. Both groups of speakers were "virtually booed off the
stage," and BMU officers were unable to control the angry discussion that
followed. According to the *Union*, Mine Mill's own newspaper, "Emotional
speakers flayed the government and the International Union for insisting
on the right of Negroes to work in the Butte mines." One miner recalled
that Robinson finally told the miners that these black men "are just as good
as you are." The men responded, "Well go down and work with them then.
We're not working with them and that's it." A vote was called, and Robinson
and Leary's resolution was soundly defeated.[27]

Just how much Robinson's continual championing of interracialism,
combined with his purported ties to Communism, cost him in Butte was
evident in Mine Mill election results announced later that November. In
the race for president of the International, Butte's miners gave Robinson
742 votes. John J. Driscoll, the vehemently anti-Communist leader of the
Connecticut Brass Works local who in late October had come out publicly against Robinson's "communist machine," earned 1,169 votes in

Butte. James Byrne, Robinson's highest-profile Butte adversary and the labor leader whom many federal officials blamed for the wildcat, received 1,838 votes.[28]

James Byrne, Race, and the Independent Masculinity of Miners

By the fall of 1942, James Byrne had come to represent the dominant perspective in Butte. While the vision of an interracial labor movement motivated Robinson, Byrne saw himself as a realist who put the desires of Butte's rank and file first. Byrne's platform, which reflected his sense of what other Butte miners believed, attacked Mine Mill's leaders for being too soft on government plans that hurt labor, specifically wage and personnel freezes, and not forceful enough in the wartime battle for workplace power against the ACM. Embedding this critique of Mine Mill strategy in a more personal condemnation of Robinson, Byrne's rhetoric suggested that Robinson was a Communist, a Roosevelt lackey, and unmanly. He argued that the union needed leaders "who can maintain some spirit of American independence," not a recent convert to the cause who, thanks to his Communist ties, had not initially supported "the war against fascism."[29]

Robinson's lack of manly independence, Byrne opined, hampered his effectiveness in contract negotiations then under way between Mine Mill and the Company. He insinuated that Robinson would follow the Communist Party line and sacrifice the workers' gains for the sake of the war effort. Robinson and his hand-picked negotiators, Byrne suggested, would also fail to push contract issues that challenged the government's policies, for fear of being deemed unpatriotic or anti-Roosevelt. Workers knew that this contract would likely go to the government for mediation. Byrne implied that Robinson's close relationship with the Roosevelt administration would hurt the BMU's ability to push its case in this arena as well, because government officials believed union members under Robinson's control would be loyal to the war program no matter what the National War Labor Board (NWLB) decided.[30]

Contract negotiations between Mine Mill and the ACM gained a deeper resonance given the contest between Byrne and Robinson, with its links to the intertwined prewar and wartime histories of racial, gender, and class ideology. In late August 1942, the joint negotiating committee for the ACM's Mine Mill Montana locals had formally demanded a wage increase of two dollars for all workers; an additional increase of fifty cents a day for afternoon- and night-shift workers; a fourteen-day paid vacation; and an impartial chairman for the top grievance committee. The Company sought to institute a central hiring system, which managers hoped would stop miners from showing so much autonomy. The wartime labor shortage had facilitated miners' longtime practice of quitting a mine because they either did not like their boss or wanted better conditions, some time off, or simply a change of scenery. Without a central hiring system, they could go to another mine in the Butte complex and be hired with no questions asked. With central hiring, the Company could more easily discipline such miners. The ACM also wanted to introduce biweekly pay, which would help the mines' overstretched administrators. The miners countered that they had a right to draw their pay at the end of each week. Even after calling in a US Department of Labor conciliator, management and union negotiators remained deadlocked over the issues of central hiring, biweekly pay, and wages. When ACM officials said they could not afford the proposed wage increase, Mine Mill responded that the Company had posted an after-tax profit of over $18 million for the first half of 1942. Following the framework mandated by the Roosevelt administration, the case went to the NWLB, where it sat without a decision until after the Mine Mill election.[31] This impasse made it difficult for Robinson to show that cooperating with the government would pay dividends, and reinforced Byrne's critique of the relationship between Robinson, the ACM, and the government.

Byrne's reading of the mood among the miners was confirmed by a report circulated just days before the hate strike by an OWI Bureau of Intelligence survey team that was sent to Butte and other area locales to gauge workers' attitudes. Men told the interviewers that the high-paying, safer, more family-friendly war work available on the West Coast seemed much more preferable to the mines. They saw themselves as victims of government policies that had produced a regional wage crisis and labor shortage. Since copper men and their Northwest mates, lumber men, were among the few workers nationally that had been frozen in place by legislative edict, threats by government officials and Mine Mill officers that absenteeism-prone men would have to either "work or fight" were received quite bitterly. The survey team reported, "The imputation of cowardice to men working in one of the most hazardous occupations in American industry is deeply resented." Referring to their Wobbly heritage, some men talked about resorting to sabotage or other forms of what they pointedly called "soldiering on the job," a term made popular by the industrial efficiency pioneer Frederick Winslow Taylor that most typically referred to instituting a production slowdown. Virtually all believed that government labor policies were controlled by employers.

Listing "independence" and "individuality" among their core values, these men articulated a view of wartime masculinity based on older labor ideas rather than the ubiquitous and government-propagated rhetoric of sacrifice that the government and corporations had mobilized against men on the home front. Even before the strike, some federal officials had apparently taken the OWI study to heart, tailoring their message to assure copper men that they recognized these workers' importance. Nonetheless, others continued to scold copper men about doing their patriotic duty (fig. 6.3).[32]

The day after the strike began, WMC chairman Paul McNutt sent telegrams to the CIO leadership, Mine Mill's international and regional officers, and the BMU, demanding an immediate end to the walkout. He saved his harshest words for Byrne, declaring that "under no circumstances [could] the government permit any group to prevent skilled miners from performing this all important work." McNutt highlighted Executive Order 8802 and reminded Byrne of the union's long history of fighting racism in the workplace.[33]

Responding the same day, Byrne telegraphed McNutt and other government officials that the situation was "critical." The withdrawal of the black soldiers from Butte was "imperative to avoid trouble and interruption of production of copper." Byrne contended that the BMU's opposition to the black soldier-miners was "not in any way involved with question of race," then added that an "attempt at rape by Negro has aroused entire citizenry." This rumored rape had not occurred, but by invoking the trope of a black man raping a white woman, Byrne actually revealed how central race was to the wildcat and how quickly interlocking white fictions about black masculinity could be mobilized to foreclose on the possibilities of interracial working-class solidarity. Miner Silvio Sciuchetti recalled what Butte's white residents were thinking when the black soldier-miners were in town: "You would see three or four together, walking the streets . . . that was kind of scary. My wife . . . wouldn't go out of the house."[34]

Another rumor that "reached the ears of some thousands, especially the miners," expressed home front copper men's material anxieties: that "the importation of the Negroes was a deep laid plan of the company who was and is now engaged in negotiations . . . for a new contract to take advantage of the situation." A federal official reported that "a great majority of the miners" believed this claim. Yet another rumor revealed the miners' distrust of the government: the Roosevelt administration, at the behest of the Company, was preparing a much larger group of black soldier-miners to follow the initial cohort. On November 16, the *Great Falls Tribune* gave further credence to this rumor by reporting that six hundred more black men were

6.3 This 1943 poster was part of the government's effort to convince white Americans, and male home front workers in particular, to put aside their racial prejudices. "United We Win," War Manpower Commission; courtesy Northwestern University Library.

on their way to Butte. This erroneous article so infuriated officials that they mobilized the FBI to trace its source.[35]

The Butte men's belief that the introduction of black soldier-miners was intended to "soften the union and put a large group in the mines to which the company could dictate terms" emerged from the miners' view of how employers functioned.[36] They remembered the ACM's repeated efforts to use racial-ethnic animosity and political tensions to fracture the workers during the 1910s, 1920s, and 1930s. Miners believed that the ACM and other corporations viewed wartime labor turmoil as an even greater opportunity. The discourse about the threat posed by the black soldier-miners spoke to this and reflected yet another set of unfounded racist assumptions about black men. Butte's miners believed that unlike the white soldier-miners they had readily accepted, they could not trust black men to join the collective and, within it, to exercise the independent masculinity that was the hallmark of copper men's gendered identity. They decided to make the black soldier-miner crisis a showpiece for white and white ethnic working-class masculine solidarity.

Father Michael English, John McCusker, and General Frank McSherry: The Local Rules

During the first two weeks of November 1942, the government shifted its strategy but did not remove the black soldier-miners. In turn, after being castigated by federal officials and their own national union leaders, the independent-minded Butte miners dug in their heels. So the government turned to the Catholic Church, one of the institutions they believed the miners most respected. On one hand, enlisting the help of religious leaders made sense, given the long-term ties between the labor movement and local churches and that the vast preponderance of Butte's white ethnic miners were Catholic. On the other hand, the churches in the mining city were not models of racial inclusiveness. Butte's African Americans had been forced to found their own churches because, like the YMCA, dance halls, and restaurants, white churches did not welcome blacks.[37] The message local white religious leaders would offer about race relations was thus an open question.

The government officials charged with finding a solution to the Butte wildcat knew very little about the local history of antiblack racism when they turned to Bishop Joseph Gilmore in the hope that he might succeed where Reid Robinson had not. His involvement reflected his desire to serve his flock as well as his kinship with copper workers—his own nephew was involved in the work stoppage. Affiliated with the National Catholic Welfare Conference's Social Action Department and the Catholic Youth Organization, two of the church's most progressive offshoots, the bishop had long shown an interest in social justice issues, particularly in regard to the working class. The war did not change that. In a late October 1942 letter to the general in charge of procurement for the War Department, Gilmore insisted that the only way to guarantee high copper output was to increase miners' wages. He advocated raising copper prices so both companies and laborers could thrive.[38]

By the second week of November, Gilmore had become a leader in the effort to find a solution to the crisis. He urged James Byrne to persuade BMU members to allow the black soldier-miners to work in Butte: "Impress upon those whose attitude has raised this question of race discrimination the urgent necessity of presenting a united front on labor's essential contribution." In addition, he directed Father Michael English, senior pastor of the Catholic clergy in Butte, to have parish priests discuss with the miners the importance of unwavering loyalty to the war production program. Gilmore wanted parishioners reminded of the "tradition of Butte labor which has always fought for the fullest opportunity and equality of the workers regardless or race, color, or creed. . . . Discrimination of this kind is un-Christian as well as undemocratic." That point was reinforced in the diocesan newspaper over the next few weeks. Gilmore asked Father English to organize a committee representing the city's labor, business, religious, and civic leaders to try to solve the impasse.[39]

English, like Gilmore, felt a strong obligation to defend the city from charges that its citizens were deficient in patriotism. He maintained a strict neutrality between the Company and its workers, and federal officials relied on his counsel and intercession. English acknowledged that the miners had "an inordinate, and sometimes unfounded suspicion that the 'Company' [was] constantly plotting to destroy the rights of the miners and to undermine their union." But he added that some Butte businessmen had similar suspicions, particularly in regard to the importation of the black soldier-miners. Local residents especially resented the fact that the government, the Company, and labor leaders such as Robinson had called the miners "Axis Agents" for opposing the black workers. English told the government that the miners were "patriotic Americans . . . loyal, almost to a fault, to any cause they consider just."[40]

While Gilmore paid more attention to the progressive views that circulated among Catholic Church officials in the nation's capital, English's approach was rooted in his local experience. He spent considerable time talking with rank-and-file miners and dealing with inflammatory statements, such as accusations that the strikers were unpatriotic and rumors about the impending arrival of more black soldiers, both of which hampered efforts to mediate a solution to the strike. More than any of the national figures involved in the crisis, English had a strong sense of what the men on the street were thinking—and, as it soon became evident, a strong desire to see them appeased.

John McCusker, the regional WMC official whom the Roosevelt administration sent to Butte, worked hand in hand with English. McCusker had already said that he believed the federal government was "powerless" when it came to ending racist employment practices in the Butte mines. He and John Hanley, head of the local United States Employment Service (USES) office, shared English's belief that white miners would never work with blacks. His efforts to bring the strike to a close indicate a pragmatism born of his assessment of local politics. At times his behavior suggests, not so much that he was compelled to compromise in order to secure production, but that he agreed with the miners' stance. The Mountain West–based McCusker quite simply did not share the commitment to Executive Order 8802 enunciated by McNutt and other federal officials.

Adding to the disconnect between officials in Washington and those in the field, federal agencies sent contradictory signals to their local offices. The USES, like the local draft boards of the Selective Service System, had representatives in towns throughout the United States who served as the local face of government's effort to manage manpower during the war. Its highest priority was to move local residents from nonessential work into essential jobs rather than to shift large numbers of workers around the country. On October 19, 1942, the very day that the officials in Washington announced the furlough plan, the head of the USES circulated a major policy document to all its offices regarding the need to promote the nondiscriminatory employment of workers of color. The statement noted that USES representatives had the responsibility to refer workers in a color-blind fashion and try to end discrimination by either employers or unions. But by emphasizing that its local agents "should make a definite effort to persuade employers to eliminate specifications which prevent the consideration of local qualified workers because of their race, color, creed, national origin, or citizenship," the directive appeared to leave open the question of how workers from outside the local area should be handled. The memo's focus on "maximum production" and the "local" left room for local officials to wonder how vigorously, and at what cost, their superiors wanted them to enforce Executive Order 8802.[41]

The committee that Gilmore asked English to form soon reached a consensus that reflected local preoccupations rather than national policy. Publicly, English, McCusker, and their committee members advocated the acceptance of the furloughed African American soldiers, but their main thrust was a behind-the-scenes effort to push the government to ship the black men out of Butte and to the Victory Lease, an ACM mining property near Wendover, Nevada.[42]

As the local committee made this decision, Paul McNutt, the head of the WMC, dispatched Brigadier General Frank McSherry, operations director of the WMC, and Major General William Hershey, head of the Selective Service, to a mining industry conference being attended by Butte labor and management leaders, with instructions to end the miners' intransigence once and for all. The *Montana Standard* carried a detailed report on McSherry's speech, including his declaration that "Negroes, Latin Americans and Indians must make up an increasing proportion" of mine workers. "If and when" employees resist this development, McSherry averred, union and management leaders must step forward and help overcome any objections. Going a step further, he said that "as a former miner," he believed that "many surface jobs [could] be handled by women," and offered WMC assistance in placing women in western mines.[43]

The decision to force Butte miners to comply with national policy may well have stemmed from President Roosevelt as well as McSherry and McNutt. Roosevelt had already become involved in the crisis, summoning Robinson and CIO president Philip Murray, a coal miner turned steelworker, to Washington to discuss the situation. Through most of November, Roosevelt insisted that the black soldier-miners had to stay in Butte, and the Butte men had to capitulate. Following this mandate, McSherry told McCusker, Hanley, and the Butte labor and management representatives that McNutt had declared the Nevada Victory Lease plan "unacceptable." McSherry said that the government would show flexibility on one point: the ACM and the BMU could segregate black soldiers in one mine as long as Mine Mill found white men to work with them. He stressed that union, management, and church leaders should prepare Butte's miners to accept African Americans as coworkers. Moreover, he volunteered to come to Butte to help convince the miners of this reality, an offer the union and the ACM accepted.[44]

The "one mine" plan, although antithetical to Executive Order 8802, Mine Mill's constitution, and Robinson's explicit denunciation of segregated work practices in his letter to the Butte miners, resembled arrangements made in a few other war plants. And, of course, the US armed forces themselves remained more segregated than the proposed "one mine" would be. McCusker, Hanley, and English seemed convinced that it was impossible to persuade the white miners to back down completely. McSherry had not faced the intransigence of the Butte men personally, but he had another powerful motivation to compromise. The government increasingly worried that the behavior of Butte's men, who because of their affiliation with Mine

Mill were widely considered racially progressive unionists as well as stalwart supporters of the Roosevelt administration, might inspire other white men to oppose the integration of war production facilities.[45]

On November 20, 1942, word about events in Butte began to leak out. The *Washington Star* reported on the strike and remarked that the black men had not been able to reenter the mines for two weeks. The paper also carried McNutt's denial that the federal government intended to force the miners to accede by using military force, which suggests yet another rumor circulating in Butte. *Time* magazine made Butte an even bigger story by focusing its scorn on Mine Mill's left-leaning leadership for its inability to enforce its progressive racial agenda at the local level.[46]

The defense of Butte's miners by the *People's Voice* reveals how the local progressive media were making sense of the situation and why they supported McCusker and English rather than McSherry and the International's leaders. The *Voice* framed its coverage as a direct response to *Time*: "First Publicity on Labor Troubles in Butte Printed by National Magazine Generally Recognized as Anti-Labor and Story as Told There, Paints the Miners Union as Prejudiced against Colored Labor." Expanding on the argument first put forward by Bill Mason, Mine Mill's regional representative in Butte, but also mobilized by Robinson in late October and early November, the newspaper claimed that the miners' actions arose not from racism but in response to the bungling bureaucracy's inability to do right by workingpeople: "The situation in Butte demonstrates the mistakes which have been made by the national administration regarding the manpower program." Instead of sending inducted Butte miners back home, the government sent other soldier-miners, including "many a southern negro." "It was only natural then that the people of Butte were disturbed. . . . The fact that disorders have occurred, and the miners have sometimes refused to work does not indicate that they have racial prejudices or that they are anti-negro," the *Voice* concluded.[47]

On Monday, November 23, the same day that *Time* carried the Butte strike story, BMU officers and McCusker scheduled two mass meetings for Wednesday, November 25, so that McSherry could bring the senior governmental perspective to the miners directly. McSherry's objective would be to convince the local men to offer, in Bill Mason's words, "the Original [mine] first, Orphan Girl [mine] second, as gifts to black Americans." Mason was given the task of assembling a group of BMU members willing to work underground with their "black brothers." McCusker and local labor leaders spent Tuesday speaking to as many groups of miners as possible in an effort to dispel the false rumors circulating in Butte and to sell the one-mine plan.

Indicating how interlocked the issues of the draft, mining labor, and home front workers' masculinity remained, they also met with the members of Butte's three Selective Service boards in order to clarify deferment rules and to reinforce the need to push all men not yet employed in essential industries to enter the mines if they wanted to avoid induction.[48]

McCusker, echoing his superiors' hard line instead of taking the more accommodating tone that had characterized his previous interactions with the miners, began each of the two November 25 meetings by insisting on the applicability of Executive Order 8802 to the local situation. The miners, instead of focusing on the issue of racial integration, asked McCusker about the Montana copper workers' wage case, which had been returned to the National War Labor Board. The miners had rejected the NWLB's first contract settlement offer as insufficient in light of the critical work they were doing and the wages received by other war workers, particularly on the West Coast. Following Mason's advice that there were other ways to indicate the firmness of the government's position than to tell the men that they either allow the black soldier-miners to work "or we'll send in the army," McSherry mentioned his miner's roots to show he understood the world Butte men occupied; then he dwelled on his experience as a military man and war planner to argue that patriotic duty required the Butte men to set aside their concerns and allow the black soldier-miners to work alongside them. McCusker described McSherry's speech as amazingly effective: it "will be long remembered in Butte by all those who heard it." From the perspective of a number of government officials in attendance, it appeared that McSherry's oratory swayed the night-shift men. They voted 164 to 122 in favor of allowing the black soldier-miners to work in Butte. Father English believed that a "cross-section of the miners of Butte" now supported the employment of black miners. None of the officials present made much of the fact that 450 men had abstained.[49]

Over one thousand day-shift men attended the second special meeting, which took place that evening at the Fox Theater. McSherry spoke for almost an hour and, in McCusker's eyes, "fully answered all questions that should have eliminated any doubts" about rumors that the government planned to send hundreds more furloughed black soldier-miners to Butte. He also explained why more Butte miners in the armed forces were not being furloughed and sent home to work. His argument on this latter issue found support from at least one former Butte miner who had returned on furlough. Kent McFarland insisted that the government was not to blame for more Butte men not returning. "Where are these Butte miners who were inducted into the army? Well, they were at Camp Kearns also, those who are not already serving overseas. The ones who did not come back to Butte, either elected to stay in the army or to go to some other copper camp. Seems strange, doesn't it, but a fact nevertheless." Rebukingly he added, "I'm proud of the uniform I wore and I'm also proud that I can do a job that is so important. I'm driving drift in the Butte Hill now, and liking it, but for other men who don't like our Butte hot-boxes, I for one object to trying to force them to come back. That, Brothers, is really forced labor!"[50] But both McSherry's and McFarland's arguments fell on deaf ears.

After more presentations by union and WMC officials, supporters of the plan to employ black miners in Butte appeared surprised that all these reassurances and remonstrations failed to strike a chord with the miners. Hours of heated debate followed. One Mine Mill representative described the meeting as "very disorderly." Someone finally succeeded in offering a motion supporting the plan. The day-shift miners defeated the motion by at least a 9-to-1 ratio, an "overwhelming" loss that stunned both federal officials and local leaders.[51] Would the government send in troops to enforce Executive Order 8802? Would an angry McSherry send hundreds more African American soldier-miners to Butte? Would the white miners resort to racial violence?

The next day was Thanksgiving, but government and union officials held an emergency meeting to find another solution to the three-week-old crisis. According to McCusker's memorandum, they decided to push forward with the plan to place the black soldier-miners in one of Butte's mines. After the meeting adjourned, however, McSherry pulled English aside and told him something quite different: McNutt had decided that "the best and easiest way out of a situation that might be explosive was to have the negroes state of their own volition that they did not want to work in Butte." The government wanted English to secure such a statement. McSherry cautioned that "no pressure of any kind was to be exercised" on the black soldier-miners to make this decision. Afraid that Butte's copper workers might create an even more serious political problem, the Roosevelt administration had abdicated its principled stand against home front racism.[52]

Hezekiah Jones and the Wartime Struggle for Black Equality

Given their treatment ever since their arrival, getting the black soldier-miners to state that they did not want to work in Butte should not have been a difficult task. Indeed, they had already signaled that they were ready to depart. On November 25, between the two mass meetings, a black furloughed soldier met with McSherry and told him that a large majority of the black men wanted to be transferred. The day after McSherry had asked English to facilitate the black men's "voluntary" withdrawal, Hezekiah Jones, one of the leaders of the thirty-nine soldier-miners, delivered to McCusker a written list of the men who were requesting removal from Butte.[53]

McSherry, the federal official most supportive of employing the soldier-miners in that city, seemingly did not have a higher opinion of the black men's independent masculinity than the BMU did. He refused to legitimate this list, because he was concerned that the men had not arrived at their decision independently. He wanted to ascertain that the group had not been "forced . . . or persuaded" to choose this course of action, and asked McCusker to tell them that the government wanted an impartial party to meet with officials and confirm this. When McCusker informed the soldier-miners of McSherry's concerns, they suggested Lewis Stewart, the minister who had written McNutt about Hi Brown's being barred from the mines. But Stewart was a little too independent for the government and, ironically, for the BMU.[54]

Like many African American leaders, Rev. Stewart had seen the decision against integrating the military and the weakness of the Fair Employment Practices Commission as evidence of the Roosevelt administration's limited commitment to racial equality. But he went much further than most activists to make his anger known. In January 1942, Stewart formally renounced his US citizenship in a document entitled "DECLARATION OF RENUNCIATION OF AMERICAN CITIZENSHIP" and addressed "TO WHOM IT MAY CONCERN and particularly to the MEMBERS OF ORGANIZED LABOR." Referencing the Declaration of Independence, he argued that the policies of the US government ran counter to Christian ideals of an "equal station among men." He concluded that "repeated injustices and injuries" and an "attitude of contempt" marked the Roosevelt administration's relationship with "those citizens it has designatedly classified as 'Negroes' on all its public records." Referring to his own experience, he contended that the government had denied him "the fruit of [his] labor" solely because of the color of his skin. Intriguingly, Stewart's letter addressed Butte's union members in particular. The men who would later both support Brown's petition for employment and fight against allowing black soldier-miners to work among them had, he asserted, "unfailingly given me the privilege of presenting the various causes which I have supported."[55]

Citing Stewart's letter renouncing his US citizenship, BMU officials said they "feared" his influence on the black soldiers. John McCusker told these troops bluntly that Stewart's "feeling toward the government" ruled him out as an impartial party. He offered Father Michael English, whom Frank

McSherry had already chosen, as the "neutral" party to communicate with the black soldiers.[56] On Saturday, November 28, English went to the Baltimore Hotel in Butte, where almost all the men were staying; then, because he said there was insufficient room for a proper conversation, he hired cabs and brought the men to his rectory. Awaiting them there were two cases of beer. After telling the men to help themselves, English flourished Bishop Joseph Gilmore's telegram empowering the Butte priest to attempt to solve the crisis. According to English, the black soldier-miners "applauded heartily." Almost all the men asked him why they could not work in Butte, and English replied that as citizens they had the right to do so, but the Butte miners believed the black men were part of a Company-led effort to break the union. Eventually, the men asked him: "Reverend, if you was us, would you leave for another mine where you would be more fitted, or would you take a chance on going down in the hole in Butte where you wasn't wanted?" English recalled that he "paused for a moment, then said, 'I wouldn't care to go down in the hole in Butte.'" The priest reported that the soldier-miners "shouted, 'that's all we want to know—let's get out.'" Then, with English's assistance, they wrote and signed a statement to this effect. English, seemingly without a sense of paradox, later told McCusker and McSherry that the men stated their desire to leave Butte "freely, openly, and frankly."[57]

Hezekiah Jones's account of what occurred both at the rectory and in other meetings differed markedly from that produced by McCusker and English. Jones revealed that McCusker and English, sometimes together and sometimes separately, had repeatedly attempted to persuade him and the other leaders of the black soldier-miners to leave Butte voluntarily. On November 26, McCusker was joined by an ACM executive who added his voice to the chorus of locals urging the black men to vacate the city. After the executive left, Jones said that McCusker told him and fellow soldier-miner William Bogle that "the Butte miners hate us boys and won't let us get on the jobs." Then McCusker said "the whole thing is a communist plot . . . and . . . that Reid Robinson is a Communist and that he does not like us Negroes, no matter what he says."[58]

In his account, English did not evince the same disdain for Robinson, but he echoed McCusker's description of the white miners' feelings toward the black men. Jones reported that in the meeting with the black soldier-miners, English spent considerable time discussing Butte's past "strikes and troubles." He believed that English sought to scare them with his tales "about riots and bloodshed and how bad and radical the Butte people are."[59] English omitted that part of the meeting from his report.

Despite English's and McCusker's obfuscations and McSherry's disbelief that the soldier-miners could represent themselves without a white intermediary, Jones and other independent-minded soldier-miners fought to make their view heard. On November 28, 1942, in response to the one-mine plan, the proposal to ship the black soldier-miners to Nevada, and the meeting earlier that day with English, Jones submitted a statement from "the members of the United Mine Workers of America who had contracted to work in the Butte Mines." The statement bluntly noted that UMW principles stood strongly against workplace discrimination, as did those of Mine Mill. The black UMW members added, "If we are worthy of wearing the uniform of the United States Army, we are sufficiently worthy to work with the Butte Miners in all the mines here." Appealing to the wartime hierarchy of masculinity that placed soldiering above home front labor, they indicated their opposition to the plan that would create a segregated underground space in Butte. They concluded by requesting time to consult with their own union leadership regarding the situation in Butte.[60]

Both government and Mine Mill officials had reason to fear the involvement of the UMW, especially its president, John L. Lewis. The country's best-known and most controversial labor leader during World War II, Lewis had refused to sign the no-strike pledge that virtually every other union had accepted. Left-led unions such as Mine Mill told their members that they had accepted the no-strike policy for the duration, because they realized that "fascism is the worst enemy of the working people . . . that the war against the fascist enemy is a people's war and cannot be won if production is interrupted by stoppages of work." Lewis's unwillingness to bend to government demands made the UMW a potentially appealing alternative to workers interested in more militant unionism. His union, in fact, did launch a wartime organizing campaign in Montana, telling workers that affiliating with the UMW would "give the boys the right to go on strike." In August 1942, Bill Mason warned the Mine Mill staff, "That guy [Lewis] and his stinking outfit are really out to cause us some trouble in Montana."[61] Nonetheless, the statement submitted by Jones and other UMW members fell on deaf ears.

On Monday, November 30, McSherry reported to English, McCusker, and Mason that the Roosevelt administration accepted the black soldier-miners' decision and approved the plan to send those men desiring to leave Butte to the ACM's Victory Mining Lease in Nevada.[62] Yet although the government had given up trying to persuade Butte's miners to accede to federal policy, Jones did not give up the struggle for racial equality. On December 1,

28 of the 39 black soldier-miners left for Nevada. Of the remaining 11, 2 had gone AWOL and 4 had taken ill and been transferred out of Butte. That left 5 men. One was Richard Brown, Hiawatha Brown's brother and also a Butte native. The other 4, led by Jones, refused on principle to let the government's surrender to workplace discrimination drive them out of Montana. That same day, McCusker instructed them to report to the Orphan Girl mine. With most of the black soldier-miners on their way out of Butte, government and union officials believed they could employ a few black workers underground as long as they worked with a crew of progressive white miners whom Mason had recruited. But instead of going to the Orphan Girl, Jones and the three others reported for work at 4:00 p.m. on December 1 at the Tramway Mine—the very place where the hate strike had begun. They said, perhaps disingenuously, that they did so because that was where their mining clothes were.[63]

The arrival of Jones and his peers at the Tramway caused so much consternation that mine bosses immediately called ACM vice president Dan Kelly in New York. He called McCusker, who in turn called Jones. "Using some strong language," McCusker sent the four black men back to their hotel. Another hate strike seemed imminent, and the BMU president later said he feared a "race riot." English described Jones as "a stubborn individual" who refused to countenance exclusion and segregation. He was certainly brave. Jones and the three other men acknowledged that they feared for their safety. They were right to feel so. In mid-December the BMU leadership had to take the unusual step of forbidding members from "interferring (sic.) with the colored men." English speculated that the black men's decision to go to the Tramway was "the result of suggestions made by outside influence," by which he meant someone affiliated with the Left. In so doing, English joined white miners, local leaders, and federal officials in believing that these men of color could not exemplify the independent masculinity that Butte men believed was the cornerstone of their racialized gender identity. Yet when McCusker told the men later that day to report to him at the Finlen Hotel, they once more showed that independence by ignoring his demand.[64]

Yet again, local union, management, church, and government officials met to address the crisis. This time they decided, with the blessing of both the Anaconda smelter's management and labor representatives, to send the four black men to work at the smelter, where the ACM already employed twenty-nine other African Americans from the local community. Afraid of how the smelter's white workers might respond, the ad-hoc committee "agreed that the best procedure was to take one a day, starting with

Hezekiah Jones." For English, that decision "seem[ed] to clear up the very explosive situation caused by the sending of thirty-nine negroes to Butte." But as soon as Jones learned he would be placed on a segregated crew, he and another black soldier-miner refused to work at the smelter. The two men returned to Butte, and continuing to draw a paycheck from the ACM, they waited to hear what the Company and the government would do with them. Jones, working with Mason, recorded an affidavit indicting the BMU's leadership, McCusker, and English as those most responsible for the federal government's inability to employ black men in Butte.[65]

Mason's hope that Jones's affidavit would provide the evidence Mine Mill needed to oust McCusker from his position as the WMC's regional representative was not realized, although the International had come to see him as an obstacle to the fight against discrimination throughout the Mountain West. In mid-January 1943, Mason enlisted Jones and William Bogle, the other black soldier-miner who had stood resolutely with Jones, in Mine Mill's battle against racism within its own ranks. He told Robinson he wanted to make sure "these two boys [did] not get left out after having guts enough to stay with me in this fight." He recommended that the International ask the government if it could borrow Jones and Bogle so it could send them to Mine Mill locals to speak about "national unity" and the International's "readiness to support Negro workers." That way, it could "get something out of the fight, some satisfaction at least."[66]

Conclusion

In the end, racial progressives could not wrest even a consolation prize from the Butte crisis. Three months after every other black soldier-miner had either left for the Victory Lease in Nevada, gone AWOL, fallen ill and been sent home or back to the army, or agreed to work at the Anaconda smelter, Jones and Bogle remained in Butte, out of work but still drawing paychecks from the ACM. Finally, on March 5, 1943, Father English wrote his final memorandum on the Butte racial crisis: "Hezekiah Jones and companion ordered back to the Army and left last night."[67] The Butte miners who wanted to keep the mines all white had beat both their own international union and the US government.

The significance of hate strikes to the social politics of the home front has been largely overlooked. These wildcats certainly do not conform to the popular picture of "the greatest generation" or, when they involved progressive unions like Mine Mill, to perceptions of the Popular Front. While the CIO's no-strike pledge has received the lion's share of attention by those writing about wartime labor, wildcat strikes occurred much more often than has been commonly thought. The NWLB's Strike Section did not track these strikes, and even its data on formal work stoppages are incomplete. NWLB statistics do suggest the general trends, however. In 1942 the board noted 640 formal strikes, with the loss of almost 1 million man-days of labor. In November, the month of the Butte stoppage, 97 strikes occurred across the country, costing over 91,000 man-days. The OWI and the NWLB hailed this number as the lowest level of man-days lost since Pearl Harbor, and officials added that a surprising number of these conflicts arose from grievances, not wage issues. Although President Roosevelt and a slew of high-ranking federal officials were involved in the Butte crisis, it does not appear in the NWLB's records, because neither the BMU nor Mine Mill had officially called for a strike. We must wonder how many other wildcats were launched by working-class white men to contest the introduction of women and of people of color into the wartime labor force. Racial conflicts occurred nationwide, from Beaumont, Texas, and Memphis, Tennessee, through Chicago and Detroit to San Francisco. The number of official strikes rose in 1943 and 1944, with over 2 million and 4 million lost man-days, respectively.[68] At the most general level, then, the conflict in Butte belies the popular notion that during World War II, patriotic Americans united against racism at home as well as fascism abroad.

The aftermath of the Butte wildcat reveals even more about the social politics of Butte and suggests some of the needed revisions to the national story of the home front. The fear—or, for some progressives, the secret hope—that the government would punish Butte turned out to be unfounded. The WMC and the War Department followed through on their November 1942 offer to furlough more soldiers and send them to the mining city. Over the next year, Butte's miners welcomed upward of eight hundred furloughed white soldiers, along with hundreds of white home front men whose only mining experience came from the training they received in the ACM's new-miner training program (fig. 6.4). But Hi Brown was still the only African American in the mines' eight-thousand-man workforce, and fully a quarter of those workers had been employed for less than twelve months. More important to Butte's rank and file, in January 1943 the NWLB's Nonferrous Commission issued a wage decision that finally showed the agency's receptiveness to the miners' concerns. The dollar-a-day raise applied to back wages even during the strike, making "January like Christmas."[69]

When federal policy came into conflict with local institutions, government officials often deferred, preferring consensus to coercion even when core principles were violated. For those within the Roosevelt administra-

6.4 The ACM ran a school to teach men having no previous experience the skills necessary to be a miner. Although they grumbled about the danger of "greenhorns" and about men using the mines to hide from military duty, Butte miners accepted these workers as long as they were white. Photograph by Robert I. Nesmith, *Penn School*, 1942; Montana Historical Society Research Center Photograph Archives, Helena.

tion and the international union who wanted principles of equality placed before expediency, the resolution of the Butte crisis did not bode well. The continuing decentralization of WMC and NWLB activities made these agencies even more receptive to local opinion.

The virtual absence of the Fair Employment Practices Commission (FEPC) from the Butte crisis is revealing. The FEPC, the administration's chief watchdog on racism in the workplace, was born from the activism of A. Philip Randolph and other black labor leaders less than eighteen months before the Butte wildcat. Not only did the new agency lack enforcement mechanisms, but it deferred to more powerful agencies such as the NWLB. The only trace of the Butte conflict in FEPC records is a letter from the inimitable Rev. Lewis Stewart. In his December 1942 correspondence with Lawrence Cramer, executive secretary of the FEPC, Stewart upbraided the Roosevelt administration for its lack of commitment to racial justice. He emphasized the potent combination of local-oriented men like John McCusker and Father Michael English, who acted without "honor," and "political charlatans" from the federal government like Paul McNutt and Brigadier General Frank McSherry. Together, these men had perpetrated a "complete nullification of the previous good offices" of the FEPC.[70] Stewart's analysis highlights the importance of looking at both national and local actors and policies, progressive and otherwise, to create a more accurate account of race relations during World War II. His letter expresses the anger many black activists felt by the end of 1942, and it foreshadowed the difficulties that the FEPC would continue to encounter.

Yet this letter serves as reminder of the remarkable resilience marking the wartime struggle against discrimination by African Americans and their allies, including progressive union leaders such as Reid Robinson. Stewart told Cramer that he hoped "the real men and women of America" would rise up and beat back the "parasite" of discrimination that Butte had exposed. While other commentators, including the *New York Post*, blamed the BMU for what had happened in Butte, Stewart remained optimistic about the white rank and file. He thought they had been misled by English, McCusker, and a few "renegades" within their own ranks. Bill Mason, Stewart's ally in Mine Mill's regional leadership, saw the coalition between McCusker, English, and a powerful faction within the BMU as a continuing obstruction to a potentially progressive future for Butte.[71]

Father English, in conjunction with John Hanley, Butte's local USES representative, worked to protect the BMU from any fallout from the hate strike. The two men had learned of Jones's affidavit and of Mason's effort to use it to bring down McCusker. They responded by convincing the black soldier-miners who had accepted employment at the Anaconda smelter to record their own statements countering Jones's claims. According to Mason, the BMU's officers were also "interested in clearing English and Hanley of charges in the affidavit of Jones." The BMU credited Father English and Bishop Joseph Gilmore with mediating the crisis. In a December 2, 1942, letter offering profuse thanks to the two men, BMU officers wrote that without English's intercession, "the whole matter could have easily turned into a race riot." While Mason and Stewart condemned McCusker for his role in facilitating the removal of the black soldier-miners, the BMU offered high praise to WMC chairman McNutt for the work done by McSherry, McCusker, and Hanley. BMU leaders told McNutt in a letter that the government representatives and the miners "differed very sharply and most emphatically," but they "must in justice sincerely state that these men won the respect and praise of the miners and their officers for their views, sincerity, honesty, and fairness in a matter in which there are many deep, local convictions."[72]

This letter reveals what James Byrne and the rest of the BMU leadership thought had ultimately caused the wildcat: the "mass weight of sentiment, both inside and outside the ranks of the miners," against the presence of black men in the Butte mines. Rank-and-file accounts reinforce and add nuance to this claim. Italian American miner Silvio Sciuchetti distanced himself from his fellow strikers—and by implication, from his own views at that time—by saying that "a whole bunch of white men" went on strike because "people are funny that way." Sciuchetti, the miner who also reported that his wife was afraid to leave the house when the black furloughed soldiers were in Butte, wanted it known that he personally was not "funny that way."[73]

Miner William Bartholomew's version of what transpired in Butte and what it meant was quite different from Sciuchetti's. Bartholomew's narrative hinged on a series of justifications built on an alternative history. He claimed that the BMU had told the Company, "You can take any mine you want and give it to them, but we're not working with them. . . . You can give them the Con, the Stewart, the Leonard, the Belmont, any mine and we'll go to the others." But the ACM would not accept this solution. Bartholomew, careful to avoid depicting the miners as treasonous bigots, added that he and his fellow workers could have got any raise they wanted during the war, but "we [were] too patriotic." Then, shifting gears, he offered the argument made by many of Butte's white miners that the black miners sent in by the government "didn't know anything about mining, they would have killed us," adding, "These buggers didn't want to mine, they didn't want to come in here." For good measure, he claimed the black solder miners "were just scared to death in the mine," because they had never been underground before. According to Bartholomew, the government forced black men to come to Butte, and miners' strike or no, they were "tickled" to leave.[74]

Although these rank-and-file miners told different stories about the wildcat, their elaboration of what happened reveals the awkward fit between local racial discrimination and the national narrative that developed after the war. Sciuchetti's simple account has the ring of honesty: "If you let them in they would turn Butte into a black town. More and more of them would keep coming. So we didn't let them stay." BMU officials attempting to explain themselves to Bishop Gilmore after the black soldier-miners left town echoed this sentiment: the miners regarded black workers in the mines as an issue affecting "the welfare of the entire community."[75]

Given their adamant opposition to the introduction of black soldier-miners from elsewhere, why had Butte's white miners supported Hi Brown's employment underground? The explanation is to be found in the moderate concessions to racial integration made in Butte during the 1930s. Hi Brown and his brothers went to school with white youth, and the miners' familiarity with them laid the groundwork for their being welcomed in the mines. "Ya, we'd work with him. He was just like one of us," concluded William Bartholomew. Perle Watters said that the white miners accepted the Browns because "they were natives."[76]

Watters, and virtually every other miner who later spoke about the Browns, recalled one story in particular that, because of the frequency of its telling, suggests why the Browns were accepted when other blacks were not. Watters's version of the story has him meeting Hi Brown immediately after a shift. Brown had just left a hot raise, where very low-grade ore would leave a man covered with white dust rather than the usual black dust that, in Watters's racist lingo, "[made] you look like a Jigaboo when you came out of the mine." Watters asked Brown how he was doing, and if he and his brother had made any money in the hot raise. Brown replied, "No, we ain't making any money. We're workin' like a couple of niggers."[77] All the men who told this story thought the incident hilarious, particularly because the black man was effectively in whiteface. For Brown, the reference to "workin' like a couple of niggers" may have emphasized that white miners' difficult work and incommensurate pay afforded them common ground with black workers. But for the white men who laughingly retold the anecdote, the comment affirmed their own conviction that white privilege and its attendant benefits, including higher wages and better working conditions, must be preserved. Brown's words not only acknowledged the dangers for white men of being associated with a denigrated blackness—literalized in the black dust that often made white miners "look like a Jigaboo"—but confirmed Brown as a "whitened" black man who could be accommodated within a white workplace without destabilizing its workers' class aspirations and the racism that supported them. From the perspective of white miners, Brown's stand against Company employment practices earlier in the war also aligned him with their sense of independent white masculinity rather than the degenerate black masculinity of their imaginations.

This story indicates the difficulty that national unions faced in changing racial practice through a class-based movement, since lower-class status was, in the minds of many white workers, tied intimately to nonwhite racial identity. Robinson was hopeful that commonalities between white and black workingmen might diminish Butte's segregation.[78] But he also knew that the white miners' decision to support Hi Brown's employment did not mean that the majority supported progressive racial ideals. The Browns represented only a token presence, so the miners could think of them as "one of us." In contrast, the fact that some of the black soldier-miners were members of Mine Mill or the United Mine Workers apparently made no difference.

Byrne and other BMU leaders claimed that they were compelled by the rank and file to take the stance they did. They assured Bishop Gilmore that they understood that "the question of the negroe (sic.) people going to work in the Butte mines cannot be overcome by a motion or resolution, it takes more basic ground work and education of the workers as well as the people of the whole community." Local union leaders claimed that they had not given up on interracialism, but much work had to be done before white men would be willing to work with black men. In Butte, assumptions about racial progressivism had been made without thought given to the particular local history and human geography of the place. Robinson himself conceded that the political education interracial unionism required had not been carried out there. On the day after the start of the wildcat, Allan McNeil, one of the supposed Communists on the Mine Mill staff, saw it as a national problem: "I would also suggest that a good deal of stress be placed on the need for a general CIO educational program for the purpose of familiarizing workers with the problems arising from the war. This is very essential in order to arouse the consciousness of organized labor."[79] Not only was racial progressivism largely absent from Butte's white working class, but even racial liberalism was seldom in evidence.

Hi Brown, his brother, and one or two other "native" black men were eventually welcomed underground, but Butte's white miners continued to believe that keeping African Americans away from the highest-paying and highest-status working-class jobs in town was essential to protecting their white privilege and their "independent" masculinity. While the wildcat focused on the question of race, at the national level the government continued its multipronged approach to the home front labor shortage. The WMC built its next manpower campaign around eight major themes, including the employment of women (even "housewives") in war production, the utilization of retired and disabled workers, and the curtailment of absenteeism and discrimination.[80] Each of these categories had featured prominently in Butte's efforts to solve its labor woes. The next chapter of Montana's wartime copper saga, which was unfolding ninety miles to the north in Black Eagle, hinged mainly on the employment of women.

SEVEN

Black Eagle, 1943: Home Front Servicemen, Women Workers, and the Maintenance of Immigrant Masculinity

Like Butte, Black Eagle faced a significant labor shortage in the fall of 1942. The town had achieved full, steady employment for the first time in a decade during wartime mobilization in the United States, but the nation's formal declaration of war and the expansion of the draft strained local manpower resources beyond their capabilities. In the first half of 1942, the reduction works succeeded in keeping at least 1,500 men on its daily rolls, and April saw a wartime peak of 1,618. From July onward, however, those numbers dropped to below 1,500. In 1943, after a brief resurgence, the workforce again fell below that level. With the growing demand for copper, zinc, and the smelter's other products, which were essential to virtually every facet of the Allied war machine, the dearth of workers at Black Eagle had become critical by early spring 1943.[1]

The government did not try to send black soldiers to work in Black Eagle, seemingly as a direct consequence of the hate strike by Butte's white ethnic miners. Instead, federal authorities decided in early 1943 to push local white women as the primary solution to the Black Eagle labor problem. Unlike the employment of black soldiers in the Butte mines, the potential hiring of women at the Black Eagle plant did not challenge smeltermen's claims to whiteness. On the contrary, by taking positions that could have been filled by workers of color, particularly locally available Indian workers, white women could help solidify the whiteness of Black Eagle's immigrant community. However, women working in previously all-male production jobs would directly challenge the smelter workers' masculine status, which was already under siege because they were not fulfilling the military obligations that defined ideal masculinity in wartime. This was a particularly acute issue in the Black Eagle–Great Falls area, because in November 1942 a large number of soldiers and airmen began arriving at the Great Falls Army Air

Base and at Gore Field, another local military installation, making the comparison of smeltermen's masculinity with manhood in the armed forces much more tangible. The masculine identity of first- and second-generation immigrant men, moreover, was deeply tied to male dominance in the labor force. As Marie (Palagi) Godlewski put it, "Women stayed in the home and didn't get jobs outside the home. Man was wage earner." Likewise, Olanda Vangelisti remembered her husband telling her that women were meant "to be home and take care of the house."[2] Thus, the government's desire to employ women at the smelter could have been as explosive as its effort to employ black soldiers in Butte's mines.

Yet beginning in the spring of 1943, women did enter production jobs there. This chapter explains why the plan to employ women in Black Eagle was successful even though it faced considerable obstacles—and even though a similar initiative in Butte had been utterly disregarded in the summer and fall of 1942, and in Anaconda it was considered such an anathema by smeltermen that it would be blocked for another year. I argue that smeltermen in Black Eagle, while carefully avoiding critiques of military service on the front lines, which exemplified the wartime masculine ideal, responded to the presence of home front servicemen with a local narrative about the danger and importance of smelter work that was well received by the community. Smeltermen were also reassured of their masculine status by the difference between national and local media presentations of the threat posed by women's wartime employment, as local sensibilities promoted a conservative gender order. Equally or even more important, smeltermen ensured that only women from outside Black Eagle were hired for production jobs and that within the smelter they were segregated from men. A specific local politics grounded in community history facilitated both smeltermen's acceptance of women workers and their argument that the masculine character of their home front labor compared favorably with that of home front servicemen. These strategies did not go uncontested, but they did defuse the threats posed by women at the plant and soldiers and airmen in the vicinity, and allowed Black Eagle to appear—and perhaps even to be—more accommodating to wartime change than Butte or Anaconda.

Hometown Men and Home Front Servicemen

In Great Falls and Black Eagle, as in most parts of the United States, recruiting offices initially served as the primary connection between the townspeople and the military. A few Black Eagle men volunteered for, or were drafted into, the armed forces before the official US entry into the war. The town was too small to have its own office, but recruiting offices in Great Falls noted an upsurge in enlistments in the days immediately after the Japanese bombing of Pearl Harbor. Expectations that men would demonstrate their masculinity through military service quickly mounted, and those who did enlist found themselves praised. Although government officials dismissed the rumor that the Japanese might target Montana's copper towns, reports from the front lines indicated growing US losses, so men faced increasing pressure to prove their masculine worth by entering the military. After the initial surge, however, few at the smelter did so voluntarily.[3]

Adding to this problem for the men employed in war industries, the Black Eagle plant, like the Butte mines, received an influx of men hoping to avoid the draft. Smeltermen like Lyle Pellett, one of the few who volunteered for the military after the Selective Service granted deferments to Black Eagle workers, were well aware that "there was many, many, many people—shoe salesmen, clerks, and one thing or another—that come out there to that smelter to get the blanket [deferment]." As soldiering came to represent what scholars call "hegemonic masculinity" and some men used the smelter to avoid the draft, smeltermen's claim to masculine status was called into question.[4]

The arrival of large numbers of military men at Great Falls in the fall of 1942 intensified the stresses for local civilian home front men. As a local USO publication remarked, "The city was virtually flooded with khaki." Great Falls even turned its Civic Center into a massive dorm until the United States Army constructed housing on base. Civilians generally held men in uniform in high esteem. Towns near military installations and towns that had military personnel passing through their rail stations eagerly provided hospitality. But a number of factors complicated the relationship between civilians and members of the armed forces, including varied perceptions of different types of duty, especially frontline versus home front. Many of the military personnel serving near Black Eagle were in the Seventh Ferrying Group, which moved aircraft and supplies to Alaska as part of the Lend-Lease program supporting the Soviet Union. Local newspapers covered the activities at the air bases closely. While articles during the first year of the war regularly suggested the dangers and difficulties facing men overseas, those about the nearby air bases revealed the mundane character of home front military duty. A headline in the *Great Falls Tribune* announced, "Air Corps Officers Have Many Ground Duties," and the accompanying story added that "many officers . . . seldom see the inside of a plane because their duties keep them on the ground." Even the military was forced to admit that its stateside duty lacked the risk integral to wartime claims to masculine status.[5]

7.1 Black Eagle smeltermen and other home front men did not
necessarily believe that military men serving on the home front,
such as this Army Air Corps officer, deserved more masculine
status than they did as "soldiers of production." Photograph
by Arthur Siegel, *Wayne County Airport, a United States Army Air
Corps Air Ferry Command Base Sixteen Miles from Detroit,
Michigan: Captain Harry Algernon Baker*, 1942; Library of
Congress, Prints & Photographs Division, FSA-OWI Collection,
LC-USW3-008731-C DLC.

Nonetheless, men in uniform on the home front received greater pres-
tige, a fact that caused tension between male civilians and servicemen
(fig. 7.1). The practice of the Great Falls Victory Belles, a five-hundred-strong
organization of area women who held weekly dances for military men, amplified one of the principal worries of civilian men: they could not compete
for the local women's affections. Friction between home front servicemen
and workers boiled over at the Oasis Club in Black Eagle. Just before midnight on December 25, 1942, two members of the military police (MPs)
were making their normal rounds of bars frequented by men from the base.
When Corporal Joe Campbell and Private John MacMillan entered the Oa-

sis Club, "all present joined in declaring only civilians were in the establishment." This did not stop the MPs from coming into the bar to confront Ray Gardner, a civilian from Great Falls, "concerning his wearing of an Army flight jacket." Other customers resented the military men's effort to exert their power over a civilian space. In the ensuing altercation, the MPs shot four people. Two men sustained minor gunshot injuries, while two women, one an eighteen-year-old and the other a waitress whose husband was from a well-known Italian family, suffered serious wounds. In retaliation, a group of local men severely beat the two MPs.[6]

Decades later, this story still circulated in Black Eagle and Great Falls. Memory blurred the details about how many locals were shot and even the fact that two of the victims were women. Old-timers remembered clearly that the fight involved a military jacket, suggesting that the event was discussed as a highly localized competition over the symbols of wartime masculinity. Locally, the meaning of military uniforms had changed since World War I, when the United States Navy had suggested that servicemen and miners faced equivalent dangers and emphasized that unlike miners, men who served in uniform would find reliable work, guaranteed pay, and free medical care. In World War II, on the other hand, the armed forces placed the uniform at the center of its campaign to champion military masculinity over its civilian counterpart. A navy advertisement that ran in Montana papers on November 1, 1942, informed civilian men that servicemen were not just doing their duty, but "are fighting for *you*. If you are not yet in uniform, your place is with them NOW!" Besides demonstrating their honor by protecting their own family and home, the navy insisted, military service gave men "something else, too—something you've never known before—something you can realize only when you step out in your own Navy uniform." What was it that a uniform provided? Simply put, a "grand feeling—a proud feeling." For those still unsure about what a uniform would do for them, the navy offered to send them a free book whose title said it all: *Men Make the Navy . . . the Navy Makes Men.*[7]

The MPs involved in the Oasis shooting felt that Gardner was not entitled to the trappings of military manhood. His purchasing and wearing a uniform put into high relief the thin veneer separating civilian and military masculinity. Uniforms offered the most visible way for servicemen to set themselves apart. Without uniforms they appeared to be ordinary men, perhaps even slackers. Gardner's unwillingness to take off the jacket at the MPs' command challenged the supremacy of military masculinity. Tellingly, the concern about uniforms legitimating masculinity for men who did not deserve that status also marked relations among home front men. Seven months after the Oasis shooting, Montana's copper men vetoed a government official's request to dress as a miner when he presented the case for miners and smeltermen deserving a larger meat ration.[8]

For civilians like Gardner, increasing familiarity with the mundane reality of the home front military experience undermined the notion that stateside servicemen deserved special status. Why should a civilian man who did difficult work in a critical national defense industry not be allowed to wear whatever jacket he liked? Since government propaganda called war workers "soldiers of production," why should they not be treated as equal to other home front servicemen both by the authorities and by local women?

Montana's copper men could certainly claim that their labor was as hazardous as military service at home (fig. 7.2). In 1943, the first year in which the Great Falls Army Air Base was fully operational, 109 smelter employees were injured severely enough to be sent home or to the hospital. National statistics were even more dramatic. According to the consulting physician for the National Association of Manufacturers, during the first year of the war "42,000 war plant workers . . . lost their lives in accidents . . . a casualty rate immensely greater than that of the US armed forces." As more Americans entered combat, however, daily newspaper reports highlighted their casualties, making it more difficult for the work of Montana's copper men to measure up to military service. Stories about the air base also began to paint a more hazardous picture of local military life, especially after the addition of bomber units training for combat overseas. Casualty figures for local men in uniform reported by local newspapers testified to the growing differential between the risks faced by soldiers of production and by soldiers on the front lines.[9]

Still, civilian men in Black Eagle could argue that their masculinity was affirmed by the army and the navy's decision to award them an "E" Production Award for "meritorious service on the home front," and by the War Department's furlough program, which recalled soldiers from training or other home front military duties to take up industrial work. The inversion of the wartime masculine hierarchy represented by furloughs was strikingly on display in a fall 1942 *Time* article that covered the beginning of the program. The magazine reported that mining companies rejected some military men who volunteered for furloughs because the companies did not believe they had the physical capability to mine. In a March 1943 modification of the furlough process, the government allowed companies in a few vital industries to request the return from military service of "key men" over thirty-eight years of age. Manpower officials hoped that this policy might leave men best suited for combat in uniform while filling critical labor shortages

7.2 As this photograph indicates, Black Eagle's smeltermen had good reason to believe that their labor was as dangerous and manly as that of military men serving on the home front. Photograph by Robert I. Nesmith, *Steve Antonich Burning Out Hole in Casting Oven with Oxygen Torch*, 1943; Montana Historical Society Research Center Photograph Archives, Helena.

with experienced workers. Black Eagle received five furloughed men by April 1943 and fourteen by November. Their removal from uniform provided perhaps some ammunition for home front men to claim masculine equivalency to home front servicemen, but the age specification negated the effectiveness of such an argument.[10]

Manpower officials were aware that the furlough program was unlikely to solve the labor shortage in places like Black Eagle. Consequently, in early 1943 the War Production Board began demanding a serious effort to employ women in the western copper industry, and the ACM passed this message on to all its Montana managers. WPB copper officials, following War Manpower Commission (WMC) estimates, told the Company that of the 6 million workers needed nationally for war production, only 3 million could come from men employed in nonessential industries. "The balance or 3,000,000 must be women," wrote Frank Ayer, the WPB's Copper Division Chief.[11]

Ayer understood the prevailing gender ideology in Montana's copper communities and the likelihood of resistance to women's entry into formerly all-male workplaces. He told the ACM, "We realize that, in general, it is the opinion that women do not fit into mining operations. It is, however, known that this is not correct and we suggest that you analyze all of your surface jobs to see where women can be substituted for men." Ayer intuited that plant managers, prodded by their workers, could use this analysis to delay the introduction of women, which is exactly what the Anaconda smelter did. Attempting to prevent repeated procrastination, he urged the Company to schedule training programs for women through regional vocational training offices, and concluded by reminding the ACM that women were already employed in the industry elsewhere in the West: "One large copper company has found that many surface jobs can be filled by women. At present they have working or training about 120 women for the following classes of work: mill operators, mill sampler[s], screen scratchers, mill laborers, electricians' helpers, drill press operators, pipe fitter helpers, boiler maker helpers, power house oilers, power house laborers, bolt threading machine operators, janitors, timekeepers, and clerical workers."[12] In 1942, similar lists of, by implication, less manly jobs had sparked heated debates in Butte, but there is no evidence of this sort of controversy in Black Eagle.

Black Eagle men were more inclined to cooperate with ACM and government requests for a number of reasons. Anger at the government on the part of all Montana copper men had dissipated noticeably. In January 1943, the National War Labor Board's (NWLB's) Nonferrous Metals Commission finally authorized a pay increase of a dollar a day for all ACM daily wage workers. The government had also moved quickly to correct a misperception that some believed had hindered men's willingness to support their wives' desire to do war work. Regional WMC director John McCusker told reporters that men "will not be reclassified under Selective Service if their wives go to work in an essential industry." He emphasized that "a marital relationship is the determining factor in a man's draft status," not the "financial relationship" between him and his wife. Black Eagle men were also more receptive than Butte's miners and Anaconda's smeltermen to the government's efforts to define sacrifice for the good of the state as the cornerstone of wartime patriotism. As the Black Eagle local of the International Union of Mine, Mill, and Smelter Workers (Mine Mill) told the NWLB, "We accept the mandate of the nations war time powers without question." It also reported that it had "approved Internationals program of no stoppage of production until victory is achieved." As for its greater willingness to work with the ACM, the local's telegram argued, "Our contractual relations and local settlements of all grievances is outstanding in the annals of organized labor."[13] There was, however, a sizable distance between agreeing with a general principle and acting on it in a concrete case such as the employment of women in previously male-only jobs. Just as was the case with Butte and the question of changing racial norms, persuading Black Eagle's home front men—and Americans more generally—to take this next step and see the good of the state as more important than the interest of the individual was one of the central goals of wartime propaganda.

National Popular Culture: *Punch In, Susie!*

Like other Americans on the home front, Black Eagle's residents found that little on movie screens or the printed page did not pertain, directly or indirectly, to expectations about their wartime behavior. In 1943 an especially large percentage of this propaganda focused on women's place in American society and the home front gender order more broadly. Lary May has argued that in order to alter attitudes and behavior, Hollywood propagated what he calls "conversion narratives" throughout the war. An important subset of these narratives showed men renouncing independent masculinity for a collective sacrificial masculinity that was more responsive to the government's desire to reshape the social order.[14]

One of the best examples of this subset is William Wellman's 1943 film *The Ox-Bow Incident*, which played in Montana's copper towns when the debate over gender in Black Eagle was keenest. The first critical scene occurs when news arrives in a small western town that cattle rustlers have murdered a popular local cowboy, Larry Kinkaid. Men of the town assemble to form a posse, even though the sheriff is absent. A storekeeper named Arthur Davies implores the men to "act in a reasoned and legitimate manner, not like a lawless mob." One member of the posse calls Davies, a local judge also promoting restraint, and any other man afraid to do his manly duty a "whining old woman." More masculine discourse and clouded facts overwhelm the argument to wait for local authorities and follow their lead. Eventually, the vigilantes come across what are presumed to be the stolen cattle and three exhausted homesteaders by their campfire in Ox-Bow Valley. The homesteaders are immediately put on trial, and when a few men from the posse attempt to defend the accused they are silenced by the mob and by Ma Grier, a boardinghouse proprietor who speaks of doing one's duty and is reputed to be stronger than any man in town. When another local questions the proceedings, he gets a gun butt in the face from his father for being a sissy and refusing to take part in the lynching. Moments later the three men are hung. On the way back to town, the posse meets the sheriff. The shocked lawman explains that he had been with Kinkaid, who was only wounded and was being treated by a doctor. The real rustlers have been arrested. The sheriff condemns the posse for its action: "God better have mercy on ya. You won't get any from me."[15]

Ox-Bow is both a powerful indictment of vigilante lawlessness and a wartime conversion narrative that serves as a clarion call to subjugate individual passions to the wisdom of the state. In Montana's copper communities, the film reverberated with the ideological split over race relations within Mine Mill as exemplified by the lynching of Frank Little a quarter of a century earlier and recently reignited by the wildcat strike against government-sent black soldier-miners in Butte. Nationally, *Ox-Bow* received significant notice for addressing violence against African Americans. In its February 6, 1943, issue, the national Catholic weekly magazine *America* said that "the film drove home the brutality, the senselessness and the social evil of lynching." But *The Ox-Bow Incident* spoke equally strongly—and quite consciously—to wartime gender relations. Posters described it as "the tough, true, terrifying story of America's most ruthless manhunt . . . urged on by a woman's mocking laugh!" In the novel by Walter Van Tilburg Clark on which the film was based, mocking laughter comes from a number of female characters, and numerous scenes involve women who are willing and able to perform difficult tasks that customarily fell within the masculine domain. The film condenses these multiple female voices into a single character, Ma Grier. That she emerges in the end as unsympathetic does not dampen the strength of her gender transgressions. According to film historian Thomas Doherty, female leads in some wartime films "forcefully declare new notions of a woman's work, place, and nature." Ma Grier fits this description, and as such she was part of the "concerted effort to recruit and inspire women and to reform and reeducate men concerning heretofore hidden female proficiencies."[16]

So Proudly We Hail, which played at the same time as *Ox-Bow* and made new gender norms more acceptable by presenting them in terms of older ideals, is a good example of another propaganda strategy used widely during 1943. Promotional material for the film talked about the woman beside the man behind the gun, while stressing women's ability to be "cold killers" when in combat. Another ad had one of the film's stars asserting, "I'm going to kill every Jap I get my hands on." A third asked, "Where is the girl who lived next door?" and concluded, "This is the great romance of our girls at the fighting front . . . laughing, loving, fighting side by side with their men!" The Fox newsreel that played with *The Ox-Bow Incident*, by portraying women as sexual objects in the person of Betty Grable, showed yet another mode of depicting women's place in wartime society. *Movietone News* reported Grable's trip to Grauman's Chinese Theatre, accompanied by a soldier, a sailor, and a marine, to put her handprint in wet cement. But Grable, whose pinup photo was already wildly popular, goes a little further. As the men help lower one of her famous legs into the cement, the narrator comments gleefully, "Betty Grable's shapeliness—recorded for posterity."[17] But this newsreel was atypical. More often, newsreels mixed conventional images of women with others that showed the wartime expansion of women's activities, making them—especially in combination with films like *The Ox-Bow Incident*—a powerful part of the overall conversion message sponsored by Hollywood.

Throughout 1943, print media echoed the multiple narratives about wartime gender relations found in film. Virtually every major national magazine ran articles on the question of women entering the workplace. Their blunt titles echoed the government's recruitment pitch. *Women's Home Companion* published "Wake Up and Work" by Paul McNutt, head of the WMC, and just a month later challenged readers with "How Are You Helping?" Dorothy Parker, writing in *Reader's Digest*, asked, "Are We Women or Are We Mice?" *Newsweek* noted, "More Women Must Go to Work as 3,200,000 New Jobs Beckon." *Parents' Magazine* proclaimed, "The War Needs Women." Likewise, commercial book publishers offered *Wanted: Women in War Industry*; *Your Career in Defense*; *Hit the Rivet, Sister*; and *Punch In, Susie!* Government propagandists created and distributed a plethora of pamphlets and posters with images that urged women to enter the workforce. Similarly, newspapers across the country reported on the need for more women workers, and their daily sports sections and comics sections—like their astonishingly popular cousin, comic books—promoted bolder models of womanhood.[18]

Advertisers' use of visual and written references to women entering war-time work also peaked in 1943. Woodbury facial soap and DuBarry cosmetics, for example, linked their beauty products to women's new place in industry. An ad for a hand cream read, "Barbara is romantically lovely with her . . . white, flowerlike skin—but she's also *today's* American Girl, energetically at work six days a week in a big war plant." Messages blending feminine beauty with women's successes in war work tied conventional stereotypes to compelling new models of womanhood, mirroring similar trends in movie programs. In many instances, when articles in women's magazines mentioned women's work in industry, they coupled the commentary with a reminder that employment did not diminish women's feminine sensibility. "You'll like this girl," a *McCall's* article remarked. "She does a man's work in the ground crew, servicing airplanes, but she hasn't lost any of her feminine sweetness and charm."[19] The differences in the messages contained in these examples matter. The *McCall's* article and the hand-cream advertisement, along with a plethora of similar articles and advertising copy, do not contain the same unambiguous message as, for example, an ad which proposed that lipstick "symbolizes the reasons why we are fighting . . . the precious right of women to be feminine and lovely." Rather, they remind us of the potentially destabilizing elements contained within wartime popular culture. Women might have interpreted the *McCall's* article and the hand-cream ad as reassuring, but home front men, anxious about social changes that seemed out of their control, could have seen another message in these texts: women were succeeding at and enjoying men's work.

Norman Rockwell immortalized the home front's most famous icon in an image that reinforced women's aptitude for "men's work" (fig. 7.3). Broad-shouldered, strong-armed, competent Rosie the Riveter graced the May 29, 1943, cover of the *Saturday Evening Post*. Taking a quick lunch break, she sits in her overalls with her heavy rivet gun on her lap as her feet, clad in men's loafers, rest on a copy of *Mein Kampf*. As Leila Rupp writes, "That the ideal woman in 1943 worked at all was a change. But that she worked in a factory, in a job previously defined as 'masculine,' was unprecedented." That she was white should, however, also give us pause. Black women had long been associated with physically laborious jobs, and many sought employment in war plants and shipyards. Indeed, they are visible in contemporaneous photographs taken by government employees. Yet black women were absent from the popular depictions of this icon of female strength. Rockwell

7.3 J. Howard Miller's 1943 "We Can Do It!" is arguably the most famous World War II poster and, along with Norman Rockwell's 1943 *Saturday Evening Post* cover featuring Rosie the Riveter, the most influential image of the strength and competence of home front women workers. "We Can Do It!," N. D. Westinghouse War Production Co-Ordinating Committee.

did much to naturalize women in the workplace, but he continued to place the white family at the center of the national project.[20]

That Rosie the Riveter competed with Betty Grable's pinup for iconic primacy throughout the war could be taken to mean that Rosie represented a temporary adjustment, not a lasting change, in the feminine ideal. Yet while the pinup represented men's "dream girl," the down-to-earth Rosie was more like the women they knew.[21] In this light, belittling women's abilities, framing recruitment around patriotism instead of bread-and-butter issues, aiming labor appeals at middle-class women rather than working-class women who were already in the labor force, and suggesting to women that postwar nirvana would find them in the home appear to be as much a recipe for persuading home front men to allow women into men's domain as they do a campaign aimed at recruiting female laborers.

The most successful theme of the campaign to place women workers in previously male-only workplaces, the ubiquitous tag line "it's only temporary" or "only for the duration," spoke directly to the fears of home front men. For men, the question was whether women would want to leave these high-paying, status-conferring jobs in order to return to unpaid, and often unrecognized and unappreciated, household labor. Office of War Information (OWI) officials were aware of these fears. Male workers had good reason to believe that employers might try to use female workers to reduce wages and dilute skills in the postwar period, when job opportunities would be more limited. After resisting women's entry into their factories, managers consistently praised female employees. As General Motors president Charles E. Wilson saw it, women were "more enthusiastic" and showed "much better spirit" than men. Others noted women's loyalty, willingness to follow the rules, dedication, and care of the company's equipment.[22] Yet few women were as "docile" as the bosses declared them to be; working-class women often brought labor militancy and union loyalties into the war plants.

Nonetheless, female employees were viewed in a more favorable light than the often combative, unionized labor force that had developed in male-dominated mass-production industries during the late 1930s. A production expert employed by shipbuilding corporations thought it wise to continue employing a small number of women after the war, "mainly as an incentive for greater efficiency and accomplishment for males"; a limited number of women "could possibly serve to good advantage in establishing the required tempo of production." Such sentiments, along with the media portrayal of women succeeding in previously male-only work, affected men's perspective on the severity of the threat posed by women workers. When the OWI made a formal assessment, "Opinion about the Wartime Employment of Women," workers, union officials, and editors of labor newspapers told them that home front men were "scared stiff at the danger of widespread unemployment after the war," and that they regarded women's employment as a direct threat to their future job security.[23]

National propaganda, in short, did not assuage the fears of home front men, including Black Eagle's smeltermen. But such fears aside, the national propaganda campaigns meant to increase the number of women in war industries by, in part, simultaneously cajoling and browbeating home front men into accepting women in their previously all-male work spaces largely succeeded. Almost 5 million women entered the labor force between 1941 and 1944, when 37 percent of adult females in the United States worked for wages. Women comprised most of the new hires in defense plants, including shipyards, munitions manufacturing, and aircraft assembly, and were performing tasks previously assigned to men in lumber and steel mills. As Frank Ayer observed, women were also working at the surface for mining companies and in ore smelting and refining.[24]

Local Popular Culture: The *Commando* Kitchen

In the working-class copper communities of Montana, local popular culture provided a fertile space in which to negotiate and contest changes that some deemed unacceptable, including transformations in the gender segregation of work. Even the media controlled by local elites, such as Great Falls' two major newspapers, did little to support expanding opportunities for women. More often, they continued to emphasize housewives' participation in campaigns to conserve and recycle materials that had military uses. Women served as the principal foot soldiers in war bond drives. Other activities led by women, such as a civil defense program that ran in February 1942 and the massive Red Cross volunteer initiative the next month, reinforced the domestic character of their wartime responsibilities even while taking place within the public sphere.[25]

In Black Eagle, the media most closely affiliated with its working class during the war provided a slightly less constricted picture of women's wartime work. Because of its links to the management-labor bloc that had long controlled social politics in the three copper towns, the *Copper Commando*, a bimonthly paper jointly published by labor and management in Butte, Anaconda, and Black Eagle, offers an unparalleled window into how such local cultural vessels helped workingmen mediate rapidly evolving gender norms. In the first issue, the *Commando*'s treatment of women's place in society redirected the language of change, which appeared to be more threatening in some national media, so as to comfort masculine sensibilities. In a section titled "The Gals Do Their Bit, Too," the paper presented, not women war workers, but three glamorous actresses, noting that "Hollywood turns out not only good movie actresses but good soldierettes too." According to Montana's own Jean Parker, these women's job was to keep "the morale of the boys high." In this premiere issue, the only nod to women's entry into arenas from which they had previously been barred was a photograph of three female soldiers, suggesting that women were more appropriate for noncombat jobs in the military than for copper work. Lest the image imply an endorsement of women filling previously all-male jobs, the caption—"Three WAAC [Women's Army Auxiliary Corps] beauties in their new uniforms"—defused the threat by focusing not on their abilities but on their appearance.[26]

The *Commando*'s initial presentation of local civilian women's responsibilities was equally reassuring to area men concerned about the shifting gender order. In an article titled "Thoughts for Food—Mrs. Smith and Mrs. Johnson Talk over a Common Problem: What to Put in the Lunch Bucket?," two women exchange ideas on nutrition. Mrs. Johnson exclaims, "But my John won't eat vegetables. He wants meat." "That's just it," replies Mrs. Smith. "Neither will Bill and the boys. But Mrs. Griffith says we can put them in and teach them to like them. They need the energy and the right food so that the extra hours and the extra effort they're putting out won't be so hard on them. She told us some good diets that won't be so fattening and yet keep all the energy in them too." In addition to such reinforcement of hegemonic familial gender roles, "Thoughts for Food" appealed to a specific local social politics. Comments about men and meat foreshadowed the battle for more beef that became part of Butte miners' efforts to have the government acknowledge copper men's superior masculinity in relation to other home front men. But this article would also have found a keen audience in Black Eagle, because food was such a big part of local identity. Cooking by the town's women, which included both ethnic Italian and Croatian dishes and the American recipes that the second generation had added to their repertoire, enjoyed a reputation for excellence across the region, and women took pride in their culinary skills.[27] Conducted alongside smeltermen's competitions at community picnics, cooking contests reinforced the gender divide that had long characterized Black Eagle.

In September 1942, six months before women began to be employed in production jobs at the smelter, the *Commando* broached the matter of local women's war work. The article concentrated on women working in the

7.4 The *Copper Commando* titled this 1942 photo of the women who worked clerical jobs at the Black Eagle smelter "Office girls in the garden." Women from Black Eagle were not hired for these jobs. Photograph by Robert Nesmith, *Office Girls in the Garden*, Montana Historical Society Research Center Photograph Archives, Helena.

Black Eagle smelter office, which fit customary gender stereotypes, and did not mention the Butte or Anaconda facilities. Significantly, it called these employees "the Great Falls Girls" (fig. 7.4). If a Black Eagle smelterman saw the presence of women at the plant as transgressive of established customs, he could take comfort that they were not from his own community.[28] This reassuring fact did not entirely erase the specter of women's entry into formerly all-male workplaces, however. The article concluded by referring to women employed in factories across the United States and to the manpower problem in the copper industry.

Just one month later, as the government's first major female labor recruitment campaign was being launched, the October 23, 1942, issue of the *Commando* indicated that the possibility of women entering the wartime industrial workforce had become more real to men in Montana's copper communities. In a cartoon section called "Copper Shorts," the editors included a variety of information about the nonferrous industry. Besides finding out that "the new war nickel has no nickel in it," readers learned from the caricatured lips of a donkey-riding placer miner that women were now working in the copper mines of Arizona—the same data the WPB would cite 120 days later, when it urged the ACM to open its copper facilities to female employees. For Montana's copper men, there was little to laugh at in the image of this old-timer ogling a phalanx of well-proportioned, attractive women miners or in his lascivious comment, "Blast me for an ol' desert rat—if I wasn't born fifty years too soon."[29]

By the end of 1942, as the interlocking concerns of women's place in society and labor shortages on the home front reached a point of crisis, the *Commando* continued to present women as family caretakers. Published letters to the editor from women did not push for fuller coverage of women in the war production effort, but instead called for a family page or "a place where recipes and household hints can be exchanged." In apparent contrast, the cover of the first December issue featured a professional-looking woman in uniform. The editors explained, "The *Copper Commando* felt it was high time we had a picture of a good-looking girl on the front cover and you can imagine how delighted we were to find that Miss Virginia Hall of Fort Shaw, Montana, filled all the requirements for an attractive cover."[30] Framed in this way, the image insinuated men's acceptance of local women in uniform while minimizing any threat posed by women in nontraditional positions—although Hall's serious countenance countered the *Commando*'s captioning.

Astonishingly, the Great Falls papers did not report on the most obvious local example of women's expanding role in the military: the arrival of Women's Auxiliary Ferrying Services (WAFS) pilots at the Great Falls Air Base. Only the air base newsletter, *Tail Winds*, covered the story. The WAFS, which merged with the Women's Flying Training Detachment in 1943 to create the Women's Airforce Service Pilots (WASPs), were commanded by Nancy Harkness Love, one of the nation's best-known female military officers. Love earned her fame by demonstrating remarkable flying skills. In December 1942, shortly after Hall had appeared on the *Commando* cover, Love visited Great Falls to check on her troops. Her stopover coincided with a mission by six WAFS pilots, including "Kitty" Rawls Thompson, who had been a world-class swimmer. At that same moment, and notably just before the fight between home front soldiers and civilians at the Oasis Club, female civilian employees of the Seventh Ferrying Group unveiled their uniforms. According to the newsletter, the women had voted to wear "a blouse with a military cut, matching skirt, and a snappy flight cap." If they hoped that the new ensemble would foster greater professionalism and respect from their male counterparts at the base, they were in for a disappointment. The newsletter repeatedly referred to the women as "gals," joked that men envied the women's "snazzy" new uniforms, and commented that "everyone agreed that the girls 'looked right nice.'"[31] Taken together, the *Commando* pieces, the air base newsletter, and Great Falls newspapers indicate that as the first year of US involvement in the war drew to a close, local popular culture continued to put forward a discourse meant to alleviate the strain of changes in the national gender order.

Those changes intensified over the next year. At the beginning of 1943, the *Commando* finally covered women's industrial work in some depth. "The Gals Got Busy," a full-page spread showing a variety of women doing war production work, conveyed the multiple and contradictory nature of narratives about women's wartime work during the middle phase of the war. The paper asked its readers, "A MAN's war?," and responded, "Not so you'd notice it! The gals got into the fracas too, lots of them. Like the lady at the left shown polishing a cannon component casing." This picture showed an older woman wearing male work clothes, unglamorous but obviously competent. But the next two images were less professional. The first showed an attractive young woman in work clothes "chatting with an Army officer"; the caption labeled her an "Ordnance eyeful." Not only did this image reinforce the importance of feminine attractiveness to men, but, not incidentally, it also communicated the notion that military men on the home front had a higher status with women than did male production workers. The next showed two women in semiformal dresses mugging for the camera in a scrap yard; the *Commando* wryly described them as "scrap-conscious sweeties." Only then came photos of three more women who were unadorned and focused on their work. The montage ended by showing a woman cooking for a soldier, which was captioned, "American homes were opened up to fighting men hungry for a home-cooked meal."[32] Over the course of the war, this type of image, which both celebrated female domesticity and elevated "fighting men" to the pinnacle of masculinity, fought for dominance in local popular culture with images of home front male production workers. And, like virtually every photograph in the four-year run of the *Commando*, it naturalized these valued wartime figures as white.

During the next six months, when the national media were celebrating women's participation in production for the "Arsenal of Democracy" and when women were for the first time joining the Black Eagle smelter workforce, the pages of the *Commando* depicted local women as the mothers and wives of soldiers and male war workers rather than as workers themselves. The "*Commando* Kitchen," a special section of the paper introduced in 1943, showed cross-class masculine agreement on the importance of food by picturing wives of managers and wives of laborers working together to feed their husbands. The fact that "Mary became so interested in Dorothy's recipe for using leftovers that she forgot to eat" is not seen as troubling, instead praising feminine self-sacrifice. At the same time, area mothers mobilized the maternal ideal to critique home front masculinity as they exhorted their men to maximize copper output. The *Commando's* extensive Mother's Day coverage depicted Mrs. Ouellette onstage at Butte's Eagles' Lodge, representing all the mothers of Montana's copper communities. She was flanked by three sergeants, each in full uniform and standing at parade rest, while she sat in a stage-prop living room near the hearth and surrounded by pictures of her four children. Mrs. Oullette intoned, "I could feel the hearts break in that group of women there before me. Sitting there on the stage I just looked out on them and knew what it meant to them not to have their children with them and not know where they are, or what they need. There's one thing that we all know and that is that the boys in service need copper. That's one need that is well known. We must give it to them. We can't let them down."[33]

One woman after another at the Eagles' Lodge event presented her impressive maternal credentials and pleaded with home front men to do more. Mrs. Elizabeth Hovan, "a widow, and the mother of three sons," elaborated: "This is the first time we haven't been together on Mother's Day. Last year my son took part in this very program. . . . Tell the men they should hurry up and do all the work they can. It's up to them to bring our boys back again." The next to speak, Mrs. Naomi Cline, was described as "the mother of four children and the stepmother of three boys in service whom she raised from childhood." If any men in the audience or reading the *Copper Commando* wondered about their place relative to soldiers, Cline reminded them of the answer: "Copper must be kept rolling. If men don't want to work on the production line, they should go to the Front. Then they would know the need for copper. I know because of the letters from the boys." Cline implied that women on the home front and "boys" on the front lines questioned workers' masculinity. Still, Ouellette, Hovan, and Cline gave as much as they took. Their enactment of tightly circumscribed femininity reinforced local notions of women's proper place. Unlike Butte miner Lewis Remark's mother, who went to Tacoma, Washington, to build ships after her son was taken prisoner in the Philippines, none of these mothers suggested that women should be doing production work.

These women embodied the vision of femininity and maternity espoused by an especially powerful institution locally: the Roman Catholic Church. As Marie "Cookie" Godlewski commented, "Most of Black Eagle's life centered around the church," which served as a spiritual, social, and educational center for adults and children. The church used the pulpit and, like the ACM's Victory Labor-Management Committee's *Copper Commando*, it also used its own local publication, the *Montana Catholic Register*, to contest the new image of women that pervaded government propaganda and popular culture. While the Catholic Church waged a warlong crusade against women's entering the workplace, a development it deemed a major threat to the sanctity of the family and, implicitly, to the rule of the father, during the period in question the weekly *Register* constantly reminded women of the church's expectations. In November 1942, for instance, the newspaper carried a story commending Catholic women for "rais[ing] your voice against the destroyers of the Christian family" and concluding, "Today the mother who has boys to give to the Stars and Stripes is giving the biggest thing." In concert with the Mother's Day rituals of Black Eagle and Great Falls, the Catholic Church valorized motherhood and used it symbolically to direct and limit women's aspirations.[34]

Street parades in the copper communities before, during, and after World War II provided yet another local reinforcement of the differences between men's and women's worlds. Miners' Union Day, held every June thirteenth and reported on in the *Commando* immediately following its 1943 Mother's Day edition, saw costumed female drum corps and marching bands parading down Main Street in Butte. After them came the main attraction: thousands of miners marching in their Sunday best and being recognized as the town's royalty by the cheering women and children thronging the parade route.[35] Similar events occurred in Black Eagle and Anaconda, reinforcing the notion that these men defined the copper towns' identity. In contrast to the story of the World War II home front told in textbooks, the women of these towns appeared as supporting actors in a drama starring home front men.

In July 1943, the *Commando* finally felt compelled to cover women who were performing copper-production jobs once restricted to men. The cover showed a woman assembling ammunition. Inside, a headline asked, "Who Says It's a Man's War?" But rather than reporting women's arrival at the Black Eagle smelter, the article exemplified the local media's support of the copper community ideology: "Every now and then you have to admit that some of the so-called weaker sex are getting right in there and pitching in and doing a man's job. At Great Falls, gals are relieving the messenger boys in the general office." Reporting on women relieving "boys" occupied safe terrain, while covering women's incursion into the pinnacle of Black Eagle masculine labor—smelter work—did not. Indeed, the latter story was never covered in the *Commando*. Instead, as women were proving they could handle smelter jobs previously done only by men, the paper devoted an entire issue to "Joe Copper," the collective embodiment of all the men working selflessly in Montana's copper industry.[36] The visual and linguistic discourse that suffused "Joe Copper" made explicit the focus on heroic male workers that defined the entire wartime run of the *Copper Commando* and helped perpetuate the institutionalized gender regime in Montana's copper towns. In so doing, it also helped make the employment of women in smelter production jobs seem more temporary and less revolutionary.

Smelterwomen

A local cultural milieu that supported a masculinist ideology by sublimating women's incursions into formerly all-male workplaces and hyping home front men's contributions to the war effort does not fully explain how Black Eagle smelter management was able to begin hiring women in mid-1943 without arousing significant opposition or precipitating a wildcat strike. A number of other factors were crucial. The necessity of hiring more workers played a part in male workers' acquiescence to the employment of women at the smelter. As personnel manager Eugene Cox put it, by 1943 the smelter was "gloriously short of people." In addition, despite differences between national and local perspectives on gender relations, Black Eagle's men responded to the patriotic imperative to increase production by accommodating women in the workplace, especially after national labor leaders' endorsement. Congress of Industrial Organizations (CIO) president Philip Murray, just as he joined Mine Mill president Reid Robinson in advocating the end of racial discrimination during the war, took a socially progressive though cautious position regarding the use of women in war industries. Through national resolutions made public in late 1942, the CIO as a whole stated its support for the employment of women to solve the wartime labor shortage, though it advocated the hiring of mothers only after the government provided appropriate child care. Local managers' decision not to hire women from Black Eagle but to draw on those regarded as outsiders was even more vital to their ability to bring women workers into the smelter with so little controversy, for that move defused any imminent threat to the local gender order. The particularly close bonds and regular communication between management and labor in Black Eagle facilitated this decision, and meant that local workingmen felt their concerns were being heard and their desires considered.[37]

Also key to facilitating the acceptance of women on the Black Eagle production line was the long-term presence of women working in the smelter office. Before the turn of the century, men had primarily held clerical positions. Then employers such as the ACM began to offer women jobs as stenographers and typists at lower pay than their male counterparts. Non-managerial male office workers, unable to control their white-collar workplace in the same way as working-class male unionists, shifted to other types of office work, particularly clerking, from which they successfully excluded women. Unable to call upon the physicality of their work to shore up their masculinity, they claimed masculine privilege by segregating themselves from women in positions that were more highly paid and perceived as more skilled, confirming their status as breadwinners. Women's employment in the smelter office rose dramatically during the 1920s. By 1926, when Eugene Cox started work in the timekeeping department, he remembered about thirty-two female stenographers and telephone operators in the main office, still the only place at the plant where women could work.[38] These women earned lower salaries than most men in the office ranks, although the differential was less than it would be in later years and a few women outearned less experienced male coworkers.[39] While both men and women might work as stenographers, only men held the more highly paid clerk jobs, and women's and men's wages were determined by different scales.

Experienced women earned relatively high wages, but they could also find themselves in trouble if they pushed for equality too forcefully. The case of Mary Pestana illustrates the limits placed on women's advancement by the ACM. Pestana, a single woman who had worked at the Black Eagle plant since 1904, had, by 1924, been earning $150 a month for twelve years, a base rate of pay that increased only by adjustments for inflation. She sought a raise, and superintendent A. E. Wiggin personally pushed for her pay to be increased to $190 a month. But the ACM personnel office balked, and when Pestana told her bosses that she was insulted by the amount they recommended, they responded that "she should not act hastily in this matter and that we thought she would find it very difficult to obtain employment any where else at a salary at all near the one which we were paying her." Pestana angrily resigned. But her managers' assessment proved to be true. Unable to find equal or better employment conditions in California, Pestana went to Butte to discuss her situation with R. D. Cole, a higher-level ACM executive. Despite Pestana's efficiency, experience, and longevity at the Company, Cole refused to grant her the wage she requested. Rather than comparing Pestana with long-term male office employees, the Company asserted that it paid Pestana considerably more than any other woman in a similar position at the ACM's other facilities. Six months later, Pestana admitted she had made a "serious mistake" and asked for her job back, but Black Eagle had hired another woman at a lower pay rate and would not reemploy her.[40] ACM managers, in short, had experience ensuring that male workers' status remained above that of their female counterparts.

In the 1930s, Black Eagle management continued to not only restrict but even reduce women's pay rates. First, a base rate of $180 per month became the highest allowable salary for female stenographers. After the plant's 1932 shutdown, when base salary rates were cut across the board, the maximum salary for stenographers employed by the Company before the Great Depression fell to $170, and new hires had their salaries capped at $150 per month.[41]

Equally significantly, and foreshadowing what would occur with production jobs during the war, ACM managers hired women from Great Falls to work in the office, while women from Black Eagle found other jobs in Great Falls. By the 1930s, Great Falls High School, which Black Eagle teenagers also attended, was offering female students a vocational track that allowed them to learn secretarial skills. This training, along with the contraction of job opportunities during the Depression, generated significant competition for office jobs at the smelter. But women from Black Eagle were not included among those hired. Apparently without exception, they were employed in Great Falls businesses instead. Emelia Tabaracci Qunell recalled that "most of us [women] went to Great Falls and worked, but . . . a lot of the young men" were hired for industrial work up at the smelter.[42] Local gender norms reigned in Black Eagle: women could work for pay as waitresses and cooks, but those who worked outside these occupations, even in jobs typed as feminine, did so only beyond the town's boundaries.

During World War II, with a labor shortage and competition for female as well as male workers, the ACM did adjust some of its attitudes toward female office workers. In 1943 R. B. Caples, the Black Eagle smelter manager, recommended that the maximum salary for stenographers "carry the same range as that for Filing Clerk. . . . i.e., $175.00 to $235.00." Perhaps managers like Caples always saw female stenographers as on par with the lowest-level clerk. But the articulation of gender parity was consonant with changes in national gender norms, as well as the rising demand for office workers after several male employees had left for the military. During the war, women for the first time occupied positions with *clerk* in the title. Still, in 1943 even the most experienced women did not earn as much as any of the men, except for one.[43] Male office workers still could claim masculine privilege. That women were being contained in gender-segregated positions at wage levels lower than those of men reassured workingmen that male privilege could be maintained despite the presence of women at the smelter.

Each of these factors helped facilitate women walking onto the shop floor at the Black Eagle smelter starting in the spring of 1943, at which point the debate shifted from whether the smelter should employ women to how to manage and assess their work. The Company quickly built separate washrooms, locker rooms, and showers for their new female industrial employees. Since they were on the union laborer pay scale, these women received pay equal to what union men had made doing the same work.[44]

Among men at the plant, managers were more complimentary than laborers regarding women's contributions. Cox described the tasks assigned to smelterwomen as "godawful heavy" work. He recalled that one woman had her leg and foot crushed when a three-hundred-pound anode—a large sheet of unrefined copper—dropped on her. He estimated that many of the forty-seven women who worked as laborers at the plant were injured.[45] From one perspective, Cox's appraisal affirms wartime women's achievements and their equality with home front men, differentiating him from some other managers across the United States who belittled women's accomplishments in war work as the product of their domestic skills, such as sewing, or, following a perverse bodily logic, as the result of their small hands and nimble fingers. But from another perspective, Cox was reinforcing the dangerousness inherent in men's industrial work and arguing that women were unable to perform these tasks safely.

In contrast, the recollections of the women workers themselves asserted their capabilities and achievements. Dorothy Moran Anderson worked on an all-woman crew of twelve to fifteen. Her memories of her experiences at the smelter and the contrast between that job and the traditionally female occupations she formerly held undermined the idea that men's work was more difficult or dangerous. Anderson's job at the plant was to "rack," or move, anodes that arrived in Black Eagle from Anaconda in railroad boxcars. Working both indoors and out, though away from the acidic fumes that made much of the plant environment unhealthy and uncomfortable, women hooked a chain block onto each anode's ears, hitting the extensions with a hammer to bend them for proper positioning on the rack before being dipped into acid. Having heard men describe smelter work before she began her job there, Anderson recalled, "I used to think that it would be a hard job out there. . . . These men that go out and work all day, they have to be coddled and everything else at night 'cause they're so tired 'cause they worked all day." Laughing, she continued, "Heck I wasn't tired when I came home from doing that job." Anderson contended that her previous job, wrapping doughnuts at the Sweetheart Bakery, was much more physically demanding and difficult even though it was classified as "light" work suitable for women. "My hands couldn't take it," she said, and she developed carpal tunnel syndrome. This condition drove her to the smelter employment office, where she was hired on the spot at a much higher wage and told to perform tasks that many local men believed women could not do safely—or at all.[46]

Despite Cox's recollection that women were often injured, the evidence suggests that they did not experience higher rates of injury than men. Only four women appeared on the smelter's monthly accident reports between 1943 and 1945: two missed two days each for bruised feet and were not compensated; Audrey Mclemore fractured her leg working in the Electrolytic Copper Refinery; and Ruth Parr, while working in the zinc leaching section on Christmas Eve, suffered a burn on her arm that later became infected. Management compensated Mclemore $168, or $17 a week for eight weeks. She apparently left the smelter afterward. Parr was paid for almost a year of missed work, at which point the Company elected to discontinue compensation, even though the doctor advised that the wound was not completely healed. Of the eleven workers listed in the "Compensation to Injured Employees" report for 1945, Parr was the only woman.[47]

Nor were the smelterwomen any more prone to absenteeism than their male counterparts, despite widely circulated assumptions about women war workers. Black Eagle management, with the help of the Montana Division of Industrial Hygiene, kept careful watch over illness and absenteeism statistics over the course of the war. Their figures reinforce the claim that women were able to handle smelter work as well as men. In 1943, the year that women entered the smelter production labor force, workers reported two thousand cases of illness, with respiratory problems ailing the largest number. On average, each of these cases cost the plant a little more than five workdays. However, illnesses were concentrated in the early part of the year, before the women's arrival. The number of workdays lost because of illness declined in 1944 and 1945, when a sizable number of women were still employed in production jobs at the smelter.[48]

The smelter's female workers made some inroads into local assumptions about their capabilities and social place. Eugene Cox ultimately concluded that these women "did a damn good job." Production records bear him out. At the height of women's participation in the workforce at Black Eagle, WPB statistics indicate slightly higher production levels for refined copper. While other factors, including quota allotments, could have contributed to this difference, the figures nonetheless show that women were clearly not a hindrance to the operation of the plant. Women's experiences there also challenged their own views about their abilities. They greatly appreciated the smelter's higher wages, took a sense of pride in their work, and enjoyed the camaraderie they found among fellow smelterwomen.[49]

Home Front smeltermen described women's contributions differently and for good reason: women's evident ability to perform physical tasks previously understood as men's work violated local ideas that smelter labor conferred masculine status. Anderson's comments destabilized both the division between men's and women's work and their unequal valuation; she punctured both the notion that conventionally feminine jobs were "light" and the myth that smelter labor was uniformly difficult. While women's experience with wartime industrial work bolstered their confidence, it also confirmed home front men's fears that some women hoped the war would permanently change the sex-typing of jobs and gender-linked wage differentials. In order to contain such a threat, men in Black Eagle exerted significant control over women's work at the smelter and offered a strenuous counter-argument regarding how that work should be perceived.

Home Front Masculinity, Space, and the Acceptance of Women Workers

The advent of women in previously male-only employment at the smelter, as well as the proximity of men in uniform, jeopardized the masculine status of Black Eagle's smeltermen. Yet it proved possible for the workingmen, in concert with smelter management, to contain the destabilization of gender relations that this first shift might have signified. The limitations placed on women office workers at the smelter reinforced the conservative gender politics practiced in Black Eagle and promoted by local popular media. Building on these pillars, smeltermen secured their masculine privilege in the face of wartime female employment in production jobs through four key measures: the smelter's policy of hiring only women from outside Black Eagle; the segregation of women from men within the plant; Mine Mill's strict enforcement of contractual agreements that provided benefits that the men considered part of the wages of masculinity; and a hiring policy at the smelter that excluded married women. These measures in turn promoted a local set of values that associated working women with the possibility of inappropriate sexual behavior and, by undergirding the family wage, helped ensure that these women would not become a long-term threat to male dominance in the workplace and the heterosexual family.

Mirroring its approach to employing female office workers at the smelter, the ACM did not hire women from Black Eagle for production jobs during the war. Instead, the smelter recruited women from Great Falls and from farms in the region to fill its labor shortage. Their presence, nonetheless, did challenge the smeltermen's claim of working in a manly industry. Cox admired the farm women who worked at the plant, declaring that one who came in "off the farm" from near the town of Belt "could outwork most of the men." He also expressed surprise that the female workers who had not been raised on farms could handle the work at the smelter too. But the threat posed by employing women from outside Black Eagle was far less imposing than it would have been if the smelter employed a significant number of women from town, because it diminished the sense that gender norms were changing there.[50]

Black Eagle women, like the men, regarded the female smelter workers as interlopers whose values were inconsistent with those of the local community. The smeltermen's wives, who contributed to the war effort through sewing and other domestic projects coordinated by women's groups such as the Home Demonstration Club, questioned the intentions of women who sought employment at the smelter. Lois Nicholls said that the wives "wonder[ed] about the respectability of these women," and whether they would try to lure male workers into inappropriate relationships. Many of the women who joined the smelter's workforce did have a different sensibility from that of the town's women. One smelterwoman remarked of her female coworkers, "I didn't think that women . . . could talk the way they did." Laughing, she added, "Oh dear, there was never any swearing around our house. [But the smelterwomen] told some of the rankest stories!" Tellingly, Montanans in other locales similarly questioned the ethics of women, including some from Black Eagle, who enlisted in the armed forces. One woman told a twenty-two-year-old neighbor who had enlisted "to free a man for overseas duty to win the war sooner" that she had heard that women in uniform were "all prostitutes." Such comments reflect one aspect of what the historian Leisa Meier found in regard to views of women in uniform.[51] As women left the controlling environment of their hometowns, they were freed of certain gendered restrictions, yet men and women took it upon themselves to police apparent gender transgressions by publicly disapproving of unconventional behavior. There was a spatial politics to this. Casting aspersions on the sexual reputation of working women enabled Black Eagle locals to distinguish their women from the supposedly different value system of women laboring in the male space of the smelter.

The spatial politics through which Black Eagle men ensured that their community's women would not work alongside them translated into an even more localized gender segregation scheme within the smelter itself. While men like Cox asserted that the work women tackled there was too difficult for them to handle and female workers like Dorothy Anderson contended that they had found the work relatively easy, smeltermen refuted the idea that women did heavy or skilled labor, arguing that they were given the easiest jobs at the plant.[52] In sum, smeltermen contended that these women did not do real men's labor, so their presence did not degrade the masculine nature of smelter work.

Smeltermen could claim that their work was more demanding, because ACM management and labor agreed to segregate female workers and assign them to tasks deemed less taxing—a tactic also used by home front men in other wartime industries. For instance, workers thought of the tankhouse as the site of the smelter's most abject labor, "blackening" the "husky" Croatians who undertook it. But the gritty physicality of work in the tankhouse elevated these men's masculine status. Because this sort of work was so deeply at odds with local concepts of femininity, the tankhouse remained off-limits to female workers; they performed sex-segregated tasks in places such as the Electrolytic Copper Refinery. The smelterwomen sometimes suspected the motives behind this gendering of tasks. Anderson acknowledged that working in the tankhouse "might have been a pretty tough job," but she did not think it was any harder than the work she had done as a farm laborer, nor did she believe it would cause the same damage to her hands as her previous job wrapping doughnuts. Black Eagle's male copper workers also rationalized gender segregation and elevated the status of work done by home front men by insisting that women would prove to be a danger to other workers if they were allowed to work in tasks perceived as more difficult and requiring skills women did not intrinsically have.[53] But given the similarity of this argument to the one used by Butte's white miners against employing black soldier-miners underground, the exclusion of women from certain spaces and types of work seems less a matter of safety or female capability than an effort to protect the local home front male ego.

Indeed, one of the risks implicit in women's entry into smelter work was the likelihood that they would realize the contradictions between the image of hard, masculine physical labor that the smelter represented to the community and the perks and privileges of unionized masculinity vehemently protected by the smeltermen. Women were well aware of the less desirable aspects of the smelter's hardest work, particularly as their husbands' toil intensified their own. Recalled Amelia Polich, "I remember when the men used to come home with their clothes and they would just be green from that solution that they used to soak the copper in and all that, you know. And then, oh, the women used to have to wash all those clothes out, especially underwear and things. It used to be terrible!" Despite the fact that particularly dirty or physically difficult tasks ostensibly conferred greater masculine status, most smeltermen valued their ability to avoid or rise above such work while still being associated with its status-conferring properties. Lawrence Tessman explained that in the smelter's many different sections, "practically every place had a job" that workers considered the dirtiest and most exhausting. "But," he acknowledged, men "weren't on it too much because the new men had to take that job."[54] For smeltermen, establishing their masculinity to their coworkers involved passing through that type of work and moving on to less unpleasant tasks.

This perspective suggests a localized redefinition of masculinity in terms of progression toward higher-paying and more skilled work. Yet at the Black Eagle smelter, as in Montana's other copper production facilities, some men chose to "deadhead" on a job: that is, to halt their efforts to get a promotion by remaining in a middling position that involved an easy task they had thoroughly mastered. For these men, masculinity meant affirming their independence and choosing their own tasks rather than climbing the skill ladder. Their masculine victory was to get the Company to pay them a decent wage for work they found easy. As a result, at any one time during the war, only 35 or 40 of the 125 men in the smelter furnace had progressed from basic labor positions to a point where they had the skills, if called upon, to cover the vast majority of section jobs. Some smeltermen complained about coworkers who deadheaded, believing they made the work lives of the highly trained more arduous. Black Eagle workers appointed a subcommittee of stewards to meet with foremen and decide on the legitimacy of a deadhead employee's reasoning. If the group judged his reasoning to be illegitimate, then it would have the power to discipline him. Friction arose between different versions of working-class masculinity. A man's body and bodily history—that is, age, injury, or other disability—determined whether others deemed his deadheading legitimate. If before the war better-skilled smeltermen had little recourse against deadheaders, during the war they joined with foremen, itself a telling alliance, in using patriotic expectations to discipline those they believed were illegitimate deadheaders.[55]

In so doing, these more accomplished smeltermen asserted another definition of masculine worth, built on the acquisition of skills and larger pay envelopes. But deadheaders could counter that their better-skilled peers were meekly doing the Company's bidding by acquiring expertise that could facilitate workforce consolidation through the dismissal of the less skilled. Moreover, while deadheaders avoided the smelter's ostensibly more masculine tasks, which were particularly arduous or required greater skill, they still benefited from outsiders' assumptions about the masculine status of their work.[56] These men had the most to lose if women were employed throughout the plant, including in jobs that management deemed relatively easy—in other words, their own.

The smeltermen's strategies of employing only women from outside Black Eagle and of segregating women on the shop floor into particular kinds of tasks also worked to minimize the women's knowledge of and interference with hard-won concessions that, in the men's eyes, protected their masculine privileges, breadwinner status, and future employment prospects. As it was, the smelterwomen were struck by how little work was done by all their male peers. Anderson quickly discovered that the smelter ran by strict, union-imposed, communally enforced limits on how much work could be completed, even during a period when men were supposed to be producing to their maximum ability as "soldiers of production." Smelterwomen recalled that after they finished their assigned day's work, they would shower, change, and still have "an hour and a half at least before [they] could go home." For those who believed that even this restricted amount of toil was too great, men circulated tricks on how to avoid work. Anderson painted a stunning picture of the smelter's collective male wartime work ethic: "There was all kinds of loafing around, all kinds of loafing around! I worked harder at home than I did out there."[57] The ACM accepted these norms. When foremen or other bosses came into a worker's area and found that he or she had already completed the amount of labor set out by the union, they did not push the worker to do more.

Anderson's perspective was that of a self-employed farmer; she did not understand why workers stopped working if time was still left in the day. But smeltermen, unlike such farmers, did not work for themselves. Rather, they worked for a corporation that they knew was making huge profits but refused to raise their wages substantially—a position supported by the federal government, which told home front men they should be working harder. Workingmen saw assertions of power such as controlling the pace of work as vital to their own definitions of masculinity. But these priorities did not make sense to many women workers, particularly when an ethos of patriotic sacrifice defined hegemonic masculinity at the national level. For many women with a son, husband, boyfriend, brother, or some other relative in the military, work at the smelter highlighted the clash between the masculinity of relatively autonomous workers and that of patriotic soldiers. Influenced by propaganda campaigns that questioned the dedication of home front men to the cause, these women believed that workingmen's masculinity did not measure up to their previous claims about their jobs, and certainly not to that of men in uniform.

The ACM's stated policy of not employing married women reassured the smeltermen that the Company did not intend to infringe upon the family wage. It took this policy to extraordinary lengths, firing a female telephone operator who had secretly married one of Black Eagle's war heroes, a young man locally famous for being the first aviator to fly a plane off a battleship. Although a few married women did, in fact, work at the smelter during the war, most Black Eagle townspeople interviewed in later years remembered a complete ban on the employment of married women. Their testimony in itself illuminates the enduring effects of the town's conservative gender ideology, especially since everyone was familiar with the figure of Rosie the Riveter, who was often represented as a married woman. The ACM upheld this policy at a time when many other firms actively recruited married women, and many experts, including Black Eagle's own personnel manager, believed that married women would prove to be more reliable than single women and more dedicated to their work than some men. Notably, the unwritten agreement between management and labor that barred married women at the smelter further validated local men's gender values and assuaged their fears about women's postwar employment.[58]

The exclusion of married women from smelter employment also reinforced local assumptions that women working in predominantly male workplaces were improperly sexual. The association of sexual promiscuity with gender-mixed workplaces had a long history throughout the United States, but it was reinforced in this place and time by a scandal that inflamed anxieties about changing gender norms and prompted Montanans to reassert them. In 1943 the Great Falls area experienced a venereal disease epidemic. Reported cases of gonorrhea and syphilis in Cascade County, which included Great Falls and Black Eagle, rocketed from 79 in 1941 to 122 in 1942, and 389 in 1943. Public health officials expressed the most concern about servicemen stationed at the Great Falls Army Air Base, once again suggesting the greater import of men in uniform compared with home front men. It also might have suggested that few expected Black Eagle men, with their strict Catholic moral code, to wander. Officials did not blame prostitutes, a significant number of whom called Great Falls home, but rather "so called 'victory girls,' large numbers of whom flocked to [Great Falls] during the summer of 1943," the very time that women were entering the smelter. City officials felt a personal "responsibility . . . [for] safe-guarding the health of the soldiers," so they mobilized the Police Department's vice squad to exclude the "'victory girl' and so-called 'good-time girl'" from taverns, halls, and hotels frequented by the troops stationed in the area. Authorities applied for funding to construct and staff a Venereal Disease Quarantine Hospital to deal with the ostensible emergency. The application contended that these women came from "small towns located within a radius of 150 miles of Great Falls." Officials in Great Falls replicated the strategy employed in Black Eagle, suspecting female outsiders of disrupting the town's gender and sexual norms. This geography of suspicion inverted the idyllic image of small towns and farming communities, condemning the areas from which numerous women came to work at the smelter. It also placed under further scrutiny those young, unmarried women workers who began stopping off at the bars after their shift, making inroads into what had been exclusively masculine spaces in Black Eagle.[59]

The VD epidemic generated another development linking the devaluation of working women to the reestablishment of local values. In petitioning for a hospital, Great Falls health officials based their request on the Lanham Act, which provided federal funding for child-care facilities. Social historians often represent the Lanham Act as a sign of public acknowledgement that mothers needed publicly funded child care in order to work full time. The effort to use these funds to build a VD hospital counters the national drive to reconceptualize women as mothers *and* workers, articulating instead a need by local men to mitigate the harm they believed that female outsiders and working women were inflicting.[60]

Conclusion

The most telling opinion about the smelterwomen and their effect on local gender relations came from the women of Black Eagle, after they overcame their initial fears that these workers would cause extramarital affairs. Olanda Vangelisti articulated the conclusion reached by some of the town's women: "Men had always maintained that the woman's place was in the home. And also that [men] were the only ones that could really work and operate that equipment in [the] smelter and here were these women!"[61] Her comment intimates that women's success at the smelter challenged long-held assumptions about Black Eagle's sex-segregated and male-dominated workplaces. That success, however, did not apparently lead to local women attempting to push their way into working there.

Despite these shifts in opinion, prevailing gender beliefs in the area were too ingrained to be dismantled by the smelter's wartime employment of women. Smelterwomen themselves had internalized gender norms too deeply to challenge them beyond the extraordinary circumstances of the war. Female workers such as Dorothy Anderson, even though they had the ability to be successful long-term employees of ACM, agreed that women did not belong at the smelter except at wartime, because "it's not the way God made us[;] [women's] bodies are not made for that heavy kind of work." A mother of three in her midthirties, she concluded, "I had a home to go to and I felt that is where I belonged." This sentiment, along with the ACM's refusal to employ Black Eagle women at the smelter, local and religious representations of women's domestic responsibilities, smeltermen's ability to retain their working privileges, the Company's restriction on hiring married women, and the disparaging associations of working women with sexual impropriety, ensured that what might have provoked a long-term crisis in masculinity passed without having done so. Paradoxically, then, the employment of women at the smelter did more to reveal the sustainability of Black Eagle's entrenched patriarchal value system, even amid the war's social dislocations, than to catalyze change. Indeed, it appears that the town's home front men, like the Anaconda men discussed in the next chapter, used their acceptance of women into their plant as leverage to obtain further gains in shop-floor control.[62] Nationally, workingmen's ability to win more power on the job and to mobilize a "we showed the company" rhetoric was a proven critical measure of masculinity.

The masculine status of home front workers was again at stake after the war, when they had to assert their manhood relative to that of returning veterans. Some male workers tried to strengthen their masculinity by favorably comparing their wartime labor with that of uniformed home front men. But in Black Eagle, it was the ability of home front men to mitigate the potential disruption of wartime changes to their racialized gender regime that sustained their defense of their own masculinity. Women had been ousted from smelter production jobs by 1946. Moreover, the potential wartime threat to local privileges of whiteness by workers of color, particularly American Indian workers, had failed to materialize. By deploying a discourse of brotherhood and honoring the service of their comrades in uniform, the smeltermen could, ironically, also point to their successful solidification of performance standards that allowed some of them to finish their work quickly and nap for the rest of the shift. Lyle Pellet, who started at the smelter in 1940 and enlisted in 1942, maintained that things "changed a lot" while he was gone. Before he left, Pellett recalled, Mine Mill had bargained for fixed workloads, but once a worker finished, he could not sleep or rest in the change house; he had to stay out on the shop floor. "After we came back from wartime, it was a different situation. You could go eat your lunch any time you wanted to, and . . . you could take a couple hours of sleep. Just so you got done that's all they cared about."[63]

These men's ability to impose such work practices at a dirty and dangerous job site during wartime was impressive indeed. It served as the basis on which men who remained in Black Eagle could assert a form of masculine status based on notions of collective union accomplishments and the honoring of worker fraternity. The acceptance of working women by the town's smeltermen, which looked like a gamble in comparison with the defensive actions of Butte and Anaconda men against similar incursions, proved an effective strategy that relied on the particularities of the local context. It paid enormous dividends for the one group of men among Montana's copper communities who appeared willing to follow new national norms, even as they, in fact, successfully reasserted prewar notions of masculinity and rendered women's employment a temporary aberration under exceptional circumstances. Anaconda's smeltermen, who faced a labor crisis involving the threat of both women and black and Mexican men, pursued a different though equally revealing set of strategies in their effort to reinforce white male status on their part of the home front.

Anaconda, 1944: White Women, Men of Color, and Cross-Class White Male Solidarity

On April 13, 1944—twelve months after women began working at the Black Eagle smelter, eighteen months after Butte's white miners refused to work with black soldiers, and almost two and a half years after the United States officially entered World War II—W. E. Mitchell, manager of the massive copper smelter in Anaconda, Montana, met with the Executive Committee of Local 117, International Union of Mine, Mill, and Smelter Workers (Mine Mill) to try to break an impasse over the smelter's labor shortage. Only a few minutes into the meeting, Mitchell announced that the War Manpower Commission (WMC) had "200,000 Mexicans in various parts of the country available for [immediate] transportation" to Anaconda. Prompted by a federal government nervous about declining mineral production, the ACM, which employed Local 117's three-thousand-plus members, proposed these Mexican men, or black men who were also part of the WMC's reserve labor pool, as a solution to the Anaconda Reduction Works' worsening manpower problem. Mitchell knew the workingmen did not believe that the ACM would actually bring in these men of color, so he added aggressively: "This is no idle conversation. You fellows know that Mexicans were imported into Montana last year. You also know that colored fellows from the Islands were imported into this country last year." He concluded by offering what he saw as a generous and more viable solution to the problem. Reassuring the union leaders that he too did not want to see racial-ethnic minority men "imported" to Anaconda, he argued that they could all avoid such a fate if the workers would simply stop "making a lot of too do [sic]" about employing women at the smelter.[1] For more than a year, the Executive Committee had shown it had no more intention of allowing women to work there than of allowing nonwhite men do to so. Instead, it had spent that time maneuvering to solidify Local 117's wartime agenda: maintenance of a status quo that guaranteed considerable overtime pay, job stability, and a strict bar against the employment of women or minority men in what they regarded as jobs belonging exclusively to themselves and to their coworkers and sons currently serving in the armed forces.

It is fitting that Anaconda came between Butte and Black Eagle as the middle step in the ACM's Montana-based mineral production empire, as the employment of workers of color, which was attempted unsuccessfully in the Butte mines, and the employment of women, which was accomplished on a small scale at the Black Eagle smelter, represent the two highest-profile solutions to the nation's wartime labor shortage. By the spring of 1944, the conditions were set for a major three-way confrontation between the Anaconda smeltermen, the ACM, and the federal government, which was taking an increasingly aggressive stance on the employment of people of color and women in industries vital to the defense effort. This chapter explores the story of this labor crisis, which ended with the continued exclusion of men of color from outside town and with the employment of no more than eighty-five women at the Anaconda Reduction Works. The choices made by these white and white-ethnic home front men when confronted by the simultaneous threats of men of color and of women entering their workplace clearly communicate the gender and racial ideology to which most of Montana's home front copper men subscribed near the end of the war. As they anticipated unsettled social and economic conditions after the war, they increased their focus on protecting the privileges of whiteness and masculinity for themselves and for their friends and relatives in uniform. That ideology, I argue, represents a critical aspect of home front society and politics that is elided in most popular histories of wartime America.[2]

"Blood and Bread"

Anacondan Edward Reynolds's "Blood and Bread," a short story he submitted for *Men at Work*, a Federal Writers' Project anthology on work in America, provides a revealing snapshot of the mindset of male workers during the wartime mobilization period. The story shows that during the war-production-driven employment boom that put a sudden end to the Great Depression, workingmen believed that providing for their families was as crucial to fulfilling their manly obligations as answering the call to join the military. Reynolds noted, "Butte and Anaconda were booming and we all had jobs. Far down underground in Butte men were digging ore from the veins of the 'richest hill on earth' and over in Anaconda men were boiling that ore down into molten copper that glowed a bloody red. 'Sinews of war,' the editorial writers call it; 'bread and butter,' say the miners and smeltermen." Drawing on his own experience as a smelterman, the author continued: "'Yes,' they agree, 'war is hell.' But work is hell, too, and starving to death is a damn sight worse.'" "Sodbusters from North Dakota, cow hands from Eastern Montana, Okies from the dust bowl, boomers from the southland and the west—and home town boys, too, who were given first preference" chose not to talk about the losses the war might bring; instead, their focus was on having stable jobs and being able to provide for the first time in a decade.[3]

Local officials estimated that Anaconda's population rose from about 12,000 to 15,000 between 1940 and 1941, the wartime mobilization period, as the smelter increased its output to keep up with the demand stimulated by war production. By the middle of 1942, smelter employment had increased by over a thousand, to 3,338. The chair of the Anaconda Housing Authority said that the city was experiencing "the biggest boom and the highest wages in the history of our town." Like many war production centers, it also faced a housing shortage. Six months into the war, one home that four people occupied in 1939 now housed eleven, while ten people crowded into a small, three-room lodging that had previously housed one person. Shortly thereafter, the employment rolls in Anaconda, like those in Butte and Black Eagle, began to shrink as more workingmen left for higher-paying war production jobs on the West Coast or joined the armed forces. Despite the industrial deferments available for many smeltermen, by late January 1943, six hundred members of Anaconda's Local 117 were in uniform. These developments not only produced a labor shortage but also indicate the eclipse of the breadwinning-based definition of masculinity that was articulated in "Blood and Bread."[4]

By the fall of 1942, the US government was actively involved in trying to solve the manpower problem at the Anaconda Reduction Works. Following the Butte debacle, federal officials accelerated the enactment of labor policies more attuned to the specific desires of local white male workers in the nonferrous sector. They modified the furlough program to make it more attractive to white soldiers, white workers, and employers, and shifted the focus of labor recruitment to army camps in the West from camps in the Southeast and Northeast, where the furloughed black soldiers had come from. According to the government's 1943 plan, nonferrous metal production facilities in the Southwest would have their needs "satisfied through the importation of Mexican workers," while Northwestern and Mountain West facilities would receive all furloughed copper workers. In July 1943, officials of the WMC and the United States Employment Service (USES) opened another forty-five hundred furlough slots for soldiers with experience in the nonferrous industry, signaling both the government's continued commitment to this method of filling labor shortages and the increasing loss of workers from western smelters and mines. The WMC also formalized an industrywide labor stabilization program that was meant to help keep home front copper workers in their jobs. Among other changes, the stabilization plan allowed regional WMC representatives like John McCusker who were friendly to the views held by white workingmen to take the reins from local USES officials when any labor troubles involved racial discrimination. It also included a "morale program" intended to broadcast the importance of copper and copper workers across the western states.[5] None of these initiatives solved Anaconda's labor shortage.

ACM management grew increasingly frustrated with the USES as these programs' ineffectiveness became evident. It seemed especially angered by the amount of overtime the Company had to pay in order to maintain capacity production—mid-1943 figures show smeltermen averaging 51 hours a week. The Company had to pay regular wages on 40 hours, time-and-a-half on 8 hours, and double time on 3 hours. At that point, management estimated that 230 more men were needed to reduce the average workweek to 48 hours. Government officials responded to the ACM's concerns about overtime by reiterating its position that women were the best solution to the labor shortage. Those salvos had no effect. In August 1943, WMC staffers noted that "to date the question of using women in the smelter is still unsettled." At the end of 1943, when the ACM was short "approximately 1,000 men," workers in Butte and Anaconda still held fast to their powerful masculine culture and continued to exclude women from production jobs.[6]

Some federal officials were reluctant to impose the employment of women on Butte and Anaconda because they were well aware of these localities' intransigence. But other officials, including members of the WMC's national bureaucracy, considered remote and often out of touch by some, did not show the same reluctance. In early December 1943, WMC headquarters released a study noting that Butte and Anaconda had a surplus of women available for employment in war production, which prompted the USES to declare it "an area of . . . labor surplus" where other employers might locate. When the *Washington Post* publicized the study, the first person to react publicly was not a member of Anaconda labor or management but H. O. King, director of the War Production Board's (WPB's) Copper Division. King feared that "any new war contracts in the Butte area would have a distinct tendency to decrease the amount of labor available for the Butte Copper mines." He was not concerned about women leaving the ACM's employ; their numbers were so minuscule even in administrative positions that their departure would not have had a significant effect. Rather, he worried about men quitting their posts in and around the mines and at the Anaconda smelter. King's letter served as a reminder that although many men wanted to avoid being drafted, some considered their wartime employment in the mines and the smelter involuntary. Given a choice, they would seek employment in other wartime industries that could also provide them deferments. King thought that the nation could not afford this exodus. In his view, the whole government manpower apparatus should follow the Copper Division's lead and allow Anaconda and Butte to play by a different set of rules.[7]

As King knew, workers and managers in Butte and Anaconda approached the employment of women in a strikingly different way than their counterparts in many industrial centers across the country, including other mining and smelting centers in the West that he oversaw. In Globe, Arizona, 150 women had taken jobs in the mines, and the USES had helped the Miami Copper Company hire just under 100. Arizona had one facility employing 200 women, a second with 70 female employees, and a smelter in which women comprised 30 percent of the crew. At two smelters in California, women made up 10 percent and 20 percent of the workforce; in total these plants employed 146 women. Closer to home in Kellogg, Idaho, 44 women worked in the lead smelter and 10 at the zinc plant. Women at Kellogg worked in the roasters; operated conveyor belts; regulated the flow of materials from the bins to the belts; served as machinist helpers; cast and strung large lead ingots; handled, cleaned, and operated electric locomotives and charge cars; and cut scrap iron with acetylene torches—performing some of the dirtiest and most physically grueling jobs at the plant. And only one hundred miles to the north, the Black Eagle smelter, with which Anaconda managers and workers had tight ties, had been employing women in production jobs since mid-1943.[8]

King's boss, Donald Nelson, whom FDR had personally chosen to head the WPB, also supported the increased employment of women in industrial work, as he made clear only a month before the *Washington Post* article appeared. At the November 4, 1943, meeting of the WPB's Operations Council, members of the WPB's leadership—its national directors in charge of particular industries and its regional directors—learned of Nelson's trip to evaluate the Soviet and British labor situation and, more important, of the effect his observations would have on WPB policy. Nelson made it clear to his staff that those who counted most—the men running the war—"emphasized to him that the larger the supply available of the material and equipment that fighting men need, the safer those men are on their dangerous missions." If this did not induce the regional and industry-specific WPB directors to "bend every effort toward the full and rapid completion" of production goals, his portrayal of the conditions Soviet laborers were willing to endure certainly should have. Nelson said that employees working "under the most difficult circumstances" put in eleven-hour shifts, and that each plant, in a display of its commitment to victory, maintained maps with up-to-date information about the Red Army's movements. Above all else, Nelson stressed the role of women in war production and, by implication, men's assent to their employment in heavy industry. As he pointed out, "The ratio of women and girls in factories rises to 85 percent in some [Soviet] airplane factories," and "in the steel plant at Magnitogorsk, employing 55,000, 45 percent are women." This message was bluntly delivered and clearly received. The officials at the meeting, all of whom were men, agreed that "the most efficient parts of the manpower pool had been exhausted," but that production gains could be made with the remaining parts of the pool—read: women.[9]

Despite their formal endorsement of this policy, other regional and locally based manpower officials shared King's reservations regarding the wisdom of pushing the ACM to hire women alongside men in the mines and smelters. A careful reading of the Monthly Report for July 1943 underscores local USES officials' understanding of the contradiction between the agency's estimates of the number of potential women workers and its failure to implement the national policy for hiring them. Instead of focusing on women's availability and the ACM's "manpower" needs, the report discussed the gendered character of the industry and cited the Company's official position on how many jobs women could do: "The nature of mine work is such that women cannot be utilized to replace men. In the smelter there are perhaps 8 jobs on which women could be utilized." The report ended with five explanations of the labor situation in the Butte-Anaconda area. The first reiterated the labor shortage but noted that the availability of women "is not a factor to provide a supply [of laborers] because of the nature of mine work." The second pointed both to the possibility that women might be the solution to the Anaconda Reduction Works' labor shortage and to local reluctance to take this step: "To date, there has been no positive action taken by either the union or the smelter officials relative to the use of women." The final comment declared categorically, "Women cannot be used to any appreciable extent in the area." September's version of the USES explanation expressed the same attitude: "The hazardous nature of mine

work and the physical strength required prevents the utilization of women."
Both reports concluded that "women cannot be used to any appreciable
extent in the area. A new type of industry would have to be started to absorb
the surplus of women workers."[10] In all likelihood, the repetition of this
point month after month led the WMC to reclassify the Butte-Anaconda
labor area and precipitated the story in the *Washington Post*.

The local USES office's decision to reproduce without comment the
ACM's estimate that women could perform only eight jobs at the smelter
suggests not only that these representatives were willing to ignore national
policy but also that they were empowered to do so. While labor at the national level had a less-than-equal place at the production planning table,
in the fall of 1943 the government signaled a growing awareness that in
order to avoid labor actions like the coal strikes then taking place, labor's
concerns had to be taken into account. Following a model first tried on the
West Coast and dubbed the West Coast Plan, the delegation of authority to
local WPB and USES manpower representatives for solving local problems
evolved as the national solution to the manpower situation. In the case of
the Mountain West, the WPB issued a press release on October 31, 1943,
announcing the "establishment of a new streamlined mining division of the
War Production Board in the Denver regional office with far-reaching authority" to assist in all production matters, including manpower problems.[11]
Although authorities in Washington, DC, still monitored the situation, formal decentralization had a major effect on copper communities for the last
two years of the war. For one thing, reporting that women might only be
able to do eight jobs at the Anaconda Reduction Works—without noting
that if one of the eight was a common laborer position, the smelter could
have easily employed hundreds of women—suggests that many Mountain
West USES and WPB officials shared a propensity to represent local instead
of national interests, and offers a partial explanation for why Anaconda
could delay incorporating new workers into its operations for so long.

Beginning in February 1944, some WPB officials reported an increasing
interest among locals in employing women at the smelter, which they hoped
could "solve, to a large degree, the pressing labor demands of the Montana
nonferrous metal smelting industry." By April they saw signs of a sea change
in local attitudes: "Slowly but surely Montana Chivalry is backing down.
Reluctant to permit its women folks to accept industrial employment, the
logic of war production necessity is forcing a decision." In addition, the
WPB trumpeted its recent success in promoting women's employment
in local war production jobs at railroads, lumber mills, and repair and

mechanical plants. However, whether local attitudes about women's work had significantly changed was an open question. By January 1944, the entire population of Deer Lodge County, which Anaconda dominated, stood at 12,883. Even with so many men at war, males outnumbered females by approximately 500. Employment figures showed a much greater disparity, with 4,200 men and 895 women listed as working. Only 50 more women had wage-earning jobs in 1944 than in 1940. Indicative of the diffuseness of government power and its contradictory policy positions even at the regional and local levels, the WPB, which through King had been angry with national USES officials for pushing the use of women for war work, now claimed that local USES officials were among the main obstacles to the employment of women in Anaconda. "Local offices of the USES," WPB officials noted, were finally "accepting the fact that the new worker in shops, mills, stations, on trucks, trailers, trains, and in most phases of industry, will be a woman."[12]

Still, the WPB agreed, "Mining demands rugged physical strength, endurance both for work and for unfavorable working surroundings, and therefore is not thinkable for women."[13] Even though women were working in mines in the West and the WMC's operations director, Brigadier General Frank McSherry, had championed the employment of women to solve mine labor shortages only the year before, WPB officials continued to claim that placing women in the Butte mines was out of the question. Whether the WPB would really try to convince the Anaconda smelter's managers and workers that "thousands of Montana women are available for work near their homes; industry must adapt itself to their employment or curtail operations," and whether Anaconda men would be receptive, remained to be seen.

The Question of White Women or Men of Color

In the fall of 1943, the Anaconda Reduction Works' general manager, offering yet another estimate, had told the government that he did "not believe that there are more than 35 to 40 operating jobs in which women could be used." His elaboration of his answer reveals the often hidden dynamics among home front men at the plant. Giving those jobs to women, he said, "would raise serious problems in plant labor relations," because they were "held by men at high seniority levels" who would resist being moved to more difficult work and who held considerable sway. Remarkably, three hundred smeltermen were over the age of sixty. ACM bosses told the USES that they would willingly replace thirty-five male clerks with women so that these men could be transferred to production jobs, but they feared that "it would be very difficult to develop them as effective smeltermen." Both Butte and Anaconda management did in fact add more women to their office staffs between late 1943 and mid-1944.[14]

The smelter managers' hesitancy to employ women in production jobs was rooted in the intransigence of the smeltermen. In the fall of 1943, when WPB chairman Donald Nelson was redoubling the board's efforts to place more women in industrial jobs, Local 117 finally gave a little ground and submitted a short list of jobs to smelter managers that the workingmen felt women could handle. For the ACM, the union's list did not go nearly far enough. By early 1944, management had come to believe that it had to make at least a token effort to allow female workers into more types of production jobs if it was going to stop the government from imposing its own solutions to the labor shortage. So the Company hired a few women to work in the sampling department's laboratory, one of the places the smeltermen had agreed women could work.[15] Although these laboratory jobs had been held by men, they were outside the production-work sector that smeltermen were most keen to keep exclusively male. This step was not followed by a greater initiative to hire women at the smelter, however. The smeltermen continued to delay that process through their tacit refusal to submit an expanded list of jobs in which they would accept women as coworkers.

A number of developments in early 1944 increased the pressure on all parties to put aside their differences and find a solution to the labor shortage. In January WPB officials announced a scarcity of copper in the national stockpile and attributed the problem entirely to the industry's manpower shortage. The government renewed its efforts to gather copper, bronze, and red brass scrap through salvage and scrap drives. A WPB memo issued just before the critical April 13, 1944, meeting between labor and management at the Anaconda Reduction Works relayed the bad news that copper production for January and February had fallen short of estimates. Moreover, the estimates for March and April had not included the "probable loss of civilians and enlisted reservists" caused by the recent shift in draft regulations. Copper workers' tendency to leave their jobs during the summer months to do agricultural work worried the WPB, which foresaw a "serious production crisis" and reminded labor and management that "we must not let down the boys on the battle fronts." Pulling out their most powerful weapon, federal and state manpower representatives, along with employers, spread the word that "if this practice is entered into this year, it is likely these men will have their deferments cancelled, and be subject to Army call."[16]

In early 1944, the Committee on Military Affairs conducted hearings about the National War Service Act that brought a renewed critique of union masculinity to the fore and pressured home front men to practice the sacrificial masculinity that was the new national ideal. Montana senator James Murray, who had close connections to the copper men, took the lead in defending workers by charging that the military had not propagated labor's excellent performance or management's role in production problems. Murray was featured in a *March of Time* newsreel segment, where he contended,

> The record shows that we are winning the war on the brawn, skill and loyalty of American workers. Strikes and threatened strikes have been magnified out of all proportion. Meanwhile, costs of living have steadily increased and scandalous war profits have been concealed or minimized. This has been a clear injustice to labor. Undue emphasis on civilian conscription at this time reflects on the integrity and loyalty of American workers. Conscription of labor without conscription of property would be one-sided and oppressive.

In the hearings, he highlighted the ACM's recent fine for manufacturing faulty products. When asked by Murray whether "there is widespread, bitter resentment in the minds of the armed forces" toward labor, secretary of war Henry Stimson said, "Yes, I know that." Murray repeated, "Against American labor?" Stimson confirmed, "Yes, I know that." An April 17, 1944, editorial in *Life* magazine supported Stimson's assessment, arguing that antipathy had grown among those in the military. "Civilians and servicemen are living in two separate worlds," *Life* contended, adding, in the words of "a young lieutenant," "Lots of people don't realize it, but many servicemen are getting so they hate civilians." "Men who had experienced battle" had the darkest view. They saw male home front civilians and men in uniform who had not been in the fight as "gold-brickers," and had contempt for both.[17] But the potential ramifications, especially conscription, for home front men were far more dire.

Finally, on April 13, 1944, at the watershed meeting that opens this chapter, the battle over who would fill the growing labor shortage at the Anaconda Reduction Works reached a turning point. Anaconda manager W. E. Mitchell began by updating the Mine Mill representatives on the personnel situation. "Last week we worked 367 men, seven days. We were short, as of April 12, 123 men for a six-day operation. We have 80 men in the draft age group, 22 through 25. At the present time we need 150 men, steady, in the plant from now until the first of October to take care of vacancies, an indicated shortage of something over 500 men." He told the local Mine Mill Executive Committee, composed of Charles "Bubs" McLean, John Donovan, Owen McNally, and Walter Dooley—all Irish and all veteran smelter workers—that the ACM could foresee only four solutions to the manpower crisis at the smelter. First, the Company could curtail production, which all parties had pledged not to do. Second, the ACM could hire women. Its other two options were to get Mexican or black men from the USES.[18] The suggestion that women should join the smelter's all-male production workforce had been bandied about for two years, but the idea of hiring men of color to alleviate the labor shortage had not been mentioned since the Butte wildcat.

It was not clear whether Mexican workers would be welcome in Anaconda. Small numbers of Mexican American men had been hired by the ACM, and had worked in Butte and Anaconda for decades. Mine Mill had taken the lead in organizing Mexican American and Mexican workers in the Southwest in the 1930s and early 1940s. Since mid-1942, the government had contracted to use Mexican workers in western agriculture and industry, and mining was considered among the most likely sites for their employment. Many federal officials believed that because Montana's copper facilities had a history of employing Mexican Americans as well as transient Mexican copper workers, Anaconda or Butte would allow braceros into the mines or the smelter. In contrast, Reid Robinson, president of Mine Mill, expressed his concern that the importation of a large number of Mexican workers would allow mining corporations to continue their discriminatory practices and provide mine and smelter managers with a tool to keep everyone's wages low. Robinson knew that those actions could spur resistance from union locals. He eventually supported their implementation, but only in the Southwest and only because he believed that from the Butte debacle the WMC had "learned from its experience with furloughing of miners in the United States army that shifting of men from place to place and occupation to occupation can not be successfully done arbitrarily, without consideration of human factors involved." Robinson worried that the racist views of some white copper workers in the Mountain West and Northwest would mean they would not welcome braceros, a view that none other than Brigadier General Frank McSherry of the WMC had also come to hold. Government officials were also aware that other groups of white industrial workers in the West had resisted the introduction of Mexicans. An incident on the Santa Fe Railroad in late 1943 was so serious that a special commission was formed to investigate the allegations of racism; the US and Mexican governments settled the case shortly before the April 13 meeting of Mitchell and the Local 117 Executive Committee. The question was probably moot. By 1944 braceros were in high demand for both agricultural and railroad work.[19] Thus, if the USES sent men of color to Anaconda, it was likely to send black men from the Caribbean rather than Mexicans.

Unlike Butte's mines, which did not employ a black miner until Hiawatha Brown began in 1942, the Anaconda smelter had had a long history of employing black workers.[20] Some of these men may have worked alongside white and white ethnic smeltermen earlier in the century, but by World War II the approximately twenty-five black men who labored there did so only in segregated crews and only in the arsenic, acid, and calcine sections and as janitors. With the cooperation of management, white and white ethnic workers promoted the idea that the acid, calcine, and arsenic sections were the worst jobs at the plant, because maintaining the privileges of whiteness and avoiding being labeled nonwhite required such a demarcation.

The initial debate that occurred over the use of Anaconda's black janitors in production jobs suggests that workers and management differed on the racial politics of wartime employment. During the April 13, 1944, meeting, Mitchell proposed putting the black janitors, all of whom had previously worked in the arsenic, calcine, and acid sections, back to work on a production crew. The union first responded by suggesting that before management pulled working-class blacks off positions they had earned, Mitchell should place timekeepers, who were white-collar management types, in laborer jobs. Just a week later, however, the smeltermen decided not to put class solidarity above racial considerations. John Donovan told Mitchell, "If there is enough work for those 7 men to work as a crew, under the supervision of a white foreman in the Surface, I don't think the Union has any objection."[21] Although smeltermen enjoyed indicting middle-class masculinity and calling for an equality of sacrifice by white-collar workers, when push came to shove the white workingmen of Anaconda chose to join white management in forcing their fellow black workers to make a sacrifice. Putting these local black men back at work might ease the pressure to either import minority men from outside the community or hire local women to fill the shortage. Placing a white man in charge of this small group of blacks ensured that racial distinctions were maintained, and no one would think that black men were working in jobs regarded as reserved for whites. Management and workers seemed to agree that black men did dirtier, lesser work and were in need of supervision—unless they were working in jobs that were too dirty for whites.

Management knew that the smeltermen's reasoning in regard to black workers already at the plant extended to the potential importation of black men. Within the smelter, there were not enough jobs labeled as "black work" to contain a large group of minority men. If men of color were brought in to relieve the manpower shortage at the reduction works, they would have to work in jobs previously typed as white. This move could, by association, denigrate the white men who previously held these jobs. A quick exercise in rhetorical gymnastics by the smeltermen could, in theory, reinscribe these jobs as nonwhite. Other white workers during the war had opted for just such a solution. But accomplishing such a maneuver in Anaconda would be difficult. The seniority system, one of the fundamental planks of the Congress of Industrial Organizations' (CIO's) national fight with employers, enabled white smeltermen to resist being moved to a new job. Black workers would be part of the union and would gain seniority, and there was no guarantee that they would leave after the war. Indeed, white smeltermen would no longer be able to use the seniority system to deny the plant's black workers access to better jobs. Most problematically, white men from Anaconda serving in the armed forces who had previously been employed at the smelter or were planning on working there after the war would return to jobs now associated with blacks, which tended to be lower paid as well as stigmatized. White home front men felt it was their duty to defend their friends and relatives against such an occurrence.

Management's and smeltermen's common views in support of maintaining racial distinctions within the plant's workforce as well as excluding men of color from other regions ran counter to aspects of each group's national cohort. Creating competition between different races and ethnicities was a tactic favored by managers across the United States, and Mine Mill was committed to racial-ethnic equality and inclusion, making managers' and laborers' shared opposition to the arrival of workingmen of color at the Anaconda Reduction Works all the more remarkable. Anaconda management believed that the ACM derived economic benefits from a stable workforce, and local workers valued security of employment as well. Mitchell, who had grown up in Anaconda and worked as a laborer at the smelter, thought of himself as much a fellow community member and friend of his workers as an ACM manager. His own bias against men of color and his sense of the workers' and the community's bias drove his actions in the spring of 1944. As he put it, "We only want to employ these women because of the manpower shortage, and we prefer to employ them on jobs they can do rather than open ourselves up—you fellows and the management—to the possible influx of minority groups."[22]

Mitchell believed that the bond between management and labor provided all the reassurance the men should need. He asked defensively,

"Aren't we good enough friends that we can sit down here and discuss [any problems with the women] at the time they happen?" For the smeltermen, the answer was no. ACM managers, seemingly surprised by this response, appealed to Mine Mill's progressive political principles. "Your own International is signing contracts with no discrimination as to sex, creed, or color, aren't they?" asked Mitchell. Walter Dooley, in the spirit of autonomy that characterized the Anaconda workers, would not take the bait. "That isn't the first time it has been put to us," he replied. Sensing a bit of us-versus-them camaraderie in Dooley's comment, Mitchell leapt at the chance to find common ground. "The one thing you and I are facing is that there is nothing to stop the United States Employment Service sending colored men in here this morning." But it was for naught. Dooley, in an emblematic bit of sarcasm, replied, "Colored women also."[23]

National Narratives of Masculinity and Patriotism

ACM managers frequently referred to local and national norms of race and masculinity and to the local version of national patriotic ideals, which tellingly omitted racial equality, as a way of shaming the workingmen into cooperating with the plan to employ larger numbers of women. Mines manager Ed McGlone told the smeltermen, "I consider myself lucky to be able to stay on this side—on American soil, and make a living while our sons, brothers, and relatives are over there struggling, sacrificing and risking their lives." Smelter supervisor E. A. Bernard expanded on this point: "It doesn't seem to me that the boys up there are very patriotic. Naturally they hate to give up those soft jobs up there, but suppose some newspaper got out and published that the Anaconda Mill & Smeltermen would only allow women to work on dirty jobs at the Mill. I would be very much ashamed. You certainly don't want to import some of this Mexican and negro labor and stuff like that in order to supply labor to keep this plant going" (fig. 8.1). Anaconda management's version of the parameters of wartime patriotism and what it demanded of home front men circa 1944 had certain similarities with the national narratives in circulation at the time, but also some glaring differences.[24] National popular culture's depiction of gender norms, shaped by and reflecting government desires more so than perhaps at any other time in US history, provided an influential backdrop to the drama that played out at the smelter that spring.

During the week before the April 13 meeting between W. E. Mitchell and the union representatives, *A Guy Named Joe*, starring Spencer Tracy, Irene Dunne, and Van Johnson, played at Anaconda's Washoe Theatre, as

8.1 Montana's copper men resented claims that they were unpatriotic. They contended that their wartime working-class values supported the men in the military more than the brand of patriotism proffered by corporations. The large quantity of war bonds purchased by Anaconda's smeltermen, and other home front men, provided further evidence that they backed the national war effort. Photograph by Robert I. Nesmith, *Men in Line for "Group 1"—Buying War Bonds*, circa 1942; Montana Historical Society Research Center Photograph Archives, Helena.

the five Sullivan brothers
"missing in action" off the Solomons

THEY DID THEIR PART

8.2 Before the story of the five Sullivan brothers became a Hollywood film, the federal government used their example to compel home front men to follow the dictates of sacrificial masculinity. *"They* Did Their Part," Office of War Information, 1943; courtesy Northwestern University Library.

it did across the country. This Hollywood film, along with newsreels showing fighting in Europe and the Pacific, government shorts such as *The Negro Soldier*, and other feature films including *The Sullivans*, demonstrates the federal government's remarkable power in crafting cinema's wartime message (fig. 8.2). Simultaneously, the content of each of these moving pictures mirrored the unsettled gender and race relations of wartime America. In *A Guy Named Joe*, Spencer Tracy plays Pete Sandidge, a middle-aged man fulfilling the requirements of hegemonic masculinity first by being in uniform even though he was well past the typical draft age, and then by making the ultimate sacrifice for his fellow soldiers and his country by flying his stricken plane into a Japanese battleship. The plot largely revolves around Sandidge, who gets called into God's army as a guardian angel, helping Ted Randall, a wealthy young management type played by Van Johnson, to become a pilot and also an ideal husband for Dorinda Durston, Sandidge's former love interest, played by Irene Dunne. Concluding with a scene in which Durston, a ferry pilot, steals a P-38 fighter and successfully flies a dangerous mission to destroy a heavily fortified Japanese ammunition storage site, *A Guy Named Joe* suggests that women could ably perform even the most rigorous, formerly male-only tasks.[25]

Central themes of work and ethnicity in *The Sullivans* resonated with the wartime experiences of many white ethnic families, including those in Anaconda, Butte, and Black Eagle. During the Depression, four of the Sullivan brothers go to work at the local plant instead of finishing school, a situation familiar to working-class audiences. *The Sullivans* also echoed ethnic and heteronormative masculine ideals of the time, with Mr. Sullivan labeling his sons "Wild Micks" who "wouldn't be legal Sullivan[s] if [they] didn't have an eye for the girls." Yet the decision by all the Sullivan boys, including Al, who has a baby and a wife, to enlist the moment they hear radio reports from Pearl Harbor challenged the course taken by other men, such as Montana's copper workers, who stayed at work rather than going to war.[26]

Of all the components of a movie program, which included cartoons, shorts, serials, and movies, newsreels had the most direct influence on the message audiences received, largely because of their journalistic quality. During World War II, American newsreels had over 3 billion viewers a year, and 95 percent of the country's 20,230 cinemas showed them. As one wartime viewer wrote, newsreels offered "a college first-hand education, [and played] a big part in awakening and arousing the American public to a greater understanding and responsibility." The Fox newsreel that preceded *The Sullivans* lent credence to the idea that home front men, including copper workers, had lost significant masculine status. The lead story ran under the title "Yank Paratroopers Dazzle Churchill." It began by playing on national tensions as the D-Day invasion neared. The narrative then segued to a more reassuring mode while cutting to footage of a confident, smiling paratrooper chomping on a cigar during a rehearsal jump, an image mirrored by the swagger of the Sullivan boys. In the final sequence of this first story, the newsreel shifted to extended panoramic shots that moved across the massive number of men and aircraft involved. The narrator reinforced the manly danger of the operation by referencing an image of two jumpers with tangled chutes and noting the crucial role these soldiers would have in the invasion.[27]

The newsreel that ran before *The Sullivans* was not an anomaly. Male soldiers, sailors, airmen, and marines practicing, performing, or recovering from their missions were ever present in newsreels and movies. Their ubiquity implicitly questioned the masculinity of men serving on the home front instead of the front lines, but in 1944 the problem became more acute when an increasing proportion of newsreels alluded to the mortal danger of manly military service. For example, the lead story of Universal's last newsreel in March centered on the danger of flying medium-range bombers by showing a nineteen-year-old "youngster" piloting a damaged plane and performing a belly landing. The next story of this newsreel told about the Anzio Beachhead, where "every single minute of every day and night is lived . . . within range of Nazi artillery." At the same time, a Paramount newsreel offered a story about a cameraman, Private Byron Tower of Dearborn, Michigan, who was wounded in the assault of Los Negros, in the Pacific's Admiralty Islands. The segment showed Tower being given plasma and then evacuated. It concluded by noting that after Tower's evacuation, he died at sea, "a symbol of all such men who go to face the enemy with a camera so that this story may be told."[28]

In contrast to the depiction of male soldiers, the sixth story of the newsreel that played with *The Sullivans* highlighted women war workers in a less serious tone. The narrator began by opining, "The eternal feminine isn't going to be denied by a mere war, even if she spends it in a shipyard. And if you want the truly chic in welders, riveters, and what have you, gaze on this lunchtime fashion show at the Philadelphia Navy Yard holding its own Easter Parade." After showing the parade and fashion show, the camera zoomed in on a female worker tilting her head. The narrator, speaking directly to the audience, remarked, "Coy, what? Even a bit flirtatious. And don't think the so-called stronger sex doesn't like it. Yes, fellow citizens, [these women seem to say] we'll do our bit, but we'll do it the glamorous way."[29]

Newsreels mirrored movies in presenting a mix of radical, moderate, and conservative representations of wartime womanhood. The *MGM-Hearst News of the Day* newsreel that screened minutes before *A Guy Named Joe* included stories about women working in war plants and United States Army nurses receiving praise for their valor in Pacific combat zones, reinforcing the idea that women had seized new opportunities. Two weeks before the *A*

Guy Named Joe screenings in Montana, a Universal newsreel contained a segment on "hero" nurses, and its Fox newsreel counterpart covered the same nurses receiving Air Medals for their service in Guadalcanal. Two weeks after *A Guy Named Joe* opened, a Metro-Goldwyn-Mayer newsreel showed army nurses in the Pacific going through special basic training, including long ruck marches and gas-attack training. A Universal newsreel that ran twenty days later provides an example of perhaps the most common version of wartime womanhood and, not coincidentally, mirrors the handling of women industrial workers in the Fox newsreel that screened with *The Sullivans*. This newsreel referred to the nurses on Guadalcanal not as heroes but as "Girls in [the] Solomons" welcomed by GIs with "smiles and cameras." This segment immediately cut to another about a fashion show of service uniforms, and then to a story about 190 California girls who decided to "Follow the Boys to Victory" by enlisting in the WACs. "It's stylish to be a WAC," the narrator intoned, hinting at how newsreels helped in the attempt to deradicalize the drive to recruit women. Other newsreels segments showed women in domestic settings or as "bathing beauties" to be ogled.[30]

"From My Personal Experience, I Would Rather Work alongside a Woman Than a Mexican"

The aim, if seemingly not always the outcome, of government propaganda was to support local efforts like the ACM's to employ women—but to make sure that the smeltermen finally accepted women, the Company primarily relied on the threat that the government would send men of color to the Anaconda Reduction Works. The ACM was its own worst enemy when it came to selling the legitimacy of this threat. In conversations between labor and management, management time and again revealed more than it intended. Early on, for example, Mitchell had attempted to illustrate the flimsiness of the local's position by referring to another situation that was close to home. "I saw a statement in an Eastern paper last night—I read under a Montana date line—how pleased the farmers were with the Mexican labor—a two column story on how wonderful they were." Dooley's response to Mitchell—"Yet a couple of years ago you read about the zoot-suit trouble in California and other places"—led the smelter manager to reiterate that he shared the workingmen's racist perspective. "I don't want to see them in Anaconda," Mitchell replied. The manager erased any lingering uncertainty about the Company's position in June 1944. "Now, I have thought many times," he argued, "that it was far better for us to string along here indefinitely, as far as 7 days are concerned and employing what local women were available on jobs they can do, rather than [leave] ourselves open to an order from the U.S. Employment Office, which can very easily be a bus load of colored fellows or a bus load of Mexicans." In so noting, Mitchell undercut his repeated assertion that the Company could not afford to continue paying overtime and thus had to bring in a large number of new workers.[31] Instead, he was seemingly agreeing to continue allowing smeltermen to accumulate massive overtime, because he desperately wanted to avoid what he saw as the two real threats facing the smelter: more government involvement in the Company's affairs, and the possibility that federal officials might bring men of color to the community.

The smeltermen agreed with Mitchell that black and Mexican men were a greater threat than women. One smelterman voiced the opinion many shared: "From my personal experience, I would rather work alongside a woman than a Mexican." But neither union leaders nor the majority of the rank and file believed that Mitchell would act or that the government would send men of color to Anaconda. After what had happened with the black soldier-miners in Butte, the smeltermen thought that the government would worry that any effort to force a new group of workers on the smelter would prompt more labor unrest and result in an even greater downturn in Montana's nonferrous minerals production. After all, the Butte hate strike was not an anomaly. National War Labor Board (NWLB) statistics, which tended to dramatically underestimate the number of strikes, suggest just how often home front workers violated the no-strike pledge. Between the beginning of the war and mid-1944, the NWLB had recorded 7,842 strikes. In the months before the April 13 meeting between Mitchell and Mine Mill representatives in Anaconda, male workers from coast to coast had shown an increasing proclivity for launching larger strikes, placing the government on the defensive. One set of NWLB figures indicates that 222 significant strikes—those that went beyond brief wildcats or that local mediation did not resolve—occurred during this period. The most important causes were grievances over discharges, wage rates, and workloads (97 strikes); protests against NWLB decisions (73); and protests against employers (16) and unions (24) for failure to comply with NWLB decisions. Averaging 8.24 days in length, strikes took place across the country and in virtually every sector of the economy. Seventy unions, including the Cigarmakers, Boilermakers, Garment Workers, Packinghouse Workers, and Upholsters, were involved, with the United Automobile, Aircraft, and Agricultural Implement Workers of America (CIO affiliate) leading the field with 18 strikes. Other NWLB documents indicate that more than twice as many significant strikes occurred among workers involved in production for the War Department. Mine Mill affiliates led 3 of the 222 job actions.[32]

Adding to the government's and ACM management's perception that they needed to deal with Anaconda delicately, in the spring of 1944 Montana's copper men were fighting an NWLB decision just as they had been in the fall of 1942, when the Butte hate strike occurred. The NWLB had issued a directive regarding Mine Mill's contract with the Company in early 1944 that granted copper workers a 25-cent daily increase in wages and two weeks' paid vacation. While the Great Falls and Anaconda locals voted to accept the terms, Butte refused by a ratio of 2 to 1; in solidarity, Great Falls and Anaconda workers refused to ratify the contract until the appeal process concluded. The appeal dragged on through the spring. The WPB worried that the issue was "causing unrest" and lowering "workers morale" in all three copper towns.[33]

That simmering anger boiled over on May 16, when thirty-five to forty miners from the St. Lawrence Mine walked out, refusing to work any longer for a shift boss they despised. In solidarity the rest of the men in the mine joined them on strike. The ACM had employed the shift boss in question on and off since 1938. The mines manager, E. S. McGlone, told the local WPB representative that the miners "just didn't like [the shift boss]. Figured he asked them to do too much work." He added, "They've violated every contract and even violated the law." The workers told a different story. As the *Miner's Voice*, published by the Butte Miners' Union (BMU), put it, "On May 11th the experienced and hard-working crew of miners on the lower levels of the St. Lawrence shaft, driven to action by the abusive tactics of Shift Boss Saunders, requested the mine management remove him." Contrary to McGlone's assertions, the union contended that it had acted through the appropriate grievance channels and that the ACM had removed Saunders from the St. Lawrence. Four days, later word spread that management was sending Saunders back to work, and union and Company leaders made their way to the scene. The BMU suggested that until the grievance could be formally adjudicated, both parties agree to take "practical steps" to defuse the situation. The ACM refused to keep Saunders out of the St. Lawrence, and at that point, according to the workers, the walkout began.[34]

The WPB was not interested in recriminations, but was worried about whether the strike would spread throughout Montana's copper communities. "We're sure as Hell not going to let it spread if we can help it," McGlone answered. Then he added that the ACM "can't let these men collectively walk off because they don't like a boss . . . . We're going to take a stand against that." McGlone and ACM chairman D. M. Kelley reiterated that the Company would not discuss the matter with the BMU until the men returned to work and filed a formal grievance. After Kelley remarked to the press how much copper production was being lost by idling the mine, the men responded: "Neither Mr. Kelley nor any of the company officials nor Shift Boss Saunders produced a single pound of this copper. It was all produced by miners working there." The ACM-owned *Montana Standard* reported the Company's version of events, claiming in bold type, "This is first collective stoppage of work in the Butte mines in 10 years," and, in so doing, erasing the massive 1942 walkout against the Company and the government's efforts to employ black soldier-miners. This time local WPB officials stepped in and brokered a compromise. The BMU had to admit that "the men erred by walking off the job." The ACM also capitulated. "In the interests of production," the Company agreed to "immediately withdraw the shift boss involved in the dispute from the job." Although the strike only lasted three days, it reminded the government and the Company that Montana's copper workers would ignore the wartime no-strike pledge and walk off the job if provoked. The WMC was especially concerned about the national labor situation at this precise moment. Agency leaders announced that "industries requiring able bodied workers are confronting the most serious difficulties in holding and recruiting manpower than at any time since we entered the war."[35]

Even amid this atmosphere of labor unrest and government unease, W. E. Mitchell did not share the smeltermen's confidence that the government would avoid taking action to address the Anaconda labor shortage.[36] He felt that in order to prevent government intervention, he could no longer delay hiring women for production jobs at the smelter. Just after the April 13 meeting, he began doing so on a small scale. Rather than launch a wildcat or declare a formal strike, the smeltermen decided to focus their efforts on minimizing the effect of women's entry into their workplace. Tracing the process they undertook and the arguments they offered to attain this objective does much to reveal the gendered beliefs of working-class men on this part of the home front.

Smeltermen, Smelterwomen, and the Equality/Difference Paradox

After stalling for months on providing a list of jobs they felt women could occupy at the Anaconda Reduction Works, the next phase of the smeltermen's campaign to control women's employment centered on the Mine Mill membership's call for a written agreement on the terms of this employment. The union's recording secretary, John Donovan, first presented Mitchell with the proposed supplementary agreement at the April 13 meeting. The nine-point proposal specified that the union and the Company would agree to the following:

1 The employment of all available men on a seven (7) day or fifty six (56) hour per week basis.
2 The employment of women in jobs their physical capability will permit. (a) Provided, however, said employment of women will not deprive any member of the union of his full seniority rights.
3 Men who have started on jobs within a certain department will not be moved off these jobs to other departments in order to make places for women, unless otherwise agreed upon.
4 All women going to work on Smeltermens' jobs will be under the jurisdiction of the Mill & Smeltermens' Union No. 117, and will be required to have a permit from the union in order to continue to work. The permit fee will be $10.00 and $1.25 per month thereafter. The same fee is charged as dues and will be covered by the same provisions as in the contract concerning the "check off."
5 Women can be employed for the period of the manpower shortage or the duration of the war, whichever shall be the shortest period of time, unless amended by mutual agreement of both parties.
6 Women will be employed on jobs that do not affect the seniority set-up. That is, that they will start in a laborer's pay at the bottom of the seniority flow sheet on jobs as vacancies occur.
7 Any controversy that may arise which is not covered by this agreement shall be taken up and disposed of through the regular grievance procedure.
8 In the event the above steps do not correct the manpower shortage the Union and the Company agree to hold further negotiations with the end in view of correcting the shortage.
9 Anaconda women will be given the first preference by the Company in their order of hiring women.

Mitchell immediately refused point one, but said he would be happy to consider the rest of the proposal. The meeting adjourned on this note.[37]

Union and management representatives continued to meet, but over the next month little progress was made on the agreement. All the while, management introduced more women into production jobs. By May 18, the rank and file had reached a breaking point, and Mine Mill local representatives Charles McLean, Walter Dooley, John Donovan, and Owen

McNally met with Mitchell. Donovan spoke first: "We were ordered here this morning to see if we can't get some kind of agreement along the lines of that agreement we presented you some time ago as regards women." There were two major reasons the union so badly wanted this agreement ratified. One focused on the wartime context, the other on the postwar. First, some smeltermen were worried about what the employment of women would mean to their current working conditions. Men who had gained plum jobs through seniority feared the ACM would soon replace them with women. Other smeltermen worried they would have to do more work to cover for women unable to handle their assigned duties. As McNally told Mitchell, the men "want a specific agreement in regards to the jobs women take [and] that jobs would not be changed to suit the women. That[,] I believe, [the membership] is watching very closely." Union representative Mike Sestrich also called out Mitchell for not sending some members of his male office staff onto the production floor: "You have a lot of big husky men working in the time office. There are lots of women who could handle jobs there; lots of women who could handle jobs like that and be put in as clerks."[38]

On April 19, Mitchell had asked the local if it was serious about its demand that new smelterwomen be treated the same as new smeltermen. He queried, "Would it not be better for a woman to work some place in the Mill than it would for her to work in the Roasters?" Dooley's snide reply, "Maybe it would be a good thing if some of these smeltermen's wives worked there for a while," suggests that the men believed that local women did not understand the difficulty of smelter work and needed reminding that their husbands deserved respect for the physically demanding jobs they did. A month later, when he asked the same question again, the representatives told Mitchell the rank and file had not changed their position. If a man started at the plant by doing heavy labor, then a woman should too.[39] This response, viewed as extraordinary for the time, marked a defining moment in the relationship between the sexes in Anaconda. It did not gel with local conceptions of gender, and also made no sense in the context of the copper workers' long-stated claim that women could not handle men's work.

In mass-production industries such as auto and electrical that employed large numbers of women during the war and converted their plants for military production, the sex-labeling of specific jobs—assigning a task to workers based on their gender—was fluid, but the practice of sex-typing jobs, which ensured that women and men did not perform the same jobs in the workplace, was not. The smelter shop floor, in contrast, was exclusively male before the war, and smeltermen fought the introduction of women into production jobs for two and a half years. Now the smeltermen not only claimed that they were willing to work with women but also refused to follow the sex-typing practice typical of home front men who wanted to protect male privilege by defining specific jobs that could be held by women.[40]

One catalyst for the smeltermen adopting this approach was the ACM itself. When Mine Mill proposed defining the terms and conditions of women's employment through a special agreement, Mitchell responded, "We have a contract with the Mill and Smeltermen's Union, and we expect [women] will be accepted as any other employee." Charles McLean responded promptly that the union contract made "no mention of women," so a separate agreement "covering the women question" was needed.[41] While the Company emphasized equality between male and female workers, the union stressed that women were different from men.

Smeltermen believed that women were physically incapable of performing the same jobs as men, so their stance implicitly, and seemingly deliberately, set newly hired smelterwomen up for failure. Mitchell was well aware that the union's new position was contrary to local masculine customs that called for chivalric attitudes toward women, and expressed genuine surprise at the union's hard line. He could not believe that men he had known for years really wanted women to go to work on "Joe Thomas's bull gang," a crew comprising the smelter's newest workers who were farmed out to the plant's dirtiest and most grueling tasks until a permanent spot could be found for them. Some smeltermen shared Mitchell's concern about the implications of having new smelterwomen treated the same as new smeltermen. Union representative Charles McCarthy put into words the bind he experienced as a local man and as a union member: "It is kind of hard to say to put the women out handling these heavy liners, at the same time it is pretty hard to see a man who has worked two or three years and worked on a job on which he was satisfied, and the boss was satisfied with him and have the boss come and say—'you go down there' . . . [because] a woman will have to take his place." Shocked by the inflexibility of the membership's position, Mitchell asked, "Why don't you say you don't want women in the Mill?"[42] McCarthy lamely argued that this was not the men's contention, but it was exactly their point.

The second reason the smeltermen desired a written agreement arose from their concerns about the shape of postwar society. As Walter Dooley put it on May 18, the smeltermen wanted "to see some kind of an agreement that women would be allowed to stay on the job only for the duration" of the war. In order to ensure that principle and in the hope that it would convince management to agree to the smeltermen's other conditions, the union said it would remove points one, four, and nine of the original agreement. None of these three points altered the union's basic stance on women working at the smelter, but the membership's willingness to back down on them provides valuable clues to the rank and file's priorities and to how labor and management, two-thirds of the way through the war, handled the wartime relationship with the government.[43] Their compromise on points one and nine is particularly revealing. Mitchell had previously stated that because of its excessive costs, he would never agree to giving men so much overtime, although only a few weeks later he had agreed to continue the overtime pattern. The smeltermen's acquiescence on this issue meant that they were dropping their "money at all costs" philosophy. Like many Americans on the home front, they had seen the war as an opportunity to put themselves and their families on firm financial footing. For the first time in a generation, labor had become the number-one commodity on the market, and Anaconda's workers had taken full advantage of the labor shortage. Now the smeltermen seemed willing to sacrifice immediate gains in order to help secure their position in the postwar period.

Striking point nine of the agreement regarding preferential hiring of local women signifies the smeltermen's concern for Anaconda's social structure during and after the war. On its face, it appears that the workers had a change of heart and decided to pursue Black Eagle's strategy of employing only women from outside the community. Following this logic, Local 117 could have reasoned that women from outside Anaconda would more easily be viewed as a temporary and transitory workforce; they would return to their homes when the war ended or, if they did not, it would be easy to argue that they were hired only for the duration of the war and should leave the smelter. Women without local attachments would garner far less support if they sought to keep their jobs after the war, whereas local women who had to work to support a family were sure to attract some supporters. But the situation in Anaconda differed from that in Black Eagle. The smeltermen of the Anaconda Reduction Works still supported giving local women priority. They volunteered to remove point nine because Mitchell had told them, "Well, I think we should mutually agree that these women are being employed during the emergency . . . I am not going to agree to write it down—that Anaconda women will be given first preference by the company, although that is what I intend to do. I am not going to set it down that way and have the United States Employment tell me that that can't be done." In direct opposition to the position of the WMC, the smelter's unwritten policy also favored married women with children. Furthermore, management almost exclusively hired women whose husbands were either in the military or disabled smeltermen.[44]

Many smeltermen were aware of the economic pressures facing some local women, and supported their working at the plant. Indeed, one of the women who wanted to work at the smelter was union representative Charles McLean's mother. In other places, gaining access to well-paid, previously male-only jobs made the war a boon to working-class women who had to support themselves and others. Because Anaconda was a company town, the smelter's policy of barring women dramatically reduced local women's opportunities to benefit from the wartime labor shortage. Men who opposed the employment of women at the smelter were not deaf to the reasons these women might want to work, but they feared that once the door was opened it could not be closed. The union's position that women should work only during the wartime emergency was an open admission that men had control of the workplace and that women might choose to work there if given the opportunity. In the third week of April 1944, Walter Dooley had bluntly conceded that fear. "Yes, we are starting to think if you took a survey of the whole country, I think you would find that women who will want to work after the war is around 65 to 85 percent. We know the women's place is in the home but in times like this it is different."[45]

One of the critical aspects of what the smeltermen believed they were fighting for, which underlines why they believed their "equality" stance was necessary, emerged in May 1944, when McLean emphasized to Mitchell the Mine Mill membership's concern that Anaconda boys who had completed high school and gone into the military would not be hired at the smelter when they returned from the war because women had taken those jobs. The smeltermen "won't want to see women holding jobs, and possibly where two or more are working in the same family keeping these young fellows out of work because they have no rights. Of course, that situation was here before—after the last war." When smelter supervisor E. A. Bernard asked, "Can we legally draw up an agreement that has prejudice against women?," Donovan shot back that the proposed agreement was not prejudiced toward women but simply protected the men who were currently employed. Mitchell, referring to the smeltermen's concerns for their sons' job prospects, asked whether Donovan meant "protection for the man who never saw the plant." "Well, we aren't drawing up an agreement for men who have never seen the plant," replied Donovan, apparently aware that such a contract was illegal. Mitchell rejoined, "That's the idea behind the 18 year old boy situation." Owen McNally interceded to point out that such a setup was the idea of the boys' parents. Mitchell asked, "What about the parents of the girls?" "Well, some of these girls may have some other means of income such as two, three, or four in the family working, and they may have other means of income but they may decide to stay on those jobs after the war is over," explained McNally.[46]

Even more telling than McNally's admission that some of the "girls" might want to keep their jobs was the construction of gendered social roles implied by his comment that these girls did not need jobs, because others in their family would be working. It was a straightforward proposition and a common assumption that women would depend financially on their fathers, brothers, and husbands. Male breadwinning was the essential element in local definitions of masculinity. McNally recognized the problems inherent in this schema: some local women needed to work to support their families. Yet what these women should do was apparently too uncomfortable a question to discuss openly. Women at the smelter jeopardized the smeltermen's ability to provide their sons the opportunity to work in the same place they did and earn a family wage, perpetuating the gender norms that the smeltermen strongly supported and from which they benefited.

The desire to look after the interests of boys in uniform was equally apparent in Butte, where in September 1943 local men formed a chapter of American War Dads. Although the national organization championed sacrifice as one of the principal duties of home front Americans, the Butte chapter used the more aggressive language of the local working class to describe itself as a "militant union of Service fathers." That was no accident; the leadership included prominent miners such as Stanley Babcock, who assumed the presidency in late February 1944, and applications for American War Dads membership were available at the Butte Miners' Hall. Care and rehabilitation of the wounded and postwar jobs for veterans were the major objectives of the Butte's War Dads. They added, "As War Dads we demand that our flesh and blood who wear the uniform of their country shall come home to live self-reliant American lives; with work sufficiently remunerative to sustain a family in the best of American standards, able to own a home and decently raise and educate their children." In their official literature, the War Dads contended they sought to serve their sons and daughters in uniform, but the male breadwinner was almost always at the center. Daughters, for example, tended to disappear in the organization's more informal pronouncements, as a speech by the Butte chapter's first president indicates: "As fathers of men who have dedicated their lives to their country, you enjoy a great distinction, an eminence of citizenship." Echoing the national organization's description of its membership as "**fighting** fathers" (emphasis in original), his comments also reveal that being the father of a veteran had become another way to claim status for home front men.[47]

When at a later meeting the parties returned to the topic of former and would-be Anaconda smeltermen in uniform, Mine Mill continued to put them first and oppose the inclusion of more women at the plant. Mitchell, in a futile attempt to end the debate, made it clear that the mill and the smelter would remain a male domain. "We ought to get the confusion out of the men's head,—that we aren't trying to make a women's job out of the Mill here." He confirmed that "any boy who worked at this plant and went into the Armed Forces, as far as I am concerned, all he will have to do is present himself and he will go back to work when he comes back. That not only means the women who will have been employed, but some men who have been employed since will have to find someplace else" to work. "The main idea is only to put a woman on a job that she can do and hope that the boys come back so that we won't have to have her at all." Turning to the union's social concerns, Mitchell continued, "I think the women here have grown up in an atmosphere where I don't know very many would care for these operating jobs around here permanently."[48] But he could not change the opinion of many smeltermen who remained adamant that women at the smelter jeopardized Anaconda's prewar value system and threatened their vision of the postwar gender order.

On June 13, 1944, one week after the Allied invasion at Normandy, a moment when discourse about patriotism and sacrifice was at an apex, union representatives told management that the rank and file felt that the employment of women had gone too far. In short, the membership really *did* want Mitchell to start women on physically difficult manual work and to fire them if they could not handle the job assigned to them. Mitchell was startled at the men's brash demand. His anger barely under control, he said to Mine Mill representative John Donovan, "What, John? They want their jobs back on the screens and the mills, if their seniority entitles them to it and let the women take whatever is left until a vacancy occurs and the women can be moved on the screens? And if the women can't do the work—then God help the women!" "I can't make it any plainer than that," replied Donovan. At this point Ed McGlone, manager of the Company's Butte Operations, blew up at the union representatives: "God help the women! God help production! God help everything! In other words you don't want women employed here is that it, John?" "I wouldn't say that, Ed," Donovan replied. "[But] if she can't do the work it looks like she is out in the cold." McGlone regained his composure and asked the union representatives to use a little common sense; he felt it was not a real sacrifice for the men to "rustle around" from one part of the plant to another in order to allow women to work and thereby keep production high. Donovan could only reply, "I will admit I have gone as far as I can in this thing. I'm at the end of my rope."[49]

In peacetime, Anaconda Reduction Works' managers and workers had acted in concert to uphold the gender order that prevailed in local society. In wartime, although they shared a perspective on race, these men ultimately held different views on gender. Comments by the smelter's assistant manager, Bob Lemmon, during the union-management meetings indicate the problem. Lemmon told the smeltermen that the question of what to do with the women who were hired to work at the smelter was best left for later discussion, and he reassured the men that management would protect their and their sons' job prospects. The union representatives insisted that the issue had to be dealt with immediately, not at some nebulous future point: "That's what the membership wants—they feel it is easier to do it now than argue about it years from now."[50] The middle-class manager did not seem to grasp why the working-class smeltermen felt such a sense of urgency. There was a good reason for Lemmon's thickheadedness: the employment of women at the smelter threatened neither his job nor his masculinity.

Because physical labor had long been considered the province of working-class men, women toiling at the smelter could diminish the status of smeltermen's work. The amount of masculine status derived from the actual work involved in managing the smelter was more questionable. Nonetheless, when women moved into jobs previously held by men, they moved into manual labor or lower-level office jobs. Whether Rosie the Riveter largely came from a middle-class background, as print and motion picture propaganda suggested, or from working-class roots, as the statistics demonstrate, she almost never stepped into managerial work.[51] Jobs in management remained sex segregated throughout the war. Bob Lemmon's wife or daughter did not enter the managerial class to free him for war duty or to fill vacancies in the front office. Middle-class managers not only kept their masculine privileges but never even had to defend them.

Whether or not managers ever fully understood workers' anxieties about the advent of women at the smelter, it was the more fundamental masculine bond between them, reinforced by their regular meetings during the war, that solved the impasse. The fact that managers and workers concurred that the employment of white women was far preferable to the introduction of workingmen of color, and that women were already working production jobs, virtually ensured that the two parties would find some way to work

8.3 The *Copper Commando* highlighted local women's domestic roles during the war
through features such as the paper's "Platter Chatter" column, where this image
appeared in July 1943. Photograph by Robert I. Nesmith, *Food—Glynn Family*,
Montana Historical Society Research Center Photograph Archives, Helena.

out their differences over the terms of women's employment. At the end of
June 1944, the rank-and-file smeltermen who would be most affected by the
employment of additional women agreed to sit down with the foremen in
their sections of the plant. Shortly thereafter they came to an understanding
regarding how women would be incorporated onto the shop floor.[52]

The way that local popular culture portrayed women's wartime roles
over these decisive months had played an important part in reassuring
the smeltermen that war-driven changes that were occurring nationally in
gender relations were unlikely locally. Local media celebrated not wom-
en's work in war production but rather their domestic accomplishments in
support of the war, such as stretching meat rations and collecting fats for
military use (fig. 8.3). Soon after more substantial numbers of women entered the plant, the *Copper Commando*, a bimonthly newspaper produced by
the ACM Victory Labor-Management Committee, minimized the disruption
and mitigated the threat posed to men by reinforcing the dominant gender
ideology. The *Commando* did not report the presence of female industrial

workers at the Anaconda smelter during their first four months there, just as it ignored the presence of women production workers at the Black Eagle smelter for the entirety of the war.[53]

Finally, on August 18, 1944, the *Copper Commando* introduced Anaconda's smelterwomen via "Ladies' Day," a strangely but tellingly titled article. Virtually every aspect of "Ladies' Day" seemed orchestrated to smooth ruffled male feathers (fig. 8.4). The article began by observing, "In war production factories from coast to coast, women have been freeing men for more strenuous production jobs and for the Armed Forces." After setting this context of normalcy, the article mentioned that in facing the threat of male workers from outside Anaconda being sent to the smelter by the USES, local men had followed the lead of industrial men all over the country and made a wiser choice: "Imported male labor has been available, and still is, but the prevailing sentiment among both members of labor and management is that preference should be given to local people. . . . The usual grumbling over the advent of women into industry was heard to some extent at the Smelter, just as it always is when women move in on men's jobs, but the men at the Smelter were smart enough to know that this was an emergency measure, that Uncle Sam needs every able-bodied person to help win the war and that the admission of women into labor ranks means no threat to organized labor."[54]

"Ladies' Day" said plenty of what the smeltermen wanted to hear about the women who had entered their domain. Mary Blaz, who had one of the more strenuous jobs at the plant, shoveling grinding balls into the mill, said she liked "the idea of finding out for herself just how things are done, for when her boyfriend and brother get back she figures she'll be a lot more interesting to them and will know what they're talking about." Lola Harrington, a "tank man" at the smelter, had worked in a restaurant in Anaconda, but when she heard the smelter was hiring women "she felt that she'd be doing a lot more toward winning the war by changing work even though, as she said, 'I always felt that feeding war workers was helping, too.'" This sort of innocuous rationale for working in traditionally masculine jobs took the sting out of the smeltermen's prophecies of doom. It was no accident that only a few of the women interviewed were not initially defined by their relationship to a man. For example, Zita Robison was introduced by noting that her "husband worked in the Zinc plant before he was transferred to the timekeeper's office. He was sent to Europe in September, 1943, and now has fifty-one missions to his credit." Only Ruth McEachran and Erma Crom were defined as individuals. Ruth, a college student at St. Mary's in Kansas, was "doing her bit while on summer vacation"; she presented no

Mary Blaz   Frances Scott   Lola Harrington

T HE writer who called this a man's/ world has had to back off in the past few years and think it over a little more. In war production factories from coast to coast, women have been freeing men for more strenuous production jobs and for the Armed Forces. In many civilian jobs, women have taken the places of men so men could be made available for more essential work, either in the production army or in the Armed Services.

At the Reduction Works at Anaconda, women have recently b e e n brought in to do war jobs. The drains caused by the manpower s h o r t a g e throughout the copper industry have been so heavy that it has been essential, in the interest of maintaining production, that girls and women go to work at the Smelter, Imported male labor has been available, and still is, but the prevailing sentiment among both members of labor and management is that preference should be given to local people.

When the decision was finally reached to enlist the services of women, top priority was given to the wives of service men who were former employees at the Reduction Works. Every effort was made to establish members of the Anaconda Company family in available positions.

The usual grumbling over the advent of women into industry was heard to some extent at the Smelter, just as it always is when women move in on men's jobs, but the men at the Smelter were smart enough to know that this was an emergency measure, that Uncle Sam needs every able-bodied person to help win the war and that the admission of women into labor ranks means no threat to organized labor. As a matter of fact,

the spirit of the men toward the women has been fine from the beginning—these women, who are doing essential war jobs, are made welcome.

Now, let's take a little journey around the Hill and get acquainted with some of these gals:

That's Mary Blaz in the upper left shot. Mary, as you can see in the picture, has a wheelbarrow full of grinding balls. No doubt you recognize the balls as those used in the Hardinge ball mills. Part of Mary's work is to load the wheelbarrow and take them over to the Hardinge ball mills and load the mills once per shift. Another job of Mary's is to oil the mills every hour. She's been on the job for the last two months and likes this work which in the old days before the advent of women to the Plant was called a "mill man's job."

Mary felt she knew quite a lot about the Plant even before she started to work there for her brother worked on the elevators in the Plant before he joined the Army, and her boy friend, now in the Army overseas, worked in the Zinc Plant. She likes the idea of finding out for herself just how things are done, for when her boy friend and brother get back she figures she'll be a lot more interesting to them and will know what they're talking about. She says it was pretty strange at first but she's gotten all over that and now she likes it fine.

Frances Scott, shown in the top center picture picking pieces of wood from the vibrating screen, has been at her job for two and a half months. This operation too you'll probably remember from previous issues of Copper Commando. The copper ore, you may recall, drops through the screen if it's ground suf-

LADIES'
DAY

Kay Groshong and Ernest Johnson

ficiently, and goes to the grinding mills. If it isn't sufficiently ground, back it goes to the rolls and then comes back to the screen.

In the upper right shot we take you to the tank house to see Lola Harrington carrying on a "tank man's" job. Lola worked in a restaurant in Anaconda but when she heard that women could work at the Smelter she felt that she'd be doing a lot more toward winning the war by changing her work even though, as she said, "I always felt that feeding war workers was helping, too." Lola now watches the valves in the tank house and thus tends the Dorr thickeners where the

Ruth McEachran   Zita Robison   Helen McElroy and Helen Heath

8.4 The *Copper Commando*'s story on Anaconda's smelterwomen featured photos of women working throughout the plant. "Ladies' Day," *Copper Commando*, 18 Aug. 1944, 4; Montana Historical Society Research Center—Library, Helena.

threat to the masculine value system, because the *Commando* covered her work in patriotic terms and as very temporary. On the surface, Erma Crom, who was also single, represented exactly what these men feared. She was a teacher who moved into the copper industry because it offered higher pay, and she said she hoped to stay on after the war. It seems extraordinary that the union's editorial board would include Crom's profile in the story. Crom may have had some preexisting connections with men who had worked at the plant, which would have reassured readers who recognized her local history. Or, perhaps the editors felt that she represented a group of women workers who deserved to be included. After all, she had given up a career for a job at the smelter and affirmed that she "really likes this new work of hers."[55]

This issue of the *Commando* closed with a series of thoroughly uncontroversial domestic images that emphasized these women's good citizenship. Viola Malone, whose husband, Bill (who, the *Commando* tells its readers, was affectionately known as "Duke"), was in the South Pacific, said she was just doing her part. Mary Stinger echoed Viola's words, but added that she also worked to stop herself from worrying. The *Commando* concluded, "The seventy or so gals working at the Smelter in Anaconda are doing a fine job and here's hats off to all of them who have shouldered their war responsibility by joining the workers at the Reduction Works."[56]

Conclusion

The language and process of negotiation in Anaconda suggest that men's experiences on the home front during World War II significantly shaped facets of the conservatism that became apparent among the white and white ethnic working class after the war. Rather than relegating race- and gender-based wildcat strikes to the margins of history, this analysis sees these actions and, in the case of Anaconda, the threat of such actions as key to understanding labor's wartime and postwar history. Explaining why workers shifted from the CIO's ethnically and racially inclusive "culture of unity," to borrow Lizabeth Cohen's phrase, to promoting gender and racial exclusion is at the heart of this history. Anaconda's male workers changed their stance when the war challenged them to practice on their own turf the principles that Mine Mill and the CIO required them to preach. Paradoxically, it was the full wartime employment enjoyed by the workingmen of Anaconda, not the unemployment of Depression America, that destabilized the CIO's culture of unity in this western town. Because of the dearth of jobs in Anaconda during the Depression, no significant migration of new workers occurred. It was easy for copper workers to support the CIO's social platform during the 1930s. The CIO's conservative gender politics, which promoted a family wage for male breadwinners, were compatible with the masculine culture of the smelter city.[57] In contrast, the war, with its manpower crisis and simultaneous assault on parts of the New Deal, put new stresses on progressive unionism.

Local circumstances that had developed over time combined with the national political context to shape the community's reaction to the prospect and presence of racial and sexual others in the workplace. In regard to race, it was far from alone. Across the country, different workers at different times adopted what Thomas Sugrue has called "the not-in-my-backyard attitude toward racial equality."[58]

In another set of ironies, the combination of a reinvigorated sense of union power fostered by the success of the CIO and the bond between the Anaconda Reduction Works' labor and management enabled smeltermen to meet the perceived threat posed by the employment of white women and men of color. They sought to defend some of the specific gains won by the CIO's national power, particularly seniority rights and a unified voice in bargaining, and they relied on those provisions in their contract to exclude these new groups of workers.

Franklin Roosevelt's wartime government does not look like the cornerstone of New Deal progressivism when viewed from the local and regional instead of the national level. In his drive to employ women, smelter manager W. E. Mitchell cited government pressure, and noted that the USES had workers of color available to fill the labor shortage in Anaconda, but the USES—or the WPB or the WMC, for that matter—did not actively combat racial exclusion at the smelter. In fact, the Fair Employment Practices Commission often saw the government's regional and local offices as among the weakest links in federal efforts to enforce the desegregation of war plants.[59] For the first thirty months of the war, local and regional government officials were apparently satisfied to apply only slight pressure on the smelter to employ women, and to wait for other developments to prompt change. The final year of the war tested home front workers and managers and the government in similar ways, and they responded similarly.

The Man in the Blue-Collar Shirt:
The Working Class and Postwar Masculinity

One of the unexpected results of a close look at home front men is that it has suggested a previously veiled continuity between the Great Depression, World War II, and the early postwar period: the influential role of working-class masculinity on the social politics of each of these eras. Our current sense of the history of masculinity over these three decades is characterized by disjuncture. Working-class masculinity dominated the 1930s. Military masculinity dominated World War II. And white-collar corporate masculinity quickly came to dominate the latter 1940s and 1950s.

This book complicates that understanding of the Depression decade by emphasizing the importance of working-class masculine practices and the role of local gender and racial orders *before* the 1930s in shaping that decade's racialized masculinity. In the case of Montana's copper communities, the strength of immigrant gender norms and workers' assertion of an independent working-class masculinity in the face of the ACM's overwhelming power translated to support for their radical parent union, based not on that union's well-known campaign for racial equality but on its much lesser-known championing of militant masculinity. World War II saw these men resist the sacrificial masculinity demanded of home front men in favor of the working-class masculine ideology they had solidified in the 1930s. They shored up their privileges of whiteness and masculinity by containing the challenge posed by the introduction of women and workers of color into wartime industry. But what of the postwar period?

The early postwar history of Montana's copper communities shows that men who had stayed on the home front during the war took the lead in establishing a postwar working-class masculine ethos, and that working-class veterans integrated themselves into this form of masculinity. Yet postwar working-class masculinity, and its effect on the social politics of the era, has been largely ignored. This is due to a host of factors, but two play an especially large part: the myth that places all veterans in the middle class after the war thanks to the college and mortgage benefits of the GI Bill; and the powerful influence of films such as *The Man in the Gray Flannel Suit* and television shows such as *Leave It to Beaver* that made it seem as though postwar America's entire population was middle class.[1]

In this conclusion, I will use evidence from Montana's copper communities during the early postwar era to elaborate on the link between home front men and veterans, the working-class masculinity they came to share, and that masculinity's relation to its middle-class counterpart. I argue that what transpired in this part of the West affirms a received history of the postwar that has male employees and employers continuing to fight about bread-and-butter issues and control of the shop floor. But it also suggests another aspect of the postwar relationship between blue-collar and white-collar men: an alliance between workers and management to protect privileges of whiteness and masculinity. If Montana is any indication, working-class men took an active role in forging these partnerships and profoundly shaped postwar gender and race relations in the process.

It was apparent from the beginning of the war that home front copper men, even as they questioned whether all men in uniform deserved to be considered as occupying the pinnacle of manliness, felt a sense of responsibility and brotherhood toward local men in the military (fig. 9.1). For their part, servicemen from Montana's copper towns may have joined others in generally questioning home front men's devotion to the war effort. But when it came to home front men in their hometowns, they tended to think of them as relatives and friends instead of as slackers.[2] In Montana's copper communities in the postwar era, this bond between a town's veterans and home front men trumped wartime differences and facilitated a shared politics.

The question of accommodating the employment of veterans at the smelters and mines had become a major issue for home front copper men by the spring of 1944, as indicated by the struggle between labor, management, and the federal government over whether the Anaconda Reduction Works would employ women or men of color to address the manpower shortage. Copper men's desire to defend the interests of working-class men in the military was given another push in 1944 and into 1945 when the Selective Service, responding to the military's needs, drafted a significant number of younger home front miners and smeltermen, including many with wives and even some with children. By early 1945, local newspapers

9.1 This 1941 poster was one of the first to show the bond between home front male workers and military men. "Men Working *Together!*," Division of Information, U.S. Office for Emergency Management, 1941; courtesy Northwestern University Library.

were reporting more frequently that some of these men, as well as others from the copper communities, had either been taken prisoner, gone missing, or been killed in action, further catalyzing the drive by home front copper men to protect jobs for men in uniform.[3]

A special issue of the *Copper Commando*, a bimonthly newspaper jointly published by the International Union of Mine, Mill, and Smelter Workers (Mine Mill) and ACM management in Butte, Anaconda, and Black Eagle, published at the end of March 1945 and dedicated to "Joe Copper," shows how far this concern for veterans had advanced. The paper declared, "It is the part of every civilian Joe, and Joe knows it, to make sure that all these men figure the costs of war were not too great for the comforts of peace they will have won for us." Certain rights defined that peace and the vision of postwar society shared by copper men—past, present, and future. They were not constitutional rights or notions of equality championed by New Deal progressives but rather "the right to hunt and fish and sit around a campfire" and to "[raise] a few chickens and [plant] a garden." Although the *Commando* painted a picture of postwar masculinity fulfilled through homosocial leisure and heterosexual domesticity, it also asserted that for veterans "to have the full fruits of peacetime when they return from the battle fronts where they fought for him" required Joe Copper to secure workplace rights for men in uniform. The paper told home front miners and smeltermen that they needed to behave like men and treat the veterans like men. "That means no pity, no stupid or maudlin tears." Most important, "it means that our fighting men must have an honest chance at good jobs, assuring them of security and their own self-respect." The paper reiterated that it was Joe Copper's job to make sure that happened.[4]

Veterans began to return to Montana's copper communities in large numbers in September 1945, a month after World War II had ended. In another sign of the growth of government influence in American lives, these men turned first to a federal agency, the United States Employment Service (USES), to help them find work. But the USES's Montana office had little to offer working-class veterans besides jobs in the mines and smelters. According to officials, veterans showed "a reluctancy (*sic.*) to accept employment in these industries." In this they mirrored the home front men who had also turned to the USES for assistance in finding employment after having been released from other war production jobs. Local USES officials reported a "staggering increase" in unemployment claims by October 1945, but men continued to resist being placed in copper work.[5]

Working-class veterans across the United States showed a similar tendency, asking the USES to find them clerical or service positions instead of factory jobs. In a remarkable comment about the power of hegemonic working-class masculine ideals, Detroit's USES office told male veterans— who presumably were considered to have already proved their manhood— desiring these positions that "opportunities in the field were limited and that pay levels were inappropriately low for men." It asked these applicants to submit a preference card "indicating their availability for more traditional 'men's' work."[6]

In Montana working-class veterans and out-of-work former home front men soon realized that in a state whose economy was built around resource-extractive industries, other more attractive job opportunities were not likely to materialize. Thanks to the GI Bill, veterans had more opportunities than their unemployed home front brethren. They could use their benefits to pursue higher education or vocational training, they could leave the state in search of better work opportunities, or they could accept positions in mineral production. Popular mythology, of course, holds that most went to college. But in fact, only 37 percent, or 2,232,000, of eligible World War II veterans did so. Nonetheless, this was a far higher number than expected by officials and experts who knew well the working-class composition of the armed forces and the constraints those men would face. Indeed, of those veterans who used the higher-education benefit, only 10 percent said they would not have gone to college, and 10 percent said they might not have gone, without the GI Bill. Over 3.5 million—over 50 percent more than went to college—attended a trade or vocational school, and many of these men entered higher-skilled but nonetheless working-class positions afterward. It appears that an even larger number of veterans simply decided to take whatever positions they could find, and the vast majority of these men also entered the postwar working class. In Montana many in this group eventually settled for jobs in the local mines and smelters.[7]

Home front copper men who had shown their opposition to sacrificial masculinity throughout the war rejected it even more forcefully in the postwar, and working-class veterans, even though sacrifice had also been a key component of the military masculine ideology, followed their lead. Veterans in Montana's copper towns, facing a lifetime of work at the smelters and mines, were thankful for home front men's defense and occasional extension of Depression-era gains in benefits and shop-floor control. One veteran recalled that before the war, "you had a fixed amount of work to do and once you finished it you were done. But you couldn't go in and sleep or rest in the change house, you had to stay out there. But after we came back from wartime, it was a different situation. You could go eat your lunch any time you wanted to, and . . . you could take a couple hours of sleep." Decades later, he still laughed in appreciation of the victories achieved by his male workmates on the home front who had succeeded in bolstering an idea of working-class masculinity built in part on controlling the workplace, not proving one's bodily abilities in it.[8]

For many veterans, the most powerful reintroduction to working-class masculine values came during the unprecedented wave of strikes that former home front men initiated across the United States in 1946 and 1947. These men remained furious at the government for holding down wages, and at corporations such as the ACM that made massive profits during the war but would not share that windfall with workers. Workingmen's resentment had been building for some time before the war's end, and a goodly number of workers—seeking to make gains for both themselves and their friends in uniform while they still had the leverage created by the wartime labor shortage—unilaterally terminated the no-strike pledge well before peace was declared. More than a year before the war ended, analysts in the National War Labor Board's Strike Section noted that as "the problems of post-war conversion become more acute," the number of job actions would multiply. "In many cases," they added, "the issues will be fought out on a 'showdown basis,'" producing longer, larger-scale, and more contentious work stoppages. The "showdown" strike at Butte, Black Eagle, and Anaconda took place in April 1946, and was among the most contentious in the history of the copper towns. Striking miners in Butte went the furthest, attacking Company property and the homes of residents they thought were scabs, including managers who had crossed picket lines to keep the mines running. However, the activities of copper men in all three towns reminded participants and onlookers that militance and solidarity were core principles of local working-class masculinity.[9]

Postwar miners and smeltermen very much believed that there were differences between managerial and working-class masculinity, a point the strike crystallized. Workers did accept some aspects of postwar middle-class masculinity, but they made it clear that they were producers, and middle-class managers were not. Copper men saw no contradiction between this claim and their continuing fight to reduce the amount of work they had to do and to improve the conditions in which they labored. Every time they achieved those objectives, they saw it as an expression of the independence and militance at the heart of local working-class masculinity. And at the most basic level, male copper men felt strongly that the Company's effort to hold down wages was the prime impediment stopping all miners and smeltermen from fully achieving the breadwinner ideal.

These areas of disagreement notwithstanding, workers and managers shared a common perspective regarding postwar gender relations that saw men as breadwinners and women as homemakers. This shared view did not represent a dramatic shift from that held during the war. Company officials, along with local and regional Roosevelt administration representatives, had played a decisive part in limiting the number of women employed in Montana's home front copper industry. Even Black Eagle managers, who had shown the greatest willingness to employ women, never wavered from supporting the male breadwinner ideology. In 1944, for instance, when the Black Eagle smelter, desiring more female workers, changed its policy prohibiting the employment of married women, the smelter's supervisor made sure his staff understood that "the wife cannot replace the husband as the family head." And, just as they had promised home front copper men, managers at both the Anaconda and the Black Eagle smelters released all female production workers soon after the war ended.[10]

The brief moment of postwar tension between labor and management over women's work ultimately reinforced the sense that most local men of all classes agreed on women's appropriate sphere. In the late spring and summer of 1946, Mine Mill leaders in Anaconda and Black Eagle initiated

a campaign to get former smelterwomen back pay based on contract stipu-
lations that had just been signed between the ACM and Montana locals.
The men's motivation was to gain economic justice for the women and to
return more Company dollars to the working-class community. The ACM
contended that for employees to qualify for back pay, they must have been
working at the smelter after March 1946—by which time all smelterwomen
had been released. The union representatives, prompted by the male rank
and file, responded that the Company had a "moral obligation" to the
women, because "they did a good job" and "helped during the war effort."
Management called the men's bluff, and told the union leaders that they
could solve the impasse by allowing women to return to production jobs so
they could meet the post–March 1946 requirement. The smelter manager
asked the union representatives, "Shall we put the women to work? We
might put the women in the Mill, we need some men there. What do you
think the gang in the Mill would do?" Black Eagle smelterman Gordon Dial
asked Company managers why they were so dead set on having smelterwomen return to work in order to receive back pay. "Why should this group
of people be forced to come back? They have served their duty and purpose
very worthily. . . . We don't like to see women in our country working in
smelters. We are even surprised that Mr. Kelly would use the argument—let
them go back to work. We have more respect for them—we don't want them
to work in smelters." Dial, in fact, offered the view of both copper men
and managers regarding women's place in the postwar gender order. Both
groups made it clear that this issue had escalated to the point of a formal
hearing only because each had come to see it as precedent-setting for future
battles between male laborers and male managers.[11]

Local managers and the majority of the postwar rank and file—veterans and former home front men alike—also shared a racial ideology built
around protecting the whiteness of the three copper towns, the mines and
smelters, and the workers who labored in them. The Butte miners who believed the Company was behind the plan to introduce black soldier-miners
into Butte's mines in November 1942—and, indeed, believed the initial
cohort was only the vanguard of a much larger contingent of black miners
sponsored by the ACM and the government—would not agree with this
assessment of management. Neither would some of the Anaconda smeltermen who perceived smelter manager W. E. Mitchell as threatening such
an importation into their plant in the spring of 1944. But Mitchell's open
admission, "I don't want to see them in Anaconda," more accurately represents the view of managers in all three towns. In the years immediately after
the war, the ACM did not change its approach to race in Montana's copper

towns. It did hire two other men from Butte's African American community as miners and continued to employ a small cohort of African American smeltermen in Anaconda, but it made no attempt to introduce a large group of workers of color. Critics within the working class would describe the protection of the prerogatives of whiteness and masculinity through such a relationship as paternalism. That term, however, does not adequately reflect white male workers' agency in creating and maintaining a cross-class alliance that, while antithetical to the development of a movement of the entire working class regardless of race or gender, provided what many smeltermen saw as real benefits.[12] Events in Montana suggest that such cross-class alliances represent one of the dominant approaches by white and white ethnic men to protecting racial and masculine privilege during—and after—World War II.

Mine Mill's postwar leadership opposed this alliance, especially its solidification of white privilege. Indeed, the union's fight for equality for workers of color in the postwar era further expanded its reputation, at the time and among scholars today, as one of the most radical unions in the United States. It included the International's leaders taking an even more aggressive line than they had during the war. Maurice Travis, who succeeded Reid Robinson as Mine Mill president, embodied this amplification. Travis went to the front lines of postwar labor and racial conflict and lost an eye when defending the rights of African American Mine Mill members in Alabama against white supremacists affiliated with the Congress of Industrial Organizations (CIO).[13]

Travis told Mine Mill's membership that working-class racism was more than just a southern issue, and that unionists who defended the privileges of whiteness in any way were the labor movement's central problem. He called on white workers to stop supporting corporate paternalism, which he believed destroyed their ability to create class-based change. And he consistently reiterated his view that progress could only be made when working-class white men and men of color came together as they did in some places in the 1930s. Not surprisingly, the majority of Montana's copper men were as opposed to Travis's racial politics as they had been to Robinson's. As Laurie Mercier points out, "Many second-generation ethnic Montanans were uncomfortable with the multicultural union's civil rights efforts." One prominent Anaconda smelterman, for instance, "felt that the union they had nurtured was slipping away to 'others.'" He "asserted that the 'colored group' and 'Mexican group' received more respect than the Montanans."[14]

Montana's copper men had the opportunity to change the direction of the union or to leave it, but they accepted this turn of events for a number of reasons. The fight for racial equality in the postwar period had evolved in a way that replicated what had occurred during the 1930s, not World War II. The struggle was at a distance from Montana, and there was little concern that black or Mexican American workers would arrive in large numbers in Butte, Black Eagle, or Anaconda and thereby challenge white masculinity on multiple levels. Moreover, white and white ethnic workers remembered that ACM managers had been tepid toward or downright hostile to the introduction of black and Mexican men. They also knew that the government's interest in pushing for racial equality had waned, and that it was unlikely that a large number of workers of color would seek employment at the smelters and mines.[15] As they looked back on the war, they were further reassured by their treatment as part of the white American mainstream. Even the divisions among smeltermen and miners during the war were typically based on political disagreements instead of racial-ethnic ancestry. Together, these developments made most second-generation white ethnic smeltermen and miners—and even their first-generation relatives and friends still working in the industry—confident in their white status and less willing to allow the race issue to determine their union loyalty.

Of equal importance to Mine Mill's revived popularity with the rank and file was the leadership's emphasis on its history of advocating for independent, working-class masculinity. During the war, Robinson and Mine Mill had shown some progressivism in regard to improving women's opportunities in war work, but any support the International gave to the employment of women in the copper industry during World War II all but vanished in the postwar era. Even the remarkable 1954 Mine Mill–produced film *Salt of the Earth*, which has been hailed for its compelling depiction of class solidarity in the face of racial oppression and for its feminist sensibility, ultimately reinforced a gender order that had the male copper worker as breadwinner and his wife as responsible for the family's unpaid domestic labor.[16]

The importance of masculinity and the diminishing influence of race, at least in this part of the West, are clearly seen in Montana copper men's reaction to the CIO's expulsion of Mine Mill and ten other radical unions in 1949 and 1950. The United Steelworkers of America (USWA), which remained affiliated with the CIO and whose postwar leadership shared the CIO's more conservative politics, sought to take over some key Mine Mill locals, including those in Butte, Anaconda, and Black Eagle. One of the cornerstones of its campaign was affirming white privilege by attacking Mine Mill's interracial position. But another cornerstone of the campaign, the USWA's and CIO's use of anti-Communist rhetoric, with its inherent links to a discourse that questioned the masculinity of those supposedly affiliated with Communism, angered as many Montana workers as it swayed. A large cohort in Montana had seen employers use this very tactic repeatedly in the past to try to stamp out militant unionists. Former home front men and veterans who put the values of community unionism first and who saw Mine Mill as a paragon of independent masculinity and the longtime protector of the local male breadwinner system joined progressives in successfully opposing the USWA's CIO-supported takeover. But it is critical to recognize that Mine Mill and the CIO, while arguing over the particulars, both put a working-class masculine ideology at the center of their campaigns.[17] The importance of this issue to local men suggests that working-class masculine values played a determinative part in the politics that dominated this and many other workplaces and communities across the United States in the postwar era. It reminds us that unions, and the working-class men who dominated them, combined with the GI Bill, Cold War containment, and a middle-class-oriented popular culture in creating the conservative gender order of the time.

Women living in Butte, Black Eagle, and Anaconda in the postwar era struggled against the limits that came as part of this masculine ideology. They found ways to assert a greater voice in community affairs; to question the negative effects of the prevailing gender order; and to use the values of community unionism to support greater equality for themselves within the local economic system. But their world remained highly circumscribed because of it. Not until the early 1970s would Montana's smelters and mines, compelled by national social and political changes catalyzed by the women's movement, again provide women the opportunity to work in production jobs.[18] There was nothing accidental about the longevity of this gender order. Its effects on the social politics of the twentieth century are indisputable. And it was home front men—until now sidelined in histories of World War II and midcentury liberalism—who most strongly defended it and who defeated the greatest challenge to it.

Likewise, it took the 1960s civil rights movement and its effect on federal legislation to prompt an increasing openness to the employment of black men, including their acceptance at the Black Eagle smelter for the first time. Indicating the methods used by managers and workers to continue to protect the interlocking privileges of whiteness and masculinity during the postwar era, smelter personnel manager Eugene Cox recalled, "My fellas were coached on just exactly what to say and they wouldn't be breaking any law or anything else that way. And that's what we did, we did that until I would say, roughly like, '65 or '66. And then we had to break down. . . . We began to take on, try to take on, some Black ones. . . . When we started to take on a black or two, why, dammit you give 'em a card to go to work and the next morning . . . they wouldn't show up." Angry, Cox went down to see his boyhood friend Gene, to whom he had given a card: "What's the matter with you? I bend over backwards getting you on and now you don't show up and this is twice you did it. What is it, what's wrong Gene? He said, 'Well, I'm actually'—and he meant it—'I'm afraid those white guys will kill me.' So, I took him by the hand and took him up to the mill again, the wire mill, a choice place to work, and went in with the superintendent of the mill and one or two of his foremen and we talked it over and finally Gene came to work." Laughing, Cox concludes, "That's the way we got the first one." But "there never was too many that wanted to work out there." The same sort of attitudes by workers and managers continued to foreclose on the possibility that black men, other than a few locals such as Hiawatha Brown, could gain employment in Butte's mines. It also drove most of Anaconda's remaining black smeltermen out of the plant during the 1950s.[19] As when they excluded women from copper production jobs, it was home front men who had defeated the greatest challenge to this long-running racial order.

What took place in Butte, Black Eagle, and Anaconda, Montana, in the two decades after World War II affirms the continuation of power relations in the United States that this study has shown were rooted in the pre–World War II history of local racial-ethnic and gender orders, and that were also dramatically influenced by the war. *Meet Joe Copper* has shown that in Montana's copper towns, the conservative political and social vision that many scholars attribute to the postwar era emerged among home front men during the war and was carried forward by them and by working-class veterans in the years that followed. Rather than developing in opposition to the Popular Front and New Deal liberalism, these social politics emerged from within them, affirming working-class masculine solidarity but diverging from Mine Mill's racial progressivism. By continuing to support one of the most radical unions of the war and postwar era, Montana's copper men reinforce the emerging picture of an entangled liberal and conservative American ideology that has as its central feature the protection of whiteness and masculinity. Joe Copper's history, and that of the many home front men he represents, is riddled with contradictions and paradoxes, but it is ultimately no less a part of the greatest generation's legacy and of the American national story.

ABBREVIATIONS

ACM	Anaconda Copper Mining Company
AFL	American Federation of Labor
AMPAS	Academy of Motion Picture Arts and Sciences, Los Angeles
AUCBL	Archives, University of Colorado at Boulder Library
BMU	Butte Miners' Union
BSBA	Butte-Silver Bow Public Archives, Butte
CC	*Copper Commando*
CCHS	Cascade County Historical Society, Great Falls
CIO	Congress of Industrial Organizations
DOHA	Diocese of Helena Archives, Helena
FEPC	Fair Employment Practices Commission
FSA	Federal Security Agency
GFT	*Great Falls Tribune*
Grievance Committee	Anaconda Smelter Workers' Union-Management Grievance Committee
IWW	Industrial Workers of the Worlds
Local 117	Anaconda, Montana, local of the International Union of Mine, Mill, and Smelter Workers
Local 16	Black Eagle, Montana, local of the International Union of Mine, Mill, and Smelter Workers
MGM	Metro Goldwyn Mayer
MHSRC	Montana Historical Society Research Center, Helena
Mine Mill	International Union of Mine, Mill, and Smelter Workers, Denver

MPAA	Motion Picture Association of America, Washington, DC
MS	*Montana Standard*, Butte
NARA	National Archives and Records Administration, Washington, DC
NARA–Denver	National Archives and Records Administration, Denver Office
NWLB	National War Labor Board
OWI	Office of War Information
USCFA	University of Southern California Film Archive, Los Angeles
USES	United States Employment Service
Victory Committee	ACM Victory Labor-Management Committee
WB	Warner Brothers
WFM	Western Federation of Miners, Denver (founded in Butte)
WMC	War Manpower Commission
WPA	Works Progress Administration
WPB	War Production Board
WPB–Helena	War Production Board's Helena Office

NOTES

INTRODUCTION

1. Tom Brokaw, *The Greatest Generation* (New York: Random House, 1998), 9, 11. *The Greatest Generation* was the best-selling book, fiction or nonfiction, in the United States for much of 1998. By 2005, Brokaw had authored two more books about the "greatest generation." Combined, these three works sold over 5 million copies, and his television special on the topic was watched by millions more. See Tom Brokaw, interview by Brian Lamb, "Booknotes: Tom Brokaw, *The Greatest Generation*," March 7, 1999, http://www.booknotes.org/Watch/121264-1/Tom+Brokaw.aspx, accessed January 21, 2013. See also Christopher Hayes, "The Good War on Terror," *In These Times*, September 6, 2006, http://www.inthesetimes.org/article/2788/the_good_war _on_terror/, accessed January 21, 2013.

2. Brokaw, *Greatest Generation*, 9, 12, 137.

3. There are countless films that depict military masculinity during World War II. The most influential of the recent titles is *Saving Private Ryan* (DreamWorks, 1998). Three memorials are especially indicative of this trend: the National World War II Memorial, http://www.nps.gov/nwwm/index.htm, accessed January 21, 2013; the Women in Military Service for America Memorial, http://www.womensmemorial .org/, accessed January 21, 2013; and the Rosie the Riveter/World War II Home Front National Historical Park, http://www.rosietheriveter.org/ and http://www.nps.gov /rori/index.htm, both accessed January 21, 2013. Other than Brokaw, Stephen Ambrose is the most widely read author on World War II. His books on the subject include *Band of Brothers: E Company, 106th Company, 101st Airborne; From Normandy to Hitler's Eagle's Nest* (New York: Simon & Schuster, 1992); *D-Day, June 6, 1944: The Climactic Battle of World War II* (New York: Simon & Schuster, 1994); and *Citizen Soldiers: The U.S. Army from the Normandy Beaches to the Bulge to the Surrender of Germany, June 7, 1944–May 7, 1945* (New York: Simon & Schuster, 1997). Ambrose's scholarship has been under a cloud since other historians accused him of plagiarism and factual inaccuracies. He and his publisher have apologized. There is a vast trove of scholarly work on the World War II home front. See, for example, Richard Polenberg, *War and Society: The United States, 1941–1945* (New York: J. B. Lippincott, 1972); John Morton Blum, *V Was for Victory: Politics and American Culture during World War II* (New York: Harcourt Brace Jovanovich, 1976); Richard R. Lingeman,

Don't You Know There's a War On? The American Homefront, 1941–1945 (New York: Capricorn, 1976); John Patrick Diggins, *The Proud Decades: America in War and in Peace, 1941–1960* (New York: W. W. Norton, 1988); and Allan M. Winkler, *Home Front U.S.A.: America during World War II* (New York: Harlan Davidson, 2000). The sale of Norman Rockwell's original painting, *Rosie the Riveter*, in 2002 for $4.96 million, the highest price ever paid for a Rockwell work, reinforced the interest in Rosie and suggested her continued popularity. See http://www.rosietheriveter.org/painting .htm, accessed January 21, 2013.

4. Brokaw, *Greatest Generation*, xvii, 5–6, 11–12. Brokaw notes that his perception of the greatest generation is colored by his family's World War II experience. "My first impressions of women were not confined to those of my mother caring for my brothers and me at home. I can still see in my mind's eye a woman in overalls carrying a lunch bucket, her hair covered in a red bandanna, swinging out of the big Army truck she had just parked, headed for home at the end of a long day" (ibid., 9).

5. Ibid., xvii, 11–12, 94, 96. Officially known as the Black Hills Army Ordnance Depot, Igloo's location was in far southwestern South Dakota. Construction of the depot started early in 1942. At its peak, 7,100 people were employed there, most by the Army Supply Service. For more on the history of the base, see http://www.igloo -sd.org/, accessed January 21, 2013. For more on Red Brokaw and the Brokaw family's time at Igloo, see Tom Brokaw, *A Long Way from Home: Growing Up in the American Heartland* (New York: Random House, 2002), 63–66. The story of Charles Briscoe, a Boeing engineer who helped design the B-29 bomber, provides the one extended treatment of a man on the home front. Fittingly, given the dominance of military manhood in Brokaw's book, in 1945 Briscoe volunteered for the United States Navy as a twenty-nine-year-old even though his job in a vital war industry protected him from the draft. "I had two sons and I wanted the world to be safe for them," Briscoe explained. Quoted in Brokaw, *Greatest Generation*, 94.

6. This study has been deeply influenced by the historians who in the 1970s and 1980s wrote so ably about women's World War II experiences: William H. Chafe, *The Paradox of Change* (New York: Oxford University Press, 1974); Leila Rupp, *Mobilizing Women for War: German and American Propaganda, 1939–1945* (Princeton, NJ: Princeton University Press, 1978); Karen Anderson, *Wartime Women: Sex Roles, Family Relations, and the Status of Women during World War II* (Westport, CT: Greenwood Press, 1981), 23–25; Susan M. Hartmann, *The Home Front and Beyond: American Women in the 1940s* (Boston: Twayne, 1982); Sherna Berger Gluck, *Rosie the Riveter Revisited: Women, the War, and Social Change* (Boston: Twayne, 1987); Maureen Honey, *Creating Rosie the Riveter: Class, Gender, and Propaganda during World War II* (Amherst: University of Massachusetts Press, 1984); D'Ann Campbell, *Women at War with America: Private Lives in a Patriotic Era* (Cambridge, MA: Harvard University Press, 1984); and Ruth Milkman, *Gender at Work: The Dynamics of Job Segregation by Sex during World War II* (Urbana: University of Illinois Press, 1987).

7. I drew inspiration partly from Gerald Nash's call for more research on the impact of World War II on the West. For his own groundbreaking examination, see Gerald Nash, *The American West Transformed: The Impact of the Second World War* (Lincoln: University of Nebraska Press, 1990).

8. Anaconda Smelter Worker's Union-Management Grievance Committee Meeting Transcript, 13 Apr. 1944, 4, Marcus Daly Historical Society, Anaconda, Montana. Copies of these transcripts are also in the possession of the author and available as well at the Montana Historical Society Research Center, Helena (hereafter MHSRC).

9. The scholarship on African Americans during World War II includes Neil Wynn, *The Afro-American and the Second World War* (London: Paul Elek, 1976); George Lipsitz, *Rainbow at Midnight: Labor and Culture in the 1940s* (Urbana: University of Illinois Press, 1994); Robin D. G. Kelley, "The Riddle of the Zoot: Malcolm Little and Black Cultural Politics during World War II," in Kelley, *Race Rebels: Culture, Politics, and the Black Working Class* (New York: Simon & Schuster, 1996), 161–82; Nikhil Pal Singh, "Culture/Wars: Recoding Empire in an Age of Democracy," *American Quarterly*, September 1998, pp. 471–522; Eileen Boris, "'You Wouldn't Want One of 'Em Dancing with Your Wife': Racialized Bodies on the Job in World War II," *American Quarterly* 50, no. 1 (1998), 77–108; Barbara Dianne Savage, *Broadcasting Freedom: Radio, War, and the Politics of Race, 1938–1948* (Chapel Hill: University of North Carolina Press, 1999); Steve Estes, *I Am a Man!: Race, Manhood, and the Civil Rights Movement* (Chapel Hill: University of North Carolina Press, 2005); and Lauren Rebecca Sklaroff, *Black Culture and the New Deal: The Quest for Civil Rights in the Roosevelt Era* (Chapel Hill: University of North Carolina Press, 2009). On Mexicans and Mexican Americans during World War II, see Mauricio Mazón, *The Zoot-Suit Riots: The Psychology of Symbolic Annihilation* (Austin: University of Texas Press, 1984); Rodolfo Acuña, *Occupied America: A History of Chicanos* (New York: Harper & Row, 1988), 251–98; Edward J. Escobar, *Race, Police, and the Making of a Political Identity: Mexican Americans and the Los Angeles Police Department, 1900–1945* (Berkeley: University of California Press, 1999); Erasmo Gamboa, *Mexican Labor and World War II: Braceros in the Pacific Northwest, 1942–1947* (Austin: University of Texas Press, 1990); Barbara Driscoll, *The Tracks North: The Railroad Bracero Program of World War II* (Austin: CMAS Books, Center for Mexican American Studies, University of Texas at Austin, 1998); Mae Ngai, *Impossible Subjects: Illegal Aliens and the Making of Modern America* (Princeton, NJ: Princeton University Press, 2004), 127–66; Zaragosa Vargas, *Labor Rights Are Civil Rights: Mexican American Workers in Twentieth-Century America* (Princeton, NJ: Princeton University Press, 2005), 203–51; Thomas Guglielmo, "Fighting for Caucasian Rights: Mexicans, Mexican Americans, and the Transnational Struggle for Civil Rights in World War II," *Journal of American History* 92, no. 4 (March 2006): 1218–38; and Emilio Zamora, *Claiming Rights and Righting Wrongs in Texas: Mexican Workers and Job Politics during World War II* (College Station: Texas A&M University Press, 2009).

10. Historians and other scholars of gender have urged a greater focus on men as gendered subjects. Following this prompt, recent histories of the Spanish-American War and World War I have illuminated the ways in which those conflicts challenged, reinforced, and transformed masculinity in America. Joan W. Scott, "Gender: A Useful Category of Historical Analysis," *American Historical Review* 91, no. 5 (December 1986): 1053–75, and in specific regard to World War II, Scott, "Reconceptualizing the Two World Wars," in *Behind the Lines: Gender and the Two World Wars*, ed. Margaret Randolph Higonnet, Jane Jenson, Sonya Michel, and Margaret Collins Weitz (New Haven, CT: Yale University Press, 1987), 19–30; Kristin Hoganson, *Fighting for American Manhood: How Gender Politics Provoked the Spanish-American and Philippine-American Wars* (New Haven, CT: Yale University Press, 1998); Sandra Gilbert, "Soldier's Heart: Literary Men, Literary Women, and the Great War," in Higonnet et. al., *Behind the Lines*, 197–226; and Michael C. C. Adams, *The Great Adventure: Male Desire and the Coming of World War I* (Bloomington: Indiana University Press, 1990). Adams's study, however, neglects to consider the home front. See also Mary Renda, *Taking Haiti: Military Occupation and the Culture of U.S. Imperialism, 1915–1940* (Chapel

Hill: University of North Carolina Press, 2000). For an overview on the relationship between war and gender formation, see Joshua S. Goldstein, *War and Gender: How Gender Shapes the War System and Vice Versa* (New York: Cambridge University Press, 2001).

11. The local magazine was the *Copper Commando*, which was published by the Victory Labor-Management Committees of the Butte mines and Black Eagle and Anaconda smelters during the war. A full run of the *Commando* is available at the Butte-Silver Bow Public Archives. "Montana State Guide," Works Progress Administration (hereafter WPA) Papers, box 26, folder 21, MHSRC; Patrick F. Morris, *Anaconda Montana: Copper Smelting Boom Town on the Western Frontier* (Bethesda, MD: Swann, 1997), 178–83; Black Eagle Book Committee, *In the Shadow of the Big Stack: Black Eagle* (Black Eagle, MT: Black Eagle Book Committee, 2000), 7–14.

12. Besides copper, essential for ammunition and dozens of other war items; zinc; and manganese, necessary for steel, Montana mines also provided a number of other minerals critical to war production: chromite, needed for chrome steel used in armor plate, among other products; industrial sapphire, used in scientific instruments; vermiculite, a key component in fireproof products; bentonite, a clay used especially for alsifilm, a sheet mica replacement necessary for vital electronic equipment; tungsten, used for high-speed-tool steel; and antimony, a lead "stiffener" incorporated in artillery and ammunition. Each of these minerals also had countless other wartime uses. Montana School of Mines, "Brief Memoranda concerning War Minerals in Montana," 16 Apr. 1941, War Production Board–Helena Office Records, box 7, folder 3, MHSRC; Black Eagle Book Committee, *In the Shadow of the Big Stack*, 7–14.

13. E. Anthony Rotundo, *American Manhood: Transformations in Masculinity from the Revolution to the Modern Era* (New York: Basic Books, 1983); Michael Kimmel, *Manhood in America: A Cultural History* (New York: Oxford University Press, 2006); Peter N. Stearns, *Be A Man! Males in Modern Society* (New York: Holmes and Meier, 1990). See also Peter Filene, *Him/Her/Self: Gender Identities in Modern America*, 3rd ed. (Baltimore: Johns Hopkins University Press, 1998), 173. Filene mentions men on the home front very briefly, but comes to different conclusions than does this study. Christina S. Jarvis, *The Male Body at War: American Masculinity during World War II* (DeKalb: Northern Illinois University Press, 2004), is the best study of American masculinity during World War II, but focuses on military manhood. Two essential sources on the intersection between gender identity and sexuality during the war are Allan Bérubé, *Coming Out under Fire: The History of Gay Men and Women in World War II* (New York: Simon & Schuster, 2000), and Leisa Meyer, *Creating GI Jane: Sexuality and Power in the Women's Army Corps during World War II* (New York: Columbia University Press, 1996).

14. David R. Segal, *Recruiting for Uncle Sam: Citizenship and Military Manpower Policy* (Lawrence: University Press of Kansas, 1989).

15. Historians who focus on the working class in particular places and regions have revealed the rich insights and new perspectives on gender and racial formation that in-depth, locally focused studies can yield. See Elizabeth Faue, *Community of Suffering and Struggle: Women, Men, and the Labor Movement in Minneapolis, 1915–1945* (Chapel Hill: University of North Carolina Press, 1991); Lizabeth Cohen, *Making a New Deal: Industrial Workers in Chicago, 1919–1939* (New York: Cambridge University Press, 1990); Ilene DeVault, *Sons and Daughters of Labor: Class and Clerical Work in Turn-of-the-Century Pittsburgh* (Ithaca, NY: Cornell University Press, 1990); and Michael Honey, *Southern Labor and Black Civil Rights: Organizing Memphis Work-*

ers (Urbana: University of Illinois Press, 1993). There are innumerable examples of place-based studies in the historiography of the West. I have been particularly influenced by David Emmons, *The Butte Irish: Class and Ethnicity in an American Mining Town, 1875–1925* (Urbana: University of Illinois Press, 1989); Mary Murphy, *Mining Cultures: Men, Women, and Leisure in Butte, 1914–41* (Urbana: University of Illinois Press, 1997); Elizabeth Jameson, *All That Glitters: Class, Conflict, and Community in Cripple Creek* (Urbana: University of Illinois Press, 1998); Susan Lee Johnson, *Roaring Camp: The Social World of the California Gold Rush* (New York: W. W. Norton, 2000); Laurie Mercier, *Anaconda: Labor, Community, and Culture in Montana's Smelter City* (Urbana: University of Illinois Press, 2001); and Thomas G. Andrews, *Killing for Coal: America's Deadliest Labor War* (Cambridge, MA: Harvard University Press, 2009). Gary Gerstle points out that the trend toward locally and regionally focused scholarship on the 1940s is again occurring. Gary Gerstle, "The Crucial Decade: The 1940s and Beyond," *Journal of American History* 92, no. 4 (March 2006): 1292–99. On place, gender, and class, see also the foundational essays in Ava Baron, ed., *Work Engendered: Toward a New History of American Labor* (Ithaca, NY: Cornell University Press, 1991).

16. R. W. Connell, *Masculinities: Knowledge, Power, and Social Change* (Berkeley: University of California Press, 1995), 76–81 (quotation is from p. 76); R. W. Connell and James W. Messerschmidt, "Hegemonic Masculinity: Rethinking the Concept," *Gender & Society* 19, no. 6 (December 2005): 829–59. On the importance of situating gender analysis, see Scott, "Gender," and in specific regard to World War II, Scott, "Reconceptualizing the Two World Wars."

17. Others are working in this vein. See, for example, Dean Lusher and Garry Robins, "Hegemonic and Other Masculinities in Local Social Contexts," *Men and Masculinities* 11 (June 2009): 387–423.

18. My effort to focus on power has been influenced by a variety of scholars, including Herbert G. Gutman, *Power and Culture: Essays on the American Working Class*, ed. Ira Berlin (New York: Pantheon, 1987), and Toby Ditz, "The New Men's History and the Peculiar Absence of Gendered Power: Remedies from Early American Gender History," *Gender & History* 16 (April 2004): 1–35.

19. Gail Bederman, *Manliness and Civilization: A Cultural History of Gender and Race in the United State, 1880–1917* (Chicago: University of Chicago Press, 1996). Eileen Boris's scholarship on the intersections of race, gender, and class has strongly influenced my work. Among other essays, see Eileen Boris, "From Gender to Racialized Gender: Laboring Bodies that Matter," *International Labor and Working-Class History*, no. 63 (Spring 2003): 9–13. There has been considerable scholarly interest in this area. For an excellent critical overview, see Ava Baron, "Reflections on Class, Gender, and Sexuality: Masculinity, the Embodied Worker, and the Historian's Gaze," *International Labor and Working-Class History*, no. 69 (Spring 2006): 143–60. A useful early critique of the analysis of working-class masculinity is found in Steven Maynard, "Rough Work and Rugged Men: The Social Construction of Masculinity in Working-Class History," *Labour/Le Travail* 23 (Spring 1989): 159–69.

20. "Montana State Guide," WPA Papers, MC 77, box 26, folder 21, MHSRC.

21. The US Bureau of the Census counted 1,834 African Americans in Montana out of a total population of 243,329 in 1900, and 1,256 out of a total population of 537,606 in 1930. For this and other information about the African American community in 286 the state, see the "African Americans in Montana" resources available at the Montana Historical Society's webpage: http://mhs.mt.gov/research/AfricanAmerican

/AfricanAmericanInMT.asp, accessed January 21, 2013; Bureau of the Census, *Fifteenth Census of the United States: 1930 Population*, p. 633. Oral histories, buttressed by other sources, suggest a sizable Latino presence, but exact numbers are not available because the census did not ask about individuals' Hispanic background. For American Indian data, see "Montana State Guide."

22. Matthew Guterl, *The Color of Race in America, 1900–1940* (Cambridge, MA: Harvard University Press, 2001). The scholarship on European immigrants and the question of assimilation is vast. For a useful overview, see Peter Kivisto, "The Transplanted Then and Now: The Reorientation of Immigration Studies from the Chicago School to the New Social History," *Ethnic and Racial Studies* 13, no. 4 (1990): 455–81. Thomas Guglielmo, *White on Arrival: Italians, Race, Color, and Power in Chicago, 1890–1945* New York: Oxford University Press, 2003. Guglielmo's immigrants also evidenced strong and continuing ties to their specific immigrant identity.

23. A considerable amount of scholarly work has now been done on the question of whiteness. My analysis draws especially from David Roediger, *The Wages of Whiteness: Race and the Making of the American Working Class* (New York: Verso, 1991); Cheryl I. Harris, "Whiteness as Property," *Harvard Law Review* 106 (1993): 1709–91; Matthew Frye Jacobson, *Whiteness of a Different Color: European Immigrants and the Alchemy of Race* (Cambridge, MA: Harvard University Press, 1998); Guterl, *The Color of Race in America*; Eric Arnesan, "Whiteness and the Historian's Imagination," *International Labor and Working Class History* 60 (Fall 2001): 3–32; and Guglielmo, *White on Arrival*.

24. The term *white ethnic* usually refers to the children and grandchildren of immigrants mainly from southern and eastern Europe, who desired both to be considered white and to hold on to some vestiges of their past through their community identification and cultural traditions. Barry Goldberg and Colin Greer have traced the emergence of a "pan-ethnic" ideology among white ethnics in the 1950s that "did not emphasize cultural distinction but the shared values of a white immigrant heritage." Goldberg and Greer, along with Tom Sugrue and Arnold Hirsch, note that this pan-ethnic mobilization occurred as an opposition movement to defeat racial integration of white ethnic neighborhoods in the fifties. Cited in David Roediger, "Whiteness and Ethnicity in the History of 'White Ethnics' in the United States," in his compilation of essays, *Towards the Abolition of Whiteness* (London: Verso, 1994), 183. See also Jacobson, *Whiteness of a Different Color*, 93–96.

25. The research of Nelson Lichtenstein, *Labor's War at Home: The CIO in World War II* (New York: Cambridge University Press, 1982); Gary Gerstle, *Working-Class Americanism: The Politics of Labor in a Textile City, 1914–1961* (New York: Cambridge University Press, 1989); Lipsitz, *Rainbow at Midnight*; and Bruce Nelson, *Divided We Stand: American Workers and the Struggle for Black Equality* (Princeton, NJ: Princeton University Press, 2000), proved especially crucial to my understanding of the working class during the war. Those scholars as well as Elaine Tyler May, *Homeward Bound: American Families in the Cold War Era* (New York: Basic Books, 1988); L. Cohen, *Making a New Deal*; Alan Brinkley, *The End of Reform: New Deal Liberalism in Recession and War* (Cambridge, MA: Harvard University Press, 1994); Thomas J. Sugrue, "Segmented Work, Race-Conscious Workers: Structure, Agency and Division in the CIO Era," *International Review of Social History* 41 (1996): 389–406; Thomas J. Sugrue, *The Origins of the Urban Crisis: Race and Inequality in Postwar Detroit* (Princeton, NJ: Princeton University Press, 1996); Michael Denning, *The Cultural Front: The Laboring of American Culture in the Twentieth Century* (New York: Verso, 1997); David M. Kennedy, *Freedom from Fear: The American People in Depression and War, 1929–1945*

(New York: Oxford University Press, 1999); Michelle Brattain, *The Politics of Whiteness: Race Workers, and Culture in the Modern South* (Princeton, NJ: Princeton University Press, 2001); Alice Kessler-Harris, *In Pursuit of Equity: Women, Men, and the Quest for Economic Citizenship in 20th Century America* (New York: Oxford University Press, 2001); Robert Self, *American Babylon: Race and the Struggle for Postwar Oakland* (Princeton, NJ: Princeton University Press, 2005); and Margot Canaday, *The Straight State: Sexuality and Citizenship in Twentieth-Century America* (Princeton, NJ: Princeton University Press, 2009), have deeply influenced my sense of the era's politics.

26. L. Cohen, *Making a New Deal*; Robin D. G. Kelley, *Hammer and Hoe: Alabama Communists during the Great Depression* (Chapel Hill: University of North Carolina Press, 1990); Mario T. Garcia, *Mexican Americans: Leadership, Ideology, and Identity, 1930–1960* (New Haven, CT: Yale University Press, 1991); Michael Goldfield, *The Color of Politics: Race and the Mainsprings of American Politics* (New York: New Press, 1997); Nelson, *Divided We Stand*; Denning, *The Cultural Front*.

27. During the war the government, in the guise of an enormous number of agencies, entered citizens' lives to an unprecedented degree. Wartime agencies now largely forgotten, such as the Office of Price Administration, which administered the wartime rationing program, impacted the daily existence of all Americans and even played a direct part in the drama surrounding home front masculinity. Meg Jacobs, *Pocketbook Politics: Economic Citizenship in Twentieth-Century America* (Princeton, NJ: Princeton University Press, 2005) 179–220; James T. Sparrow, *Warfare State: World War II Americans and the Age of Big Government* (New York: Oxford University Press, 2011).

CHAPTER ONE

1. Rufus A. Coleman, "Mark Twain in Montana, 1895," *Montana Magazine of History* 3, no. 2 (Spring 1953): 9–17. Michael P. Malone, *The Battle for Butte: Mining and Politics on the Northern Frontier, 1864–1906* (Seattle: University of Washington Press, 2006), 62. Michael Malone, Richard Roeder, and William Lang, *Montana: A History of Two Centuries* (Seattle: University of Washington Press, 1991), 207, 274; Joseph Kinsey Howard, "Boisterous Butte," *Survey Graphic* 28, no. 5 (May 1939): 316–20, 348–51. Likewise, Josephine Roche and Ella Gardner in 1927 labeled Butte "typically a man's world." Quoted in Mary Murphy, *Mining Cultures: Men, Women, and Leisure in Butte, 1914–41* (Urbana: University of Illinois Press, 1997), 106.

2. Ronald C. Brown, *Hard-Rock Miners: The Intermountain West, 1860–1920* (College Station: Texas A&M University Press, 1979), 20–23. Howard calls Butte a "northwestern metropolis." Howard, "Boisterous Butte," 316–317. Malone, *The Battle for Butte*, 11–33; and Writers Project of Montana, *Copper Camp: The Lusty Story of Butte, Montana, the Richest Hill on Earth* (Helena, MT: Riverbend, 2002 [first published 1943]), 13–18. Paul F. Brissenden, "Butte Miners and the Rustling Card," *American Economic Review* 10, no. 12 (December 1920), 755; M. Murphy, *Mining Cultures*, 5–6.

3. Many Butte residents recalled the ethnic character of particular neighborhoods. Joe Navarro remembered, "The Dublin Gulch was Irish, and Broadway Street was all Finlanders. Meaderville was strictly Bohunks and Italians." Joe Navarro, interview by Laurie Mercier, 25 Mar. 1983, Montana Historical Society Research Center, Helena (hereafter MHSRC); "Montana State Guide—Butte," 15 June 1938, Works Progress Administration Records, box 26, folder 27, MHSRC; Pat Kearney, *Butte Voices: Mining, Neighborhoods, People* (Butte, MT: Skyhigh Communications, 1998), 161–258. Mark Wyman, *Hard Rock Epic: Western Miners and the Industrial Revolution, 1860–1910* (Berkeley: University of California Press, 1979), 3–16, 35; Brown,

Hard-Rock Miners, 4; Writers Project of Montana, *Copper Camp,* 12, 21; M. Murphy, *Mining Cultures,* 9.

4. Federal Writers' Project, *Montana: A State Guide Book* (New York: Hastings House, 1939), 137.

5. Malone, Roeder, and Lang, *Montana,* 202–5, 209–11.

6. Ibid., 210–11, 222–31.

7. Ibid., 207–9.

8. David Emmons, *The Butte Irish: Class and Ethnicity in an American Mining Town, 1875–1925* (Urbana: University of Illinois Press, 1989), 223. Matthew Basso, "Another Look at Burke's Butte: The Great Depression and William Allen Burke's 'Greenhorn Miner,'" *Montana: The Magazine of Western History* 56, no. 4 (Winter 2006): 18–31.

9. Brown, *Hard-Rock Miners,* 6. Gail Bederman, *Manliness and Civilization: A Cultural History of Gender and Race in the United States, 1880–1917* (Chicago: University of Chicago Press, 1996); Kevin Murphy, *Political Manhood: Red Bloods, Mollycoddles, and the Politics of Progressive Era Reform* (New York: Columbia University Press, 2008); Kevin White, *The First Sexual Revolution: The Emergence of Male Heterosexuality in Modern America* (New York: New York University Press, 1992); Elliott J. Gorn, *Manly Art: Bare Knuckle Prize Fighting in America* (Ithaca, NY: Cornell University Press, 1989); Kim Townsend, *Manhood at Harvard: William James and Others* (New York: W. W. Norton, 1996); Howard, "Boisterous Butte," 316.

10. M. Murphy, *Mining Cultures,* 111–12. The mantra of one group of boys sent home from school for disobeying the rules—"We wasn't going to be sissies. We were tough guys"—articulated the beliefs of many.

11. Emmons, *The Butte Irish,* 151. *Rickettsia,* the bacteria that causes typhoid fever, was among the many bacteria found in the mines. Federal Writers' Project, *Montana,* 136.

12. Emmons, *The Butte Irish,* 141–53. M. Murphy, *Mining Cultures,* 18, 106–7. Writers Project of Montana, *Copper Camp,* 169. Gunther Peck, "Manly Gambles: The Politics of Risk on the Comstock Lode, 1860–1880," in *Across the Great Divide: Cultures of Manhood in the American West,* ed. Matthew Basso, Laura McCall, and Dee Garceau (New York: Routledge, 2001), 73–96. D. Hand Wayland et al., "Songs of the Butte Miners," *Western Folkore* 9, no. 1 (1950); S. Page Stegner, "Protest Songs from the Butte Mines," *Western Folklore* 26, no. 3 (1967). Miners' songs hint at what families and friends thought of hard-rock mining; lyrics beseeched, "Don't go down in the mine, Dad," and described Butte as a place "where the streets were paved with Irish bones."

13. By way of illustration, beginning in 1919 contract miners earned "approximately $1.50 a day over day's pay"—that is, the daily base wage. Nonferrous Metals Commission of the National War Labor Board, "Transcript of Hearing: NWLB Case No. 527," 14 and 15 Dec. 1942, 58–59, National War Labor Board Records, box 7, folder 4, National Archives and Records Administration (hereafter NARA)–Denver. Malone, *The Battle for Butte,* 76; *Nineteenth Annual Report of the Commissioner of Labor 1904* (Washington, DC: Government Printing Office, 1905), 40–209.

14. Writers Project of Montana, *Copper Camp,* 19. Berton Braley in *Pegasus Pulls a Hack* (1934), quoted in ibid., 76. On cowboys' low status in Butte during these years, see ibid., 155.

15. Emmons, *The Butte Irish,* 149–56, 265. Interestingly, there is no record that Shannon himself mined, even though he was a member of the BMU. Thomas Andrews found

some suggestive similarities in masculine ideals in Colorado's coal mines. Thomas G. Andrews, *Killing for Coal: America's Deadliest Labor War* (Cambridge, MA: Harvard University Press, 2009), 139. Perle Watters, interview by Laurie Mercier, 25 Mar. 1983, MHSRC.

16. Howard, "Boisterous Butte," 318. On working-class men, including immigrants, and the idea of breadwinning more generally, see Robert L. Griswold, *Fatherhood in America: A History* (New York: Basic Books, 1993), 34–87. For further context and a telling comparison, see Lawrence Glickman, "Inventing the 'American Standard of Living': Gender, Race, and Working-Class Identity, 1880–1925," *Labor History* 34, nos. 2–3 (Spring–Summer 1993): 221–35; and Mary H. Blewett, "Manhood and the Market: The Politics of Gender and Class among the Textile Workers of Fall River, Massachusetts, 1870–1880," in *Work Engendered. Toward a New History of American Labor*, ed. Ava Baron (Ithaca, NY: Cornell University Press, 1991), 92–113. On miners' positive view of the contract system, see John Conners, interview by Laurie Mercier, 9 Dec. 1982, MHSRC.

17. Nancy Quam-Wickham, "Rereading Man's Conquest of Nature: Skill, Myths, and the Historical Construction of Masculinity in Western Extractive Industries," *Men and Masculinities* 2, no. 2 (October 1999): 135–51; Fran Shor, "'Virile Syndicalism' in Comparative Perspective: A Gender Analysis of the IWW in the United States and Australia," *International Labor and Working Class History* 56 (October 1999): 65–77; Todd McCallum, "'Not a Sex Question'?: The One Big Union and the Politics of Radical Manhood," *Labour* 42 (Fall 1998): 15–54; David Roediger, *Towards the Abolition of Whiteness: Essays on Race, Politics, and Working Class History* (London: Verso, 1994), 127–80; Todd DePastino, *Citizen Hobo: How a Century of Homelessness Shaped America* (Chicago: University of Chicago Press, 2003), 121; Emmons, *The Butte Irish*, 221–54; Vernon H. Jensen, *Nonferrous Metals Industry Unionism, 1932–1954* (Ithaca, NY: Cornell University Press, 1954), 1–9.

18. Emmons, *The Butte Irish*, 13, 63; the proportion of Irish immigrants in Butte's population was higher than that in Boston. Malone, *The Battle for Butte*, 64–67. Writers Project of Montana, *Copper Camp*, 6, 11, 61, 222.

19. Matthew Guterl, *The Color of Race in America, 1900–1940* (Cambridge, MA: Harvard University Press, 2001), 15–19; Kevin Kenny, "Race, Violence, and the Anti-Irish Sentiment in the Nineteenth Century," in *Making the Irish American: History and Heritage of the Irish in the United States*, ed. J. J. Lee and Marion R. Casey (New York: New York University Press, 2006), 364–78; Noel Ignatiev, *How the Irish Became White* (New York: Routledge, 1995); Matthew Frye Jacobsen, *Barbarian Virtues: The United States Encounters Foreign Peoples at Home and Abroad, 1876–1917* (New York: Macmillan, 2001), 180–95. The power of the black-white binary in the South is one of the exceptions that made racial categorization in this era confusing and contradictory.

20. Madison Grant, *The Passing of the Great Race; or, The Racial Basis of European History* (New York: Charles Scribner's Sons, 1916), 86, 107–11. Grant's book continued to be so popular after its original 1916 publication that by 1937, over 1.5 million copies were circulating in the United States alone. Guterl, *The Color of Race in America*, 32–55; Roediger, *The Wages of Whiteness*.

21. Brown, *Hard-Rock Miners*, 134; Emmons, *The Butte Irish*, 246–47. On the battles, political, economic, and otherwise, among the "Copper Kings," see C. B. Glasscock, *War of the Copper Kings* (Helena, MT: Riverbend, 2002).

22. Writers Project of Montana, *Copper Camp*, 33; M. Murphy, *Mining Cultures*, 136–68. Malone, *The Battle for Butte*, 76; Jerre C. Murphy, *Comical History of Montana*, quoted

in Patrick F. Morris, *Anaconda Montana: Copper Smelting Boom Town on the Western Frontier* (Bethesda, MD: Swann, 1997), 137; Emmons, *The Butte Irish*, passim, 223–31.

23. Emmons, *The Butte Irish*, 223–31. Robert. R. Swartout Jr., "Kwangtung to Big Sky: The Chinese in Montana, 1864–1900," *Montana: The Magazine of Western History* 38, no. 1 (Winter 1988): 42–53; Stacy A. Flaherty, "Boycott in Butte: Organized Labor and the Chinese Community, 1896–1897," *Montana: The Magazine of Western History* 37, no. 1 (Winter 1987): 34–47; Ronald Takaki, *Strangers from a Different Shore: A History of Asian Americans* (Boston: Little, Brown, 1998); Erica Lee, *At America's Gates: Chinese Immigration during the Exclusion Era, 1882–1943* (Chapel Hill: University of North Carolina Press, 2004); Robert G. Lee, *Orientals: Asian Americans in Popular Culture* (Philadelphia: Temple University Press, 1999), 1–14, 51–82.

24. Carrie Schneider, "Remembering Butte's Chinatown," *Montana: The Magazine of Western History* 54, no. 2 (2004): 67–69; Karen Leong, "'A Distinct and Antagonistic Race': Constructions of Chinese Manhood in the Exclusion Debates, 1869–1878," in *Across the Great Divide: Cultures of Manhood in the American West*, ed. Matthew Basso, Laura McCall, and Dee Garceau (New York: Routledge, 2001), 131–48; David Eng, *Racial Castration: Managing Masculinity in Asian America* (Durham, NC: Duke University Press, 2001).

25. Wyman, *Hard Rock Epic*, 37–41; Writers Project of Montana, *Copper Camp*, 48. Emmons, *The Butte Irish*, 224. *Dago* and *bohunk* are derogatory terms used to describe, respectively, Italians and immigrants from southeastern Europe. Malone, *The Battle for Butte*, 67. Butte's sizable Finnish community, nominally "northern European," was nonetheless marginalized by English-speaking settled miners who saw the Finns as too politically radical.

26. Isaac F. Marcosson, *Anaconda* (New York: Dodd, Mead, 1957), 90–119; Emmons, *The Butte Irish*, 245, 257; Malone, *The Battle for Butte*, 69.

27. Malone, *The Battle For Butte*, 65.

28. Writers Project of Montana, *Copper Camp*, 140–44; Richard White, *It's Your Misfortune and None of My Own* (Norman: University of Oklahoma Press, 1993), 289; "The Story of the Butte Bo-hunk—The Dark Skinned Invader," *Butte Evening News*, 24 July 1910.

29. "The Story of the Butte Bo-hunk."

30. Ibid.

31. Ibid. Writers Project of Montana, *Copper Camp*, 141–44.

32. Emmons, *The Butte Irish*, 245. On the padrone system, see Gunther Peck, *Reinventing Free Labor: Padrones and Immigrant Workers in the North American West, 1880–1930* (New York: Cambridge University Press, 2000).

33. Rex C. Myers, "Montana's Negro Newspapers, 1894–1911," *Montana Journalism Review*, no. 16 (1973) (quotations are from p. 17); Lucille Smith Thompson and Alma Smith Jacobs, *The Negro in Montana 1800–1945: A Selective Bibliography* (Helena: Montana State Library, 1970). On Butte's African American community, see Matthew Basso, "Metal of Honor: Montana's World War II Homefront, Movies, and the Social Politics of White Male Anxiety" (PhD diss., University of Minnesota, 2001), 104–50. For a masterly overview of the African American experience in the West, see Quintard Taylor, *In Search of the Racial Frontier: African Americans in the American West, 1528–1990* (New York: W. W. Norton, 1998). Perdita Duncan, Walter Duncan, William Fenter, Elmo Fortune, and notes made by Mrs. Lena Brown, interview by Laurie Mercier, 24 Mar. 1983, MHSRC. One former timekeeper claims that black miners

were employed during World War I; however, no other source supports this contention. Hedley "Hap" Halloway, interview by Laurie Mercier, 9 Mar. 1982, MHSRC.

34. "Colored Man on the Police Force," *Butte Miner*, 7 July 1911, and "Mayor Has Faith
in Colored Cop," *Butte Miner*, 8 July 1911, both in "Afro-Americans in Montana"
vertical file, MHSRC. The mayor was a Democrat, and Cassell a Republican.

35. Duncan, Duncan, Fenter, Fortune, and Brown, interview; Nina Mjagkij, *Light in the
Darkness: African Americans and the YMCA, 1852–1946* (Lexington: University of Kentucky Press, 2003); Taylor, *In Search of the Racial Frontier*, 194–96.

36. Duncan, Duncan, Fenter, Fortune, and Brown, interview. One of Butte's oldest African American residents contended that this policy had more to do with money
than with racial attitudes: it would have been prohibitively expensive to build a
separate school for a relatively small group. Indeed, Montana had school segregation
laws as well as antimiscegenation laws on its books well into the twentieth century.
Thompson and Jacobs, *The Negro in Montana*, 1. Duncan, Duncan, Fenter, Fortune,
and Brown also noted that the wealthy wanted their domestic servants—white or
black—within walking distance of Butte's affluent Westside residential district.

37. Hugo Kenck and Margaret McMann Kenck, interview by Laurie Mercier, 8 Dec.
1982, MHSRC. Eduardo Bonilla-Silva argues that in a "racialized social system," "the
placement of people in racial categories involves some form of hierarchy that pro-
duces definite social relations between the races." Quoted and expanded in Thomas
Guglielmo, *White on Arrival: Italians, Race, Color, and Power in Chicago, 1890–1945*
(New York: Oxford University Press, 2003), 6–7. Morris, *Anaconda Montana*, 77.

38. Kenck and Kenck, interview.

39. Ibid.

40. Jerry Calvert, *The Gibraltar: Socialism and Labor in Butte, Montana, 1895–1920* (Helena:
Montana Historical Society Press, 1988). Vernon Jensen attributes the demise of the
Western Federation of Miners (WFM) in part to masculinity, arguing that the WFM
could have secured its future if it affiliated with the American Federation of Labor
(AFL). But WFM leaders would not do so, "because the AFL was considered effete,
misguided, and improperly conceived and led." Jensen, *Nonferrous Metals Industry
Unionism*, 3; Laurie Mercier, *Anaconda: Labor, Community, and Culture in Montana's
Smelter City* (Urbana: University of Illinois Press, 2001), 18–19.

41. Marcosson, *Anaconda*, 78–136. Morris, *Anaconda Montana*, 169, 196. Ironically,
when the Amalgamated holding company took control of the mines and smelters
in 1899, it stopped requiring Anaconda smeltermen to shop at the Company store.
M. Murphy, *Mining Cultures*, 24–25, 128. The ACM also tried to blame radicals for
Butte's woes.

42. Michael Punke, *Fire and Brimstone: The North Butte Mining Disaster of 1917* (New
York: Hyperion, 2007). Emmons, *The Butte Irish*, 364–67.

43. M. Murphy, *Mining Cultures*, 2, 33, 125–28. Joseph Kinsey Howard, and later the
eminent Montana historian K. Ross Toole, both argued that Montana as a whole had
become for all intents and purposes a colony of the East. Joseph Kinsey Howard,
High, Wide, and Handsome (New Haven, CT: Yale University Press, 1943); K. Ross
Toole, *Montana: An Uncommon Land* (Norman: University of Oklahoma Press, 1959).
Calvert, *The Gibraltar*.

44. M. Murphy, *Mining Cultures*, 10, 108; Griswold, *Fatherhood in America*, 34–87; Kimmel, *Manhood in America*, 191–222. Joseph Bolkovatz, interview by Laurie Mercier,
12 Aug. 1986, MHSRC. The same was true in Montana's other copper towns.

45. M. Murphy, *Mining Cultures*, 19–21, 74–76, 138–48; quotations are from p. 76. On

women's subordination and agency in Butte earlier in the century, see Paula Petrik, "She Be Content: The Development of Montana Divorce Law, 1865–1907," *Western Historical Quarterly* 18, no. 3 (July 1987): 261–91. On fashion as a contested working-class site, see Nan Enstad, *Ladies of Labor, Girls of Adventure: Working Women, Popular Culture, and Labor Politics at the Turn of the Twentieth Century* (New York: Columbia University Press, 1999).

46. M. Murphy, *Mining Cultures,* 99, 121. As Dana Frank has shown, consumership in its own right was a political and gendered arena for working-class families in this era. Dana Frank, *Purchasing Power: Consumer Organizing, Gender, and the Seattle Labor Movement, 1919–1929* (Cambridge: Cambridge University Press, 1994). On labor and the politics of consumership and production earlier in the century, see Eileen Boris, *Home to Work: Motherhood and the Politics of Industrial Homework in the United States* (Cambridge: Cambridge University Press, 1994), 81–123.

47. On the Great Depression's effect on working-class masculinity, see Kimmel, *Manhood in America,* 132–33; and Lara Campbell, *Respectable Citizens: Gender, Family, and Unemployment in Ontario's Great Depression* (Toronto: University of Toronto Press, 2009), 57–83. David Emmons, "Hard Times and War Times," in "Expert Report of David Emmons, Ph.D.," *United States of America v. Atlantic Richfield Company, et. al.,* US District Court, District of Montana, Helena Division, Case No. CV-89-039-PGH, 15 July 1996, 236–44. Howard, "Boisterous Butte," 319; M. Murphy, *Mining Cultures,* 201–5, 208–9.

48. Relief cases doubled in the same 1937–38 period. Howard, "Boisterous Butte," 319; M. Murphy, *Mining Cultures,* 201–5, 208–9. Government relief work in Butte included, most prominently, a tannery and a storm and sanitary sewer project. Emmons, "Hard Times and War Times," 236–44. The tensions between conservatives and liberals in Montana's Democratic coalition would emerge dramatically after 1940. Malone, Roeder, and Lang, *Montana,* 306–11.

49. Gary Fink, ed., *Biographical Dictionary of American Labor* (Westport, CT: Greenwood Press, 1984), 488–89. Reid Robinson, "Resignation Statement," 10 Mar. 1947, WFM-International Union of Mine, Mill, and Smelter Workers (hereafter Mine Mill) Collection, box 29, folder 19, Archives, University of Colorado at Boulder Library (hereafter AUCBL); Calvert, *The Gibraltar;* Reid Robinson, interview by Ronald Filippelli, Dec. 1969, Labor Oral History Collection, Historical Collections and Labor Archives, Pennsylvania State University Libraries, University Park.

50. Robinson, interview. Jensen, *Nonferrous Metals Industry Unionism,* 6–9. "Montana State Guide," 76–77.

51. Michael Denning, *The Cultural Front: The Laboring of American Culture in the Twentieth Century* (New York: Verso, 1997), 3–11, 23–25; Joseph Kinsey Howard, "Butte Remembers Big Bill Haywood," *Nation,* 30 Oct. 1936, 514–15. For tensions over diversity, see "Transcript of the Proceedings at the Meeting of the Mine-Mill Executive Board, August 1, 1941," WFM Mine Mill Collection, box 29, folder 1, AUCBL. Robin Kelley sees Mine Mill as "a union with a longstanding radical tradition" whose "policy of racial egalitarianism remained unmatched." Robin D. G. Kelley, *Hammer and Hoe: Alabama Communists during the Great Depression* (Chapel Hill: University of North Carolina Press, 1990), 145. Michael Goldfield, *The Color of Politics: Race and the Mainsprings of American Politics* (New York: New Press, 1997), 193–96. Jim Robinson left Butte in the 1930s and became one of Mine Mill's most important organizers, especially among workers of color in the Southwest; he continued in that capacity into the 1940s. Fink, *Biographical Dictionary,* 488–89. Mario T. Garcia,

Mexican Americans: Leadership, Ideology, and Identity, 1930–1960 (New Haven, CT: Yale University Press, 1991), 183–87, 339, note 30. Robinson, interview. Of the seven times Reid Robinson ran for union president, one of his challengers was from Butte in three elections (1936, 1942, 1946), and one was from Anaconda in a fourth (1940). Robinson, "Resignation Statement." On Communism and Mine Mill, see the history of the union by Vernon H. Jensen, the staunchly anti-Communist Cold War labor scholar, in his *Nonferrous Metals Industry Unionism*. Jensen did not believe that Jim Robinson was a Communist (33, note 6). For Jensen's take on Reid Robinson's relationship to Communism, see 34–35, 46, 50–53, 75, 95–96, 146, 150–51, and 277. Among many examples of Jensen's own politics emerging in his scholarship, see his speculation of why Communists supposedly targeted Mine Mill (xiii).

52. Walter Valacich, interview by Laurie Mercier, 17 July 1986, MHRSC; Denning, *Cultural Front*, 3–11; Harvey A. Levenstein, *Communism, Anticommunism, and the CIO* (Westport, CT: Greenwood Press, 1981), 65; Jensen, *Nonferrous Metals Industry Unionism*, 54.

53. Butte's Hibernian Lodge, founded in 1884, provides a good example of the breakdown of the Irish bond. In 1905 the order counted six hundred members, but by 1922 there were only sixty left. Irish opposed to the Free State and those who supported it ended their business and even their personal connections. M. Murphy, *Mining Cultures*, 113, 151, 152; Writers Project of Montana, *Copper Camp*, 144. On pan-ethnicity between Irish and other immigrants, see David Roediger and James Barrett, "Making New Immigrants 'Inbetween': Irish Hosts and White Panethnicity, 1890 to 1930," in *Not Just Black and White: Historical and Contemporary Perspectives on Immigration, Race, and Ethnicity in the United States*, ed. Nancy Foner and George M. Frederickson (New York: Russell Sage Foundation, 2004), 167–96.

54. Duncan, Duncan, Fenter, Fortune, and Brown, interview.

CHAPTER TWO

1. "Shack Towns on River near New Town Spur Hill into Action," *Great Falls Leader*, 11 Nov. 1959; Walter Valacich, interview by Laurie Mercier, 17 July 1986, MHRSC. Similar push-and-pull factors were common regionally and nationally. Joseph Bolkovatz, interview by Laurie Mercier, 12 Aug. 1986, Montana Historical Society Research Center, Helena (hereafter MHSRC); Gary Gerstle, "Liberty, Coercion, and the Making of Americans," *Journal of American History* 84, no. 2 (September 1997): 524–58; Black Eagle Book Committee, *In the Shadow of the Big Stack: Black Eagle* (Black Eagle, Montana: Black Eagle Book Committee, 2000), 109, 164, 302. Company documents and workers from Anaconda and Butte often referred to the "Great Falls smelter," but I will call it the Black Eagle smelter—both because that is where it was actually located, and to acknowledge the town and people that most shaped the social politics of the plant and, likewise, that the plant most influenced.

2. Black Eagle Book Committee, *In the Shadow of the Big Stack*, 6–12; Walt Valacich, "First Croats and Slovenes Came to Area in 1890 to Work at Smelter," *Great Falls Tribune* (hereafter *GFT*), 25 Mar. 1984; "[Photograph of 'Croatian Nightingale Band' from 1908,]" *Great Falls Leader*, 11 Nov. 1959; Jennie Signori, interview by Laurie Mercier, 23 Apr. 1987, MHSRC. Black Eagle residents noted that Bribir was "not far from the Italian border." Black Eagle Book Committee, *In the Shadow of the Big Stack*, 43. George J. Prpic, *The Croatian Immigrants in America* (New York: Philosophical Library, 1971). Anne Prebil, interview by Laurie Mercier, 10 July 1986, MHSRC. For a helpful framing of chain migration, networks, and push-and-pull factors, see Lucie

Cheng and Edna Bonacich, eds., *Labor Migration under Capitalism: Asian Workers in the United States before World War II* (Berkeley: University of California Press, 1984).

3. Valacich, "First Croats"; Olanda Rinari Vangelisti and Claire Vangelisti Del Guerra, interview by Laurie Mercier, 16 July 1986, MHSRC; Amelia Polich, interview by Laurie Mercier, 13 Mar. 1986, MHSRC. Swedes and Germans also had a presence in Black Eagle. Joan Earl, interview by Laurie Mercier, 19 Jan. 1988, MHSRC; Emelia Tabaracci Qunell, interview by Laurie Mercier, 6 Feb. 1986, MHSRC; Black Eagle Book Committee, *In the Shadow of the Big Stack*, 24–27; John Bodnar, *Workers' World: Kinship, Community, and Protest in an Industrial Society, 1900–1940* (Baltimore: Johns Hopkins University Press, 1982), 63–66; Kathleen Conzen, "Mainstreams and Side Channels: The Localization of Immigrant Cultures," *Journal of American Ethnic History* 11 (1991): 5–20; Rudolph J. Vecoli, ed., *Italian Immigrants in Rural and Small Town America* (New York: American Italian Historical Association, 1987).

4. Vangelisti and Del Guerra, interview (the source of the "shoes" quotation); William Tonkovich, interview by Laurie Mercier, 27 Feb. 1986, MHSRC; Qunell, interview; Ronald Bayor, *Neighbors in Conflict: The Irish, Germans, Jews, and Italians of New York City, 1929–1941* (Baltimore: Johns Hopkins University Press, 1978); Polich, interview; Qunell, interview; Black Eagle Book Committee, *In the Shadow of the Big Stack*, 109, 319, 388; Prebil, interview; Nancy C. Carnevale, *A New Language, A New World: Italian Immigrants in the United States, 1890–1945* (Urbana: University of Illinois Press, 2009); Philip Gleason, *Speaking of Diversity: Language and Ethnicity in Twentieth Century America* (Baltimore: Johns Hopkins University Press, 1992).

5. Black Eagle Book Committee, *In the Shadow of the Big Stack*, 433–35. Desmond S. King, *Making Americans: Immigration, Race, and the Origins of the Diverse Democracy* (Cambridge, MA: Harvard University Press, 2002), 29–30, 35, 44; Johnathan Zimmerman, "Ethnics against Ethnicity: European Immigrants and Foreign-Language Instruction, 1890–1940," *Journal of American History* 88, no. 4 (March 2003): 1383–1404; Vangelisti and Del Guerra, interview; Black Eagle Book Committee, *In the Shadow of the Big Stack*, 35, 433, 436, 442; Tonkovich, interview; Qunell, interview.

6. Richard Jules Oestreicher, *Solidarity and Fragmentation: Working People and Class Consciousness in Detroit, 1875–1900* (Urbana: University of Illinois Press, 1989). On the history and practice of associational life in Montana, see David Emmons, *The Butte Irish: Class and Ethnicity in an American Mining Town, 1875–1925* (Urbana: University of Illinois Press, 1989), 94–132; and Mary Murphy, *Mining Cultures: Men, Women, and Leisure in Butte, 1914–41* (Urbana: University of Illinois Press, 1997), 136–62. See also Lizabeth Cohen, *Making a New Deal: Industrial Workers in Chicago, 1919–1939* (New York: Cambridge University Press, 1990); Mary Ann Clawson, *Constructing Brotherhood: Class, Gender, and Fraternalism* (Princeton, NJ: Princeton University Press, 1989); Mark C. Carnes, *Secret Ritual and Manhood in Victorian America* (New Haven, CT: Yale University Press, 1989); Robert Putnam, *Bowling Alone: The Collapse and Revival of American Community* (New York: Simon & Schuster, 2000); Valacich, "First Croats"; and Black Eagle Book Committee, *In the Shadow of the Big Stack*, 27–29, 39, 501.

7. Tonkovich, interview; Signori, interview; Black Eagle Book Committee, *In the Shadow of the Big Stack*, 27–28.

8. Tonkovich, interview; Signori, interview; Black Eagle Book Committee, *In the Shadow of the Big Stack*, 27–28.

9. "The History of Blessed Sacrament Parish, Black Eagle, Montana," n.d., and "The Church History of the Black Eagle Parish for the 50th Anniversary of the Blessed

Sacrament Church," 16 Dec. 1972, both in Diocese of Great Falls–Billings Archives, Great Falls, Montana; Vangelisti and Del Guerra, interview; Tonkovich, interview; Qunell, interview; Earl, interview; Black Eagle Book Committee, *In the Shadow of the Big Stack*, 5, 27, 34, 109 (the source of the Garrity quotation), 164, 424–26; Signori, interview. For a fuller picture of the relationship between Catholicism, immigrants, and gender, see Colleen McDannell, "True Men as We Need Them: Catholicism and the Irish Male," *American Studies* 27, no. 2 (1986): 19–36; Colleen McDannell, "Catholic Domesticity, 1860–1960," in *American Catholic Women: A Historical Exploration*, ed. Karen Kennelly, CSJ (New York: Macmillan, 1989), 48–80; James K. Kenneally, *The History of American Catholic Women* (New York: Crossroads, 1990), 113–30; Robert A. Orsi, *Thank You, St. Jude: Women's Devotion to the Patron Saint of Hopeless Causes* (New Haven, CT: Yale University Press, 1996), 71–94; and Mary Jo Weaver, "Feminists and Patriarchs in the Catholic Church: Orthodoxy and Its Discontents," in *Catholic Lives, and Contemporary America*, ed. Thomas J. Ferraro (Durham, NC: Duke University Press, 1997), 187–204.

10. Black Eagle Book Committee, *In the Shadow of the Big Stack*, 38, 43, 120, 154, 254, 302, 345. Signori, interview; Qunell, interview.

11. Vangelisti and Del Guerra, interview; Signori, interview. On immigrant women's migration and labor, see Donna R. Gabaccia, *From the Other Side: Women, Gender, and Immigrant Life in the U.S., 1820–1990* (Indianapolis: Indiana University Press, 1994). Ilene DeVault, *Sons and Daughters of Labor: Class and Clerical Work in Turn-of-the-Century Pittsburgh* (Ithaca, NY: Cornell University Press, 1990). Lawrence Tessman, interview by Laurie Mercier, 28 Feb. 1986, MHSRC. The same dynamic was true in Butte and Anaconda. Eugene Cox, interview by Laurie Mercier, 16 July 1986, MHSRC. Bob Vine, interview by Laurie Mercier, 27 and 29 May 1986, MHSRC. Tonkovich, interview.

12. Marie "Cookie" Palagi Godlewski, interview by Laurie Mercier, 7 May 1987, MHSRC. Polich, interview; Signori, interview.

13. Christina Simmons, *Making Marriage Modern: Women's Sexuality from the Progressive Era to World War II* (New York: Oxford University Press, 2009); Elizabeth Clement, *Love For Sale: Courting, Treating, and Prostitution in New York City, 1900–1945* (Chapel Hill: University of North Carolina Press, 2006), 13–44; Paula Fass, *The Damned and the Beautiful: American Youth in the 1920s* (New York: Oxford University Press, 1979); Beth Bailey, *From Front Porch to Back Seat: Courtship in Twentieth-Century America* (Baltimore: Johns Hopkins University Press, 1989); Zaira Stefani Lukes, interview by Laurie Mercier, 28 Feb. 1986, MHSRC. For more on gendered space locally, see Black Eagle Book Committee, *In the Shadow of the Big Stack*, 4, 328; and Vangelisti and Del Guerra, interview. Rinari was Vangelisti's father. Godlewski, interview.

14. McDannell, "True Men as We Need Them"; Kevin Murphy, *Political Manhood: Red Bloods, Mollycoddles, and the Politics of Progressive Era Reform* (New York: Columbia University Press, 2008), 38–103.

15. Immigration Commission (William P. Dillingham et al.), *Reports of the Immigration Commission: Immigrants in Industries, Part 25; Japanese and Other Immigrant Races in the Pacific Coast and Rocky Mountain States* (Washington, DC: Government Printing Office, 1911). Black Eagle Book Committee, *In the Shadow of the Big Stack*, 212, 460–73.

16. Black Eagle Book Committee, *In the Shadow of the Big Stack*, 6–12.

17. Clarence Silloway, interview by Laurie Mercier, 15 July 1986, MHSRC. Cox, interview. For a fuller description of areas in the plant, see Black Eagle Book Committee,

In the Shadow of the Big Stack, 9–11. Eric Foner, *Free Soil, Free Labor, Free Men: The Ideology of the Republican Party before the Civil War* (New York: Oxford University Press, 1970); David R. Roediger, *The Wages of Whiteness: Race and the Making of the American Working Class* (New York: Verso, 1990).

18. Tonkovich, interview; Signori, interview; Matthew Guterl, *The Color of Race in America, 1900–1940* (Cambridge, MA: Harvard University Press, 2001); Thomas Guglielmo, *White on Arrival: Italians, Race, Color, and Power in Chicago, 1890–1945* (New York: Oxford University Press, 2003). Fights did occur occasionally between Croatians and Italians. Silloway recalled the knifing of a Croatian in Black Eagle in the 1920s or early 1930s. Silloway, interview.

19. Great Falls was home to a large Anglo population as well as a substantial number of first-, second-, and third-generation immigrants, a small African American community, and a sizable American Indian community. Del Guerra says that ethnics in Black Eagle "were much closer as a community because of the pressure to abandon" their culture and assimilate. Vangelisti and Del Guerra, interview. Valacich, interview. Richard B. Roeder, "A Settlement on the Plains: Paris Gibson and the Building of Great Falls," *Montana: The Magazine of Western History* 42, no. 4 (Autumn 1992): 4–19. Godlewski, interview; Tonkovich, interview. Valacich claims that Black Eagle's immigrants were refused work in Great Falls.

20. Cox, interview; Black Eagle Book Committee, *In the Shadow of the Big Stack*, 119.

21. David Roediger, *Working toward Whiteness: How America's Immigrant Became White; The Strange Journey from Ellis Island to the Suburbs* (New York: Basic Books, 2006). Cox, interview. Lawrence Tessman, a longtime smelterman, confirmed Cox's assessment and argued that "the railroad never discriminated," a point that many African American veterans of railroad employment would surely contest. Residents suggested that the Company saw Black Eagle's ethnic groups as "valuable people to society and the community." Vangelisti and Del Guerra, interview; Silloway, interview; Guglielmo, *White on Arrival*.

22. Tessman, interview. Division of Indian Education, Montana Office of Public Instruction, "Montana Indians: Their History and Location," April 2009, http://opi.mt.gov /pdf/indianed/resources/MTIndiansHistoryLocation.pdf, accessed January 21, 2013. A precise historical accounting of the shifting population of Great Falls's Landless Indian community is virtually impossible, but the following sources are enlightening: "Population of Hill 57 Tribal Affiliation," 6 Nov. 1955, available in "Hill 57" vertical file, MHSRC; "Large Percentage of Hill 57 Residents Originally Turtle Mountain Chippewa," *GFT*, 6 Sept. 1955. Those with links to the Little Shell Band were among the victims of the infamous "Ten Cent Treaty" that fraudulently removed approximately 10 million acres from the tribe's possession. Roland Marmon, "Last Card Played: A History of the Turtle Mountain Chippewa and the Ten Cent Treaty of 1892" (PhD diss., University of Arizona, 2009); Donald Smythe, *Guerrilla Warrior: The Early Life of John J. Pershing* (New York: Charles Scribner's Sons, 1973); Peter Johnson, "Landless Indian Roots Date to 1890" and "Hill 57," *GFT*, 10 Aug. 1986; D'arcy McNickle, "Hill 57," *Indians at Work* magazine, 1 Feb. 1937; and Jim Tracy, "Landless Tribe: After Nearly a Century Recognition of Chippewa Finally Nears Reality," *Montana Standard*, 3 Jan. 1988.

23. Tessman, interview. Tessman confirms that "there were a lot of Indians" who worked at the smelter. He adds that there were also three or four Filipinos, but no other sources mention this group. P. Johnson, "Landless Indian Roots" and "Hill 57"; McNickle, "Hill 57"; Tracy, "Landless Tribe." On Charlie Russell's influence locally, see

"Montana State Guide—Great Falls," June 17, 1938, Works Progress Administration (hereafter WPA) Records, box 26, folder 28, MHSA. Alexander Nemerov, *Frederick Remington and Turn-of-the-Century America* (New Haven, CT: Yale University Press, 1995).

24. Valacich, interview. On the connection between the IWW and Indian employment, see Silloway, interview. "Montana State Guide—Great Falls," WPA Records, box 26, folder 28, MHSRC; Melvin Dubofsky, *We Shall Be All: A History of the Industrial Workers of the World* (Urbana: University of Illinois Press, 2000), 106; Philip S. Foner, *History of the Labor Movement in the United States, World War I, 1914–1918* (New York: International Publishers, 1987), 247; Michael Punke, *Fire and Brimstone: The North Butte Disaster of 1917* (New York: Hyperion, 2007), 202. Michael P. Malone, *The Battle for Butte: Mining and Politics on the Northern Frontier, 1864–1906* (Seattle: University of Washington Press, 2006); Emmons, *The Butte Irish*.

25. The story of Guy Palagi (found on p. 259 of *In the Shadow of the Big Stack*) represents well the Company's reputation for assisting the town's immigrant population long before the high period of paternalistic management practices. Black Eagle Book Committee, *In the Shadow of the Big Stack*, 259, 275, 299. R. B. Caples to A. E. Wiggin, correspondence re: honoring workers, 9 June 1939, and "General Sheet," 1 Mar. 1939, both in ACM Co. Records, box 208, folder 9, MHSRC. Wiggin, who took his first position at the smelter in 1907, and who also had experience at the Anaconda plant, took over the top position in Black Eagle in 1929. Townspeople remember him as "a highly popular executive who won the respect and friendship of thousands who had been employed" at the plant. Wiggin's paternalistic management methods were featured in the industry's leading journal in 1939. He was also a well-known "progressive citizen" in Great Falls. His death at age fifty-six in April 1942 saw "nearly all stores in Great Falls" close their doors on the day of his funeral and flags at the Montana ACM properties fly at half-staff (Black Eagle Book Committee, *In the Shadow of the Big Stack*, 398). Albert E. Wiggin, "Making Employment Attractive at Anaconda's Great Falls Plant," *Engineering and Mining Journal* 40, no. 3 (1939): 35–37. L. Cohen, *Making a New Deal*; Gerald Zahavi, *Workers, Managers, and Welfare Capitalism: The Shoemakers and Tanners of Endicott Johnson, 1890–1950* (Urbana: University of Illinois Press, 1988). Tom Dickson, interview by Laurie Mercier, 30 May 1986, MHSRC. Ties to immigrant identity were also maintained into the World War II period by shopping at Black Eagle's local ethnic markets. The continuation of this practice put the town outside national trends. Black Eagle Book Committee, *In the Shadow of the Big Stack*, 406–7.

26. "More than 1,100 Now Employed at Smelter," *Educator*, 24 Mar. 1932; R. B. Caples to A. E. Wiggin, 26 May 1932, and A. E. Wiggin to J. R. Hobbins, 4 Feb. 1932, both in ACM Co. Records, box 219, folder 1, MHSRC; Walter C. Teagle to Roy D. Chapin, 14 Dec. 1932, ACM Co. Records, box 229, folder 8, MHSRC. ACM had instituted a policy at all its US facilities mirroring the national "Share-the-Work" initiative. Teagle to Chapin, 14 Dec. 1932, and R. B. Caples to W. B. Daly, 11 Jan. 1932, ACM Co. Records, box 219, folder 1, MHSRC; "Notice to Employees," 23 Apr. 1930, and "Share the Work" worksheet, 20 Dec. 1932, ACM Co. Records, box 229, folder 8, MHSRC.

27. Silloway, interview. L. Cohen, *Making a New Deal*; and Elizabeth Faue, *Community of Suffering and Struggle: Women, Men, and the Labor Movement in Minneapolis, 1915–1945* (Chapel Hill: University of North Carolina Press, 1991). In contrast, Anaconda's white and white ethnic smeltermen bragged about taking whatever they pleased

from the plant. Frank Zogarts, interview by Laurie Mercier, 18 November 1982, MHSRC. Black Eagle's second-generation immigrant children "played Indian" during this same period—a practice, as Philip Deloria has argued, that was part of claiming whiteness. Black Eagle Book Committee, *In the Shadow of the Big Stack*, 441. Philip Deloria, *Playing Indian* (New Haven, CT: Yale University Press, 1998), 95–107.

28. Ward Kinney, "Montana Challenges the Tyranny of Copper," *Nation*, 25 July 1934, 98–99; Polich, interview. The resulting contract included a closed shop, a $4.75 base daily wage for eight hours, with sliding scale of increases tied to copper prices, and a forty-hour workweek. "Montana State Guide—Great Falls," June 17, 1938, WPA Records, box 26, folder 28, MHSRC. See also "'Beautiful People of Little Chicago' Face Long Winter with the Closing of 'the Company,'" *GFT*, 5 Oct. 1980; and US Department of Labor to Anaconda Copper Mining Company, Great Falls, 16 June 1934, ACM Co. Records, box 229, folder 8, MHSRC. Michael Denning, *The Cultural Front: The Laboring of American Culture in the Twentieth Century* (New York: Verso, 1997); Anthony Tyeeme Clark and Joane Nagel, "White Men, Red Masks," in *Across the Great Divide: Cultures of Manhood in the American West*, ed. Matthew Basso, Laura McCall, and Dee Garceau (New York: Routledge, 2001), 109–30; Deloria, *Playing Indian*; Tonkovich, interview; "Montana State Guide—Great Falls."

29. Lyle Pellett, interview by Laurie Mercier, 13 Mar. 1986, MHSRC; Tonkovich, interview. Wiggin's paternalistic approach lasted into the early 1940s, and included supporting his Croatian and Italian employees if they had a conflict with a local business. The result was that, in his words, "the relations between management and employees are, we think, very satisfactory." R. B. Caples, Wiggin's second in command throughout the 1930s, continued this approach when he took the top job following Wiggin's death. R. B. Caples to A. E. Wiggin, 9 June 1939, and "General Sheet," 1 Mar. 1939, both in ACM Co. Records, box 208, folder 9, MHSRC. Signori, interview. Black Eagle Book Committee, *In the Shadow of the Big Stack*, 64, 479–82.

30. Tonkovich, interview. The same employment dynamic was true in Anaconda. Robert J. Kelly, interview by Laurie Mercier, 2 October 1986, MHSRC. Not until 1940, when the Company started hiring again, did Pellett make his way into the smelter workforce. Pellett, interview. Tessman, interview. On the other hand, Albert Clark contended that "boys looked forward to working in the smelter." Albert Clark, interview by Laurie Mercier, 19 Nov. 1982, MHSRC.

31. Robert Rossberg and Muriel Rossberg, interview by Laurie Mercier, 18 Jan. 1988, MHSRC; Vangelisti and Del Guerra, interview; Godlewski, interview. Black Eagle Book Committee, *In the Shadow of the Big Stack*, 12–13.

32. Vangelisti and Del Guerra, interview; Earl, interview.

33. P. Johnson, "Landless Indian Roots" and "Hill 57"; McNickle, "Hill 57"; Tracy, "Landless Tribe."

34. Denning, *The Cultural Front*; Michael Goldfield, *The Color of Politics: Race and the Mainsprings of American Politics* (New York: The New Press, 1997), 193–96; W. E. Mitchell to K. B. Frazier, 6 Mar. 1937, and ACM Number of [Daily Wage] Employees by Month for 1937, 10 Dec. 1937, both in ACM Co. Records, box 208, folder 9, MHSRC.

35. D'arcy McNickle, "Indians of Hill 57 May Teach Lessons of Production for Use," *GFT*, 7 Feb. 1937; P. Johnson, "Landless Indian Roots" and "Hill 57"; Joan Bishop, "From Hill 57 to Capitol Hill: 'Making the Sparks Fly'; Sister Providencial Tolan's Drive on Behalf of Montana's Off-Reservation Indians, 1950–1970," *Montana: The Magazine of*

Western History 43, no. 3 (Summer 1993): 16–29; McNickle, "Hill 57"; Tracy, "Landless Tribe."

36. McNickle, "Indians of Hill 57"; Black Eagle Book Committee, *In the Shadow of the Big Stack*, 125.

37. W. E. Mitchell to K. B. Frazier, 6 Mar. 1937; ACM Number of [Daily Wage] Employees by Month for 1937, 10 Dec. 1937, and E. B. Larsen to K. B. Frazier, 17 Jun. 1940, all in ACM Co. Records, box 208, folder 9, MHSRC.

CHAPTER THREE

1. Isaac F. Marcosson, *Anaconda* (New York: Dodd, Mead, 1957), 46–47. At that time, the only large-capacity copper smelter was in Wales. Daly initially had copper shipped there for processing.

2. Ibid., 51–54; Laurie Mercier, *Anaconda: Labor, Community, and Culture in Montana's Smelter City* (Urbana: University of Illinois Press, 2001), 10–11; Patrick F. Morris, *Anaconda Montana: Copper Smelting Boom Town on the Western Frontier* (Bethesda, MD: Swann, 1997), 26–48; "Edward B. Reynolds—Sketch Autobiography" (the source of the block quotation), 24 Mar. 1941, Works Progress Administration (hereafter WPA) Records, box 18, folder 6, Montana Historical Society Research Center, Helena (hereafter MHSRC).

3. Morris, *Anaconda Montana*, 33–38.

4. Ibid., 27, 33, 108, 109 (the source of the "owned and operated" quotation); Marcosson, *Anaconda*, 53–54 (the source of the "Anaconda lay deep" quotation).

5. Mercier, *Anaconda*, 14; Bob Vine, *Anaconda Memories, 1883–1983* (Butte, MT: Artcraft Publishers, 1983), 8, 13, 24; David R. Roediger and Philip S. Foner, *Our Own Time: A History of American Labor and the Working Day* (London: Verso, 1989); Roy Rosenzweig, *Eight Hours for What We Will: Workers and Leisure in an Industrial City, 1870–1920* (New York: Cambridge University Press, 1985).

6. *Polk's Anaconda (Deer Lodge County, Mont.) City Directory, 1941* (Salt Lake City, UT: R. L. Polk, 1941), 11, 13–15; Mercier, *Anaconda*, 15, 19; Michael P. Malone, *The Battle for Butte: Mining and Politics on the Northern Frontier, 1864–1906* (Seattle: University of Washington Press, 2006), 159–62; Morris, *Anaconda Montana*, 109–11; Matt Kelly, *Anaconda, Montana's Copper City* (Anaconda, MT: Soroptimist Club, 1983), 35 (the source of the "[each] new man" quotation).

7. Morris, *Anaconda Montana*, 79, 128 (the source of the block quotation). In the press, Anaconda also found itself described repeatedly as a "a city of mechanics and laborers." Mercier, *Anaconda*, 28. Matt Kelly described Anaconda of this period as "a bachelor's town of big boarding houses, saloons that stayed open all night, gambling houses running wide open on Main Street" (Kelly, *Anaconda*, 5).

8. Montana's Socialists also played on masculine ideals as they situated their politics in relation to competitors. Jerry Calvert, *The Gibraltar: Socialism and Labor in Butte, Montana, 1895–1920* (Helena: Montana Historical Society Press, 1988); Mercier, *Anaconda*, 15 (the source of the quotation); Vine, *Anaconda Memories*, 13. Nationally see Julie Greene, *Pure and Simple Politics: The American Federation of Labor and Political Activism, 1181–1917* (Cambridge: Cambridge University Press, 1998), 139.

9. Jerry Calvert, "The Rise and Fall of Socialism in a Company Town: Anaconda, Montana, 1902–1905," *Montana: Magazine of Western History* 36, no. 4 (Autumn 1986): 6–12; Morris, *Anaconda Montana*, 208–12; Vine, *Anaconda Memories*, 13; Mercier, *Anaconda*, 17.

10. Calvert, "The Rise and Fall"; Morris, *Anaconda Montana*, 208–12; Elizabeth Jameson, *All that Glitters: Class, Conflict, and Community in Cripple Creek* (Urbana: University of Illinois Press, 1998).

11. Calvert, "The Rise and Fall," 6–12 (quotation is from p. 12); Morris, *Anaconda Montana*, 208–12; Vine, *Anaconda Memories*, 13; Mercier, *Anaconda*, 17.

12. Immigration Commission (William P. Dillingham et al.), *Reports of the Immigration Commission: Immigrants in Industries, Part 25; Japanese and Other Immigrant Races in the Pacific Coast and Rocky Mountain States* (Washington, DC: Government Printing Office, 1911), 176–78.

13. Ibid., 173–74, 176–78; John Luke McKeon, interview by Laurie Mercier, 29 July 1986, MHSRC; M. Kelly, *Anaconda, Montana's Copper City*, 30–31.

14. Morris, *Anaconda Montana*. A parallel settlement model described the northern Italians. As of 1909, fifty-eight men, or 43 percent of the total northern Italian workforce, had come to the United States within the previous five years. Immigration Commission, *Reports*, 174–76; Ruth Meidl, comp., and George P. Wellcome, ed., *Anaconda, Montana: A Century of History, 1883–1983* (Anaconda, MT: n.p. [1983]), 17.

15. McKeon, interview; M. Kelly, *Anaconda, Montana's Copper City*, 18. On Goosetown's name, see Vine, *Anaconda Memories*, 24–25; and M. Kelly, *Anaconda, Montana's Copper City*, 68. Morris, *Anaconda Montana*, 33–35, 42, 100, 158–59.

16. Howard Rosenleaf, interview by Laurie Mercier, 29 July 1986, MHSRC; Morris, *Anaconda Montana*, 193–94; Mercier, *Anaconda*, 22–23; Robert J. Kelly, interview by Laurie Mercier, 2 October 1986, MHSRC. Kelly contended that Anaconda schools helped overcome ethnic separatism.

17. For more on ethnic Anaconda, see Mercier, *Anaconda*, 21–28; Immigration Commission, *Reports*, 174–76; McKeon, interview; and Katie Dewing, interview by Laurie Mercier, 11 Aug. 1986, MHSRC. Anaconda management tended to live on the West Side, in what one member of the working class described as "mansions" with "servants" and "chauffeured cars" (Dewing, interview).

18. Mercier, *Anaconda*, 23; John Phillip, interview by Laurie Mercier, 24 Nov. 1981, MHSRC; Joseph Bolkovatz, interview by Laurie Mercier, 12 Aug. 1986, MHSRC. The Irish controlled a number of areas in the plant—particularly in the mill—considered the best in which to work, and they tended to hire other Irish. Austrians controlled a few less sought-after areas, and also hired fellow countrymen. Bob Vine, interview by Laurie Mercier, 27 and 29 May 1986, MHSRC; Albert Clark, interview by Laurie Mercier, 19 Nov. 1982, MHSRC; M. Kelly, *Anaconda, Montana's Copper City*, 31; Meidl and Wellcome, *Anaconda, Montana*, 27; McKeon, interview; David Emmons, *The Butte Irish: Class and Ethnicity in an American Mining Town, 1875–1925* (Urbana: University of Illinois Press, 1989), 94–132; Mary Murphy, *Mining Cultures: Men, Women, and Leisure in Butte, 1914–41* (Urbana: University of Illinois Press, 1997), 136–62.

19. Meidl and Wellcome, *Anaconda, Montana*, 13–14, 32, 46, 57, 60; Morris, *Anaconda Montana*, 100, 110 (the source of the quotations); Mercier, *Anaconda*, 15.

20. R. J. Kelly, interview. On boxing in Butte, see M. Murphy, *Mining Cultures*, 114–18 (quotation is from p. 118); and M. Kelly, *Anaconda, Montana's Copper City*, 4. In Black Eagle, see Black Eagle Book Committee, *In the Shadow of the Big Stack: Black Eagle* (Black Eagle, MT: Black Eagle Book Committee, 2000), 28–29.

21. M. Kelly, *Anaconda, Montana's Copper City*, 4.

22. Immigration Commission, *Reports*, 179–81.

23. Ibid., 179–82; Malone, *The Battle for Butte*, 161; Vine, *Anaconda Memories*, 124; Mercier, *Anaconda*, 31.

24. Morris, *Anaconda Montana*, 113–24.

25. Ibid.; Alexander Saxton, *The Indispensable Enemy: Labor and the Anti-Chinese Movement in California* (Berkeley: University of California Press, 1995); Robert. R. Swartout Jr., "Kwangtung to Big Sky: The Chinese in Montana, 1864–1900," *Montana: The Magazine of Western History* 38, no. 1 (Winter 1988): 42–53; Stacy A. Flaherty, "Boycott in Butte: Organized Labor and the Chinese Community, 1896–1897," *Montana: The Magazine of Western History* 37, no. 1 (Winter 1987): 34–47.

26. Nicholas Peterson Vrooman, "Sundance in Silver Bow: Urban Indian Poverty in the Shadow of the Richest Hill on Earth," *Drumlummon Views* 3, no. 1 (Spring 2009): 361–94; William H. Gustafson, interview by Laurie Mercier, 10 Mar. 1983, MHSRC; M. Kelly, *Anaconda, Montana's Copper City*, 48–49; Morris, *Anaconda Montana*, 23–25.

27. Southern Italians were less successful. Mercier, *Anaconda*, 26.

28. M. Kelly, *Anaconda, Montana's Copper City*, 71; Vine, *Anaconda Memories*, 39–40. Smelterman George Bertsch, who began at the smelter in 1883 and worked until 1944, provides one of many good examples of the "steady smelterman." There were 105 other men with over forty years' experience at the smelter in 1943. Mercier, *Anaconda*, 19; craft unions did survive this period.

29. Mercier, *Anaconda*, 21, 26–28. The Hibernians' practice of marching in the Mesopust parade is a wonderful example of this. Immigration Commission, *Reports*, 174–76.

30. Writers Project of Montana, *Copper Camp: The Lusty Story of Butte, Montana, the Richest Hill on Earth* (Helena, MT: Riverbend, 2002 [first published 1943]), 229–50; quotation is from p. 236. Morris, *Anaconda Montana*, 84–96. Anaconda's status vis-à-vis Butte was not as straightforward as that of rival city. Because transit between the two places was constant, thanks to the Butte, Anaconda, and Pacific Railroad, in some ways Anaconda self-identified, and was thought of in the mining city as another Butte neighborhood. Anaconda sports teams played in leagues against those from Meaderville, Walkerville, Dublin Gulch, and other Butte areas. But they also took on Butte combined teams in virtually every sport popular at the time.

31. R. J. Kelly, interview; Writers Project of Montana, *Copper Camp*, 235–36; Patrick F. McDevitt, *"May the Best Man Win": Sport, Masculinity, and Nationalism in Great Britain and the Empire, 1880–1935* (New York: Palgrave MacMillan, 2004), 14. According to Patrick McDevitt, for men in Ireland, Gaelic football "assisted in the formation of an Irish conception of a nationalist masculinity during the period from 1184 to 1916" that countered "the English belief that Irish men were inferior." See also Sara Brady, "Home and Away: The Gaelic Games, Gender, and Migration," *New Hibernia Review* 11, no. 3 (Autumn 2007): 28–43.

32. Writers Project of Montana, *Copper Camp*, 60–61; Morris, *Anaconda Montana*, 96 (the source of the quotation), 137, 220. At the time, the smeltermen acknowledged that the danger of underground work deserved a higher base rate of pay than their surface labor.

33. Writers Project of Montana, *Copper Camp*, 60–61. Vine, interview. Suggesting a later amalgamation of identity around shared status as copper towns, Bob Vine reports that Anaconda and Butte youth fought each other, but "there isn't too much difference" between the two communities. "When one cut, the other bled," he summarized. Morris, *Anaconda Montana*, 84–93; quotation is from p. 84.

34. Morris, *Anaconda Montana*, 293–94; McKeon, interview. Southeastern European languages continued to be widely used throughout and even after the 1940s. Meidl

and Wellcome, *Anaconda, Montana*, 69–70. The story of Steve Trbovich represents the changes in attitude revealed by Bohunkus Day as well. Mercier, *Anaconda*, 31. On smeltermen's cross-ethnic male bond, see Sister Gilmary Vaughan, interview by Laurie Mercier, 30 July 1986, MHSRC.

35. Mercier, *Anaconda*, 21, 34–37. Women in Anaconda were outnumbered. In 1900 they comprised only 41.6 percent of the population; by 1920 they comprised 46 percent, and by 1940 48 percent. Vaughan, interview.

36. Mercier, *Anaconda*, 21, 24–25, 29, 35–41.

37. Meidl and Wellcome, *Anaconda, Montana*, 12.

38. Laurie Mercier, "Smelter City: Labor, Gender, and Cultural Politics in Anaconda, Montana, 1934–1980" (PhD diss., University of Oregon, 1995), 147, 157–59; David Montgomery, *The Fall of the House of Labor: The Workplace, the State, and American Labor Activism, 1865–1925* (New York: Cambridge University Press, 1988); Janet Ore, "Labor and the New Deal in Butte, Montana: The IUMMSW Strike of 1934" (MA thesis, Washington State University, 1987), 57–70.

39. Mercier, "Smelter City," 151, 164. See, for example, Elizabeth Faue, *Community of Suffering and Struggle: Women, Men, and the Labor Movement in Minneapolis, 1915–1945* (Chapel Hill: University of North Carolina Pres, 1991).

40. David Montgomery, *Workers' Control in America: Studies in the History of Work, Technology, and Labor Struggles* (New York: Cambridge University Press, 1979); Ava Baron, ed., *Labor Engendered: Toward a New History of American Labor* (Ithaca, NY: Cornell University Press, 1991); Peter Way, *Common Labor: Workers and the Digging of North American Canals, 1780–1860* (Baltimore: Johns Hopkins University Press, 1997); and especially, Steve Meyer, "Rough Manhood: The Aggressive and Confrontational Shop Culture of U.S. Auto Workers during World War II," *Journal of Social History* 36, no. 1 (Fall 2002): 125–47. For an example of the use of the term *company boys*, see William Tonkovich, interview by Laurie Mercier, 27 Feb. 1986, MHSRC. Clark Davis, *Company Men: White-Collar Life and Corporate Cultures in Los Angeles, 1892–1941* (Baltimore: Johns Hopkins University Press, 2001); Meidl and Wellcome, *Anaconda, Montana*, 25; "Mining Jargon," WPA Records, box 18, folder 12, MHSRC; "Mill and Smelter Jargon," US Work Projects Administration, Montana Writers Project Records for 1939–1941, MF 250, reel 5, MHSRC.

41. A. Clark, interview; Frank Zogarts, interview by Laurie Mercier, 18 November 1982, MHSRC; Bolkovatz, interview; Morris, *Anaconda Montana*, 188–89.

42. For more on the plant's operation and the type of workers employed there, see Matthew Basso, "Metal of Honor: Montana's World War II Homefront, Movies, and the Social Politics of White Male Anxiety" (PhD diss., University of Minnesota, 2001), 247–49; and Morris, *Anaconda Montana*, 178–83. On the material and psychological privileges of masculinity, see Simone de Beauvoir, *Second Sex* (New York: Bantam, 1961), and R. W. Connell, *Masculinities: Knowledge, Power, and Social Change* (Berkeley: University of California Press, 1995).

43. Edward Reynolds, "Anaconda," in *Men at Work: Stories of People at Their Jobs in America*, ed. Harold Rosenberg; unpublished manuscript, "Writers' Program, Work Projects Administration," 1941, box A-852, folders 1 and 2, Records of US Work Projects Administration, Library of Congress, Washington, DC. Also available in Matthew L. Basso, ed., *Men at Work: Rediscovering Depression-Era Stories from the Federal Writers' Project* (Salt Lake City: University of Utah Press, 2012), 254–68.

44. Reynolds, "Anaconda"; Charles Chaplin, dir., *Modern Times*, Charles Chaplin Productions, 1936. Chaplin's *Modern Times* is the best-known meditation on the issue

from the 1930s, but journalism and proletarian fiction of the era also focused on the question. Leo Wolman, "Machinery and Unemployment," *Nation* 136, no. 3529, 22 Feb. 1933, 202. On 1930s proletariat fiction, see Daniel Aaron, *Writers on the Left* (New York: Avon, 1961), and Barbara Foley, *Radical Representations: Politics and Form in U.S. Proletarian Fiction, 1929–1941* (Durham, NC: Duke University Press, 1993). For another local view on the subject, see Bolkovatz, interview.

45. Reynolds, "Anaconda." His other writings on the topic underscore this. Edward B. Reynolds, "Blood and Bread," WPA Records, box 9, folder 7, MHSRC. Zogarts, interview; Gustafson, interview. Smelterman William Gustafson recalled a death occurring at the hot-metal section of the plant before the war.

46. Reynolds, "Anaconda"; ACM Co. Claim Department to D. M. Kelly, December 31, 1942, National War Labor Board Records, box 7, folder 3, National Archives and Records Administration–Denver. Craftsmen occupied among the least dangerous production jobs in the copper industry. From 1939 to 1942, men in the crafts at all three production facilities suffered "only a few accidents that caused a loss of time beyond a few weeks" (ACM to Kelly). Because of this and because of the elevated pay that came with those positions, many smeltermen wanted to join the crafts. Before that, the Anselmo Mine was the site of the last fatal accident to a craftsman, in 1938.

47. Jerry Hansen, interview by Matthew Basso, 23 Apr. 1996, notes in the possession of the author. "Black skin" quote from Vine, interview. On Anaconda's African American community, see Morris, *Anaconda Montana*, 127, 187, 281, 290.

48. Gustafson, interview (the source of the quotation); Bolkovatz, interview; Phillip, interview; Vine, interview; Zogarts, interview; A. Clark, interview. Adding to the complexity of how race and place worked in this instance, men who labored in the arsenic section received between $.75 and $1.00 more per day, making this a preferred position for some. Joe Bolkovatz described this supplement as "blood money." It is unclear whether black men received this bump in wages. There is also some debate regarding exactly where black men worked at the plant. John Phillip argued that besides hauling calcine and working on the air line, one held a position on the air engine and another handled switching. Bob Vine, who was personnel director of the smelter after the war, placed them also in the treaters, arguing that black workers "got all the dirty jobs . . . any job that a white man didn't want, a black got." Former foreman Frank Zogarts echoed this point. Albert Clark remembered the air line being a mixture of different ethnicities and races.

49. Melvyn Dubofsky contends, "Only the Negro's presence kept the Italian, the Pole and the Slav above society's mudsill." Melvyn Dubofsky, *We Shall Be All: A History of the Industrial Workers of the World*, 2nd ed. (Urbana: University of Illinois Press, 1988), 8. See Zogarts, interview, and A. Clark, interview on black-white relations in plant. Clark confirmed that white and black men worked together, adding that Austrian foremen were especially antagonistic to black smeltermen.

50. "Anaconda Woman Passes in Butte," *Montana Standard*, 28 June 1929; "Mrs. Reynolds Taken by Death," *Anaconda Standard*, 27 June 1929. "Claude Reynolds Called by Death," *Montana Standard*, 13 Aug. 1933. "Mrs. Marie R. Reynolds," Certificate of Death, State of Montana Bureau of Vital Statistics, 29 June 1929. W. H. Gibson Sr., *History of the United Brothers of Friendship and Sisters of the Mysterious Ten* (Louisville, KY: Bradley and Gilbert, 1897), 21.

51. 9th Decennial Census Office, "Population Schedules for the 1870 Census, Orleans County, Louisiana," NARA microfilm publication M593, National Archives and

Records Administration, Washington, DC, n.d., p. 77. 10th Decennial Census Office, "Population Schedules for the 1880 Census, Cuyahoga County, Ohio," NARA microfilm publication M432, National Archives and Records Administration, Washington, DC, n.d., p. 239. 12th Decennial Census Office, "Population Schedules for the 1900 Census, Jefferson County, Kentucky," NARA microfilm publication M432, National Archives and Records Administration, Washington, DC, n.d., p. 12. Patty Dean to Matt Basso, e-mail correspondence regarding Reynolds family, 10 Feb., 11 Feb., and 23 Mar. 2009. Montana Historical Society, "African Americans in Montana Heritage Resources: Census Data," http://mhs.mt.gov/research/AfricanAmerican /AAInMTCensusData.asp, accessed January 22, 2013.

52. Anaconda smelterman Joe Bolkovatz described copper men of this era as "hardworking, no education, tough on their kids, master and lord of the house." Bolkovatz, interview.

CHAPTER FOUR

An earlier form of this chapter appeared as Matthew Basso, "Man-Power : Montana Copper Workers, State Authority, and the (Re)drafting of Manhood during World War II," in *Across the Great Divide: Cultures of Manhood in the American West*, ed. Matthew Basso, Laura McCall, and Dee Garceau (New York: Routledge, 2001), 185–210. Reprinted by permission of Taylor & Francis Group LLC-Books.

1. "Draft Registration for Montana 58,777," *Great Falls Tribune* (hereafter *GFT*), 19 Oct. 1940. Of 3,216 Anaconda smelter employees, 1,294 were liable for the peacetime draft. W. T. Maston to W. E. Mitchell, 5 Oct. 1940, ACM Co. Records, box 72, folder 2, Montana Historical Society Research Center, Helena (hereafter MHSRC). J Garry Clifford and Samuel R Spencer Jr., *The First Peacetime Draft* (Lawrence: University Press of Kansas, 1986). During the peacetime phase of the World War II–era draft, less than 1 million men were inducted. In 1942 and 1943, over 3 million men each year were placed in the armed forces through the draft. In 1944, as the supply of available men with uncontroversial draft classifications dwindled, only 1.5 million men entered the military. In 1945, the last year of the war, 900,000 were inducted. Selective Service System, http://www.sss.gov/induct.htm, accessed January 22, 2013. "5,107 County Men Register for Arms Duty," *GFT*, 18 Oct. 1940.

2. "5,107 County Men Register"; "Joseph Sanders, Samuel Cislo are County's No. 1 Draftees," *GFT*, 30 Oct. 1940; "First County Draft Group Leaves Today," *GFT*, 23 Nov. 1940.

3. Donald Jackson, "Evading the Draft: Who, How and Why," *Life*, 9 Dec. 1966, 40–49; Christian Appy, *Working Class War: American Combat Soldiers and Vietnam* (Chapel Hill: University of North Carolina Press, 1993), 35–37; Darren K. Carlson, "Public Support for Military Draft Low," Gallup, 18 Nov. 2003, http://www.gallup.com /poll/9727/public-support-military-draft-low.aspx, accessed January 22, 2013; Michael C. C. Adams, *The Best War Ever: America and World War II* (Baltimore: Johns Hopkins University Press, 1994); Studs Terkel, *The Good War: An Oral History of World War II* (New York: New Press, 1997); Stephen Ambrose, *Citizen Soldiers: The U.S. Army from Normandy Beaches to the Bulge to the Surrender of Germany, June 7, 1944–May 7, 1945* (New York: Simon & Schuster, 1997); Michael Kimmel, *Manhood in America: A Cultural History* (New York: Free Press, 1996); Peter Filene, *Him/Her/Self: Gender Identities in Modern America*, 3rd ed. (Baltimore: Johns Hopkins University Press, 1998).

4. Clifford and Spencer, *The First Peacetime Draft*, 1–6, 200–219; Beth Bailey, *America's Army: Making the All-Volunteer Force* (Cambridge, MA: Harvard University Press,

2009), 1–33. James Graham to James O'Connor, 3 Sept. 1944, *The People's Voice* Records, box 4, folder 29, MHSRC. For example, thirty-year-old Jack Kraft enlisted in January 1941, and Lewis Remark in March 1941. "Butte Soldier Is Prisoner of Japs," *Montana Standard* (hereafter *MS*), 17 Feb. 1943; "Pvt. John Kraft Is Liberated," *MS*, 15 Sept. 1945; "Prisoner of Japs," *MS*, 30 Apr. 1943; "Soldier Rescued in Philippines," *MS*, 24 Feb. 1945.

5. Christina S. Jarvis, *The Male Body at War: American Masculinity during World War II* (DeKalb: Northern Illinois University Press, 2004). For the use of "soldiers of production," see ACM Victory Labor-Management Committee (hereafter Victory Committee), *Report to Donald Nelson*, 27 June 1942, ACM Co. Records, box 71, folder 3, MHSRC. See also James T. Sparrow, *Warfare State: World War II Americans and the Age of Big Government* (New York: Oxford University Press, 2011), 160–200.

6. Barbara Dianne Savage, *Broadcasting Freedom: Radio, War, and the Politics of Race, 1938–1948* (Chapel Hill: University of North Carolina Press, 1999), 21–62; Bryan D. Booker, *African Americans in the United States Army in World War II* (New York: McFarland, 2008) 45, 52–53; Nancy Gentile Ford, *Americans All!: Foreign-Born Soldiers in World War I* (College Station: Texas A&M Press, 2001), 137–46; Matthew Guterl, *The Color of Race in America, 1900–1940* (Cambridge, MA: Harvard University Press, 2001), 39–56.

7. In May 1941, a large audience at Butte's Fox Theater cheered senator Burton K. Wheeler's contention that "this is not our war." But Wheeler was fast losing favor with many copper men. Some found his isolationism unmanly. He angered others by his opposition to Roosevelt and his drift toward conservatism. Vernon H. Jensen, *Nonferrous Metals Industry Unionism, 1932–1954* (Ithaca, NY: Cornell University Press, 1954), 61; Michael Malone, Richard Roeder, and William Lang, *Montana: A History of Two Centuries* (Seattle: University of Washington Press, 1991), 304–12; Gerald E. Shenk, *"Work or Fight": Race, Gender, and the Draft in World War I* (New York: Macmillan, 2005), 85, 97–101; Nelson Lichtenstein, *Labor's War at Home: The CIO in World War II* (New York: Cambridge University Press, 1982); W. E. Mitchell to W. H. Hoover, 23 June 1941, ACM Co. Records, box 70, folder 2, MHSRC. One smelterman recalled that between 1915 and 1939, his father, also a smelterman, had not "worked a full year without getting laid off and it was only after World War II started in Europe" that this changed. John Luke McKeon, interview by Laurie Mercier, 29 July 1986, MHSRC.

8. Comparing military and civilian pay rates was challenging, but most men, especially those with dependents, thought that entering the military meant taking a pay cut. Malvern Hall Tillitt, "Army-Navy Pay Tops Most Civilians': Unmarried Private's Income Equivalent to $3,600 Salary," *Barron's National Business and Financial Weekly*, 24 Apr. 1944, available at http://www.usmm.org/barrons.html, accessed January 22, 2013; Olanda Rinari Vangelisti and Claire Vangelisti Del Guerra, interview by Laurie Mercier, 16 July 1986, MHSRC; Tom Brokaw, *The Greatest Generation* (New York: Random House, 1998), 9–12.

9. Kimmel, *Manhood in America*, 134; R. W. Connell, *Masculinities: Knowledge, Power, and Social Change* (Berkeley: University of California Press, 1995), 28–29, 90; Joshua S. Goldstein, *War and Gender: How Gender Shapes the War System and Vice Versa* (New York: Cambridge University Press, 2001), 1–57; Edward B. Reynolds, "Sketch Autobiography" and "Hot Metal," 1, Works Progress Administration (hereafter WPA) Records, box 18, folder 6, MHSRC.

10. Reynolds, "Hot Metal," 1.

11. Ibid., 1–2.

12. David Emmons, *The Butte Irish: Class and Ethnicity in an American Mining Town, 1875–1925* (Urbana: University of Illinois Press, 1989), 148–59; Ronald C. Brown, *Hard-rock Miners: The Intermountain West, 1860–1920* (College Station: Texas A&M Press, 1979), 75–98; Patrick F. Morris, *Anaconda Montana: Copper Smelting Boom Town on the Western Frontier* (Bethesda, MD: Swann, 1997), 188–89. Black Eagle smelter injury and death data are available in ACM Co. Records, box 243, folder 10, and box 228, folder 8, MHSRC. James H. Hallas, *Doughboy War: The American Expeditionary Force in World War I* (Boulder, CO: Lynne Reinner, 2000). David Emmons points out that just before the United States' official entry into World War I, the navy used advertisements to recruit Butte miners that argued that navy jobs were safer and held considerably more benefits than working in the mines; Emmons, *Butte Irish*, 167. The danger of contracting miners' consumption did not decline with the advent of mechanization and wet drilling as much as companies claimed. David Rosner and Gerald Markowitz, *Deadly Dust: Silicosis and the Politics of Occupational Disease in Twentieth-Century America* (Princeton, NJ: Princeton University Press, 1991), 203–5. Industrial accidents were commonplace across the United States during the war; Geoffrey Perrett, *Days of Sadness, Years of Triumph: The American People 1939–1945* (New York: Coward, McCann & Geoghegan, 1973), 399.

13. Frank Zogarts, interview by Laurie Mercier, 18 Nov. 1942, MHSRC; Joe Navarro, interview by Laurie Mercier, 25 Mar. 1983, MHSRC. In the mines, for instance, one group of "elite" were men who worked in the "raises," a type of mine shaft driven upward to the next level. "Mining Jargon," WPA Records, box 18, folder 12, MHSRC; Reynolds, "Hot Metal," 1–2.

14. "1,123 Aliens Registered Here; U.S. Total Near 5,000,000," *GFT*, 27 Dec. 1940.

15. "Alcohol Tax Unit Agents Destroy Still and Arrest Operator in Black Eagle," *GFT*, 5 June 1941; "The Story of the Butte Bo-hunk—The Dark Skinned Invader," *Butte Evening News*, 24 July 1910. Indicating the continued vitality and long history of ethnic identification, in 1941 the local Cristoforo Colombo Lodge celebrated its fiftieth anniversary, and the Croatian Brotherhood rebuilt its hall, which had burned down in 1916. Residents also founded the Civic Club of Black Eagle in 1940. Black Eagle Book Committee, *In the Shadow of the Big Stack: Black Eagle* (Black Eagle, MT: Black Eagle Book Committee, 2000), 476–78. Felix Schreiber, American Institute of Fraternal Citizenship, to Anaconda Copper Mining Co., 15 July 1942, S. I. Blair to W. E. Mitchell, 17 Mar. 1942, and S. S. Rodgers to W. E. Mitchell, 24 Feb. 1942, all in ACM Co. Records, box 113, folder 1, MHSRC.

16. J. L. DeWitt to Sam Ford, 19 Dec. 1941, and Sam Ford to J. L. DeWitt, 7 Jan. 1942, both in Montana Governors' Papers, box 121, folder 15, MHSRC; "Alien Curfew Law to Become Effective Today," *GFT*, 23 Dec. 1943; "Curfew Rule Will Affect 100 Aliens in this Area," *GFT*, 26 Mar. 1942; "Comparatively Few, Less Than 150 Believed in Enemy Alien Class," *GFT*, 27 Mar. 1942. In comparison with Black Eagle, Anaconda had twenty-two men come forward in early 1942 acknowledging their alien status but claiming permanent US residence. Figures are not available for Butte. "List of Aliens Who Have Executed Form 1078," 20 Feb. 1942, ACM Co. Records, box 113, folder 1, MHSRC.

17. Tracy Thornton, "Butte Man First to Die in State," *MS*, 7 Dec. 1991; "LeRoy Carpenter of Butte"; "Cited Posthumously [Norman J Fetherolf]," *MS*, 2 Apr. 1943; "Honored Posthumously [James M. Gill, Jr.]," likely *MS*, date unknown; and "Additional List

of Prisoners Issued," likely *MS*, 3 July 1943, all in "Montana in the Wars" clippings file, Butte-Silver Bow Public Archives (hereafter BSBA).

18. "LeRoy Carpenter." On Butte miners as a type, see Mary Murphy, *Mining Cultures: Men, Women, and Leisure in Butte, 1914–1941* (Urbana: University of Illinois Press, 1997), 106–35.

19. John Buckley, *Air Power in the Age of Total War* (Bloomington: Indiana University Press, 1999), 42–69; Denis Winter, *Death's Men: Soldiers of the Great War* (New York: Penguin, 1985), 128; "Missing and Killed in Action, World War II (A–H, I–Z), 1942–1946," ACM Co. Records, box 132, folder 1, MHSRC.

20. George Q. Flynn, *Lewis B. Hershey, Mr. Selective Service* (Chapel Hill: University of North Carolina Press, 1986), 76, 84. Significantly, the strongest proponents for peacetime conscription came from the East; see Flynn, 66–69. Burton K. Wheeler to James D. Graham, 29 July 1940, *The People's Voice* Records, box 52, folder 3, MHSRC. On Wheeler see Clifford and Spencer, *The First Peacetime Draft*, 70–82, 180; and J. Leonard Bates, *Senator Thomas J. Walsh of Montana: Law and Public Affairs, from TR to FDR* (Urbana: University of Illinois Press, 1999), 195–202, 250–52. Some 44,048 Montanans served in World War I. "Montana, upon Population Basis, Supplied More Men for Army than any Other State," *Rocky Mountain Husbandman*, 3 Nov. 1938, 1. Malone, Roeder, and Lang, *Montana*, 309. On the West during World War II generally, see Gerald Nash, *The American West Transformed: The Impact of the Second World War* (Lincoln: University of Nebraska Press, 1990).

21. William T. Paull, *From Butte to Iwo Jima: The Memoirs of William T. Paull*, http://www.sihope.com/~tipi/chap4.html, accessed January 22, 2013.

22. Ibid.

23. "Alleged Draft Dodger Is Overtaken by Posse," *GFT*, 15 Feb. 1942; David M. Kennedy, *Freedom from Fear: The American People in Depression and War, 1929–1945* (New York: Oxford University Press, 1999), 631. By the end of the war, only 1,533 eligible men had evaded classification. Jarvis, *The Male Body at War*, 57.

24. Adapted from "Selective Service Classifications Revised to Include New Category: List Is Released by Office of War Information," *GFT*, 12 Dec. 1942.

25. Cited in Jarvis, *The Male Body at War*, 60; "Many Draftees Not Physically Fit for Army," *GFT*, 27 Nov. 1940. In October 1941, preliminary figures from the Selective Service showed that only 40 percent of registrants were "physically and mentally fit for general military service"; "Everyone Must Have a Stake in the Nation," *People's Voice*, 29 Oct. 1941. Sam Ford to Henry Stimson, 9 Apr. 1942, Montana Governors' Papers, box 122, folder 3, MHSRC; Adams, *Best War Ever*, 78.

26. Flynn, *Lewis B. Hershey*, 126–31. Thomas Doherty, *Projections of War: Hollywood, American Culture, and World War II* (New York: Columbia University Press, 1993), 100–111.

27. Unknown author, "Effect of Alien's Filing of Claim for Exemption from Military Service upon Subsequent Petition for Naturalization," *Columbia Law Review* 55, no. 5 (May 1955): 748–51.

28. William M. Tuttle Jr., *"Daddy's Gone to War": The Second World War in the Lives of America's Children* (New York: Oxford University Press, 1993), 19–21, 25; Elaine Tyler May, *Homeward Bound: American Families in the Cold War Era* (New York: Basic Books, 1988), 59–60; Karen Anderson, *Wartime Women: Sex Roles, Family Relations, and the Status of Women during World War II* (Westport, CT: Greenwood Press, 1981), 76–78.

29. Tuttle, *"Daddy's Gone to War,"* 19–21, 25; E. May, *Homeward Bound*, 59–60; Kennedy, *Freedom from Fear*, 634–35; Lee B. Kennett, *G.I.: The American Soldier in World War II* (Norman: University of Oklahoma Press, 1997), 12–14.

30. Allan Bérubé, *Coming Out under Fire: The History of Gay Men and Women in World War II* (New York: Simon & Schuster, 2000); Leila Rupp, *Mobilizing Women for War: German and American Propaganda, 1939–1945* (Princeton, NJ: Princeton University Press, 1978).

31. The question of when a young man gained the responsibilities of a male citizen affected more than the draft. In 1942 the War Manpower Commission (WMC) considered how young was too young for a boy to enlist in the military or go to work in industry. Bernard C. Gavit to Paul V. McNutt, 22 Dec. 1942; Paul McNutt to Dr. P. Phillips Co., 20 Nov. 1942; Office of War Information Advance Release, WMC 2037, "For Sunday Papers, February 7, 1943"; and Bernard C. Gavit to Thomas J. Close Jr., 29 May 1943, all in WMC Records, RG 211, box 156, folder 2, National Archives and Records Administration. "Congressional Delay in Enacting 'Teen-Age Draft Bill' to Cause Induction of 200,000 Married Men," *MS*, 8 Nov. 1942. The protection of husbands and fathers is another aspect of what Sonya Michel has called "the discourse of the democratic family." Sonya Michel, "American Women and the Discourse of the Democratic Family during World War II," in *Behind the Lines: Gender and the Two World Wars*, ed. Margaret Randolph Higonnet, Jane Jenson, Sonya Michel, and Margaret Collins Weitz (New Haven, CT: Yale University Press, 1987), 154–67.

32. Flynn, *Lewis B. Hershey*, 108–9; Tuttle, *"Daddy's Gone to War,"* 19, 31. Draft statistics can be a source of confusion because they often cover different periods, and draftees often changed categories.

33. Elaine Tyler May, "Rosie the Riveter Gets Married," in *The War in American Culture: Society and Consciousness during World War II*, ed. Lewis Erenberg and Susan E. Hirsch (Chicago: University of Chicago Press, 1996), 137. See also Drew Gilpin Faust, "'Altars of Sacrifice': Confederate Women and the Narratives of War," *Journal of American History* 76, no. 4 (March 1990): 1200–1228. On October 1, 1943, the Selective Service abolished classification 3-A. Just two months later, fathers comprised over one-quarter of inductees, and by April 1944 they were a majority. Those between the ages of eighteen and thirty-seven were the most likely to serve on active duty, but only one in five fathers did so. Kennedy, *Freedom from Fear*, 634–37; Tuttle, *"Daddy's Gone to War,"* 31.

34. Flynn, *Lewis B. Hershey*, 90–92 ("thousands of young" quotation is from p. 91); David A. Horowitz, *America's Political Class under Fire: The Twentieth Century's Great Culture War* (New York: Routledge, 2003), 88–89 (the source of the "characterized his supervisors" quotation).

35. By the end of the war, young farmworkers had three times more deferments than young industrial workers. Flynn, *Lewis B. Hershey*, 110–14 (quotation is from p. 111); R. Douglas Hurt, *The Great Plains during World War II* (Lincoln: University of Nebraska Press, 2008), 154.

36. Flynn, *Lewis B. Hershey*, 103–42; figures on 107–9.

37. Most historians, following Allan Winkler, characterize wartime propaganda as constantly seeking "to generate an appreciation for the American way of life." Allan M. Winkler, *The Politics of Propaganda: The Office of War Information, 1942–1945* (New Haven, CT: Yale University Press, 1978). See also Adams, *Best War Ever*, 73–75.

38. Attempting to overcome other workplace divisions, participants decided to include plant tradesmen affiliated with the American Federation of Labor (AFL). "Devel-

opment and Progress of Victory Labor-Management Committees at the Anaconda Reduction Works," in Victory Committee, *Report to Donald Nelson*, 27 June 1942, ACM Co. Records, box 71, folder 3, MHSRC. On these committees nationally, see Lichtenstein, *Labor's War at Home*, 89–93. "Give Us a Lift," *Copper Commando* (hereafter *CC*), 18 Aug. 1942, 18, BSBA.

39. "Development and Progress of Victory Labor-Management Committees"; John Davis Morgan Jr., *The Domestic Mining Industry of the United States in World War II* (Washington, DC: National Security Resources Board, 1949), 271–75.

40. "A Message from Lieutenant General Somervell," *CC*, 22 Aug. 1942, 2, and "Chiefs of Four Top War Agencies Appeal to Metal Miners to Remain on Jobs," *CC*, 5 Sept. 1942, 13, 15, both in BSBA.

41. "Boys away from Home," *CC*, 5 Sept. 1942, 5–6; see also "Let us Give Thanks," *CC*, 20 Nov. 1942, 2, both in BSBA. See also "Address by Donald M. Nelson, Chairman, War Production Board, on the Mutual Broadcasting System," 10 Mar. 1942; "Address by Rear Admiral Clark H. Woodward," Office of Civilian Defense Publicity Release, PM-2892, 9 Apr. 1942, both in War Production Board (hereafter WPB)–Helena Office Records, box 2, folder 7, MHSRC.

42. "A Dying Jap Speaks," *CC*, 7 Oct. 1942, 8–9; see also "Objective: 100,000,000 Dead Japs," *CC*, 18 Feb. 1944, 12, both in BSBA. Most of the five categories of Anglo-American anti-Japanese racism identified by John Dower appear here. John Dower, *War without Mercy: Race and Power in the Pacific* (New York: Pantheon Books, 1986).

43. "Officer Talks to Miners," *CC*, 22 Aug. 1942, 18, BSBA. On homosociality see the pioneering work of Heidi Hartmann and Eve Sedgwick: Heidi Hartmann, "The Unhappy Marriage of Marxism and Feminism: Towards a More Progressive Union," in *Women and Revolution: A Discussion of the Unhappy Marriage of Marxism and Feminism*, ed. Lydia Sargent (Boston: South End Press, 1981); Eve Kosofsky Sedgwick, *Between Men: English Literature and Male Homosocial Desire* (New York: Columbia University Press, 1985). Specific to miners, see the three quite different homosocial worlds depicted in Susan Lee Johnson, *Roaring Camp: The Social World of the California Gold Rush* (New York: W. W. Norton, 2000), and M. Murphy, *Mining Cultures*; and Thomas Klubock, *Contested Communities: Class, Gender, and Politics in Chile's El Teniente Copper Mine, 1904–1951* (Durham, NC: Duke University Press, 1998).

44. Tubie Johnson, "Remember Our Boys," *CC*, 19 Sept. 1942, 7, BSBA. See also Ida E. Staples, "One of Them," *CC*, 6 Nov. 1942, 15, BSBA. The *Miner's Voice*, newspaper of the BMU, also had a section called "Our Poet's Corner," which offered similar fare. See "To the Butte Miner," *Miner's Voice*, 11 Sept. 1942.

45. "Blows against Absentee-ism," *CC*, 22 Aug. 1942, 18, BSBA. Butte had by far the worst problem with absenteeism. Approximately 29% of miners and 70% of surface men worked all their assigned workdays each month during fall 1942. Typically, over 95% of smeltermen in Anaconda and Black Eagle worked all their shifts in the same period. Nonferrous Metals Commission of the National War Labor Board, "Transcript of Hearing: NWLB Case No. 527," 14 and 15 Dec. 1942, 115–16, 136–37, National War Labor Board Records, box 7, folder 4, NARA–Denver. Philip Gleason, *Speaking of Diversity: Language and Ethnicity in Twentieth Century America* (Baltimore: Johns Hopkins University Press, 1992), 153–87.

46. Victory Committee Meeting Transcript, 15 Oct. 1942, 6–8, 21, ACM Co. Records, box 71, folder 4, MHSRC; quotations are from p. 8 of the transcript.

47. Downsley Clark to Oscar Baarson, 23 Jan. 1942, and "Defense Bulletin Board," R-1-19, "Two Armies by '43," both in WPB–Helena Office Records, box 2, folder 7,

MHSRC. Congress of Industrial Organizations (CIO) president Philip Murray similarly described the home front production worker's role: "Your task in America is just about as important . . . as is the task of a soldier in the army." Graham Dolan, "CIO Moves ahead in Wartime Leadership of American People," *Union*, 16 Nov. 1942. On the pledge, its history, and the multiple places it appeared, see Victory Committee, *Report to Donald Nelson*, 27 June 1942, ACM Co. Records, box 71, folder 3, MHSRC; the pledge is found on p. 2 of this report.

48. "Over the Hill with Al Giecek," *Miner's Voice*, 11 Sept. 1942. For one of the many other times the ACM questioned workers' devotion to the war cause either directly or through the *MS*, the newspaper it controlled as part of its larger "copper collar" on Butte and Anaconda, see "Vast Production for War By Anaconda Company," *MS*, 21 Apr. 1942. Dennis Swibold, *Copper Chorus: Mining, Politics, and the Montana Press, 1889–1959* (Helena: Montana Historical Society Press, 2006).

49. Martin Glaberman, *Wartime Strikes: The Struggle against the No-Strike Pledge in the UAW during World War II* (Detroit: Bewick, 1980); Mark H. Leff, "Politics of Sacrifice on the American Home Front in World War II," *Journal of American History* 77, no. 4 (March 1991): 1296–1318; "Unanswered Questions on Production," *Miner's Voice*, 11 Sept. 1942, 1.

50. Byron E. Shafer, "The Two Majorities and the Puzzle of Modern American Politics," in *Contesting Democracy: Substance and Structure in American Political History, 1775–2000*, ed. Byron E. Shafer and Anthony J. Badger (Lawrence: University Press of Kansas, 2001), 225–37.

51. Victory Committee, *Report to Donald Nelson*, August 1942, ACM Co. Records, box 71, folder 3, MHSRC.

52. Victory Committee Meeting Transcript, 3 Sept. 1942, 1, 5–6, ACM Co. Records, box 71, folder 4, MHSRC. Between January and the end of September 1942, four hundred Anaconda smeltermen entered the armed forces; officials expected this rate of withdrawal to "be much lower in the future." "Anaconda, Montana, Locality War Housing Program No. 3," report, n.d. [ca. 30 June 1942], WPB Records, RG 183, box 219, folder "Butte, Montana," NARA.

53. Victory Committee Meeting Transcript, 3 Sept. 1942, 1, 5–6. The War Manpower Stabilization Act signed in September 1942 theoretically ended the ability of copper men to choose where they worked, as those that went through the process of gaining a Certificate of Separation from the United States Employment Service found out. See the case of nineteen-year-old James Dunston in David Emmons, "Hard Times and War Times," in "Expert Report of David Emmons, Ph.D.," *United States of America v. Atlantic Richfield Company, et al.*, US District Court, District of Montana, Helena Division, Case No. CV-89-039-PGH, 15 July 1996, 253–4. "Alleged Draft Dodger."

54. Victory Committee Meeting Transcript, 3 Sept. 1942, 6.

55. Victory Committee Meeting Transcript, 15 Oct. 1942, 12–18; Katie Dewing, interview by Laurie Mercier, 11 Aug. 1986, MHSRC. White-collar men in the copper industry also received deferments and faced scrutiny and, sometimes, condemnation. Robert Corbett, interview by Laurie Mercier, 17 Apr. 1984, MHSRC.

56. Victory Committee Meeting Transcript, 15 Oct. 1942, 12–18. See the case of Harold Edward Perkins; "Butte Marine Is Killed in Action," *MS*, 24 Dec. 1943.

57. Selective Service System, "Occupational Bulletin No. 12," 28 July 1942, in memorandum "Re: Deferment Order—Metal and Non-Metallic Mines," 3 Aug. 1942, ACM Co. Records, box 70, folder 4, MHSRC.

58. Flynn, *Lewis B. Hershey*, 60, 77.

59. Victory Committee Meeting Transcript, 15 Oct. 1942, 14–18 (quotation is from p. 17); "Anaconda Reduction Works Classification of Labor and Time Required to Train for Jobs," 27 May 1942, ACM Co. Records, box 72, folder 6, MHSRC; S. H. Mitchell to W. E. Mitchell, 19 Aug. 1942, ACM Co. Records, box 72, folder 2, MHSRC.

60. Victory Committee Meeting Transcript, 15 Oct. 1942, 14–18; quotation is from p. 18.

61. Ibid.; quotation is from p. 15.

62. Victory Committee Meeting Transcript, 22 June 1943, 2 (the source of the quotations), ACM Co. Records, box 71, and folder 4, MHSRC; "People and Places," CC, 2 July 1943, 8, BSBA; Victory Committee Meeting Transcript, 3 Aug. 1943, 6–8, ACM Co. Records, box 71, folder 4, MHSRC. Mine Mill's newspaper, the Union, carried Arthur Redfield's popular labor-friendly cartoon "The Upper Crust," which also remarked on the meat question, but focused on the class politics of the issue by depicting a rotund upper-class man and woman eating while two waiters stood at the ready. The caption read: "These horrid meatless days! I'm fed up with caviar and turkey." "The Upper Crust," Union, 30 Nov. 1942. On Redfield see Gary Gerstle, Working-Class Americanism: The Politics of Labor in a Textile City, 1914–1961 (New York: Cambridge University Press, 1989), 171–72.

63. Victory Committee Meeting Transcript, 22 June 1943, 3–8.

64. Ibid., 3–11; quotations are from p. 4.

65. Skipper Scriven to F. R. McGregor, telegram, 24 Apr. 1942, WPB–Helena Office Records, box 1, folder 7, MHSRC.

66. Victory Committee Meeting Transcript, 22 June 1943, 4–5.

67. Ibid., 5–7, 11.

CHAPTER FIVE

1. "Prisoner of Japs," Montana Standard (hereafter MS), 30 Apr. 1943; "Soldier Rescued in Philippines," MS, 24 Feb. 1945. The paper listed Remark's mother as "Mrs. Thomas James" and his father as "Frederick Remark," and provided no name for his sister. Kevin Starr, Embattled Dreams: California in War and Peace (New York: Oxford University Press, 2003), 147. On the difficult circumstances women found in Tacoma, see Karen Anderson, Wartime Women: Sex Roles, Family Relations, and the Status of Women during World War II (Westport, CT: Greenwood Press, 1981), 45. For the broader story of women in the shipyards, see Amy Kesselman, Fleeting Opportunities: Women Shipyard Workers in Portland and Vancouver during World War II and Reconversion (Albany: SUNY Press, 1990).

2. David Emmons, "Hard Times and War Times," in "Expert Report of David Emmons, Ph.D.," United States of America v. Atlantic Richfield Company, et al., US District Court, District of Montana, Helena Division, Case No. CV-89-039-PGH, 15 July 1996, 250–51; "Metal Mines: Application for Quarterly Quotas for Maintenance, Repair, and Operating Supplies," War Production Board (hereafter WPB) Form PD-400-A, various dates including 27 Feb. 1943, WPB–Helena Office Records, box 16, folder 19, Montana Historical Society Research Center, Helena (hereafter MHSRC); United States Employment Service (hereafter USES), "Labor Market Survey of Butte-Anaconda, Montana," 4 Apr. 1942, WPB Records, RG 183, box 218, folder 3, National Archives and Records Administration (hereafter NARA); William Manning to L. H. Hinckley, 15 July 1942, and William Manning to Marcellus Stow, 8 Aug. 1942, both in WPB–Helena Office Records, box 4, folder 6, MHSRC; Bureau of Employment Security, "Statement on the Employment Situation in the Butte-Anaconda, Montana Area," 31 Aug. 1942, WPB Records, RG 183, box 218, folder 2, NARA; W. E. Mitchell

to B. L. Sackett, 17 Aug. 1942; W. E. Mitchell to D. M. Kelley, 5 Aug. 1942; and W. E. Mitchell to Frederick Laist, 31 Sept. 1942, all in ACM Co. Records, box 70, folder 5, MHSRC. Anaconda and Black Eagle faced similar manpower shortages, though on a smaller scale and with less seasonal variation, and, in Anaconda, exacerbated by a housing shortage. The Anaconda Reduction Works reported losing over a thousand men, many to other home front jobs, in the first seven months of 1942. "Chiefs of Four Top War Agencies Appeal to Metal Miners to Remain on Jobs," *Copper Commando* (hereafter *CC*), 5 Sept. 1942, 15, Butte-Silver Bow Public Archives (hereafter BSBA); "Women in Mines," *Business Week*, 12 Sept. 1942, 35–36. *Business Week* reported that Colorado metal mines lost workers to construction jobs "paying wages that are 50% to 100% higher than mine pay." To stop the outflow of workers there, the government also appealed to miners' patriotism.

3. These men were not "independent" in the way David Montgomery alludes to in his influential treatment of nineteenth-century independent male laborers. David Montgomery, "Workers' Control of Machine Production in the 19th Century," *Labor History* 17 (1976): 491–92; Mary Murphy, *Mining Cultures: Men, Women, and Leisure in Butte, 1914–41* (Urbana: University of Illinois Press, 1997), 106–35; Nonferrous Metals Commission of the National War Labor Board, "Transcript of Hearing: NWLB Case No. 527," 14 and 15 Dec. 1942, 58–59, 196, National War Labor Board (hereafter NWLB) Records, box 7, folder 4, NARA–Denver. ACM vice president D. M. Kelly contended that as of 1942, seven thousand contract miners worked on the hill, an estimate that appears high. Contract miners made, on average, between $2.00 and $2.35 more than men on the mine's base rate of pay, with some making considerably more.

4. USES, "Labor Market Survey of Butte-Anaconda, Montana"; War Manpower Commission (hereafter WMC)/USES, "Monthly Labor Market Developments Report," various months, WPB Records, box 219, folder "Butte, Montana," NARA.

5. "Memoranda in Reply to Telegram of J. Reed Lane, May 24, 1944," 26 May 1944, WPB–Helena Office Records, box 8, folder 7, MHSRC; Mark H. Leff, "Politics of Sacrifice on the American Home Front in World War II," *Journal of American History* 77, no. 4 (March 1991): 1296–1318; Gary Gerstle, *Working-Class Americanism: The Politics of Labor in a Textile City, 1914–1960* (New York: Cambridge University Press, 1989).

6. Herbert Carlisle, interview by Laurie Mercier, 26 Feb. 1982, MHSRC; "Vacations," n.d. [ca. 1941]; for a specific example, see H. M. Doran to R. B. Caples, 11 June 1942, both in ACM Co. Records, box 178, folder 8, MHSRC. See also ACM Vacation Granted Forms for Gallagher, Garver, Hull; and E. A. Barnard to George A. Dean, 28 July 1941, all in ACM Co. Records, box 96, folder 6, MHSRC. On vacation policies for men entering the military, see K. B. Frazier, "Circular Letter No. 427," 28 Nov. 1941, ACM Co. Records, box 33, folder 3, MHSRC. Examples of the ongoing battle appear in Commission of Conciliation, "Anaconda vs. Locals 1, 16, and 117," 12 Oct. 1943, ACM Co. Records, box 320, folder 3, MHSRC; USES, "Labor Market Survey"; Nonferrous Metals Commission, "Case No. 527," 28. Mine Mill made the productivity of Butte's experienced miners versus "green" miners a significant part of its argument before the NWLB for higher wages.

7. USES, "Labor Market Survey"; Robert Patterson to Sam Ford, 19 Oct. 1942, and Ford to Patterson, 2 Dec. 1942, Montana Governors' Records, box 122, folder 3, MHSRC; Michael Malone, Richard Roeder, and William Lang, *Montana: A History of Two Centuries* (Seattle: University of Washington Press, 1991), 306–13.

8. "Address by Donald M. Nelson, Chairman, War Production Board, on the Mutual Broadcasting System," 10 Mar. 1942; see also "Address by Rear Admiral Clark H. Woodward," Office of Civilian Defense Publicity Release, PM-2892, 9 Apr. 1942, both in WPB–Helena Office Records, box 2, folder 7, MHSRC; Emmons, "Hard Times and War Times," 254 (the source of the quotation); and ACM Victory Labor-Management Committee (hereafter Victory Committee) Meeting Transcript, 3 Sept. 1942, 16, ACM Co. Records, box 71, folder 2, MHSRC.

9. Victory Committee Meeting Transcript, 1 Oct. 1942, 4, ACM Co. Records, box 71, folder 2, MHSRC.

10. Victory Committee Meeting Transcript, 17 Sept. 1942, 6–7, 11–14, and 15 Oct. 1942, 12–14, both in ACM Co. Records, box 71, folder 2, MHSRC.

11. Victory Committee Meeting Transcript, 22 June 1943, 3–8, ACM Co. Records, box 71, folder 4, MHSRC. The Victory Committee also urged the government to reinforce the Company's internal suggestions program by issuing Individual Production Merit certificates to those men who submitted particularly useful suggestions.

12. Victory Committee Meeting Transcript, 3 Sept. 1942, 16–17; Victory Committee Meeting Transcript, 6 July 1943, 1–2, ACM Co. Records, box 71, folder 4, MHSRC.

13. "Montana State Guide–Education, Religion, and Social Welfare," Works Progress Administration (hereafter WPA) Records, box 26, folder 22, MHSRC. Montana had passed pathbreaking legislation to provide pensions for older workers. Albert Clark, interview by Laurie Mercier, 19 Nov. 1982, MHSRC; Tom Dickson, interview by Laurie Mercier, 30 May 1986, MHSRC; John Phillip, interview by Laurie Mercier, 24 Nov. 1981, MHSRC. The ACM provided support to some former workers. Their system buttressed male breadwinners, but was seen as unfair by some workers.

14. R. W. Swope to Tom Connelly, 8 Aug. 1942; Paul McNutt to Josh Lee, 28 Aug. 1942; McNutt to Connelly, 31 Aug. 1942; and Ernest McFarland to Frances Perkins, 9 Sept. 1942, all in WMC Records, box 171, folder 6, NARA. On older women, see K. Anderson, *Wartime Women*, 42. "Draft Boards Reclassify Farm Workers, Men of 45," *Great Falls Tribune* (hereafter *GFT*), 2 Dec. 1942.

15. Though there are important exceptions, most studies of disability and World War II concentrate on programs for disabled veterans. David Serlin, *Replaceable You: Engineering the Body in Postwar America* (Chicago: University of Chicago Press, 2004), 21–56; Paul Longmore, "Making Disability an Important Part of American History," in *OAH Magazine of History* 23, no. 3, (July 2009): 11; Charles Davidson to S. C. Ford, 1 Feb. 1943, Montana Governors' Records, box 122, folder 8, MHSRC. Disabled veterans became a topic of concern early in the war in Montana. By February 1, 1943, five hundred Montana men had already been discharged due to disability. For the hiring of disabled workers by war industries, see WMC, "WMC 3406–7, Advance Release: For Monday Morning Papers," 30 Apr. 1945, WMC Records, box 126, folder 19, NARA; and entire "Handicapped Week 1945" folder, including "Remarks by Secretary of Labor Lewis B. Schwellenbach," 30 Aug. 1945, and Robert C. Goodwin to All Regional Manpower Directors, 7 Sept. 1945, both in WMC Records, box 144, folder 5, NARA; WMC, "Press Release 907, for Release June 3, 1942" (the source of the McNutt quotations), and Office of War Information, "Press Release ORR-WMC-2037, Advance Release for Thursday Afternoon Papers, March 11, 1943," both in WMC Records, box 128, folder 7, NARA. See, among other radio scripts, "Manpower for Victory" (the source of the "Tarzans or Supermen" quotation), 24 July 1942, WMC Records, box 138, folder 5, NARA. Other media coverage includes "For Welfare of Disabled," *Employment Security Review*, February 1942; "Hiring the Handicapped,"

Employment Security Review, April 1942; "Production Jewels," *Employment Security Review*, October 1942; and "The Physically Handicapped—Assets not Liabilities" (the source of the "Most employers" quotation), *Manpower Review*, January 1943; see also William J. Fitzgerald to WMC, "Physically Handicapped Report," 23 Mar. 1944; all in WMC Records, box 166, folder 2, NARA. Documents in this folder also outline the ill-advised practices adopted by USES managers in Connecticut, who "auctioned" disabled workers to hesitant employers.

16. "Army-Navy E Award" Book, Anaconda Reduction Department, 28 Jan. 1943, ACM Records, Cascade County Historical Society; "List of Employees who have Passed their 70th Birthday," 26 July 1944, ACM Co. Records, box 208, folder 8, MHSRC. In 1943, the ACM conferred a special award on 106 Anaconda Reduction Works employees having more than forty years of service. As of July 1944, Black Eagle employed 1 man over the age of eighty and 36 over the age of seventy, 5 of whom worked as watchmen.

17. Michael J. Ryan, "Must Place Old Timers in War Production," *Miner's Voice*, 11 Sept. 1942. The BMU argued that the ACM's rustling system hampered the employment of older men. Writers Project of Montana, *Copper Camp: The Lusty Story of Butte, Montana, the Richest Hill on Earth* (Helena, MT: Riverbend, 2002 [first published 1943]), 232–33.

18. On the iconography of the 1930s, see Barbara Melosh, *Engendering Culture: Manhood and Womanhood in New Deal Public Art and Theater* (Washington, DC: Smithsonian Institution Press, 1991), and Elizabeth Faue, *Community of Suffering: Women, Men, and the Labor Movement in Minneapolis, 1915–1945* (Chapel Hill: University of North Carolina Press, 1991). On the wartime transition to more realistic images, see William L. Bird Jr. and Harry R. Rubenstein, *Design for Victory: World War II Posters on the American Home Front* (New York: Princeton Architectural Press, 1998), and Christina S. Jarvis, *The Male Body at War: American Masculinity during World War II* (Dekalb: Northern Illinois University Press, 2004). Examples of both heroic and normal masculinity appear in the *Copper Commando*; M. Murphy, *Mining Cultures*, 128; William Burke, "Greenhorn Miner," reprinted in Matthew Basso, "Another Look at Burke's Butte: The Great Depression and William Allen Burke's 'Greenhorn Miner,'" *Montana: The Magazine of Western History* 56, no. 4 (Winter 2006): 18–31; and Perle Watters, interview by Laurie Mercier, 25 Mar. 1983, MHSRC. On older men's difficulties, see Bob Lemmon to George Dean, 20 Dec. 1943, as well as the rest of the documents in ACM Co. Records, box 100, folder 4, MHSRC; W. E. Mitchell to D. M. Kelly, 16 Feb. 1943, ACM Co. Records, box 73, folder 2, MHSRC; and Bob Vine, *Anaconda Memories, 1883–1983* (Butte, MT: Artcraft Publishers, 1983), 39–40.

19. Victory Committee Meeting Transcript, 17 Sept. 1942.

20. Phillip, interview. Anaconda smelterman John Phillip remembers that workers would "razz" watchmen, calling them "Cox's Army," an emasculating reference to the "army" of unemployed men who marched on Washington, DC, in 1932.

21. Victory Committee Meeting Transcript, 17 Sept. 1942, 14; Leff, "Politics of Sacrifice"; Gerstle, *Working-Class Americanism*.

22. Women's World War II experience had been covered remarkably well by historians; see note 6 in the introduction for a list of representative studies. Karen Anderson (*Wartime Women*, 23–26, 44–45) argues that "antagonism toward women workers was most intense among workers in fields most associated with the attributes traditionally considered 'masculine'" (44). Among the groups she studied, longshoremen, cabdrivers, and shipbuilders had the most negative response.

23. "Women Workers Earning Top Wages in Plane Factories: Secretary Perkins' Report

Praises Their Efficiency—250,000 in Jobs by End of Year," *Wall Street Journal*, 1 Sept. 1942.

24. Western Federation of Miners (hereafter WFM)-International Union of Mine, Mill, and Smelter Workers (hereafter Mine Mill) Collection, box 216, folder 22, Archives, University of Colorado at Boulder Library (hereafter AUCBL); "Copper Shorts," *CC*, 23 Oct. 1942, 15, BSBA. *The Copper Commando* tried to make light of this remarkable change in the industry by printing a cartoon that sexualized these women through the eyes of an old-time miner. "U.S. Calls for 150 Women to Take Jobs at Copper Mines," *Washington Post*, 11 Sept. 1942; "Women in Mines," *Business Week*, 12 Sept. 1942, 35; USES–Butte, Montana, "Monthly Labor Market Developments Report," July, September, October, November, December 1943, WPB Records, box 219, folder "Butte, Montana," NARA; William H. Chafe, *Paradox of Change* (New York: Oxford University Press, 1991), 138–41; K. Anderson, *Wartime Women*, 30; "WLB Orders Equal Pay to Women As Recognition of Role in War" (the source of the quotation), *New York Times*, 26 Sept. 1942.

25. Federal Security Agency, "Summary Employment Status Report," WPB Records, box 219, folder 3, NARA; Martin Reborn, "Thoughts on the War and Post-War," *People's Voice*, 16 Oct. 1942. See also "Opinions of Readers: More on the Post War World," *People's Voice*, 6 Nov. 1942.

26. "U.S. Calls for 150 Women."

27. "Women in Mines"; USES, "Labor Market Survey"; untitled USES report, n.d., WPB Records, box 219, folder "Butte, Montana," NARA; "Anaconda, Montana, Locality War Housing Program No. 3," report, n.d. [ca.30 June 1943], WPB Records, box 219, folder "Butte, Montana," NARA. Smelter managers estimated a shortfall of 302 workers as of November 1, 1942. WMC/USES, "Monthly Labor Market Developments Report"; Bayard S. Morrow to W. E. Mitchell, 10 Aug. 1942, ACM Co. Records, box 70, folder 2, MHSRC.

28. Chafe, *Paradox of Change*, 126; R. Douglas Hurt, *The Great Plains during World War II* (Lincoln: University of Nebraska Press, 2008), 62–75. The WLB and the WMC, as well as other agencies, funded training programs for women in various professions. USES, "Labor Market Survey"; untitled USES report, n.d.; WMC/USES, "Monthly Labor Market Developments Report," various months.

29. The USES heard the exact same argument in Anaconda.

30. "War Work," *CC*, 22 Aug. 1942, 18, BSBA; "Limit Number of Mothers in Industry," *Catholic Register: Western Montana Edition*, 22 Nov. 1942; "Women of the World Must Strive to Uphold Morality," *Catholic Register: Western Montana Edition*, 29 Nov. 1942; William Mason to Fellow Worker, 15 Oct. 1942, WFM-Mine Mill Collection, box 78, folder 5, AUCBL.

31. WMC, "Advance Release, PM-4044," 19 Oct. 1942, WFM-Mine Mill Collection, box 216, folder 22, AUCBL; "Three Million More Women Needed by Industry in Next Year," *Montana Labor News*, 5 Nov. 1942; Westbrook Pegler, "Fair Enough," *MS*, 21 Nov. 1942; "Pegler's Scab Manor," *Montana Labor News*, 3 Dec. 1942. On Pegler and his hostility to a host of progressives, including labor feminists and Eleanor Roosevelt, see David Witwer, "Westbrook Pegler and the Anti-Union Movement," *Journal of American History* 92, no. 2 (2005): 527–52; and Finis Farr, *Fair Enough: The Life of Westbrook Pegler* (New Rochelle, NY: Arlington House, 1975).

32. "The Amazons among Our Women," *MS*, 4 Nov. 1942.

33. "Don't Try to Be 'The Perfect Wife,'" *MS*, 8 Nov. 1942, magazine section, 1.

34. Jane Marie Sullivan, "Butte's Famous A.W.V.S. Train Service Winds Up Two Years

of Distributing Treats to Servicemen," *MS*, 9 Apr. 1944; "AWVS Train Service Gets Recognition," *Montana Labor News*, 5 Nov. 1942.

35. William Bartholomew, interview by Laurie Mercier, 2 Mar. 1983, MHSRC. The full statement, as conveyed by Bartholomew, was "'It's deep enough; let's go down to the Brass Rail and have a drink." Watters interview. On local language, see "Mining Jargon," WPA Records, box 18, folder 12, MHSRC. Perle Watters remembers that during the war he would go into the O.K. Bar, and there would be more women than miners.

36. WFM-Mine Mill Collection, box 216, folder 2, AUCBL. Mine Mill's own records show that it was very interested in the employment of women around the United States during the war. The union collected newspaper stories as well as CIO and government information. "The Women of the Scovill Brass Workers 569," *Union*, 13 Apr. 1942, 1; "Soviet Women and the War," *Union*, 27 July 1942, 9; "Women Must Be Freed for Industry," *Union*, 19 Oct. 1942, 9; [Robinson statement and photograph of woman reading *The Union*], *Union*, 9 Nov. 1942, 5.

37. John McLeod to the Board of Trustees, School District #1, 6 Feb. 1943; "Child Care Emphasized at Recent CIO Convention," *Montana Labor News*, 3 Dec. 1942; "Application for Contribution for Providing Community Services under the Lanham Act, Butte, Montana" (the source of the quotation), 5 Feb. 1943; and Bart J. Riley to Florence Kerr, 23 Feb. 1943, all in Lanham Act Records, US Federal Works Agency, Bureau of Records Collection, MC 94, box 2, folders 9 and 10, MHSRC.

38. Rudolfo Acuna, *Occupied America: A History of Chicanos*, 3rd ed. (New York: HarperCollins, 1988), 261–65; Dorothy Bohn, "Mexican Braceros 'Lent Hand' in Fields during World War II," *GFT*, 25 Mar. 1984. For more on the bracero program, see Erasmo Gamboa, *Mexican Labor and World War II: Braceros in the Pacific Northwest, 1942–1947* (Austin: University of Texas Press, 1990); Barbara Driscoll, *The Tracks North: The Railroad Bracero Program of World War II* (Austin: CMAS Books, Center for Mexican American Studies, University of Texas at Austin, 1998); Mae Ngai, *Impossible Subjects: Illegal Aliens and the Making of Modern America* (Princeton, NJ: Princeton University Press, 2004), 127–66; and Deborah Cohen, *Braceros: Migrant Citizens and Transnational Subjects in the Postwar United States and Mexico* (Chapel Hill: University of North Carolina Press, 2011).

39. Reid Robinson to Frances Perkins, 18 May 1942, WFM-Mine Mill Collection, box 34, folder 5, AUCBL.

40. Robin D. G. Kelley, *Hammer and Hoe: Alabama Communists during the Great Depression* (Chapel Hill: University of North Carolina Press, 1990), 143–47; Michael Goldfield, *The Color of Politics: Race and the Mainsprings of American Politics* (New York: New Press, 1997), 193–96; Mario T. Garcia, *Mexican Americans: Leadership, Ideology, and Identity, 1930–1960* (New Haven, CT: Yale University Press, 1991), 183–87.

41. Carey McWilliams, *North from Mexico: The Spanish-Speaking People of the United States* (Westport, CT: Greenwood Press, 1990), 178–83; Zaragosa Vargas, *Labor Rights Are Civil Rights: Mexican American Workers in Twentieth-Century America* (Princeton, NJ: Princeton University Press, 2005), 158–67, 220–23. Robinson to Perkins.

42. D. W. Tracy to Reid Robinson, 20 May 1942, WFM-Mine Mill Collection, box 34, folder 5, AUCBL.

43. Writers Project of Montana, *Copper Camp*, 6, 139. On Filipinos in Butte, see Perdita Duncan, Walter Duncan, William Fenter, Elmo Fortune, and notes made by Mrs. Lena Brown, interview by Laurie Mercier, 24 Mar. 1983, MHSRC; and Silvio Sciuchetti, interview by Laurie Mercier, 2 Mar. 1983, MHSRC. Joe Navarro, interview by Laurie Mercier, 25 Mar. 1983, MHSRC; Bartholomew, interview; "Mining Jargon."

44. "Home on Furlough–SGT. Ronald Navaro," *MS*, 1 Nov. 1942; Navarro, interview; Duncan, Duncan, Fenter, Fortune, and Brown, interview. Reports of violence against the Filipinos who worked in the mines around World War I suggest why they did not stay long in Butte and also foreshadow the reaction to new groups of workers of color. "Mining Jargon"; USES, "Labor Market Survey."

45. Frank McSherry to Carl Ulrich, 9 Dec. 1942, WMC Records, box 156, folder 6, NARA.

46. Ibid.; USES, "Bulletin No. 35, Temporary Migration of Mexican Workers to the United States for Non Agricultural Labor," 1 July 1943, WMC Records, box 156, folder 6, "Foreign and Mexican Workers," NARA. The WMC informed all USES representatives that industrial laborers from Mexico fell under the antidiscrimination clauses of Executive Order 8802.

47. Kenneth William Townsend, *World War II and the American Indian* (Albuquerque: University of New Mexico Press, 2000), 171, 176–82 (the "tribal resources" quotation is from p. 171); Alison R. Bernstein, *American Indians and World War II: Toward a New Era in Indian Affairs* (Norman: University of Oklahoma Press, 1991), 26, 39, 64–66. Although some American Indians resisted serving in the military based on the nation's historical treatment of their peoples, the majority were overwhelmingly patriotic, participating in the military and in all other aspects of the war effort. Bernstein notes that Landless Indians were one of the groups thought to oppose conscription, and that officials believed Communists had led them to that position.

48. Writers Project of Montana, *Copper Camp*, 127 (the source of the quotation). Historically, Chinese workers were found in larger numbers and had deeper roots in Butte than their Japanese counterparts. By World War II, the Chinese population in the mining city was minuscule, but attitudes toward them had changed dramatically. *Copper Camp* reported that Butte residents discussed with pride the local Chinese effort to prompt enlistments "in Uncle Sam's forces [to] help vanquish the despised Japs from the face of the earth." Sonya K. Smith, "Manipulating Limited Options to Many Choices: Internee Labor during World War II" (unpublished paper, 2000, in author's possession; quotation is from p. 8); Ronald Takaki, *Strangers from a Different Shore: A History of Asian Americans* (Boston: Little, Brown, 1998).

49. S. Smith, "Manipulating Limited Options," 12; Immigration Commission (William P. Dillingham et al.), *Reports of the Immigration Commission: Immigrants in Industries, Part 25; Japanese and Other Immigrant Races in the Pacific Coast and Rocky Mountain States* (Washington, DC: Government Printing Office, 1911); Office of General Counsel to Lawrence W. Cramer, 2 Oct. 1942, WMC Records, box 156, folder 6, "Fair Employment Practices Committee," NARA; John McLeod, "Butte Miners Union No 1 Minutes of Regular Meeting," 16 Dec. 1942, in vol. 222, BMU Minutes, WFM-Mine Mill Collection, AUCBL; "Minutes for Meeting of Local 16, IUMMSW, Great Falls, Montana," 2 Dec. 1942, WFM-Mine Mill Collection, AUCBL. In Great Falls, one smelterman "also suggested that mention should be made that as the Japs like fish an attempt should be made to clean the Missouri of Carp and Suckers and these be fed to the interned Japs" ("Minutes for Meeting of Local 16, IUMMSW").

50. Garcia, *Mexican Americans*, 187.

CHAPTER SIX

1. Lewis B. Stewart and Hiawatha Brown to Paul McNutt, 12 Sept. 1942, Western Federation of Miners (hereafter WFM)-International Union of Mine, Mill, and Smelter Workers (hereafter Mine Mill) Collection, box 78, folder 5, Archives, University of

Colorado at Boulder Library (hereafter AUCBL). For more on this community, see Matthew Basso, "Metal of Honor: Montana's World War II Homefront, Movies, and the Social Politics of White Male Anxiety" (PhD diss., University of Minnesota, 2001), 104–50; and Robert F. Jefferson, *Fighting for Hope: African American Troops of the 93rd Infantry Division in World War II and Postwar America* (Baltimore: Johns Hopkins University Press, 2008).

2. L. Stewart and Brown to McNutt; Reid Robinson, interview by Ronald Filippelli, Dec. 1969, Labor Oral History Collection, Historical Collections and Labor Archives, Pennsylvania State University Libraries, University Park, PA.

3. Robert Corbett, interview by Laurie Mercier, 17 Apr. 1984, Montana Historical Society Research Center (hereafter MHSRC); William Bartholomew, interview by Laurie Mercier, 2 Mar. 1983, MHSRC; Graham Dolan, "Bishop Seconds MMSW Appeal to Butte Local," *Union*, 16 Nov. 1942; Father M. M. English, "Thursday, November 12" [Chronological notes regarding Butte–black soldier-miner crisis], n.d. [likely Dec.1942], Diocese of Helena Archives (hereafter DOHA).

4. Robert Hayden, "Speech," from *Heart-Shape in the Dust* (Detroit: Falcon Press, 1940).

5. Kent McFarland, "Defends Army," *Union*, 30 Nov. 1942; Federal Security Agency, "Summary Employment Status Report," n.d., War Production Board (hereafter WPB) Records, box 219, folder "Butte, Montana," National Archives and Records Administration (hereafter NARA); Jessica Rhine to Reid Robinson, 21 Oct. 1942, WFM-Mine Mill Collection, box 39, folder 1, AUCBL; WPB Form FD-400-A, 27 Feb. 1943 and 25 Oct. 1943, WPB–Helena Office Records, box 7, folder 3, MHSRC.

6. "Strike against Soldier Miners," *Washington Star*, 20 Nov. 1942; Rhine to Robinson, 21 Oct. 1942; John McCusker to Frank McSherry, n.d. [likely 3 Dec. 1943], DOHA. Father M. M. English, [Chronological notes]. ACM's Dan Kelly was among the executives who had "protested the sending of the negroes but was overruled" (English, [Chronological notes]).

7. Rhine to Robinson, 21 Oct. 1942; Fowler Harper to Reid Robinson, 26 Oct. 1942, WFM-Mine Mill Collection, box 39, folder 1, AUCBL.

8. "Hit Jim Crow," *Union*, 27 July 1942; "A. Philip Randolph and Others Call on AFL to Set Up Discrimination Board b/c 'Jimcrowism' Is Retarding War Effort," *Union*, 19 Oct. 1942. Photographs in the *Union* show the interracial character of Mine Mill; see 21 Sept. 1942 and 12 Oct. 1942 editions. Robin D. G. Kelley, *Hammer and Hoe: Alabama Communists during the Great Depression* (Chapel Hill: University of North Carolina Press, 1990), 145. Also see Michael Goldfield, *The Color of Politics: Race and the Mainsprings of American Politics* (New York: New Press, 1997), 193–96; Gary Fink, ed., *Biographical Dictionary of American Labor* (Westport, CT: Greenwood Press, 1984), 488–89; and Robinson, interview.

9. Quintard Taylor, *In Search of the Racial Frontier: African Americans in the West, 1528–1990* (New York: W. W. Norton, 1998), 250; Matthew Frye Jacobson, *Whiteness of a Different Color: European Immigrants and the Alchemy of Race* (Cambridge, MA: Harvard University Press, 1998), 95. Jacobson emphasizes that by catalyzing the migration of blacks to the North and West, World War II made Jim Crow a national question.

10. Thomas Doherty, *Projections of War: Hollywood, American Culture, and World War II* (New York: Columbia University Press, 1993), 5, 39–43; quotation is from p. 5.

11. Production Code Administration to Jack Warner, 8 Oct. 1941, Motion Picture Association of America (hereafter MPAA) Collection, folder "In This Our Life," Academy

of Motion Picture Arts and Sciences (hereafter AMPAS). For a fuller analysis of *In This Our Life*, see Basso, "Metal of Honor," 84–103.

12. Mrs. Alonzo Richardson to Joseph Breen, 6 June 1942, MPAA Collection, folder "In This Our Life," AMPAS.

13. W. A. Robinson to Warner Brothers (hereafter WB), 4 Sept. 1942; John S. Holley to WB, 9 Aug. 1942; James E. Samuels to WB, 6 June 1942; and Edith McDougald to WB, 6 June 1942, all in WB Collection, file 1998: *In This Our Life* "Memos and Correspondence," University of Southern California Film Archive (hereafter USCFA).

14. Marlon Riggs, *Ethnic Notions* (California Newsreel, 1987); Donald Bogle, *Toms, Coons, Mammies, Mulattoes, and Bucks: An Interpretive History of Blacks in American Film* (New York: Continuum, 2001); Doherty, *Projections of War*, 206 (the source of the "that white men" quotation); Thomas Guglielmo, "Red Cross, Double Cross": Race and America's World War II-Era Blood Donor Service," *Journal of American History* 97, no. 15.(June 2010): 63–90; *Manpower Missing*, Office of War Information's Bureau of Motion Pictures, 29 Oct. 1942. Similar Popular Front–themed shorts were shown throughout the war (e.g., *The Good Job*, MGM, 1942). Films available at the Motion Picture, Television, and Sound Branch, Library of Congress, Washington, DC.

15. Fiche 15/229, Paramount, 19 May 1942, in K. R. M. Short, *World War II through the American Newsreels: An Introduction and Guide to the Microfiches* (Oxford: Oxford Microform Publishers, 1984), 28; Lizabeth Cohen, *Consumers' Republic: The Politics of Mass Consumption in Postwar America* (New York: Knopf, 2003), 62–110.

16. Michael Rogin, *Blackface, White Noise: Jewish Immigrants in the Hollywood Melting Pot* (Berkeley: University of California Press, 1996), 163. Paramount's *Holiday Inn* press book highlighted the blackface component of the movie: "For the first time in his screen career, Bing Crosby will be seen in blackface!" The most popular film of the war, *This Is the Army* (1943), starring Ronald Reagan, also contained extensive blackface scenes. USC Press Book Collection, USCFA; Rogin, *Blackface, White Noise*, 137, 159–208, esp. 182–83; Doherty, *Projections of War*, 205–13.

17. Vernon H. Jensen, *Nonferrous Metals Industry Unionism, 1932–1954* (Ithaca, NY: Cornell University Press, 1954), 35; Reid Robinson, "Resignation Statement," 10 Mar. 1947, WFM-Mine Mill Collection, box 29, folder 19, AUCBL. Northeast Mine Mill members also balked at Robinson's politics.

18. Lizabeth Cohen, *Making a New Deal: Industrial Workers in Chicago, 1919–1939* (New York: Cambridge University Press, 1990), 52; Joe Navarro, interview by Laurie Mercier, 25 Mar. 1983, MHSRC; Herbert Mickelson, interview by Laurie Mercier, 12 Jan. 1982, MHSRC; Bartholomew, interview.

19. Robinson, interview; *Win the War May Day Rally* pamphlet, 2 May 1942; Edward Mason to Cap Bruce, 7 May 1942; and "Reds Dishonor One of the Greatest of Our Heroes," *People's Voice*, May 1942, all in the *People's Voice* Records, box 4, folder 29, MHSRC. The Kelly story was steeped in myth. See Jerome Klinkowitz, *Pacific Skies: American Flyers in World War II* (Jackson: University Press of Mississippi, 2004), 50–56; and John L. Frisbee, "Colin Kelly: He Was a Hero in Legend and in Fact," *Valor* 77, no. 6 (June 1994).

20. Mason to Bruce; "Reds Dishonor One of the Greatest of Our Heroes."

21. "Butte Miners Union No 1 Minutes of Regular Meeting," 6 May 1942 and 10 June 1942, in vol. 222, BMU Minutes, WFM-Mine Mill Collection, AUCBL; Kelley, *Hammer and Hoe*, 141. "Copper Miners Pledge More Ore for 2d Front Action" and "Butte Irish Catholic Mayor Hails Soviets," [likely from the *Daily Worker*], 29 June 1942, WFM-Mine Mill Collection, box 198, folder 23, AUCBL; Pat Brennan, "Bustle Is the

Word to Describe Alaska's Ladd Field Where America and Russia 'Meet' on Military Skyway," *Great Falls Tribune* (hereafter *GFT*), November 1944, in "Great Falls Army Air Base 1943–1945" vertical file, Cascade County Historical Society. During the war, supporting the "Reds" often meant supporting the Soviet Union—a practice, paradoxically, that was common in Montana and the rest of the United States.

22. "Robinson Wires Army," *Union*, 2 Nov. 1942. K. McFarland, "Defends Army."

23. Reid Robinson and James Leary to Paul Fall, 27 Oct. 1942, WFM-Mine Mill Collection, box 40, folder 13, AUCBL.

24. Ibid.

25. John McLeod, "Butte Miners Union No 1 Minutes of Regular Meeting," 28 Oct. and 4 Nov. 1942, in vol. 222, BMU Minutes, WFM-Mine Mill Collection, AUCBL; English, [Chronological notes].

26. Robinson, interview.

27. John McLeod, "Butte Miners Union No 1 Minutes of Special Meeting," 8 Nov. 1942, in vol. 222, BMU Minutes, WFM-Mine Mill Collection, AUCBL; Reid Robinson to Allan McNeil, 5 Nov. 1942, WFM-Mine Mill Collection, box 108, folder 3, AUCBL; English, [Chronological notes]; McCusker to McSherry, n.d. [likely 3 Dec. 1943]. Mine Mill's newspaper coupled its report on the Butte situation with other news about the union's progressive racial position and with photos of black and white sailors together. Graham Dolan, "Tribute to NMU," "Discrimination," "Bishop Seconds MMSW Appeal to Butte Local," "Green Light," and "Another Gain for Unity," *Union*, 16 Nov. 1942; "Ask Lynch Probe," *Union*, 23 Nov. 1942. Some members considered the paper too leftist. Jensen, *Nonferrous Metals Industry Unionism*, 115.

28. Initially, Driscoll had been a strong supporter of Robinson, saying he had "seen him stand up and do his job as a man and as a leader of labor." Jensen, *Nonferrous Metals Industry Unionism*, 45. Robinson continued to be popular elsewhere. Nationally, he won more than twice as many votes as Driscoll, and Byrne trailed well behind. Robinson also won the vote in Anaconda and Black Eagle. Paul Fall, "Butte Miners Union No 1 Minutes of Regular Meeting," 18 Nov. 1942, in vol. 222, BMU Minutes, WFM-Mine Mill Collection, AUCBL. Other sources reported slightly different vote totals. "Stanley Babcock Heads Miners," *Montana Standard* (hereafter *MS*), 10 Nov. 1942; "Election Returns of Officers and Board Members," *Union*, 14 Dec. 1942; Allan McNeil to Reid Robinson, 13 Nov. 1942, WFM-Mine Mill Collection box 108, folder 3, AUCBL; International Executive Board to the Reverend Joseph F. Donnelly, 28 Oct. 1942, WFM-Mine Mill Collection, box 29, folder 3, AUCBL.

29. "Report of the Manpower Stabilization Committee of the International Executive Board," September-October 1942, ACM Co. Records, box 70, folder 2, MHSRC; "Published Statements of Candidates for International President," *Union*, 19 Oct. 1942. "What Uncle Sam Thinks of Our Union," *Union*, 14 Dec. 1942; Mine Mill leaders issued a long defense of their relationship with the government, noting that the close ties helped secure the blanket deferment and the likelihood of pay bumps. On Robinson's relationship with the Roosevelt administration, see Harvey A. Levenstein, *Communism, Anticommunism, and the CIO* (Westport, CT: Greenwood Press, 1981), 145; and Jensen, *Nonferrous Metals Industry Unionism*, 61–65.

30. "Published Statements."

31. William Mason to Ben Riskin, 9 Aug. 1942, WFM-Mine Mill Collection, box 78, folder 1, AUCBL; "Results of Local Negotiations" and "Developments and Issues in the Negotiations," *Miner's Voice*, 11 Sept. 1942; "Proposed Agreement Rejected by Anaconda Employees (*sic.*)," *MS*, 17 Nov. 1942; "Transcript of Nonferrous Metals

Commission National War Labor Board Hearing Held in Butte, December 14 and 15, 1942," WFM-Mine Mill Collection, box 217, folder 5, AUCBL. The National War Labor Board (hereafter NWLB) accepted the case on September 23, 1942, and issued the official Directive Order on January 15, 1943. It awarded an increase of one dollar a day to the base rate of all employees retroactive to October 1, 1942 (the current base pay rate was $6.75 a day), denied the ACM's request for a central hiring hall and biweekly pay, and modified the ACM request for five-day holdback to three days on quits only, not discharges. The union's request for a night-shift differential was also denied. James M. Burns to Dan M. Kelley, Paul Fall Jr. et al., 7and 12 Jan. 1943, NWLB Records, box 7, folder 2, NARA–Denver; Nonferrous Metals Commission of the National War Labor Board, "Directive Order: NWLB Case No. 527," January 15, 1943, NWLB Records, box 7, folder 3, NARA–Denver. McNutt, worried about labor unrest among miners and smeltermen, wrote to the NWLB in mid-October 1942, reminding it how important it was to resolve the dispute. Paul McNutt to William Davis, 15 Oct. 1942, War Manpower Commission (hereafter WMC) Records, box 156, folder 11, "Non-Ferrous Metal Industries," NARA.

32. McSherry, Harper, and others involved in the Butte situation received copies of the survey report on November 10, 1942. "Job Freezing in the Northwest's Lumber and Non-Ferrous Metals Industries," 2 Nov. 1942, WMC Records, box 156, folder 11, "Non-Ferrous Metal Industries," NARA. Mine Mill cited the NWLB's decision in the Utah-Idaho case to point out that the board also believed that miners' and smelter-men's pay lagged. "Transcript of Nonferrous Metals Commission National War Labor Board Hearing," 27–29. Butte miners and Anaconda smeltermen voted overwhelmingly in mid-November to reject the wage agreement proposed by the NWLB. Black Eagle's smeltermen accepted the decision, reflecting the more amicable relationships they had with the ACM and the government. Mason to Riskin, 9 Aug. 1942, WFM-Mine Mill Collection, box 78, folder 1, AUCBL. "Results of Local Negotiations" and "Developments and Issues"; "Proposed Agreement Rejected"; "Job Freezing in the Northwest"; David Montgomery, *Workers' Control in America: Studies in the History of Work, Technology, and Labor Struggles* (New York: Cambridge University Press, 1979), 12, 115. Compare "More Soldiers Arrive on Home Front," *MS,* 1 Nov. 1942, with "Nelson Praises 'Commando,'" *MS,* 5 Nov. 1942.

33. Paul McNutt to James Byrne and William Mason; McNutt to Reid Robinson, both 5 Nov. 1942, DOHA.

34. James Byrne to Donald Nelson, 5 Nov. 1942, WFM-Mine Mill Collection, box 40, folder 13, AUCBL. Silvio Sciuchetti, interview by Laurie Mercier, 2 Mar. 1983, MHSRC. Sciuchetti, twenty-one years old at the time of this incident, was one of the young deferred miners who stayed in town. Further indicating the ways that stereotypes of black masculinity and the black male body entered the picture, William Bartholomew recalled that locals said these men were "Big. Oh, great big . . . they looked like football players." Bartholomew, interview.

35. McCusker to McSherry (the source of the quotations), n.d. [likely 3 Dec 1943]; English, [Chronological notes]; Father M. M. English, "Butte Background: For General McSherry," n.d. [likely 20 Nov. 1942], DOHA.

36. McCusker to McSherry, n.d. [likely 3 Dec. 1943]; John McLeod, "Butte Miners Union No 1 Minutes of Regular Meeting," 18 Nov. 1942, in vol. 222, BMU Minutes, WFM-Mine Mill Collection, AUCBL. A union referendum found 4,400 men opposed to and 400 in favor of the contract. "Transcript of Nonferrous Metals Commission National War Labor Board Hearing," 162, 225–26, 230.

37. When Bob Logan's wife came to Butte, she went to the local Presbyterian church and was told, "Mrs. Logan, we can't have you come to our church. You go down to the colored church at the end of the street, that's where you belong." Another African American recalled, "We did not dare go into the Baptist, the Methodist . . . the Catholic Church, the Presbyterian, the Episcopalian Church." Hugo Kenck and Margaret McMann Kenck, interview by Laurie Mercier, 8 Dec. 1982, MHSRC.

38. Cornelia M. Flaherty, *Go With Haste Into the Mountains: A History of the Diocese of Helena* (Helena, MT: Falcon Press, 1984), 123–24, 138; Bishop Joseph Gilmore to Brigadier General W. H. Harrison, 30 Oct. 1942, DOHA. Gilmore's parents came from County Galway and in 1898 moved to Anaconda, where his father worked at the smelter. He grew up among the children of copper workers, was ordained in 1915, and spent the remainder of his career in Montana. In 1926 he became the pastor at St. Helena's in Meaderville, a congregation composed mainly of Italian and Slav miners and their families. His appointment as bishop of Helena ten years later did not weaken his ties with copper workers. Shortly after the black soldier-miner crisis ended, Paul J. Gilmore, the bishop's nephew, quit his job and enlisted in the army. See "Paul J. Gilmore Dies in Action," *MS*, 11 June 1945.

39. "Bishops of U.S. Work for Victory and Peace," *Catholic Register*, 22 Nov. 1942; "Listening In," and "Church Always Opposes Racial Discrimination," *Catholic Register*, 29 Nov. 1942; Bishop Joseph Gilmore to Robert Patterson, 20 Nov. 1942; Rev. John Sullivan to Bishop Joseph Gilmore, 18 and 21 Nov. 1942; Bishop Joseph Gilmore to James Byrne, 11 Nov. 1942; Bishop Joseph Gilmore to Father M. M. English, 11 Nov. 1942, all DOHA.

40. English, "Butte Background."

41. William Haber and Daniel Kruger, *The Role of the United States Employment Service in a Changing Economy* (Washington, DC: W. E. Upjohn Institute for Employment Research, 1964). Only a month before the memo was issued, the Fair Employment Practices Commission (FEPC) had launched an investigation of discriminatory employment practices within the United States Employment Service (USES) itself. John J. Corson to All Employees of United States Employment Service, "Operating Policy," 19 Oct. 1942, and R. G. Conley, "Request by President's Committee on Fair Employment Practices," 28 Sept. 1942, both in WMC Records, box 156, folder 6, "Fair Employment Practices Committee," NARA.

42. English, [Chronological notes].

43. "Metal Mine War Conference Set for Salt Lake City This Month," *MS*, 8 Nov. 1942; "Race Prejudices Must Vanish," *MS*, 18 Nov. 1942.

44. English, [Chronological notes]; "FDR Consults Robinson on Problems at Butte," *Union*, 23 Nov. 1942; "Strike against Soldier Miners."

45. Robinson argued that segregating black miners would be equivalent to practices that Mine Mill had fought in the South. It would also be "carrying out the program that Hitler wishes us to follow in having race against race, white against colored, one religion against another and general national disunity among the people." Robinson and Leary to Fall, 27 Oct. 1942. English's committee took the lead in persuading Butte's rank and file to agree to the "one mine" plan. English instructed the clergy to support the plan in their Sunday, November 22, homilies. R. A. McGowan to Bishop Joseph Gilmore, 18 Nov. 1942, and English, [Chronological notes], DOHA.

46. "Strike against Soldier Miners." "Labor: Industrial Democracy," *Time*, 23 Nov. 1942, 93–94.

47. "Corporation Papers and A.P. and U.P. Silent on Important News," *People's Voice*, 27 Nov. 1942. As national interest in the story expanded, a *New York Post* article blamed BMU president James Byrne for the crisis. Robinson wrote to the editor to complain that the paper was unfairly singling out Byrne. The editor acknowledged the mistake, noting that the membership as a whole should have been blamed, but added that after investigating the matter the *Post* believed that although Byrne had signed a resolution, "we do not find evidence of any active, effective effort to combat the discrimination evidenced by the membership of his local." Paul Tierney to Reid Robinson, 21 Dec. 1942, WFM-Mine Mill Collection, box 40, folder 13, AUCBL. Robinson repeatedly asked McNutt and Patterson to immediately return some Butte miners via the furlough system so as to curb the complaints of those resisting the black soldier-miners. The government replied that other former Butte miners were either overseas or unavailable due to "military necessity." Ben Riskin to Murray Wright, 5 Nov. 1942, WFM-Mine Mill Collection, box 40, folder 13, AUCBL; Allan McNeil to William Mason, 5 Nov. 1942, and J. A. Ulio to William Mason, November 25, 1942, both in WFM-Mine Mill Collection, box 78, folder 5, AUCBL. K. McFarland, "Defends Army."

48. William Mason, [notes to Robinson "Butte. Saturday morning."], 23 Nov. 1942, and Reid Robinson to William Mason, 24 Nov. 1942, both in WFM-Mine Mill Collection, box 78, folder 5, AUCBL; McCusker to McSherry, n.d. [likely 3 Dec. 1943]; "Butte Union to Check on Deferments," *Union*, 23 Nov. 1942.

49. English, [Chronological notes]; McCusker to McSherry, n.d. [likely 3 Dec. 1943].

50. English, [Chronological notes]; McCusker to McSherry, n.d. [likely 3 Dec. 1943]; K. McFarland, "Defends Army."

51. English, [Chronological notes]; McCusker to McSherry, n.d. [likely 3 Dec. 1943]; John McLeod, "Butte Miners Union No 1 Minutes of Regular Meeting," 25 Nov. 1942, and "Night Meeting," 25 Nov. 1942, in vol. 222, BMU Minutes, WFM-Mine Mill Collection, AUCBL. The night meeting minutes show that only 57 of the more than 1,000 men present voted in favor of the plan.

52. English, [Chronological notes] (the source of the quotations); McCusker to McSherry, n.d. [likely 3 Dec. 1943].

53. English, [Chronological notes]

54. Ibid.

55. Lewis Stewart, "Declaration of Renunciation of American Citizenship," January 27, 1942, DOHA; "What the Poll-Taxers' Victory Should Teach MMSW Members," *Union*, 23 Nov. 1942.

56. English, [Chronological notes]; McCusker to McSherry, n.d. [likely 3 Dec. 1943].

57. English, [Chronological notes].

58. Hezekiah Jones, "Affidavit," 19 Dec. 1942, WFM-Mine Mill Collection, box 78, folder 5, AUCBL.

59. Ibid.

60. Hezekiah Jones, "Statement of the Members of the United Mine Workers of America Who Had Contracted to Work in the Butte Mines," 28 Nov. 1942, DOHA.

61. Melvyn Dubofsky and Warren Van Tine, *John L. Lewis: A Biography* (Urbana: University of Illinois Press, 1986); "Developments and Issues"; Mason to Riskin, 9 Aug. 1942. On the history between the United Mine Workers of America and Mine Mill, see Jensen, *Nonferrous Metals Industry Unionism*, 25–27.

62. English, [Chronological notes].

63. John McLeod, "Butte Miners Union No 1 Minutes of Regular Meeting," 16 Dec. 1942, in vol. 222, BMU Minutes, WFM-Mine Mill Collection, AUCBL; McCusker to McSherry, n.d. [likely 3 Dec. 1943]; Henry S. Wilson et al. [Statement of Black Soldier Miners], 29 Nov. 1942, DOHA; English, [Chronological notes]. Uncertainty surrounds Richard Brown's position in Butte at the end of 1942, but he eventually worked in the Butte mines.

64. English, [Chronological notes]; one resident recalled that the building the black soldier-miners were staying in "was blasted." Bessie Towey Mulhern, interview by Laurie Mercier, 23 Nov. 1981, MHSRC. Although seemingly inaccurate, it suggests the climate of threat at the time.

65. English, [Chronological notes]; Wilson et al. [Statement of Black Soldier Miners]; Jones, "Affidavit."

66. William Mason to Reid Robinson, 17 Jan. 1942, WFM-Mine Mill Collection, box 78, folder 5, AUCBL; K. B. Frazier to Geo. A. Dean, 21 Dec. 1942, ACM Co. Records, box 113, folder 1, MHSRC.

67. English, [Chronological notes].

68. Tom Brokaw, *The Greatest Generation* (New York: Random House, 1998); Turner Catledge, "Officials Fear Wave of Labor Strife," *New York Times*, 20 Aug. 1942; "Number of Strikes . . . Affecting War Department Procurement for the Years 1942–1944," 4 Jan. 1945, and "Office of War Information . . . Man-Days Lost . . .," 29 Dec. 1942, both in War Manpower Commission, box 133, folder 936, "Strike Statistics N.W.L.B.," NARA. "Transcript of Hearing: NWLB Case No. 527," 14 and 15 Dec. 1942, p. 246, NWLB Records, box 7, folder 4, NARA–Denver. Wildcats occurred in aviation, coal, rubber, shipbuilding, steel, and in virtually every other type of wartime industry. See Nelson Lichtenstein, *Labor's War at Home: The CIO in World War II* (New York: Cambridge University Press, 1982), 54–55, 60, 107, 131–35, 163–65, 189–92. For an overview of major hate strikes, see George Lipsitz, *Rainbow at Midnight: Labor and Culture in the 1940s* (Urbana: University of Illinois Press, 1994), 69–97.

69. "Strike against Soldier Miners"; Mulhern, interview. Bessie Mulhern contends that enough white soldier-miners came to Butte to fill every hotel and apartment. They told her that they "grabbed at the chance" to leave the military for the mines, a choice that runs counter to that made by Butte men in uniform. K. McFarland, "Defends Army"; Commission of Conciliation, "Anaconda vs. Locals 1, 16, and 117," 12 Oct. 1943, WFM-Mine Mill Collection, box 320, folder 3, AUCBL; "Bureau of Mines Report Shows Drop of 11 Per Cent from 1942 in Value of Montana Ores, Gravels," *MS*, 16 Jan. 1944. Bureau of Mines figures indicate that more than twelve hundred furloughed white soldier-miners worked in Butte by 1944. "Student Stopes," *Copper Commando*, 20 Nov. 1942, 4–5; Oscar Dingman, *A Working Plan for Training Miners* (Butte: Montana School of Mines, 1943); "Great Falls Recapitulation of Payroll," December 1942, ACM Co. Records, box 210, folder 11, MHSRC; "Back Pay at A.C.M. Plants Makes January Like Christmas," *GFT*, 27 Jan. 1943. "Transcript of Hearing," 251.

70. Lewis Stewart to Lawrence Cramer, 3 Dec. 1942, WFM-Mine Mill Collection, box 40, file 13, AUCBL.

71. L. Stewart to Cramer; Tierney to Robinson, 21 Dec. 1942; Mason to Robinson. Robinson in his public assessment blamed "disunity propaganda which can be traced direct to the defeatist camp in the nation." "The President's Corner," *Union*, 7 Dec. 1942.

72. Mason to Robinson; John McLeod to Bishop J. M. Gilmore, 2 Dec. 1942, DOHA; James Byrne et al. to Paul McNutt, 19 Dec. 1942, DOHA.
73. Byrne et al. to McNutt, 19 Dec. 1942; Sciuchetti, interview.
74. Bartholomew, interview; Mulhern, interview. Throughout the war, Butte's miner training program welcomed and trained inexperienced white men. Dingman, *A Working Plan for Training Miners;* "Anaconda Company Training Program for Miners in Operation for Two Years," *GFT,* 19 Sept. [likely 1944]. Butte thought itself very much a patriotic town and flaunted signs of the patriotism. "More Than 1,600 Former Students of Butte High School in the Armed Forces, Setting Record for Community This Size," *MS,* 12 Dec. 1943.
75. Sciuchetti, interview. Sciuchetti's racial attitudes were not unusual. See, for example, Beth Bailey and David Farber, *The First Strange Place: Race and Sex in World War II Hawaii* (Baltimore: Johns Hopkins University Press, 1994), 134–35; and McLeod to Gilmore.
76. Perle Watters, interview by Laurie Mercier, 25 Mar. 1983, MHSRC; Bartholomew, interview. In their oral histories, white miners did not mention Elmo Fortune, another African American from Butte who worked in the mines after the war. On his experience, see Perdita Duncan, Walter Duncan, William Fenter, Elmo Fortune, and notes made by Mrs. Lena Brown, interview by Laurie Mercier, 24 Mar. 1983, MHSRC.
77. Watters, interview.
78. "The President's Corner."
79. McLeod to Gilmore; Allan D. McNeil to Reid Robinson, 5 Nov. 1942, WFM-Mine Mill Collection, box 108, folder 3, AUCBL. McNeil, Robinson's assistant in 1942, faced deportation for radical political activities in 1953: WFM-Mine Mill Collection, box 119, folder 6, AUCBL. On the planned educational campaign, see "Minutes for Meeting of Local 16, IUMMSW, Great Falls, Montana," 3 Feb. 1943, WFM-Mine Mill Collection, AUCBL.
80. "Manpower Campaigns in Local Labor Shortage Areas," 20 Nov. 1942, Committee for Congested Production Areas Records, box 135, folder 1, NARA.

CHAPTER SEVEN

1. W. E. Mitchell to K. B. Frazier, 6 Mar. 1937; ACM Number of [Daily Wage] Employees by Month for 1937, 10 Dec. 1937; E. B. Larsen to K. B. Frazier, 17 June 1940; and Number of Names on Payrolls, 16 Dec. 1940, 17 Nov.1941, 16 Dec. 1942, 17 Dec. 1943, all in ACM Co. Records, box 208, folder 9, Montana Historical Society Research Center, Helena (hereafter MHSRC); David Emmons, "Hard Times and War Times," in "Expert Report of David Emmons, Ph.D." *United States of America v. Atlantic Richfield Company, et. al.,* US District Court, District of Montana, Helena Division, Case No. CV-89-039-PGH, 15 July 1996, 252.
2. Bureau of Labor, Statistics Summary of Strikes in 1943, 23 June 1944, in War Manpower Commission (hereafter WMC) Records, box 133, folder 936, "Strike Statistics N.W.L.B.," National Archives and Records Administration (hereafter NARA); "Mexicans to Help Relieve Shortage," *Union,* 23 Nov. 1942. The International Union of Mine, Mill, and Smelter Workers (hereafter Mine Mill) contended that the WMC had learned its lesson. Paul McNutt, "Employment of Aliens," 12 Oct. 1943, and "Foreign Born Employees as of 12/9/42," both in ACM Co. Records, box 72, folder 6, MHSRC; Marie "Cookie" Palagi Godlewski, interview by Laurie Mercier, 7 May 1987, MHSRC; Olanda Rinari Vangelisti and Claire Vangelisti Del Guerra, interview by Laurie Mercier, 16 July 1986, MHSRC.

3. "Local Procedure Outlined for Second Draft Lottery," *Great Falls Tribune* (hereafter *GFT*), 16 July 1941; William Tonkovich, interview by Laurie Mercier, 27 Feb. 1986, MHSRC; Lyle Pellett, interview by Laurie Mercier, 13 Mar. 1986, MHSRC; ACM, "Selective Service Report," Aug. 1943, ACM Co. Records, box 70, folder 4, MHSRC. By August 1943, 412 smeltermen were in the military and 428 had been deferred. "Great Falls Citizens, Industry Ready for Call to Arms: Reaction to Jap Attack Varied, Many Volunteer," *GFT*, [ca. 9 Dec. 1942], "Misc: World War II, Great Falls" vertical file, Cascade County Historical Society (hereafter CCHS); "Falls Not Immune from Jap Attack, OCD Chief Warns," *GFT*, 25 July 1942; Pellett, interview. When management offered to release men from deferments so they could join the service, only three came forward. "Former CIO Head Now Serving in Army," *Montana Labor News*, 14 Jan. 1943. When state CIO president Sylvester Graham volunteered, his act was treated as exemplary.

4. Pellett, interview; R. W. Connell, *Masculinities: Knowledge, Power, and Social Change* (Berkeley: University of California Press, 1995), 76–81.

5. "A Thumb-Nail Sketch of Your USO Club," 15 May 1946, in "Great Falls, World War II" vertical file, CCHS; "Soldiers' Bunk at Civic Center," *GFT*, 22 Nov. 1942; "Air Corps Officers Have Many Ground Duties," *GFT*, 22 Nov. 1942; "Seventh Ferrying Group Was Launched as Offshoot of Long Beach Division," *GFT*, 22 Nov. 1942; "Pilots Frequent Recreation Room," *GFT*, 22 Nov. 1942; "Third Birthday Celebrated by Air Transport Command," *GFT*, 26 May 1944; "Special Schools Develop, Train Ferry Pilots," *GFT*, 10 Sept. 1944.

6. "Recreation Hall Opening Voted Huge Success," in the newsletter of the Air Transport command, *Tail Winds: Seventh Ferrying Group* 1, no. 1 (18 Dec. 1942), 1, available in "Seventh Ferrying Group Gore Field" vertical file, CCHS. For other examples of animus between military and civilian men in the Mountain West, see Mary Michaele Smith, "You Can't Say No to a Soldier: Sexual Violence in the American West during World War II" (MA thesis, University of Utah, 2008); "Curfew Rings at Midnight in County's Bars Tonight," *GFT*, 10 Dec. 1942; and "Black Eagle Clubs to Remain Open Until 2 for Civilians," *GFT*, 29 Dec. 1942.

7. David Emmons, *The Butte Irish: Class and Ethnicity in an American Mining Town, 1875–1925* (Urbana: University of Illinois Press, 1989), 167; see also Peter Filene, *Him/Her/Self: Gender Identities in Modern America* (Baltimore: Johns Hopkins University Press, 1998), 109–10; Writers Project of Montana, *Copper Camp: The Lusty Story of Butte, Montana, the Richest Hill on Earth* (Helena, MT: Riverbend, 2002 [first published 1943]), 173–77; and "Men 17 to 50 . . . Get in the Navy," *Montana Standard* (hereafter *MS*), 1 Nov. 1942, 7.

8. ACM Victory Labor-Management Committee Meeting Transcript, 6 July 1943, 6, ACM Co. Records, box 71, folder 4, MHSRC.

9. D. E. Lawlor to F. S. Wiemer, n.d. [likely 1943], ACM Co. Records, box 243, folder 10, MHSRC; "Great Falls Accident Report Cumulative for the Year 1945," 28 Jan. 1946, ACM Co. Records, box 228, folder 8, MHSRC. Accident rates increased significantly during 1944. In 1945, three men died in a major accident at the smelter. United States Department of the Interior, Bureau of Mines, "Reinspection Reports No. 2 and No. 3, Great Falls Reduction Department," ACM Co. Records, box 176, folder 6, MHSRC; "42,000 Workers Have Lost Lives in War Effort" (the source of the quotation), *Montana Labor News*, 3 Dec. 1942; "Industrial Accident Toll Is High," *Montana Labor News*, 14 Jan. 1943; C. E. Weed to D. M. Kelly, 5 May 1943, ACM Co. Records, box 113, folder 1, MHSRC; "Anaconda Mining Company, Employees in Military

Service," 30 Nov. 1943, ACM Co. Records, box 132, folder 1, MHSRC. Two years into the war, of the 402 Black Eagle smeltermen who had entered the service, 4 were missing in action and 5 died in training. Of the 871 Butte miners who had entered the military, 6 were missing in action, 5 were killed in action, and 4 died during training. Of the 857 Anaconda smeltermen who had gone into the armed services, 4 were missing in action, 2 were killed in action, and 2 died during training.

10. "Stirring Program Witnessed at E Awardngs in City," *Anaconda Standard*, 29 Jan. 1943. The Anaconda plant also received the "E" Award. "Data Pertaining to Labor Situation at Great Falls," 1 July 1943, 1 Oct. 1943, 1 July 1945, and 1 Oct. 1945, ACM Co. Records, box 229, folder 8, MHSRC; "Field Operating Report, Butte-Anaconda, Montana, August 1943," War Production Board (hereafter WPB) Records, box 219, folder "Butte, Montana," NARA; Emmons, "Hard Times and War Times," 255–56; "Bureau of Mines Report Shows Drop of 11 Per Cent from 1942 in Value of Montana Ores, Gravels," *MS*, 16 Jan. 1944. Bureau of Mines figures indicate that about 800 furloughed soldiers went to work in the Butte mines during 1943, and more than 1,200 eventually worked there. "Labor: Industrial Democracy," *Time*, 23 Nov. 1942, 93.

11. K. B. Frazier to E. V. Larsen, 23 Mar. 1943, and Frank Ayer to R. E. Dwyer, 2 and 4 Mar. 1943, all in ACM Co. Records, box 113, folder 1, MHSRC.

12. Ayer to Dwyer, 2 Mar. 1943.

13. "Great Falls Recapitulation of Payroll," December 1942, ACM Co. Records, box 210, folder 11, MHSRC. Average Black Eagle smeltermen's earnings rose from $7.59 to $8.59 a day. "Womanpower Need Growing, Says WMC," *People's Voice*, 8 Jan. 1943; D. M. Kelley to James M. Burns, 17 Jan. 1943; John Clark to Charles A. Graham, 18 Jan. 1943; James M. Burns to D. M. Kelley, Paul Fall Jr. et al., 7 and 12 Jan. 1943; and Reid Robinson to Charles Graham, 31 Dec. 1942, all in National War Labor Board Records, box 7, folder 2, NARA–Denver.

14. Lary May, "Making the American Consensus: The Narrative of Conversion and Subversion in World War II Films," in *The War in American Culture: Society and Consciousness during World War II*, ed. Lewis Erenberg and Susan E. Hirsch (Chicago: University of Chicago Press, 1996), 71–104.

15. William Wellman, dir., *The Ox-Bow Incident*, Twentieth Century Fox, 1943. For a fuller analysis of the reception of *The Ox-Bow Incident* in Montana's copper towns, see Matthew Basso, "Metal of Honor: Montana's World War II Homefront, Movies, and the Social Politics of White Male Anxiety" (PhD diss., University of Minnesota, 2001), 151–72.

16. "Ox-Bow Incident," *America*, 6 Feb. 1943, 478, clipping available in Motion Picture Association of America Collection, "The Ox-Bow Incident" file, Academy of Motion Picture Arts and Sciences (hereafter AMPAS); *Ox-Bow Incident* press book, 20th Century Fox, 1943, 1, 18, University of Southern California Film Archive; Walter Van Tilburg Clark, *The Ox-Bow Incident* (New York: Time Reading Program Special Edition, 1962), 113–14; Thomas Doherty, *Projections of War: Hollywood, American Culture, and World War II* (New York: Columbia University Press, 1993), 154.

17. Maureen Honey, *Creating Rosie the Riveter: Class, Gender, and Propaganda during World War II* (Amherst: University of Massachusetts Press, 1984); Leila Rupp, *Mobilizing Women for War: German and American Propaganda, 1939–1945* (Princeton, NJ: Princeton University Press, 1978); *So Proudly We Hail* press Book, AMPAS; Doherty, *Projections of War*, 155–58; Fiche 104/229, Fox Movietone News, 21 May 1943, in K. R. M. Short, *World War II through the American Newsreels: A Comprehensive Microfiche Set*

(Oxford: Oxford Microform Publishers, 1984); Robert B. Westbrook, "'I Want a Girl, Just Like the Girl That Married Harry James': American Women and the Problem of Political Obligation in World War II," *American Quarterly* 42, no. 4 (December 1990): 587–614.

18. William L. Bird Jr. and Harry R. Rubenstein, *Design for Victory: World War II Posters on the American Home Front* (New York: Princeton Architectural Press, 1998); Rupp, *Mobilizing Women for War*, 143–44, note 13; 144, note 14; and 146, note 23; Susan M. Hartmann, *The Home Front and Beyond: American Women in the 1940s* (Boston: Twayne, 1982), 189–94. Comic books sold 12 million copies a month in 1942, and 60 million a month in 1946.

19. Rupp, *Mobilizing Women for War*, notes 31 and 150, and ad page 159. Cited in Hartmann, *Home Front and Beyond*, 198–99.

20. Cover, *Saturday Evening Post*, 29 May 1943; Rupp, *Mobilizing Women for War*, 143; Eric J. Segal, "Realizing Whiteness in U.S. Visual Culture: The Popular Illustration of J. C. Leyendecker, Norman Rockwell, and the *Saturday Evening Post*, 1917–1945" (PhD diss., University of California, Los Angeles, 2002); Gordon Parks, "Women Welders at the Landers, Frary, and Clark Plant, New Britain, Conn.," June 1943, Federal Security (hereafter FSA)/OWI-D339157, Library of Congress, Washington, DC.

21. See Louise Paine Benjamin, "What Is your Dream Girl Like?," *Ladies' Home Journal*, Mar. 1942, 114, cited in Rupp, *Mobilizing Women for War*, 151.

22. "It's only temporary" was so successfully incorporated into magazine articles, books, ads, and posters that we may fail to realize it was part of a pointed propaganda effort. Rupp, *Mobilizing Women for War*, 155, 160–61; William H. Chafe, *The Paradox of Change* (New York: Oxford University Press, 1974); D'Ann Campbell, *Women at War with America: Private Lives in a Patriotic Era* (Cambridge, MA: Harvard University Press, 1984). The Wilson quotation is from Hartmann, *The Home Front and Beyond*, 62.

23. Hartmann, *Home Front and Beyond*, 63, 64.

24. Rupp, *Mobilizing Women*, 79, 178, 186; Allan M. Winkler, *Homefront U.S.A: America during World War II* (Arlington Heights, IL: Harlan Davidson, 1986), 50–51.

25. "Signs Indicating War Bond Drive Appearing in City," *GFT*, 22 Feb. 1942. "Expansion of Red Cross Program Will Offer Local Women New Activities," *GFT*, 12 Mar. 1942; "Girl Scout Leaders Training Course Planned," *GFT*, 22 Feb. 1942; "Women Urged to Back Rag, Paper Drive," *GFT*, 21 July 1944.

26. "The Gals Do Their Bit, Too," *Copper Commando* (hereafter *CC*), 22 Aug. 1942, 13, Butte-Silver Bow Public Archives (hereafter BSBA).

27. "Thoughts for Food," *CC*, 22 Aug. 1942, 15, BSBA; Tonkovich, interview.

28. "Meet the Great Falls Girls," *CC*, 19 Sept. 1942, 14, BSBA; "Busy Lines," *CC*, 13 Oct. 1944, 4–5, BSBA. When profiling local women workers in Butte and Anaconda in later editions, the *Commando* continued to concentrate on switchboard operators, a conventionally female occupation.

29. "Copper Shorts," *CC*, 23 Oct. 1942, 15, BSBA.

30. Vangelisti and Del Guerra, interview. Smelterman Dante Vangelisti told his sons and daughters that it was their "responsibility, [their] commitment as a result of [their] parents being immigrants to defend our country." However, for daughters this meant contributing to victory gardens, rationing, and saving for war bonds. "Letter to the Editor," *CC*, 18 Dec. 1942, 10; *CC*, 4 Dec. 1942, cover and 15, both in BSBA.

31. A total of 25,000 women applied for the WASPs; 1,074 were accepted and graduated, and 38 died in service. The government did not recognize them as having performed military service until 1977. Leisa Meier, *Creating GI Jane: Sexuality and Power in the*

Women's Army Corps during World War II (New York: Columbia University Press, 1998); "Ferry Division Staff Members Visit Gore Field," *Tail Winds* 1, no. 1 (18 Dec. 1942): 1; "'Snazzy' Uniforms of Gore Field 'Gals' Arouse Envy of Men," *Tail Winds* 1, no. 1 (18 Dec. 1942): 3.

32. Hartmann, *Home Front and Beyond*; D. Campbell, *Women at War with America*; "The Gals Got Busy," *CC*, 1 Jan. 1943, 10, BSBA.

33. "Union Girls Model War Work Clothes," *Montana Labor News*, 31 Dec. 1942; "Mothers Are Soldiers," *CC*, 18 June 1943, 2–4, BSBA. See also "McQueen Mothers," *CC*, 24 Nov. 1944, 12; "*Commando* for Mother's Day," *CC*, 11 May 1945, cover; and Marg Sammons, "Sounding Off," *CC*, 18 June 1943, 2, all in BSBA. Marg Sammons, the editor of the *Commando*'s women's section, wrote, "Someone might ask, 'What's all this got to do with copper production?' Well I think the answer is this: Feed a copper worker properly and production will take care of itself." "Who Says It's a Man's War?," *CC*, 16 July 1943, cover, 3; "Commando Kitchen," *CC*, 18 June 1943, 3, both in BSBA.

34. Godlewski, interview; "Their Patriotism Long Manifest, Archbishop Tells Catholic Women," *Montana Catholic Register*, 1 Nov. 1942, 4; Joan Earl, interview by Laurie Mercier, 19 Jan. 1988, MHSRC.

35. "Miners' Union Day," *CC*, 2 July 1943, 12. The paper noted that this was the sixty-fifth anniversary of the BMU.

36. "Who Says It's a Man's War?," *CC*, 16 July 1943, 3 and cover; "Meet Joe Copper," *CC*, 13 Aug. 1943, 1–15, both in BSBA.

37. William J. Furdell, "The Great Falls Home Front during World War II," *Montana: The Magazine of Western History* 48, no. 4 (1998): 63. Among other employers, the ACM was competing with the Great Northern Rail Road and with Great Falls Air Base for women workers. Eugene Cox, interview by Laurie Mercier, 16 July 1986, MHSRC; FSA, "Summary Employment Status Report, Montana," 31 Mar. 1943, and 31 Apr. 1943, WPB Records, box 219, folder "Butte, Montana," NARA; "Data Pertaining to Labor Situation at Great Falls," 1 July 1943. In March and April 1943, management reported that it needed 35 and 75 workers, respectively. By July it was down to 12. "Child Care Emphasized at Recent CIO Convention," *Montana Labor News*, 3 Dec. 1942; "CIO Adopts Resolutions on Women," *Montana Labor News*, 24 Dec. 1942; "ACM Locals Act Jointly, WLB Next," *Union*, 30 Nov. 1942. That the Black Eagle local was the only one of the three that voted to accept the fall 1942 contract negotiated between the ACM and Mine Mill reinforces the point. Black Eagle nonetheless chose to continue negotiations alongside the Anaconda and Butte locals.

38. Sharon Hartman Strom, *Beyond the Typewriter: Gender, Class, and the Origins of Modern American Office Work, 1900–1930* (Urbana: University of Illinois Press, 1992); Janet F. Davidson, "'Now That We Have Girls in the Office': Clerical Work, Masculinity, and the Refashioning of Gender for a Bureaucratic Age," in *Boys and Their Toys? Masculinity, Technology, and Class in America*, ed. Roger Horowitz (New York: Routledge, 2001), 55–90; Alice Kessler-Harris, *Out to Work: A History of Wage-Earning Women in the United States* (New York: Oxford University Press, 1982); K. B. Frazier to R. D. Cole, 21 Dec. 1927, ACM Co. Records, box 123, folder 1, MHSRC. Cox worked around women who were paid more than he. Cox, interview.

39. "Great Falls Reduction Department: Estimate of Monthly Payroll at May 1, 1921"; K. B. Frazier to R. D. Cole, 15 Dec. 1924; and J. W. Keenan to R. D. Cole, 14 Dec. 1928, all in ACM Co. Records, box 123, folder 1, MHSRC.

40. Frazier to Cole, 15 Dec. 1924 and 3 Feb. 1925, and A. E. Wiggin to J. R. Hobbins, 10 June 1925, all in ACM Co. Records, box 123, folder 1, MHSRC.

41. R. B. Caples to C. H. Boyer, 30 Dec. 1943, ACM Co. Records, box 181, folder 2, MHSRC.

42. Emelia Tabaracci Qunell, interview by Laurie Mercier, 6 Feb. 1986, MHSRC.

43. R. B. Caples to C. H. Boyer, 30 Dec. 1943, and Chief Clerk to K. B. Frazier, 16 Dec. 1943, both in ACM Co. Records, box 181, folder 2, MHSRC.

44. Lorado Maffit, interview by Laurie Mercier, 14 Mar. 1986, MHSRC.

45. Cox, interview. ACM employment statistics broke out gender only beginning in July 1944, when the Company employed 45 women out of 1,605 workers. Cited in Furdell, "Great Falls Home Front," 69.

46. Dorothy Moran Anderson, interview by Laurie Mercier, 19 Jan. 1988, MHSRC; Anne Prebil, interview by Laurie Mercier, 10 July 1986, MHSRC. Anne Prebil, who worked in the small East Helena smelter during World War II, recalled that working at a café in Helena was more trying.

47. Great Falls Reduction Works and Wire Mill Compensation to Injured Employees, 1 Dec. 1943, ACM Co. Records, box 211, folder 9, MHSRC. As early as World War I, injuries had been so common that the Company developed a consistent compensation policy, negotiating permanent partial or full disability payments based on the employee's wage level and estimated earnings lost. Like the Company's retirement system, payments to injured workers were meant to maintain men's breadwinner status. "Compensation to Injured Employees," 1 Dec. 1943, 1 Dec. 1944, 1 July 1945, and 1 Dec. 1945, and "Personal Injury Report," May 1944, Sept. 1944, Nov. 1944, and July 1945, all in ACM Co. Records, box 211, folder 9, and box 260, folder 1, MHSRC; United States Department of the Interior, Bureau of Mines, "Reinspection Report No. 2 and 3, Great Falls Reduction Department, 30 Jan. to 2 Feb. 1945," ACM Co. Records, box 176, folder 6, MHSRC. The rate of accidents per ten thousand shifts rose from 1.56 in 1943 to 1.73 in 1944 before it decreased slightly to 1.69 in 1945.

48. Karen Anderson, *Wartime Women: Sex Roles, Family Relations, and the Status of Women during World War II* (Westport, CT: Greenwood Press, 1981), 49–50. In some places women did show higher rates of absenteeism, typically due to insufficient help with housework and child care. "Absenteeism Report of the Great Falls Reduction Department," 1943 and 1945, ACM Co. Records, box 208, folder 10, MHSRC.

49. WPB Form 3729, 13 June 1944, WPB–Helena Office, box 8, folder 11, MHSRC; Cox, interview; "What Mining Officials Think about Women Workers," *Engineering and Mining Journal* 152, no. 1 (January 1951): 66–68. Smelter and mine officials interviewed after the war echoed Cox's appraisal. D. Anderson, interview.

50. Cox, interview.

51. Black Eagle Book Committee, *In the Shadow of the Big Stack: Black Eagle* (Black Eagle, MT: Black Eagle Book Committee, 2000), 479–82; Furdell, "Montana Episodes," 64; D. Anderson, interview (the source of the "I didn't think" and "Oh dear" quotations); Godlewski, interview. Meier, *Creating GI Jane*; Doris Brander, interview by Rosetta Kamlowsky (the source of the "to free a man" and "all prostitutes" quotations), 11 June 1992, MHSRC.

52. Maffit, interview; D. Anderson, interview. Anderson's rejoinder puts the lie to this claim: "Maybe they did, because the job I did was not hard." Swinging a hammer for six hours "was physical," but not too difficult.

53. Ruth Milkman, *Gender at Work: The Dynamics of Job Segregation by Sex during World War II* (Urbana: University of Illinois Press, 1987); Pellett, interview; D. Anderson, interview.

54. Amelia Polich, interview by Laurie Mercier, 13 Mar. 1986, MHSRC; Lawrence Tessman, interview by Laurie Mercier, 28 Feb. 1986, MHSRC.

55. Minutes of Labor Meeting Furnace Refinery Office, 29 Mar. 1944, ACM Co. Records, box 185, folder 11, MHSRC.

56. For more detailed discussion of the relationship between space, scale, and masculine formation, see Matthew Basso, "Context, Subjectivity, and the Built Environment at the Anaconda Reduction Works," *Drumlummon Views* 3, no. 1 (Spring 2009): 125–52.

57. During their free time, the women "[sat] there and told dirty jokes." D. Anderson, interview. "Hail Great Falls!," *CC*, 20 Nov. 1942, 15. The *Commando* also used the phrase "soldiers of production" to describe Montana's copper men.

58. K. Anderson, *Wartime Women*, 4–5; Robert Rossberg and Muriel Rossberg, interview by Laurie Mercier, 18 Jan. 1988, MHSRC. Muriel Rossberg claimed that married women could work in the smelter office.

59. "Twenty-Fourth Annual Report of the Health Department, City of Great Falls and County of Cascade, June 30, 1944" (the source of the "so called victory girls" and "responsibility" quotations), MHSRC. Cases dropped significantly in the first six months of 1944. I thank Brian Shovers for sending me this report. Marilyn E. Hegarty, *Victory Girls, Khaki-Wackies, and Patriotutes: The Regulation of Female Sexuality during World War II* (New York: New York University Press, 2008); Stephen Hull, "Helena: the Shame of Montana," *Stag* 4, no. 2 (February 1953): 16; "Application for Contribution for Providing Community Services under the Lanham Act, Great Falls, Montana" (the source of the "small towns located" quotation), Lanham Act Records, US Federal Works Agency, Bureau of Records Collection, box 2, folder 13, MHSRC; "Councilman Seeks to Probe Competency of 'Certain Law Enforcement Officers,'" *GFT*, 13 Jan. 1943.

60. "Application for Contribution for Providing Community Services. . .Great Falls"; "Application for Contribution for Providing Community Services under the Lanham Act, Butte, Montana," Lanham Act Records, US Federal Works Agency, Bureau of Records Collection, MC 94, box 2, folders 9 and 10, MHSRC. Butte's Lanham Act request for a child-care facility reasoned that local women were needed to work in grocery and retail stores and, more urgently, to get children out of the home, because "fathers cannot have proper rest, thereby causing poor health conditions, unnecessary mine accidents, and . . . a slowing down of the production of essential war materials."

61. Vangelisti and Del Guerra, interview. Vangelisti confirmed that no women from Black Eagle worked in laborers' jobs during World War II.

62. D. Anderson, interview; Furdell, "Great Falls Home Front," 73. Great Falls newspapers reported on citywide discussions about postwar readjustment as early as spring 1943. *Report to Donald Nelson, Chairman War Production Board*, May 1943, ACM Co. Records, box 71, folder 3, MHSRC.

63. Pellet, interview.

CHAPTER EIGHT

1. Anaconda Smelter Worker's Union-Management Grievance Committee Meeting Transcript (hereafter Grievance Committee), 13 Apr. 1944, 4, Marcus Daly Historical Society, Anaconda, Montana. Copies of these transcripts are also in the possession of the author and available as well at the Montana Historical Society Research Center, Helena (hereafter MHSRC).

2. Robert Vine, *The Women of the Washoe* (Butte, MT: Butte Historical Society, 1989), tells this story from a different perspective. John Morton Blum, *V Was for Victory: Politics and American Culture during World War II* (New York: Harcourt Brace Jovanovich, 1976); Richard Polenberg, *War and Society: The United States, 1941–1945* (New York: J.B. Lippincott, 1972); and John Patrick Diggins, *The Proud Decades: America in War and in Peace, 1941–1960* (New York: W. W. Norton, 1988).

3. Edward B. Reynolds, "Blood and Bread," 1, Works Progress Administration Records, box 18, folder 6, MHSRC.

4. *Polk's Anaconda (Deer Lodge County, Mont.) City Directory, 1941* (Salt Lake City, UT: R. L. Polk, 1941), 11; Anaconda Housing Survey, 1942, War Production Board (hereafter WPB)–Helena Office Records, box 2, folder 14, MHSRC; Blum, *V was for Victory*, 200; Robert Vine, *Anaconda Memories, 1883–1983* (Butte: Artcraft Printers, 1983), 39; "Monthly Field Operating Report for Montana for February 1944," and "Anaconda, Montana, Locality War Housing Program No 3," report, n.d. [ca. 30 June 1942], both in WPB Records, box 219, folder "Butte, Montana," National Archives and Records Administration (hereafter NARA).

5. Impatience with the National War Labor Board (hereafter NWLB) continued into 1943. Anaconda warned of "considerable unrest" at "worlds largest copper smelter." Walter Dooley to Charles A. Graham, 5 Jan. 1943, and John McLeod to Charles A. Graham, 5 Jan. 1943, both in NWLB Records, box 7, folder 2, NARA–Denver. "Memorandum of Understanding concerning the Release of Soldiers for Employment in Non-Ferrous Metal Mines," 15 July 1943; "USES Headquarters Bulletin No. 54," 29 July 1943; Lawrence Appley, "Non Ferrous Metals and Lumber Stabilization Program," 3 Feb. 1943 and 16 Mar. 1943, all in War Manpower Commission (hereafter WMC) Records, box 156, folder 11, NARA.

6. W. E. Mitchell to United States Employment Service (hereafter USES), 9 June 1943, ACM Co. Records, box 70, folder 2, MHSRC; "Anaconda, Montana, Locality War Housing Program No 3," report, n.d. [ca. 30 June 1943], and "Field Operating Report, Butte-Anaconda, Montana, August 1943," both in WPB Records, box 219, folder "Butte, Montana," NARA.

7. "Job Freezing in the Northwest's Lumber and Non-Ferrous Metals Industries," 2 Nov. 1942, WMC Records, box 156, folder 11, "Non-Ferrous Metal Industries," NARA; H. O. King to L. A. Appley, 4 Dec. 1943, WPB Records, box 219, folder "Butte, Montana," NARA.

8. King to Appley; "150 Women Will Take Jobs at Copper Mines," *Miles City Daily Star*, 11 Sept. 1942. My thanks to Sonya Smith for bringing this article to my attention. "How Women Can Help in Mills" and "What Mining Officials Think about Women Workers," *Engineering and Mining Journal* 152, no. 1 (January 1951): 65, 66–68; Grievance Committee, 13 Apr. 1944, 6–7. Mitchell told Anaconda labor representatives that "thirty some percent of the force in Chicago are women. There is a plant in Arizona employing 200 women. There are two plants in California—one 20%, the other 10%. There is another plant in Arizona with seventy-odd women; another plant, in the mill, 30 percent of the crew are women. Total around the plant 146. At Kellogg, 44 women at the local smelter and 10 at the zinc plant" (Grievance Committee, 6–7). He added that these women were frequently engaged in physical jobs, and that ever more women worked in such jobs in industries such as steel.

9. WPB Operations Council Meeting Transcript, 4 Nov. 1943, 6–7, 10, WPB–Helena Office Records, box 2, folder 5, MHSRC.

10. USES–Butte, Montana, "Monthly Labor Market Developments Report," July 1943, Sept. 1943, WPB Records, box 219, folder "Butte, Montana," NARA.

11. WPB Operations Council Meeting Transcript, 4 Nov. 1943, 6–7, 10, WPB–Helena Office Records, box 2, folder 5, MHSRC; WPB Denver Office Press Release, October 30, 1943, WPB–Helena Office Records , box 4, folder 5, MHSRC.

12. "Monthly Field Operating Report for Montana for February 1944, March 1944, April 1944, and May 1944," and "Anaconda, Montana, Locality War Housing Program No 3," both in WPB Records, box 219, folder "Butte, Montana," NARA. The WPB's male officials revealed their own "chivalric" ideas by proclaiming in regard to smelter work, "Distasteful as such jobs are to women, it can be said to [the] credit of Montana's womanhood that the emergency will be met."

13. "Monthly Field Operating Report for Montana for February 1944, March 1944, April 1944, and May 1944."

14. "Anaconda, Montana, Locality War Housing Program No 3"; all quotations are from this source. At the beginning of 1944, 100 women worked in the ACM's Butte offices and 64 at its Anaconda offices. By July 1944, Butte reported 120 women on staff, while Anaconda had 109. For more on masculine politics of wartime office work, see "Demand-Supply Supplement for Butte, Montana," 30 Jan. 1944, and "Monthly Field Operating Report for Montana for May 1944," both in WPB Records, box 219, folder "Butte, Montana," NARA. "Accounting Department Employees," Jan. 1942 and July 1943; Geo. A. Dean to K. B. Frazier, 7 Sept. 1943, 2 Nov. 1943, and 3 Dec. 1943; and George Dean to W. E. Mitchell, 4 Oct. 1943, all in ACM Co. Records, box 100, folder 4, MHSRC. Geo. A. Dean to K. B. Frazier, 23 Mar. 1943, ACM Co. Records, box 113, folder 1, MHSRC.

15. This list is not with the union-management transcripts for 1943. Bayard S. Morrow to W. E. Mitchell, 10 Aug. 1942, ACM Co. Records, box 70, folder 2, MHSRC. The lab manager, F. F. Frick, asked prospective female employees, "Do you drink, do you smoke, are you pregnant, do you run around, do you have a good reputation, will you make work." Katie Dewing, interview by Laurie Mercier, 11 Aug. 1986, MHSRC.

16. War Production Board Operations Council Meeting Minutes, 13 Jan. 1944; War Production Board Report T-233, 18 Mar. 1944; and R. E. Grimes to Executive Secretaries and Fieldmen, 7 Feb. 1944, all in WPB–Helena Office Records, box 4, folder 3, MHSRC. "Memoranda in Reply to Telegram of J. Reed Lane, 24 May 1944; F. C. Gilbert, "Utilization Supplement, Anaconda Copper Mining Company, Butte, Montana," 13 Jan. 1945; and James Lane to All Technical Advisers, "Memorandum No. 24, Manpower," 27 Mar. 1944, all in WPB–Helena Office Records, box 8, folder 7, MHSRC; "Monthly Field Operating Report for Montana for June 1944," WPB Records, box 219, folder "Butte, Montana," NARA; Michael Schwarz, "Copper Division Requirements—Supply Position Report," 10 Apr. 1944, 4 May 1944, 3 July 1944, 2 Aug. 1944, and 5 Sept.1944, WPB–Helena Office Records, box 4, folder 2, MHSRC; Declassified: E.O. 12356, Sec. 3.3 Commerce Dept. Guidelines, 14 Apr. 1983 (the source of the "probable loss" quotation), HR-M/FHA, 30 Sept. 1992; and Edward Rott to Regional Technical Advisers, Mine Production Service, 1 Feb. 1944 (the source of the "serious production" and "we must not" quotations), both in WPB–Helena Office Records, box 4, folder 2, MHSRC; "Monthly Field Operating Reports for Montana for February 1944 and November 1944" ("if this practice" quotation is from the February 1944 report). Internal WPB documents suggest that local and regional government officials were trying to use their influence to secure continued deferments.

Howard R. Selover to Oscar A. Baarson, 22 Mar. 1944, WPB–Helena Office Records, box 5, folder 1, MHSRC. Mine Mill's leadership was undertaking a debate about its own deferment policy at this time. Vernon H. Jensen, *Nonferrous Metals Industry Unionism, 1932–1954* (Ithaca, NY: Cornell University Press, 1954), 114–17.

17. "Hearings Held before Committee on Military Affairs, S. 666, National War Service Act," 19 Jan. 1944, and "Senator James E. Murray's 'March of Time' Statement on the National Service Act," 14 Jan. 1944, both in WPB–Helena Office Records, box 3, folder 29, MHSRC. "Labor Protests Army's Rejection of Request to Tell Troops Truth," *Treasure State Labor Journal*, 11 Apr. 1944, 1. In April 1944, the American Federation of Labor (AFL) and the Congress of Industrial Organizations (CIO) issued a joint statement regarding the depiction of union men's performance on the home front. "Soldiers and Civilians: Why Are They Growing Apart," *Life*, 17 Apr. 1944, 32.

18. Grievance Committee, 13 Apr. 1944, 1–4.

19. Reid Robinson to Frances Perkins, 18 May 1942, and D. W. Tracy to Reid Robinson, 20 May 1942, both in Western Federation of Miners (hereafter WFM)-International Union of Mine, Mill, and Smelter Workers (hereafter Mine Mill) Collection, box 34, folder 35, Archives, University of Colorado at Boulder Library (hereafter AUCBL). Carey McWilliams, *North from Mexico: The Spanish-Speaking People of the United States* (Westport, CT: Greenwood Press, 1990), 179–82; Rudolfo Acuna, *Occupied America: A History of Chicanos*, 3rd ed. (New York: HarperCollins, 1988), 261–65; USES, "Labor Market Survey of Butte-Anaconda, Montana," 4 Apr. 1942, WPB Records, box 218, folder 3, NARA. "Mexicans to Help Relieve Shortage," *Union*, 23 Nov. 1942; Ben Riskin to James J. Leary, 23 Nov. 1942; Ben Riskin to Reid Robinson, 25 Nov. 1942; and Jessica Rhine to Reid Robinson, 19 Dec.1942, all in WFM-Mine Mill Collection, box 39, folder 1, AUCBL. "Memorandum Regarding Proposed New Identification Cards for 1) Mexican Agricultural Workers, 2) Mexican Miners, and 3) Laborers from the Bahamas," 28 Dec. 1942, WMC Records, box 156, folder 11, NARA. Frank McSherry to Carl Ulrich, 9 Dec. 1942; USES, "Bulletin No. 35, Temporary Migration of Mexican Workers to the United States for Non Agricultural Labor," 1 July 1943; Office of General Counsel to J. D. Coates, 27 July 1944; all in WMC Records, box 156, folder 6, NARA. On the Santa Fe incident, see "Mexican Commission" file, WMC Records, box 156, folder 10, NARA. Officials described these men as "Mexican Nationals and Texas Mexicans," lumping the US citizens together with foreigners. "Monthly Field Operating Report for Montana" for April 1944 and June 1944.

20. Bureau of the Census, *Sixteenth Census of the United States: 1940 Population*, vol. 2 (Washington, DC: Government Printing Office, 1943), 544; Bureau of the Census, *Seventeenth Census of the United States: 1950 Population*, vol. 2 (Washington, DC: Government Printing Office, 1952), 26–39. The 1950 census counted seventy-two black men and women. Jerry Hansen and Robert Vine, interview by Matthew Basso, 23 Apr. 1996, notes in the possession of the author; see also chapter 3.

21. Grievance Committee, 19 Apr. 1944, 6, 11. On black smeltermen "earning" janitorial positions, see Vine, *Women of the Washoe*.

22. Stuart Hall, "Gramsci's Relevance for the Study of Race and Ethnicity," in *Stuart Hall: Critical Dialogues in Cultural Studies*, ed. David Morley and Kuan-Hsing Chen (New York: Routledge, 1996), 411–40; Peter Doeringer and Michael Piore, *Internal Labor Markets and Manpower Analysis* (Cambridge, MA: Harvard University Press, 1970); Suzanne A. Model, "The Ethnic Niche and the Structure of Opportunity: Immigrants and Minorities in New York City," in *The "Underclass" Debate: Views from History*, ed. Michael B. Katz (Princeton, NJ: Princeton University Press, 1993), 161–93; Bruce

Nelson, "Class, Race, and Democracy in the CIO: The 'New' Labor History Meets the 'Wages of Whiteness,'" *International Review of Social History* 41 (1996): 351–74; Isaac F. Marcosson, *Anaconda* (New York: Dodd, Mead, 1957), 67–77, 228, 288, 351. Mitchell, variously referred to as "Bill," "Willard," or more often as "W. E.," was the general superintendent of the ACM's Black Eagle operations before coming to Anaconda to serve in the same capacity. He was soon promoted to manager of the Anaconda Reduction Works. Workers respected Mitchell because he was, in their words, a "straight shooter." ACM had a history of employing managers who had at one time or another worked as laborers, including Con Kelley, chairman of the ACM board during World War II. Vine, *Anaconda Memories*; Ruth Meidl, comp., and George P. Wellcome, ed., *Anaconda, Montana: A Century of History, 1883–1983* (Anaconda: n.p., [1983]); Margaret Tracy McLean, interview by Matthew Basso, 23 Apr. 1996, notes in possession of the author. On the McLean family, see also *Anaconda Federal Credit Union, No. 4401, 25th Anniversary: March 29, 1941–March 29, 1966* (Anaconda, MT, 1966), booklet in possession of the author. On Butte's social landscape, see Mary Murphy, *Mining Cultures: Men, Women, and Leisure in Butte, 1914–41* (Urbana: University of Illinois Press, 1997), 1–41, and Janet Finn, *Tracing the Veins of Copper, Culture, and Community from Butte to Chuquicamata* (Berkeley: University of California Press, 1998). Grievance Committee, 19 Apr. 1944, 3 (the source of the "We only" quotation).

23. Grievance Committee, 19 Apr. 1944, 2–5. On black women workers during the war, see Karen Anderson, "Last Hired, First Fired: Black Women Workers during World War II," *Journal of American History* 69 (March 1982): 82–97.

24. Vine, *Anaconda Memories*, 37. War bonds provide an interesting window into patriotism. "It's Still the Treasure State: Treasury Reports Most Bonds Per Capita Bought in Montana," *Great Falls Tribune*, 9 Nov. 1943. On war bonds and workers' patriotism, see Lawrence R. Samuel, *Pledging Allegiance: American Identity and the Bond Drive of World War II* (Washington, DC: Smithsonian Institution Press, 1997), 77–93; and James T. Sparrow, "'Buying Our Boys Back': The Mass Foundations of Fiscal Citizenship in World War II," *Journal of Policy History* 20, no. 2 (2008): 263–86.

25. Clayton Koppes and Gregory Black, *Hollywood Goes to War: How Politics, Profits, and Propaganda Shaped World War II Movies* (New York: Free Press, 1987); Joseph I. Breen to Louis B. Mayer, 21 Oct. 1942, Motion Picture Association of America Collection, "*A Guy Named Joe*" file, Academy of Motion Picture Arts and Sciences. Films like *A Guy Named Joe* can also be read as an example of wartime cinema's tendency to, in the end, buttress the idea of feminine domesticity. In this view, Irene Dunne's delight in Spencer Tracy's gift of "girl clothes" and her sprint into Van Johnson's arms after completing her raid on the ammunition storage site were the movie's two most symbolic acts. Closure, not the long periods of rupture, signified the film's message. For more on the reception of wartime films, see Matthew Basso, "Metal of Honor: Montana's World War II Homefront, Movies, and the Social Politics of White Male Anxiety" (PhD diss., University of Minnesota, 2001), 22–34. On World War II films' depiction of gender roles, see Thomas Doherty, *Projections of War: Hollywood, American Culture, and World War II* (New York: Columbia University Press, 1993), 149–79; Lary May, "Making the American Consensus: The Narrative of Conversion and Subversion in World War II Films," in *The War in American Culture: Society and Consciousness during World War II*, ed. Lewis Erenberg and Susan E. Hirsch (Chicago: University of Chicago Press, 1996), 71–104; and Andrea S. Walsh, *Women's Film and Female Experience, 1940–1950* (New York: Praeger, 1984).

26. Lloyd Bacon, dir., *The Sullivans* (also known as *The Fighting Sullivans*), Twentieth Century Fox, 1944.

27. See also Matthew Basso, "'Effect by Contrast': White Male Audiences and the Reading of World War II Newsreels and Feature Films as a Unified Text," *Columbia Journal of American Studies* 4, no. 1 (Winter 2000): 128–42; T. F. Woods, "Headlines in Celluloid," *Saturday Evening Post*, 11 Aug. 1945, 22 (the source of the "a college first-hand" quotation), cited in David H. Mould, "Historical Trends in the Criticism of the Newsreel and Television News, 1930–1955," *Journal of Popular Film and Television* 12, no. 3 (1984): 122; Peter Baechlin and Maurice Muller-Strauss, *Newsreels across the World* (Paris: UNESCO, 1952); Fox, Fiche 159/229, 18–25 Apr. 1944, in K. R. M. Short, *World War II through the American Newsreels: A Comprehensive Microfiche Set* (Oxford: Oxford Microform Publishers, 1984); and "A Letter to Thomas Jefferson," *Labor-Management News*, 1 July 1944, WPB–Helena Office Records, box 5, folder 1, MHSRC. Even labor-management-affiliated popular culture could erase the home front male worker as it celebrated female industrial workers and men in uniform.

28. Fiche 156/229, Universal, 28 Mar. 1944; Paramount, 28 Mar. 1944; and Pathe, 28 Mar. 1944, all in Short, *World War II through the American Newsreels.*

29. Fox, Fiche 159/229, 18–25 Apr. 1944.

30. MGM, Fiche 159/229, 18–25 Apr. 1944; Fox, Fiche 162/229, 12 May 1944. Ruck marches usually were for long distances at a reasonably fast pace and were meant to both solidify and show fitness. Fox's version of this story added this line: "In addition to hospital work, a nurse can pose for a soldier as his pin-up girl." Universal and Fox, Fiche 156/229, 31 Mar. 1944; Universal, Fiche 162/229, 12 May 1944, all in Short, *World War II through the American Newsreels.*

31. The Los Angeles Zoot Suit Riots occurred in June 1943. Mauricio Mazón, *The Zoot-Suit Riots: The Psychology of Symbolic Annihilation* (Austin: University of Texas Press, 1984); Edward J. Escobar, *Race, Police, and the Making of a Political Identity: Mexican Americans and the Los Angeles Police Department, 1900–1945* (Berkeley: University of California Press, 1999); ACM Victory Labor-Management Committee, *Report to Donald Nelson*, May 1943, ACM Co. Records, box 71, folder 3, MHSRC; "Last Allotted Mexicans Due in Montana," newspaper and date unclear, in "Great Falls Army Air Base 1943–1945" vertical file, Cascade County Historical Society; Santos Carranza, interview by Laurie Mercier, 24 May 1984, MHSRC. Black workers from the Caribbean did work in Montana during World War II. In one particularly difficult labor shortage period, the War Food Administration supplied the state's sugar beet farmers with 3,400 Mexican nationals, 2,400 German POWs, and 164 Jamaicans to assist in the beet harvest. Grievance Committee, 19 Apr. 1944, 12 (the source of the "I saw," "Yet a couple," and "I don't want" quotations); Grievance Committee, 21 June 1944, 12 (the source of the "Now, I have thought many times" quotation).

32. Grievance Committee, 21 June 1944, 15, 21. "Number of Strikes . . . Affecting War Department Procurement for the Years 1942–1944," 4 Jan. 1945, and "National War Labor Board Editorial Opinion on Strikes," 29 June 1944, all in NWLB Records, box 133, folder 936, NARA. Robert H. Zieger, *The CIO 1935–1955* (Chapel Hill: University of North Carolina Press, 1995), 166–76; Melvyn Dubofsky and Warren Van Tine, *John L. Lewis: A Biography* (Urbana: University of Illinois Press, 1986), 302–22. No account of wartime labor militancy would be complete without mentioning the United Mine Workers, which John L. Lewis led out of the CIO in part over the no-strike pledge; the union's 1943 strike resulted in government seizure of the mines. That debacle likely was at the foremost of everyone's minds in the spring of 1944.

"January through May, 1944 (five months)," n.d. [likely June 1 944]; "Statistical Report for Strike Section for Year 1944," n.d. [likely Jan. 1945]; "Number of Strikes . . . Affecting War Department Procurement for the Years 1942-1944"; D. Stewart to Mr. Garman, 1 July 1944; "National War Labor Board Editorial Opinion on Strikes"; and "Strikes Acted on by the National War Labor Board," n.d. [likely July 1945], all in NWLB Records, box 133, folder 936, NARA.

33. "Monthly Field Operating Report for Montana for February 1944"; "Field Operating Report, Butte-Anaconda, Montana, November 1944."

34. Nonferrous Metals Commission of the National War Labor Board, "Transcript of Hearing: NWLB Case No. 527," 14 and 15 Dec. 1942, 167–69, NWLB Records, box 7, folder 4, NARA–Denver. Munzenrider, "Long Distance Call to J. J. Carrigan," 17 May 1944; S. M. Goettlich to Oscar Baarson, 20 May 1944 (the source of the McGlone quotations); and War Production Board Agreement between the Anaconda Copper Mining Company and Butte Miners Union No. 1, 20 May 1944, all in WPB–Helena Office Records, box 8, folder 7, MHSRC. "Company Action Causes Shutdown at Saint Lawrence," *Miner's Voice*, 19 May 1944; "Miners Walk Out at St. Lawrence: Action Is without Notice to Company," *Montana Standard* (hereafter *MS*), 19 May 1944.

35. Munzenrider, "Long Distance Call" (the source of the McGlone quotations); Goettlich to Baarson; War Production Board Agreement between the Anaconda Copper Mining Company and Butte Miners Union, 20 May 1944; "Company Action Causes Shutdown at Saint Lawrence" (the source of the "neither Mr. Kelley" quotation); "Miners Walk Out at St. Lawrence." Missoula White Pine SAS Co. to Oscar Baarson, 26 May 1944, WPB–Helena Office Records, box 8, folder 7, MHSRC; Vernon A. McGee to John Gross, 24 May 1944, WPB–Helena Office Records, box 7, folder 1, MHSRC.

36. David Emmons, "Hard Times and War Times," in "Expert Report of David Emmons, Ph.D.," *United States of America v. Atlantic Richfield Company, et al.*, US District Court, District of Montana, Helena Division, Case No. CV-89-039-PGH, 15 July 1996, 266. Mitchell mirrored the concern of previous smelter manager Frederick Laist, who as ACM vice president of its metallurgical operations during the war corresponded frequently with Mitchell.

37. Grievance Committee, 13 Apr. 1944, 3–4, 10, 11-appended list.

38. Ibid., 19 Apr. 1944, 7; Vine, *Women of the Washoe*, 37.

39. Grievance Committee, 19 Apr. 1944, 7; ibid., 18 May 1944, 2–9; Joseph Bolkovatz, interview by Laurie Mercier, 12 Aug. 1986, MHSRC.

40. Ruth Milkman, *Gender at Work: The Dynamics of Job Segregation by Sex during World War II* (Urbana: University of Illinois Press, 1987), 1–8, 157–59; Vine, *Women of the Washoe*. Women and men did work next to one another at the smelter.

41. Grievance Committee, 19 Apr. 1944, 3–8; quotations are from p. 1.

42. Hansen and Vine, interview; Grievance Committee, 6 June 1944, 1–3; quotations are from p. 2; ibid., 6 June 1944, 2.

43. Grievance Committee, 18 May 1944, 1–2. It is difficult to decipher why the union was willing to strike point four, regarding the permit fee for women, which was never identified by Mitchell as a sticking point. Either they thought that Mitchell would never agree to this point and they wanted to make a goodwill gesture, or, more likely, they felt that the permit was an unnecessary precaution, since women would automatically be union members. Points seven and eight addressed union-management issues, directly or tangentially shoring up the union's power by ensuring that women

would be union members and that negotiations would precede any changes in the agreement. Tom Dickson, interview by Laurie Mercier, 30 May 1986, MHSRC. One smelterman said that women were, in fact, not allowed to join the union.

44. Grievance Committee, 2 June 1944, 2; Karen Anderson, *Wartime Women: Sex Roles, Family Relations, and the Status of Women during World War II* (Westport, CT: Greenwood Press, 1981), 4–6; "What Mining Officials Think about Women Workers," 66–68. Surveyed after the war, copper plant managers said that in fact, married women were better workers than their single counterparts during the war. Dewing, interview.

45. Grievance Committee, 19 Apr. 1944, 9; Dewing, interview. Some former smelterwomen said they had to sign a document acknowledging that they would leave the plant at war's end. Others said the expectation was clear but not contractual.

46. McLean, interview; K. Anderson, *Wartime Women*, 55. Other male workers across the United States stated similar motivations in their approach toward women's wartime employment. Grievance Committee, 2 June 1944, 2.

47. Morgan H. Wright, [Speech about Butte AWD Chapter], 24 Jan. 1944; Butte American War Dads "Minutes," 2 Sept. 1943, 17 Sept. 1943, 21 Feb. 1944; and "Service Manual of American War Dads" (the source of the "fighting fathers" quotation), all in "American War Dads, Butte, (Montana)" Collection, SC 1376, box 1, MHSRC. Babcock served on the critical BMU Negotiating Committee in the fall of 1942, and was elected BMU president later that year. He had two sons in the service, one of which, Leonard Babcock, had quit the mines after enlisting in March 1942. He was killed in action shortly after his father assumed the leadership of Butte's War Dads. "Results of Local Negotiations," *Miner's Voice*, 11 Sept. 1942; "Leonard Babcock, Killed in Action," *MS*, 24 Mar. 1944; J. M. Fitzpatrick to J. W. Keenan, 25 Mar. 1944, ACM Co. Records, box 131, folder 13, MHSRC.

48. Vine, *Women of the Washoe*, 3; Grievance Committee, 21 June 1944, 14, 21. Walter Dooley noted that as of February 1943, six hundred men from the local were serving in the armed services.

49. The screens were used to sort debris from the ore before the ore went into the mill. The work was not taxing, so older workers coveted the job. Vine, *Anaconda Memories*, 38; K. Anderson, *Wartime Women*, 56. Quotations are from Grievance Committee, 13 June 1944, 10. Men in the auto and steel plants also fought against losing "lighter" jobs to women.

50. Grievance Committee, 18 May 1944, 3–5.

51. K. Anderson, *Wartime Women*, 83. Karen Anderson also astutely points out that "the opening up of high-paying industrial jobs to women threatened a greater equalization of income levels between working-class men and women than was likely in the middle-class; as a result the economic foundation for female dependence and subordination was correspondingly strained in some working-class households" (ibid.).

52. W. E. Mitchell to D. M. Kelly, 13 May 1944, 16 June 1944, 13 Sept. 1944, and 12 Dec. 1944, all in ACM Co. Records, box 73, folder 2, MHSRC.

53. "Housewives Surpass Fat Quota for May, Keeley Says," *Helena Independent Record*, 19 June 1944; "Mothers are Soldiers," *Copper Commando* (hereafter *CC*), 18 June 1943, 2–4, Butte-Silver Bow Public Archives (hereafter BSBA). See also "McQueen Mothers," *CC*, 24 Nov. 1944, 12; "*Commando* for Mother's Day," *CC*, 11 May 1945, cover; and Marg Sammons, "Sounding Off," *CC*, 18 June 1943, 2, both in BSBA.

54. "Ladies' Day," *CC*, 18 Aug. 1944, 4–5, BSBA.

55. Ibid.

56. Ibid. Dickson, interview. Many in the copper towns thought that women did well.
57. Lizabeth Cohen, *Making a New Deal: Industrial Workers in Chicago, 1919–1939* (New York: Cambridge University Press, 1989). Elizabeth Faue, *Community of Suffering and Struggle: Women, Men, and the Labor Movement in Minneapolis, 1915–1945* (Chapel Hill: University of North Carolina Press, 1991).
58. Thomas J. Sugrue, "Segmented Work, Race-Conscious Workers: Structure, Agency and Division in the CIO Era," *International Review of Social History* 41 (1996): 392.
59. R. G. Conley to Vernon McGee, 19 July 1944; and B. Lotwin, "Memorandum re: FEPC Complaint against Region VII," 19 Aug. 1944; and other documents also in WMC Records, box 156, folder 6, NARA. Tensions between the Fair Employment Practices Commission and the USES came to a head in 1944, when the equal employment agency accused the employment service of not fully enforcing Executive Order 8802.

CONCLUSION

1. One study that does look at postwar working-class masculinity is Lisa Fine, *The Story of REO Joe: Work, Kin, and Community in Autotown, U.S.A.* (Philadelphia: Temple University Press, 2004). A number of scholars of postwar culture have also considered the subject. See, for example, Arthur F. Redding, *Turncoats, Traitors, and Fellow Travelers: Culture and Politics of the Early Cold War* (Jackson: University Press of Mississippi, 2008), 79–97. On postwar middle-class masculinity and the three white-collar groups that dominate this period—corporate "organization men," suburban fathers, and academic and governmental anti-Communist "cold warriors"—see Elaine Tyler May, *Homeward Bound: American Families in the Cold War Era* (New York: Basic Books, 1988); Robert Corber, *Homosexuality in Cold War America: Resistance and the Crisis of Masculinity* (Durham, NC: Duke University Press, 1997); Susan Clark, *Cold Warriors: Manliness on Trial in the Rhetoric of the West* (Carbondale: Southern Illinois University Press, 2000); Robert D. Dean, *Imperial Brotherhood: Gender and the Making of Cold War Foreign Policy* (Amherst: University of Massachusetts Press, 2001); K. A. Cuordileone, *Manhood and American Political Culture in the Cold War* (New York: Routledge, 2005); and James Gilbert, *Men in the Middle: Searching for Masculinity in the 1950s* (Chicago: University of Chicago Press, 2006).
2. "Soldiers and Civilians: Why Are They Growing Apart," *Life*, 17 Apr. 1944. "Over the Hill with Al Giecek," *Miner's Voice*, 11 Sept. 1942.
3. Edward Rott to William Manning, 20 Mar. 1945, War Production Board (hereafter WPB)–Helena Office Records, box 8, folder 7, Montana Historical Society Research Center, Helena (hereafter MHSRC). W. E. Mitchell to E. S. McGlone, 27 Feb. 1945, ACM Co. Records, box 70, folder 6, MHSRC. As of February 27, 1945, the Anaconda Reduction Works had 612 men between the ages of eighteen and thirty-eight who fell under Selective Service categories that made them "Possible Inductees." "March 10 Deadline for Deferment Requests, WPB Release No. DWR-400," 4 Mar. 1945, WPB–Helena Office Records, box 2, folder 6, MHSRC. "David Ryan, 38, Killed in Action," *Montana Standard* (hereafter *MS*), 26 Oct. 1944; "Earl Ramsted Is Reported Lost in Italy," *Great Falls Tribune* (hereafter *GFT*), 17 Nov. 1944. "R. B. Gallagher Said Missing: Walkerville Man Was in France," *MS*, 19 Nov. 1944. "Pvt. Krsul, Black Eagle, Dies on Europe Front, Dec. 15," *GFT*, 6 Jan. 1945; "Falls Soldier, Father of 2, Dies in Action," *GFT*, 25 Feb. 1945; "PFC N. J. Jozovich," *MS*, 1 May 1945; "Second Brother Reported Lost," *MS*, 7 May 1945; Black Eagle Book Committee, *In the Shadow of the Big Stack: Black Eagle* (Black Eagle, MT: Black Eagle Book Committee, 2000), 184–85.

4. "Joe Copper," *Copper Commando*, 30 Mar. 1945, 1–16, Butte-Silver Bow Public Archives.

5. "Field Operating Report, Butte-Anaconda, Montana," March and October 1945, WPB Records, box 219, folder "Butte, Montana," National Archives and Records Administration (hereafter NARA).

6. Howard Rosenleaf, interview by Laurie Mercier, 29 July 1986, MHSRC; Karen Anderson, *Wartime Women: Sex Roles, Family Relations, and the Status of Women during World War II* (Westport, CT: Greenwood Press, 1981), 170; Ann Elizabeth Pfau, "Demonstrations and the Desire for Domestic Tranquility," in *Miss Yourlovin: GIs, Gender, and Domesticity during World War II* (New York: Columbia University Press Gutenberg e-book, 2008). The process of releasing veterans from service also further reinforced the idea that the war was fought to secure heteronormative family values.

7. Keith W. Olson, "The G.I. Bill and Higher Education: Success and Surprise," *American Quarterly* 25, no. 5 (December 1973): 596–610; Edward Humes, *Over Here: How the G.I. Bill Transformed the American Dream* (New York: Harcourt, 2006); Glenn Altschuler and Stuart Blumin, *The GI Bill: The New Deal for Veterans* (New York: Oxford University Press, 2009). On the bill's limits, see David H. Onkst, "'First A Negro . . . Incidentally a Veteran': Black World War Two Veterans and the G.I. Bill of Rights in the Deep South, 1944–1948," *Journal of Social History* 31 (Spring 1998): 517–44; Margot Canaday, "Building a Straight State: Sexuality and Social Citizenship under the 1944 G.I. Bill," *Journal of American History* 90 (December 2003): 935–57; and Lizabeth Cohen, *A Consumers' Republic: The Politics of Mass Consumption in Postwar America* (New York: Vintage, 2003), 137–46.

8. Lyle Pellett, interview by Laurie Mercier, 13 Mar. 1986, MHSRC.

9. On the 1945–1946 strikes, see George Lipsitz, *Rainbow at Midnight: Labor and Culture in the 1940s* (Urbana: University of Illinois Press, 1994), 99–155. National War Labor Board "Daily Labor News," July 3, 1944; "Statistical Report for Strike Section for Year 1944," n.d. [likely January 1945]; and "Estimate for First Quarter 1945, Strike Section," n.d. [likely May 1945], all in National War Labor Board Records, box 113, folder 936, "Strike Statistics N.W.L.B.," NARA. "Will Not Tolerate Strikes—Murray," *Montana Labor News*, 30 Mar. 1944. Robert H. Zieger, *The CIO 1935–1955* (Chapel Hill: University of North Carolina Press, 1995), 141–211. Turner Catledge, "Officials Fear Wave of Labor Strife," *New York Times*, 20 Aug. 1942. Stephen Norwood, *Strikebreaking and Intimidation: Mercenaries and Masculinity in Twentieth-Century America* (Chapel Hill: University of North Carolina Press, 2002); Janet Finn, *Tracing the Veins of Copper, Culture, and Community from Butte to Chuquicamata* (Berkeley: University of California Press, 1998), 45–47. The ACM used the *Montana Standard*, the newspaper it controlled, to condemn the strikers in gendered terms, claiming, "The rest of the nation is looking in horror and apprehension at Butte, where a man's home is no longer his castle, where defenseless women and children alone are the target of despicable actions" (*Montana Standard*, 19 Apr. 1946, cited in Finn, *Tracing the Veins*, 45).

10. K. Anderson, *Wartime Women*, 170; R. B. Caples to Dr. Irwin et al., 7 June 1944, and R. B. Caples to R. W. Kemp, 13 May 1944, both in ACM Co. Records, box 209, folder 3, MHSRC; W. E. Mitchell to D. M. Kelly, 8 Nov. 1945, ACM Co. Records, box 73, folder 3, MHSRC. Robert Vine, *The Women of the Washoe* (Butte, MT: Butte Historical Society, 1989), Anaconda Smelter Worker's Union-Management Grievance Committee Meeting Transcript (hereafter Grievance Committee), 29 May 1946, 1–3; 7 June 1946, 1; 19 June 1946, 1–2; 10 July 1946, 13, Marcus Daly Historical Society, Ana-

conda, Montana. Copies of these transcripts are also in the possession of the author and available as well at MHSRC.

11. Grievance Committee, 29 May 1946, 1–3; 7 June 1946, 1; 19 June 1946, 1–2; 10 July 1946, 13; K. Anderson, *Wartime Women*, 46.

12. Grievance Committee, 21 June 1944, 12; correspondence and notes in WPB–Helena Office Records, box 2, folder 24, and box 8, folder 7, MHSRC. The ACM's December 1944 response to the proposal to send braceros to Montana copper towns reinforces this assessment. Perdita Duncan, Walter Duncan, William Fenter, Elmo Fortune, and notes made by Mrs. Lena Brown, interview by Laurie Mercier, 24 Mar. 1983, MHSRC. Stuart Hall, "Gramsci's Relevance for the Study of Race and Ethnicity," in *Stuart Hall: Critical Dialogues in Cultural Studies*, ed. David Morley and Kuan-Hsing Chen (New York: Routledge, 1996), 411–40. This is an example of what the theorist Antonio Gramsci calls a historic bloc.

13. Zieger, *The CIO*, 277–90; Michael Goldfield, *The Color of Politics: Race and the Mainsprings of American Politics* (New York: New Press, 1997), 193–96; "Now Is the Time," M. E. Travis, with an introduction by Raymond Dennis and Asbury Howard; taken from Travis speech 28 Oct. 1951; and "The Economics of Prejudice," a special issue of *Mine-Mill Facts and Figures*, January 1952, both in Western Federation of Miners-International Union of Mine, Mill, and Smelter Workers Collection, box 207, folder 21, Archives, University of Colorado at Boulder Library.

14. "Now Is the Time"; Laurie Mercier, "'Instead of Fighting the Common Enemy': Mine Mill versus the Steelworkers in Montana, 1950–1967," *Labor History* 40, no.4 (1999): 459–80; Tom Dickson, interview by Laurie Mercier, 30 May 1986, MHSRC. Dickson, president of the Anaconda local in the 1950s, was one of the locals who argued that paternalism, not union culture, dominated Butte and Anaconda. Laurie Mercier, *Anaconda: Labor, Community, and Culture in Montana's Smelter City* (Urbana: University of Illinois Press, 2001), 151 (the source of the quotations); Vernon H. Jensen, *Nonferrous Metals Industry Unionism, 1932–1954* (Ithaca, NY: Cornell University Press, 1954), xiv.

15. Mercier, *Anaconda*, 86.

16. [Robinson statement and photograph of woman reading the *Union*], *Union*, 9 Nov. 1942, 5; Graham Dolan, "Overtime," *Union*, 7 Dec. 1942. James Lorence, *The Suppression of Salt of the Earth: How Hollywood, Big Labor, and Politicians Blacklisted a Movie in Cold War America* (Albuquerque: University of New Mexico Press, 1999), 141, 178; Finn, *Tracing the Veins*, 46; Ellen R. Baker, *On Strike and On Film: Mexican American Families and Blacklisted Filmmakers in Cold War America* (Chapel Hill: University of North Carolina Press, 2007), 119–176; Alicia Schmidt Camacho, *Migrant Imaginaries: Latino Cultural Politics in the U.S. Mexico Borderlands* (New York: New York University Press, 2008), 112–51; Carl R. Weinberg, "Salt of the Earth: Labor, Film, and the Cold War," *OAH Magazine of History* Special Online Feature, http://magazine.oah.org/issues/244/salt.html, accessed January 23, 2013. Set during the 1950 and 1951 strike by the predominately Mexican American workers at the Empire Zinc Mine, the film *Salt of the Earth* includes scenes that depict miners' wives taking over a picket line while the miners come to understand the difficulty of their wives' domestic labor. It indicates that improving work conditions in the domestic sphere is as important as struggles in the workplace. The film does not suggest that women should have access to production jobs at the smelters and mines, however. Nonetheless, its critique of copper men's masculine politics, although ultimately limited, made many Mine Mill members uncomfortable.

17. Zieger, *The CIO*, 277–90; Jensen, *Nonferrous Metals Industry Unionism*, x, xiv; Dickson, interview. Mercier, *Anaconda*, 148–66.

18. In 1962 the United Steelworkers of America finally achieved victory in Anaconda. Five years later, Butte and Black Eagle also became USWA towns when Mine Mill was forced to merge with USWA. Mercier, *Anaconda*, 88–106. Ruth Parry Meidl, interview by Laurie Mercier, 11 Aug. 1986, MHSRC. K. Anderson, *Wartime Women*, 173.

19. Eugene Cox, interview by Laurie Mercier, 16 July 1986, MHSRC; Charles Micheletti, interview by Laurie Mercier, 13 Mar. 1986; Cox interview; Micheletti interview; Earl and Charlotte Lenci, interview by Laurie Mercier, 19 January 1988, MHSRC. Earl Lenci indicated that racism was obvious in Black Eagle until the 1980s. Katie Dewing, interview by Laurie Mercier, 11 Aug. 1986, MHSRC. Suggesting the elevation of racial tensions in Anaconda during the civil rights era, Dewing claimed that four African American men were murdered by a white man in the mid-1960s.